VOLUME III

JEWISH MYSTICISM

THE MODERN PERIOD

VOLUME III

JEWISH MYSTICISM

THE MODERN PERIOD

JOSEPH DAN

JASON ARONSON INC.
Northvale, New Jersey
Jerusalem

Most of the sixty studies collected in these volumes were published in scholarly journals and other scientific publications; a few are presented here for the first time. It is my pleasant duty to thank the scores of editors and publishers who contributed in various ways to the present form of these studies. They all took part in giving the articles their final internal and external shape. Almost all of these studies are based on lectures given in American and European universities in the last thirty years, and I have benefitted from the remarks of colleagues and students who participated in the discussions.

Joseph Dan
Cambridge, Mass.

This book was set in 11 pt. Goudy Old Style by Hightech Data Inc., and printed and bound by Book-mart Press, Inc. of North Bergen, NJ.

Library of Congress Cataloging-in-Publication Data

Dan, Joseph, 1935–
    Jewish mysticism / by Joseph Dan.
        p.   cm.
    Includes bibliographical references and index.
    Contents: v. 1. Late antiquity—v. 2. The Middle Ages.
    ISBN 0-7657-6009-6
    1. Mysticism—Judaism—History.   I. Title.
BM723.D365 1998
296.7'12'09—dc20

                                                        98-42910

Printed in the United States of America on acid-free paper. For information and catalog write to Jason Aronson Inc., 230 Livingston Street, Northvale, NJ 07647-1726, or visit our website: www.aronson.com

Acknowledgments

The author gratefully acknowledges the permissions granted by the publications in which the essays in this volume originally appeared:

"Five Versions of the Story of the Jerusalemite," from *Proceedings of the American Academy for Jewish Research, Vol. XXXV* (American Academy for Jewish Research: New York 1967), pp. 99–111.

"Imago Dei," from *Contemporary Jewish Religious Thought*, Cohen and Mendes-Flohr (eds.), (New York 1987), pp. 473–478.

"In Quest for a Historical Definition of Mysticism: The Contingental Approach," from *Pharos, Studies in Spirituality, Vol. 3* (Kok: Kampen 1993), pp. 58–90.

"Jerusalem in Jewish Spirituality," from *City of the Great King: Jerusalem from David to the Present*, N. Rosovsky (ed.) (Harvard University Press: Cambridge, MA 1996), pp. 60–73, 474–479.

"Mennasseh ben Israel's Nishmat Hayyim and the Concept of Evil in Seventeenth Century Jewish Thought," from *Jewish Thought in the Seventeenth Century*, I. Twersky and B. Septimus (eds.) (Harvard University Press: Cambridge, MA & London 1987). pp. 63–75.

"Mysticism in Jewish History, Religion, and Literature," from *Studies in Jewish Mysticism*, Dan and Talmage (eds.) (Association of Jewish Studies: Cambridge, MA 1981), pp. 1–14.

"Nachmanides and the Development of the Concept of Evil in the kabbalah," from *Proceedings of the Conference on Nachmanides and His Times (Mosse ben Nahman I el seu Temps)*, (Ajuntament de Girona: Catalonia 1996), pp. 161–179.

"No Evil Descends from Heaven, The Concept of Evil in Sixteenth Century Kabbalah," from *Jewish Thought in the Sixteenth Century*, I. Twersky and B. Septimus (eds.) (Harvard University Press: Cambridge, MA & London 1987), pp. 89–105.

"The Desert in Jewish Mysticism," from *Ariel No. 40* (Ministry for Foreign Affairs: Jerusalem 1976), pp. 38–43.

"The Kabbalah of Johannes Reuchlin and Its Historical Significance," from *The Christian Kabbalah: Jewish Mystical Books and Their Christian Interpreters*, J. Dan (ed.) (Harvard University Press: Cambridge, MA 1997), pp. 55–95.

"Kabbalistic and Gnostic Dualism," from *Binah, Vol. III: Studies in Jewish Intellectual History in the Middle Ages*, J. Dan (ed.) (Praeger Publishers 1995), pp. 19–33.

"The Kingdom of Samael," from *Ariel Vol. 40* (Ministry for Foreign Affairs: Jerusalem 1976), pp. 38–43.

"The Language of the Mystics in Medieval Germany," Dan & Grozinger, (eds.) from *Mysticism, Magic, and Kabbalah in Ashkenazi Judaism, International Symposium*, (Walter de Gruyter: Berlin & New York 1995), pp. 6–27.

The Language of the Mystical Prayer," from *Pharos: Studies in Spirituality, Vol. 5*, Dan & Grozinger (eds.) (Walter de Gruyter: Berlin & New York 1995), pp. 40–60.

"The Name of God, The Name of the Rose and the Concept of Language In Jewish Mysticism," from *Medieval Encounters Vol. 2* (E. J. Brill: Lieden 1996) pp. 228–248.

"The Paradox of Nothingness in the Kabbalah," from *Agumento e*

Silento, A. Colin (ed.), International Paul Celan Symposium (Walter de Gruyter: Berlin & New York 1987), pp. 359–363.

"Rabbi Judah the Pious and Caesarius of Heisterbach," from *Scripta Hierosalymitana Vol. XXII*, J. Heinemann (ed.) (Magnes Press: Jerusalem 1971), pp. 18–27.

"Samael and the Problem of Jewish Gnosticism," from *Perspectives on Jewish Thought and Mysticism*, A. L. Ivry (ed.) (Amsterdam: Harwood Academic Publishers 1998), pp. 257–276.

"Samael, Lilith, and the concept of Evil in Early Kabbalah," from *AJS, Vol. V* (Cambridge, MA: Association for Jewish Studies 1980), pp. 17–40.

"Teraphim: From Popular Belief to a Folktale," from *Scripta Hierosalymitana Vol. XXVII: Studies in Narrative Art*, J. Heinemann (ed.) (Magnes Press: Jerusalem 1978), pp. 99–106.

Contents

Introduction

I

The studies collected in this volume all deal, one way or another, with the linguistic expression of the unexpressible: the inaccurate and oxymoronic expressions of the mystics of their experiences, which are—so they claim—beyond the power of language to present. Mysticism is a linguistic phenomenon that developed within another linguistic phenomenon—religion; yet when religious teachers speak, they believe that they successfully communicate their innermost feelings. When mystics speak, they deny their own communicative power. Still, the self-denial of mystical language does not prevent the mystics from utilizing language, which they believe to be of divine origin, for their own purpose of expression. While doing this, the mystics have an impact on religion, on culture, and on history. This impact is a subject investigated by the historians of religions and of ideas.

When there is a conflict between people or peoples, we say: "We must get them to talk to each other." When they talk, but they disagree, we say: "at least they are still talking." It is an expression of our deep, instinctive belief in the communicative power of language. Talking means communication, and communication denies exclusion. Loneliness is defined not only by solitude, but more so by "having no one to talk to." Sometimes we are more discerning: "Nobody understands me," we say, denoting that talking is not enough, that sometimes talking is not understanding, and that inclusion and communication demand "understanding" as well as talking.

The crisis of modernity in the last few generations was focused, to a large extent, on the failure of language to convey a definite meaning. The naive, Enlightenment-encouraged trust in the intrinsic communicability of language and its ability to close the abyss separating an individual from other individuals is diminishing, if it has not been completely discarded. The faith in the power of textual presentation, of defining terminology, of verbal analysis to transmit a universally understood message, has all but disappeared. Intellectuals mourn the political process in the age of television, when politicians seem to convey an image rather than a message; yet it is these intellectuals who taught us so convincingly that "the medium is the message" and that language cannot transmit an idea or a concept in a way that will be understood by all. If one cannot trust one's understanding of a text by Plato or Hegel, if their writings can support both fascism and Marxism, why should a politician devote more effort to presenting an issue than to presenting an image? Is the structure of his sentence really more important than his hairdo?

The great upholder of the power of language in western civilization was religion, which, in this culture, actually means Christianity. God created the world by language; God was incarnated and talked to people in language, and conveyed a message that is preserved in the words of the Bible. "In the beginning there was the word." If the language of scriptures was not clear enough, there came the dogma. In a series of sentences, all truth has been encompassed. To achieve truth—redemption—fulfillment, all one need do is to follow verbatim the language of the dogma. It is not the pope as an individual who is infallible; it is the truth of his words. In a religious (i.e., Christian) context, language can and should represent absolute, eternal truth. Because of this, the rebellion against the power of language to convey truth, from Nietzsche to Derrida, is an antireligious, and most particularly anti-Christian, rebellion.

At the same time, religion (again, namely, Christianity), is the ultimate expression of inclusion. In sharing the language of the gospels, studying the communion, reciting the dogma, one is included in the universal brotherhood of redemption. "One is never alone with God," because one has the language that brings him into intimate contact with God as well as with his fellow human beings. Religion, in this sense, is an almost exclusively linguistic phenomenon. It has vast ranges of metalinguistic experiental expressions, deep emotional realms, and sensual and intellectual meanings, but these are all induced by language, communicated by language, and expressed in language. Religious emotion is not verbal, but it is by language that one is instructed what to feel, how to understand one's own feelings, and how to interpret them. The language one uses in these occasions is a language of inclusion: One is supposed to feel and behave in the same way that the first disciples of Christ did, as the Church fathers and the many generations that followed them did, and as the hundreds of millions of like believers do at this very moment. Language brings past, present, and future together; at the same time, it can and should bring everybody together—all are united in the same words.

The supreme expression of this belief in the power of language is the complete faith that religion (in this case, Christianity alone) has the power of translation. Language is supernal, transcending the differences between particular groups of people, and therefore between particular languages. Christianity preserved but six words spoken by God in their original form; everything else—the Hebrew Bible and the words of Jesus Christ—are transmitted in translations: first in the "sacred" languages, Greek and Latin, and later in the vernaculars. A translation is possible only when the translated text is understood, and at least the core of its meaning can be transmitted to another language. When Christianity adopted Greek and Latin as its own, forsaking the original divine language, Hebrew, an enormous transformation occurred: Language became nothing more than a vehicle for communicating meaning by semantic means. The Hebrew concept of language (which was shared to a large extent by the Moslems concerning Arabic) was much wider, and included many semiotic aspects. The Catholic reluctance to adopt the vernacular languages was based not on problems concerned with the nature of language, but rather on social and institutional considerations. The culture created by the Christian-translated concept of language is the one we all share, including modern Jews and Muslims, and it is based on the belief in language as communication of meaning and as absolving an individual from his loneliness and separation from other people. Christianity and Enlightenment together created the illusion of a humanity that could be united by language and could progress together toward redemption, speaking many languages but conveying the same meaning. This faith has crumbled into dust in this century.

The subject of this discussion is the exception to the rule, the premodern rebels against this concept of language who believed that language is an instrument of exclusion rather than inclusion and for this reason were themselves excluded from both religion and modernity: the mystics. For the mystic, language does not convey meaning, but hides it. Words do not clarify, but obscure. Precise expression of truth is impossible, and everything expressed in language is not the whole truth, and sometimes is not even the truth. The essence of mysticism is a negative statement, like the word itself, which does not denote any positive content: Mysticism is what we do not know; it is a particular thing that we do not know, because not all things that we do not know are mystical, but in what way the things that we do not know that are mystical are different from the things we do not know that are not mystical—we do not know. The negative denotation of "mysticism," as far as we can articulate it, is the denial of sensual and intellectual knowledge as sources of truth. Truth, for the mystic, is recognized by its independence of reliance on sensual perception and intellectual discernment. Language is a means of communication because it relies on the common denominators of human sensual and intellectual experiences. When these are denied, language as communication is denied.

It is understandable that the mystic is alienated from the Enlightenment and the trust in rationalism and progress that it demands. It is much less clear how the mystic is alienated from religion; usually, mysticism is studied and understood—as far as it is understood—as a religious phenomenon. Many of the most important analyses of the mystical phenomenon, like those of Rudolph Otto and William James, have been presented in works that are studies in the nature of religion. Indeed, the vast library of mystical works that is a part of western culture was written by people who sincerely and profoundly adhered to Christianity, Islam, or Judaism, and actively belonged to the institutional structures of these religions (though in different, and sometimes rebellious, ways). The statement that the mystic is the alienated, excluded religious person has, therefore, to be explained. This explanation, as indicated above, is found in the radical difference between the religious concept of language and the mystical one. It seems to me that the relationship between mysticism and religion can be expressed by Bernard Shaw's words related to another phenomenon: Religion and mysticism are two entities separated by a common language.

This is not the place to discuss in detail the meaning of the mystical attitude and its relationship to language and religion; a few remarks will suffice, in order to illustrate the aspect of exclusion inherent in the position of the mystic within a religious framework, its institutions, and its language. The mystic is a rebel from an institutional point of view, because by being a mystic he insists that he knows a more direct and complete way for achieving knowledge and communion with God than that offered by the Church to its other believers—including the religious official hierarchy. By this claim, the mystic is viewed as one who puts himself in a higher religious position than his place in the institutionalized structure of the Church; he is regarded as an unqualified pretender to achievements that elude people who are superior to him in the established rungs of the religious ladder. Because of this claim, he is regarded with suspicion, if not direct enmity. The mystic, being a mystic, cannot but present this claim; if he forsakes it, there is nothing that differentiates him from his fellow members of the Church.[1]

Despite this suspicious position, it is interesting that in most cases it was the Church officials who described the mystics as presenting a quantitative claim, whereas the mystics themselves usually described their uniqueness in qualitative terms. Most of the definitions of mysticism presented in the writings of medieval and modern writers, religious thinkers, and scholars alike describe the mystics as those who achieve proximity with God or union with Him, have a constant feeling of His presence, etc.[2] In all these descriptions, the mystics are portrayed as those who have excelled in achieving the purposes of religion as a whole. It can be summarized by characterizing such definitions as presenting mysticism as "religion— only a little more so"; the terms are purely quantitative, because no religion will deny that it offers its adherents an avenue to the presence of God and communion with Him in various ways. In the writings of the mystics themselves, mysticism usually is described as a different way, the *via mystica*, which is qualitatively separated from that of other religious adherents. When asked to characterize this difference, however, mystics will usually claim that it is beyond language and therefore unexplainable; and, when pressed, they utilize quantitative terms, emphasizing that this is all that language can achieve when trying to describe the undescribable.

The most common characteristic of the language of mystical writings is the negative statement, apophatic language. Mystics generally describe the content of the truth they have achieved in nega-

---

[1]Undoubtedly there were many mystics throughout the history of monotheistic religions who, because of this position, did not present their claim to mystical achievement in a public forum. This will forever remain unknown, because if they did not attempt to communicate their uniqueness, there is no way to know of their existence and spiritual lives.

[2]Concerning examples of definitions of mysticism, see especially B. McGinn's detailed survey in *The Foundations of Mysticism*, New York: Crossroads 1991, pp. 342–365.

tive terms; they speak about what it is not, not about what it is. When they use positive terminology, they hasten to qualify its relevance. This is the closest they can come to informing the reader in communicative language, but it is forbidden by them to surmise that what they have just said is actually so; this is an approximate, symbolic language that may hint at the thing itself and give some impression, but it is not an accurate description of truth. Their language abounds with oxymorons and other linguistic devices, parables, and metaphors that seem to say something when they actually do not. This negative language characterizes not only the descriptions of the mystical achievement, but also those of the mystical way. Means are part of the mystical phenomenon; the inexpressible cannot be achieved by expressible means. Mystics are eloquent and precise when telling the reader what he should not do and should not feel when he aspires to achieve the mystical goal; they are vague and apophatic when they try to point out what he should do, especially those elements that are different from those demanded by institutionalized religion.

The most radical difference between religion and mysticism is found in the relationship toward scriptures. The acceptance of the language of scriptures as a direct divine revelation unites mystics and nonmystics, but the nonmystics regard the message of scriptures as a full presentation of God's message to humanity. For the mystics, scriptures represent opaque, vague series of hints at a divine truth that even God Himself cannot express by language. For the mystics, people who read scriptures and believe that they understand their message are completely wrong; they believe that the sensual and intellectual meaning of the words of the gospels indicate sensual and intellectual contents, and that these can be understood as signifiers representing earthly and human signifieds. For the mystic, these are signifiers without any definite earthly signifieds whatsoever, a group of symbols that cannot be deciphered unless one attains mystical, metalinguistic knowledge. Scriptures, according to the mystic, cannot be understood unless one has experienced their message in its divine hidden source. While scriptures seem to be a uniting factor bringing together mystics and nonmystics, they actually divide them:

They read the same words, but understand them in a completely
different manner.[3]

This abstract, rather theoretical relationship between religious
and mystical languages is translated into historical reality in many
different and complex ways. Language separates religion from mysticism, but there are many other factors that prevent this separation
from becoming, as a rule, a historical situation of exclusion. The
religious person may be irritated by the mystic's insistence that proximity to God can be achieved in ways that do not follow everyday
religious ritual, yet it is hard for him to deny divine revelation to
the mystic; religion is based on faith in such revelations, and it is
not always easy for the religious establishment to proclaim a certain
type of unity with God to be a false one. Usually, some other factors should be involved in order to render the spirituality of the
mystic an erroneous, dangerous one.[4] As noted above, it is not easy
to attribute heresy to a mystic; accusations of heresy were the most
efficient weapon available to the religious establishment in its struggles
against deviations from the accepted religious norms, yet the mystics, who did not believe that any truth can be expressed in language, did not insist on a particular linguistic formulation as being
a truth different from the dogma of the Church. Belief in the semantic power of language is necessary if one wishes to have a theological controversy, and when one side denies it, such controversy
is impossible. This is the reason we find few examples of confronta-
tions between mystics and nonmystics throughout the history of

---

[3]The mystical reading of scriptures should not be confused with methodologies
of exegesis, like allegoristic or typological interpretations. These methodologies
represent a belief that scriptures convey a finite series of meanings, deciphered
by a finite number (usually four) clearly defined methodologies. This is still a
purely semantic concept of scriptures that conceives of their meaning as a mul-
tilayered message that has to be read in several ways. Yet each of these ways is
sensual and intellectual. The mystics believe in a completely different,
metalinguistic layer of meaning that cannot be presented by any earthly means.
[4]The history of Joan of Arc is a typical example of such ambivalence. In the
end, the political needs of the French and English establishments decided their
position concerning the revelation to the Maid of Orléans, rather than any
abstract principle concerning revelation to the ignorant and uneducated.

established religion.[5] On the other hand, mystics were not given a
share in the administration of the Church's established institutions:
We have not even one example of a pope who was a mystic. When
mystics did have a historical impact on the actual organization of
the Church, it was through the endeavor of building new institutional structures. It is probable that the beginnings of Christian
mysticism are associated with the early emergence of the monastic
movement, which began as a separation from the existing institutions and the withdrawal to deserts and seeking of solitary spiritual
life far away from the institutionalized religious bodies. Only later
was the monastic structure absorbed by the Church as a central
element of its organization. During the Middle Ages, mysticism often was expressed as movements of renewal and new initiatives within
monastic structures, or the building of new orders, rather than as a
part of the ordinary development in existing institutions.[6] This was,
in fact, a mild, relatively subdued form of religious exclusion, but it
was effective nonetheless.

---

[5]A historically meaningful example of this is the historical development of the
kabbalah within Judaism. The kabbalah presents notions that, taken literally,
seem to be completely negating the basic principles of Jewish faith. The ten *sefirot*,
regarded as divine powers in the full sense of the term, may be understood as
negating the monotheistic concept of God. The kabbalistic insistence on the direction of different parts of the prayers to different realms within the divine world
could be interpreted as pure idolatry. Yet it is almost unbelievable how few and
far between are the expressions of opposition or even resentment of the kabbalah
in medieval and early modern rabbinic literature. Some misguided writers have
concluded from this fact that all Judaism was actually—though often secretly—
united in adherence to the kabbalah, a concept that is historically unacceptable.
The reason for this absence of opposition is that there was nothing tangible to
oppose: In daily practice, the kabbalah preached strict orthodoxy, and there was
nothing in the actions of the mystics that could serve as a basis for schism or
controversy. In the first moment that kabbalists preached a change in Jewish
practice—in the context of the Sabbatian movement in the seventeenth century—
such a schism immediately occurred.

[6]Gershom Scholem described this as mysticism occurring on the fringes of religious structures, and only later working its way into the centers of its governing
bodies (unlike Jewish mysticism, which, according to his description, often originated in the heart of the greatest cultural centers). See his *Major Trends in Jewish Mysticism*, New York: Schocken 1954, pp. 19-24.

Another reason for the relatively unpronounced conflict between religion and mysticism is the result of the mystics' reverence for the traditional structures and the practices of the religious authorities. A mystic, by nature, is not inclined toward historical activity and rebellious change. Revolutionaries are not mystics; they believe in history, communication, social change, and progress. Mystics seek their individual, solitary path to the union with God. When they do not like the tradition they were brought up in, they tend to withdraw and seek their individual way, rather than preaching change and inciting their fellow believers into historical activity demanding change and transformation. Because of this, the mystics did not present, in most cases, a definite threat to the authorities, and did not regard their position within the traditional structure as unbearable, demanding innovative changes.

It is not only the nonrebellious nature of the mystic that makes direct conflict with the religious establishment a rare phenomenon; another reason is the mystic's inclination to mystical exegesis. The mystic shares the nonmystic's faith in the divine origin of ritual and scriptures; he does not share the nonmystic's literal (in the wide sense of this term, as explained above) understanding of this divine message. This directs him not toward rebellion, but toward reinterpretation and spiritualization, which is not expressed in a semantic way. For the mystic, the introduction of new understanding of existing religious norms does entail the refutation of the old ones, because his novel understanding cannot be expressed completely in words. He does not demand the replacement of one formula by another, but introduces his own metalinguistic exegesis in a series of hints, metaphors, and symbols that do not posit a clear threat to the existing order. Traditional religious life does not impose on the mystic the stagnation of adherence to the governing norms; he can find within them open spaces for the introduction of mystical meaning, without demanding any radical change.

In this way, there is always the possibility of peaceful coexistence of mystics within the framework of established religion, living "happily ever after" in mutual, comforting misunderstanding.

II

The exclusionary nature of mysticism is apparent in the first appearance[7] of this phenomenon in each of the three scriptural religions. The beginnings of Christian mysticism in the second, third, and fourth centuries are strongly associated with the beginnings of the monastic movement and the adoption of the idea of virginity,[8] both of which are strong and unambiguous statements of exclusion from surrounding society. Islamic Sufism is marked by a particular dress and an outcast's way of life in seclusion.[9] In both cases, the first overt expression of the adherence to mystical ideals is separation from society and the rejection of the accepted norms of social life.[10] The examples to be discussed here in some detail relate to the beginnings of mystical phenomena in Judaism.

The first appearance of mysticism as a historical phenomenon in Judaism, expressed by distinct terminology, literary genres, and attitude toward the normative concepts of religious worship is the formation of the groups of "descenders to the chariot" and the emergence of *Hechalot* mysticism, probably at the end of the second cen-

---

[7]It is very difficult to define a "beginning" of a mystical phenomenon. The "beginning" here relates to the first appearance of mystical groups of devotees, thinkers, and writers as a distinct historical occurrence; it relates to the endeavors of groups of people who established their own modes of expression in a particular terminology and literary genres, as well as a distinct attitude toward the social and religious norms of their coreligionists. It does not relate to scattered expressions within literary works, like some of the psalms; the interpretation of such texts as "mystical" is a literary statement, based on one's definition of mysticism. See the article "In Quest of a Historical Definition of Mysticism: The Contingental Approach," *Studies in Spirituality* 3 (1993), pp. 58–90.

[8]This subject is discussed in detail in B. McGinn, *Foundations of Mysticism* (see note 2), pp. 131–185.

[9]A recent comprehensive presentation of this subject is found in S. Murata and W. C. Chittick, *The Vision of Islam*, New York: Paragon House 1994, pp. 237–264, 304–310.

[10]This is most apparent in the nature of the gnostic phenomena in Christianity. The relationship between gnosticism and mysticism is very complex and cannot be discussed here, even though it is a most powerful expression of mystical exclusion.

tury and during the third.[11] The first studies of this phenomenon tended to present it as the esoteric, mystical underlying faith of rabbinic Judaism in Late Antiquity; further research, however, clearly proves that these early mystics were separated from the mainstream schools of rabbinic tradition. They developed their own unique terminology, and their religious attitude differed most meaningfully from that of their coreligionists.

The most significant characteristic of rabbinic Judaism in Late Antiquity, which preceded similar attitudes in mainstream Christianity and Islam, was the substitution of revelation by textual exegesis to actual divine revelation to individuals and groups. Biblical Judaism represents a consciousness of constant divine presence that is revealed to patriarchs, judges, and prophets whenever circumstances demand it; similarly, Christ is present in the New Testament, and God is available to Mohammed in the Koran. Talmudic-midrashic literature, however, expresses a religiosity in which God is revealed by the reinterpretation of the texts of ancient (biblical) revelation. The presence of God is expressed by the constant discovery of new meanings in the old texts, rather than by His actual appearance, either directly or by various messengers. In some cases this literature expressed rejection of any claim of direct connection with the divine, and insisted that everything that should be known has been incorporated within the Torah, and a reliance on direct divine revelation cannot be accepted. The development of the unique Jewish concept of the Midrash, which includes the belief that every biblical verse contains within it an infinite number of correct, equally true meanings that pertain to all past, present, and future needs, is the main cultural-religious expression of this period, which dominates rabbinic Judaism to this day. This concept includes a rejection of

---

[11]This subject has received much scholarly attention in the last few decades. General descriptions are found in G. Scholem, *Major Trends in Jewish Mysticism*, New York: Schocken 1954, pp. 40–79; idem, *Jewish Gnosticism, Merkabah Mysticism and Talmudic Tradition*, New York: The Jewish Theological Seminary 1960 (rev. ed. 1965); I. Gruenwald, *Apocalypticism and Merkava Mysticism*, Leiden: Brill 1980; P. Schaefer, *The Hidden and Manifest God*, Albany, NY: SUNY Press 1993; J. Dan, *The Ancient Jewish Mysticism*, Tel Aviv: MOD 1993; and see the volume *Jewish Mysticism: Late Antiquity* in this series.

the pseudepigraphic literature, which was current during the Second Commonwealth period, in which direct divine revelation was claimed, but was attributed to ancient, biblical figures. Thus the concept of scripture as an external source of divine presence became the dominant religious feature of Judaism, to be followed by Christianity and Islam in subsequent centuries, when their epochs of direct revelation came to an end.

Hechalot mysticism represented a direct rejection of the concepts of scripture and midrash, insisting on an immediate contact with the divine, "face to face." The vision of God, sitting on his throne of glory and surrounded by the myriad powers of the celestial realms, was the ultimate aim of these mystics. The vision of the divine chariot by Ezekiel was one of their main sources of inspiration; in this they continued an old tradition of exegesis of the first chapter of Ezekiel as a description of the divine realm (maaseh Merkavah, "the work of the chariot"), but they added to the passive, midrashic process of hermeneutics an active element of "descent to the chariot," which is described as an adventurous process of spiritual ascension. While the Merkavah terminology is a traditional one, these mystics developed a unique set of terms to describe the ascension, at the center of which is the concept of seven temples or palaces (hechalot), each above the other and each inside the other. Each temple is guarded by celestial powers, and the mystic needs skill, knowledge, and luck in order to overcome them and receive permission to continue his journey. The sixth palace, especially, is a dangerous place; a group of guardians there seem to be uncontrolled by even God Himself, and they tend to harm arbitrarily the mystics seeking entrance. Hechalot treatises include detailed instructions, on several physical and spiritual levels, concerning the ways to succeed in this intricate process. The particular name that these mystics chose for themselves, yordey ha-Merkavah—the meaning of which is unknown—is not found anywhere else in rabbinic literature,[12] like the term hechalot itself, and

---

[12]See the exhaustive analysis of this subject in A. Kuyt, The "Descent" to the Chariot: Towards a Description of the Terminology, Place, Function and Nature of the Yeridah in Hekhalot Literature, Tübingen: J.C.B. Mohr (Paul Siebeck) 1995; and my review of this important monograph in FJB 22 (1995), pp. 190-194.

even their term for the supreme divine realm, the *Shiur Komah*, the anthropomorphic gigantic image of God.[13]

It is evident that the early Jewish mystics separated themselves from the religious mainstream in their refusal to adopt the midrashic way toward divine knowledge, and adopted, in its stead, a demand for a direct, visual-auditory contact with the divine realm, which included both intellectual elements—knowledge revealed—and emotional ones, the ecstatic immersion within the celestial world and the experience of meeting God Himself. This departure from the norms resulted in their using unique literary forms, in prose and in poetry, and the development of unique terminology. The absence of any reference to these mystical aspirations and activities from the vast body of talmudic-midrashic literature[14] can be viewed as a result of their withdrawal, of the mainstream rabbis' rejection of their attitudes, or both. The Talmud includes a series of strict warnings of the dangers of dealing with hidden secrets, which may also be viewed as expressions of the separation between the mystics and their coreligionists. As a result, Judaism preserved since then an attitude of suspicion and apprehension toward mystical indulgence.

All our knowledge of this early mystical trend within Judaism is found in a handful of short treatises, all of them anonymous or pseudepigraphic, that do not reveal the human side of the contact, or its absence, between the early mystics and the religious establishment. A little more can be known concerning a later group of Jewish mystics that flourished probably in the fifth or sixth century and is known mainly by its treatise, the Prince of the Torah. This group seems to have been an isolated and neglected community, envious of the powers of the religious leaders and aspiring to achieve, by magical and mystical means, a central position that would reflect their unique spiritual qualities as they saw them. In the treatise that

---

[13]Concerning the *Shiur Komah*, see G. Scholem, *The Mystical Shape of the Godhead*, New York: Schocken 1991, pp. 15–55.
[14]There may be handful of vague, indirect references to the world of the mystics for instance in the parable of "the four who entered the *pardes*" and in some of Rabbi Akiva's statements concerning the *Song of Songs*. The key terms—descent, *Hechalot*, *Shiur Komah*, etc.—are completely absent.

reached us, they seem to downgrade the spiritual value of ancient Jewish traditions, including biblical ones, and to believe that only they have been blessed by the full power of direct divine revelation.[15] In this case, the isolation and mutual rejection of the mystics from the mainstream culture is overt and pronounced in strong terms.

Mysticism remained a marginal phenomenon in the Judaism of Late Antiquity, and the schools of mystics produced a meager literature that did not have a meaningful impact on the established religious culture.[16] The situation did not change dramatically in the Middle Ages, but our knowledge concerning the relationships between mystics and nonmystics is more detailed. One tragic example should be briefly presented here.

III

Rabbi Judah ben Samuel ben Kalonymus, known as Rabbi Judah the Pious, is one of the best-known and most respected figures in the history of the Jewish communities in central Europe throughout the Middle Ages. His name was revered by many generations, and a series of hagiographic narratives was woven around him. He was regarded as the leader and the great spiritual teacher of the circle of the Ashkenazi Hasidim, the Jewish pietists in medieval Germany.[17] His father was Rabbi Samuel ben Kalonymus, who was titled by the people of the period by an unusual series of epithets: "the saint," "the pious," "the prophet," and the Kalonymus family was regarded as the most important family in German Jewry. His best-known disciple, Rabbi Eleazar ben Judah of Worms, was the main writer of that circle of pietists, whose writings exerted influ-

---

[15]Concerning the Sar Torah mystics, see my Ancient Jewish Mysticism (see note 11), Chapter 9.

[16]An exception should be made concerning the text of some Hebrew prayers and hymns that may have been meaningfully influenced by Hechalot poetry.

[17]See the brief description in G. Scholem, Major Trends in Jewish Mysticism, pp. 80–118; I. Marcus, Piety and Society, Leiden: Brill 1980, passim. See the studies on this subject in the volume Jewish Mysticism: The High Middle Ages in this series.

ence for centuries. Rabbi Judah's image in history is that of a great, respected leader; a member of a great family of leaders and writers; a great teacher; and the most important representative of medieval Jewish ethics and esoteric knowledge.

There is, however, an element of mystery in his biography. He was born and spent most of his life in Speyer, in the heart of the Rhineland, which was the most important center of Jewish culture in Germany in that period. He died in Regensburg, which was remote from any Jewish cultural center. We do not know when he moved from Speyer to Regensburg, and we have no information concerning the reason of his departure from the place where all his family and disciples resided. Our sources are completely silent concerning this major event in his life.

Scholarly work on the Ashkenazi Hasidic circle, its ethics, and its mysticism portrayed all the people who took part in it as one unified group, without discerning any individual elements in their works. The writings of Rabbi Eleazar of Worms were regarded as representing all of them, and the main ethical work that emerged from this circle, the *Sefer Hasidim* (the Book of the Pious), was regarded as a collective work to which several writers, if not many more, contributed.[18]

This picture began to change a few decades ago. Its most obvious flaw was the difference between the demand of the *Sefer Hasidim* that writers should publish their works anonymously, while Rabbi Eleazar insisted on identifying all his works, clearly and unambiguously, as his own, using acronyms and other methods. Further research led to the conclusion that the *Sefer Hasidim* was written by Rabbi Judah the Pious alone, with only two sections in the beginning probably being the work of his father, Rabbi Samuel. A detailed study by I. Marcus indicated that there is a vast difference between the positions of Rabbi Judah and Rabbi Eleazar concern-

---

[18]The view that the work was written by many writers in several generations was held by Guedemann and by I. Tishby. I. Baer, in his study, regards it as a representative, collective work. Scholem saw it as the product of the efforts of at least Rabbi Samuel, Rabbi Judah, and Rabbi Eleazar.

ing major ethical problems; Rabbi Judah emphasized the communal aspect of religious perfection, whereas Rabbi Eleazar confined it to the individual realm, between a person and God directly. More and more differences were found, clearly separating Rabbi Judah from all other teachers of that circle. While previous scholars tended to view the descriptions of the community of pietists portrayed in the *Sefer Hasidim* as historical fact, it became evident that it was just a plan that was never carried out; it was Rabbi Judah's vision, which never materialized, and it is nowhere mentioned in the works of Rabbi Eleazar and other writers of that period. It is clear today that Rabbi Judah was isolated among his family and spiritual community, a leader who was followed by no one. This could be the real explanation of his move to Regensburg: He probably wished to withdraw from the place of his "followers," who refused to follow him, and it is possible that he tried to establish a new school farther to the east.

The most meaningful difference between Rabbi Judah and the other writers of the Ashkenazi Hasidic school, which is relevant to our subject, concerns the concept of mystical prayer. Rabbi Judah wrote an extensive, eight-volume commentary on the prayers, the first such commentary ever to be written. This great work has been lost; all we have is a small treatise, written by one of Rabbi Judah's colleagues, titled *Sodot ha-Tefillah* (the Secrets of the Prayer), a selection of several paragraphs from the lost work. These quotations give us a very good idea concerning the work as a whole: Rabbi Judah developed in it a unique, intensely innovative concept of the prayers as a mystical representation of the whole universe, reflecting intrinsic harmonies that are found in every aspect of the world—in God, in scriptures, in history, in the cosmos, and within a human being. These harmonies are presented by means of numerical analysis, which demonstrates that numerical structures in the prayers—numbers of words, names of God, particular terms, numbers of letters and their numerical values—correspond to numerical structures found in scriptures and in every subject in creation. The whole vast work, so it seems from these quotations, was a recital of these numerical harmonies, which represent the underlying mystical structure of everything. The ritual of prayer includes the worshipper within the framework of this universal harmony, uniting him with the divine meaning of creation.

There is no precedent to such a concept in previous Jewish concepts of the prayers, and there was no continuation to Rabbi Judah's ideas. This seems to have been an individual outburst of mystical insight that was not followed by anyone. Rabbi Judah did not write the work merely to express his vision; he had a more immediate concern. The quotations included in the *Sodot ha Tefillah* are mostly polemical ones: Rabbi Judah criticizes in them the different versions of the daily prayers, insisting that only his own version corresponds to the true, intrinsic mystical harmony that is the essence of prayer. The most minute change, a few words or a handful of letters, suffices to destroy this harmony and render the prayers useless or even harmful. Judaism traditionally had several legitimate versions of the prayers, and the slight differences did not evoke a meaningful controversy. Rabbi Judah chastised those whose version differed from that accepted by him as people who bring exile upon the people of Israel, as liars and falsifiers, using strong language never before used in such a context. He attacked mainly "those people of France and the Islands of the Sea" (England), people who were part of the same cultural tradition and attitude to which he himself belonged. No wonder that among the manuscripts of the *Sodot ha-Tefillah* there are several from which these polemical statements have been omitted.

The part of this historical occurrence that is relevant to the subject of this discussion is found in another work—in the great commentary on the prayers that was written by Rabbi Judah's disciple, Rabbi Eleazar of Worms, the first such commentary that reached us.[19] Unlike Rabbi Judah's commentary, which seems to have been completely dedicated to the demonstration of the mystical harmony reflected in the structure of the prayers, Rabbi Eleazar presented in his work several methodologies by which every section of the texts

---

[19]It is found in three different recensions in ms. Vienna 108, ms. Oxford 1204, and ms. Paris 772. It seems that all three are originals, despite the differences, and that Rabbi Eleazar wrote several versions of his own magnum opus.

is analyzed. These include an exegetical part, in which the meaning of the key terms is discussed and the language explained; a theological part, in which the text is elaborated as an expression of the esoteric theology that Rabbi Eleazar presented in his other works; and sections dedicated to pointing out the numerical harmony found in the texts of the prayers that corresponds to that found in scriptures and in other phenomena throughout creation. This third part, obviously, was taken from Rabbi Judah's work.[20] One may say, therefore, that Rabbi Eleazar was a loyal disciple who included the main points of his teacher's doctrines in his own work.

There is, however, a vast difference between the same paragraphs as they appear in Rabbi Judah's work and in that of Rabbi Eleazar. Obviously, all of the polemical elements have been omitted. But the main difference is that what was presented in Rabbi Judah's commentary as the one true meaning of the daily prayers has been transformed—without changing the text itself—into one more aspect of the meaning of the prayers, one among many. For the reader of Rabbi Eleazar's commentary, the numerical harmony is an additional, "interesting" aspect of the meaning of the prayers, rather than the discovery of the one and only inherent mystical truth. In Rabbi Eleazar's rendition, the mystic has been tamed, and his ideas fused within the infinite possibilities of nonmystical exegesis.

The language of the mystics has not yet been studied exhaustively;[21] the apparent similarity of the mystics' discourse to that of religious language successfully hides the uniqueness, and the exclusionary nature, of this language. This is part of a more general problem: The centrality of language in processes of exclusion, and the analysis of the differences between the language of the excluded to that of the established society from which they withdrew or were

---

[20]Rabbi Eleazar copied or paraphrased whole pages from the works of Rabbi Judah, as was the custom in those days. He did not mention the name of his teacher, probably because of Rabbi Judah's insistence on anonymity. There is nothing wrong in such a practice, according to the norms accepted at that time.

[21]An important contribution toward this goal has been made recently by the publication of a monograph on this subject: Michael A. Sells, *Mystical Languages of Unsaying*, Chicago and London: Chicago University Press 1995.

rejected from, has not received the attention it deserves in studies concerning exclusion. Language not only is a means of communication; more often than not it is the main vehicle of exclusion and denial. The first step in a process of exclusion is the appropriation of language by the oppressing social segment and denying of it to the excluded; at the same time, a particular language is developed by the excluded segment. The differences between the two languages express, sometimes more than anything else, the barriers separating the two.

In some cases, this barrier is represented not only by a difference in language, but by a different concept of language; the very role of language and its nature are conceived differently by the excluders and the excluded. This is the case concerning the relationship between mysticism and religion, as explained above. In such cases, exclusion becomes much deeper and more permanent, because any hope of discourse is lost. When accent, vocabulary, or dialect separates two groups of people, they can adapt a common means of discourse; but when the very relationship between language and truth is the rock of contention, there can never be a way to achieve common understanding. Mystics are destined to be forever misunderstood, sometimes despising their coreligionists who believe that they have understood the divine message. Their only solace is that though they are excluded, they are alone with God.

ONE

In Quest of a Historical Definition of Mysticism: The Contingental Approach

I

F_{ew} basic terms used in the study of religion are so loosely defined and so widely used as the term "mysticism." In the few cases in which an author of a book or an article does define his use of the term, it usually differs from many other definitions that are found in other works.[1] The following discussion is dedicated to one pur-

---

[1] Two comprehensive surveys of the study of mysticism have been published recently: Bernard McGinn, *The Foundations of Mysticism, Origins to the Fifth Century*, New York: Crossroads 1991, and Kees Waaijman, *Mysticism from the Perspective of the Jewish-Christian Tradition, in Studies in Spirituality*, vol. 2 (1992), Kok: Kampen, pp. 5–50. These studies include up-to-date bibliographies and detailed analysis of contemporary trends in the study of the subject, which will not be repeated here. It should be noted, however, that the contingent study of mystical phenomena as a part of the history of religion appears, at best, as a marginal aspect in these surveys, dwarfed by the theological, philosophical, and psychological approaches. This is despite the fact that Prof. McGinn's own analysis of the emergence of Latin mysticism is an exemplary study of the historical context of the emergence of mysticism (see note 8), and such a tendency also can be discerned in Prof. Waaijman's work.

1

pose only: an attempt to differentiate between several fields of usages of this term, and particularly to clarify the meaning of "mysticism" in a historical context.

By "clarify" I do not mean to distinguish between "right" and
"wrong" meanings of mysticism; I do not believe that such a distinction is appropriate. My purpose is only to delineate a group of specific contexts, and to suggest some parameters for the use of the term
"mysticism" in those cases that correspond to the characteristics of
these contexts.[2]

This methodology can be characterized as *a contingent approach
to the study of mysticism*; it emphasizes the study of a specific context, striving to reach general conclusions based on a comparative
study of particular cases in detail, rather than using any abstract concept and imposing it on individual religious phenomena.

The basis of the contingental analysis is the assumption that
the term "mysticism" is used in studies of religion mainly in a descriptive sense. We read about "mystical tendencies," "mystical visions," "mystical inclinations," "mystical characteristics," etc. Only
seldom is "mysticism" discussed as a central subject, usually when
this phenomenon is the main subject of analysis. In these cases a
detailed description and definition will frequently follow.[3] The frequent—and loose—use of the term is as an adjective, and I shall focus
on this aspect alone: That is, which phenomena can be described

---

[2]The problem has become even more complicated in the last few decades, as the
term has become a popular one in general political and cultural discussions. In
Israel today, for instance, it has a very clear meaning when found in newspapers
or political arguments: Anyone who reads the bible is religious; anyone who takes
it seriously is a mystic. In contemporary usage, "mystic" is becoming more and
more a synonym of "fanatic."

[3]The contingent character of many definitions is apparent even when an attempt
is made to present a comprehensive, all-inclusive definition. The particular scholarly background of each writer is evident in his preference of emphasis and selection, and his ideological or religious agenda shapes his presentation. This is
why I regard most of such definitions as completely correct and immensely meaningful, provided that one accepts them as contingent for the particular examples
and problems discussed in that presentation. As will be stated below, some negative statements concerning mysticism (namely, what mysticism is not) may have
wide relevance, while positive statements have to be contingental.

by the adjective "mystical" and gain something from this usage? In other words, this is a quest of the contingental use of the term, focused on the historical context.

It seems that the adjective "mystical" is used by scholars studying religion mainly in two different contexts: when describing the character of a text or portion of a text, and when describing a historical religious phenomenon, a movement, a group, or the work of a religious thinker. The first context includes sentences like "The author of the psalms sometimes uses mystical expressions," or "The visions of Zachariah certainly reflect a mystical attitude," or "The parables of Jesus emphasize the ethical rather than the mystical," etc. The second context is exemplified by statements like "The mystical element became dominant in the thinking of the Eastern Church in the eighth century," or "The Enlightenment is characterized by the rejection of the mystical way of thought." In the first case, the adjective "mystical" is intended, first and foremost, to characterize the religious sentiment within a particular text or part of a text, sometimes an individual phrase or a certain verbal picture or metaphor. In the second case, the adjective is used to describe the nature of a historical phenomenon, a tendency found in a group of people and texts.

There is a meaningful difference between these two contexts. Concerning the first one, I doubt very much that there is any hope of reaching a consensus concerning the use of the term "mysticism," because it is based on the individual's sense of what mysticism is. Is the verse "From the depth I cried to you, Oh Lord"[4] "mystical" or not? Some scholars will insist that it is, others will oppose that; there is no possibility of agreement unless a universal decision of what mysticism really is or is not is reached—something that, I am afraid, it is extremely unrealistic to expect. The analysis of such a problem involves a psychological investigation of the spiritual drives behind a textual phrase, an understanding of the individual meaning of this phrase in the particular context, a literary analysis of the place of the phrase within the text, and many other elements on which, usu-

---

[4]Psalms 130:1.

ally, scholars tend to disagree. And when this analysis is completed, it has to be compared to an abstract definition of mysticism, which also includes psychological and religious elements, stating the place of "mysticism" within the soul of a religious writer—again, something about which a consensus is seldom reached.

In general, I believe, the adjective use of the term "mystical" when describing a certain element within a text is extremely subjective, and should remain as such. A writer has every right to use such an adjective if he feels that it is appropriate, and other readers and scholars may either agree that this adjective is appropriate, or deny it; the text is still there, unchanged, and open to many interpretations and descriptions.

The situation is completely different when one considers the second case, the use of the adjective "mystical" to describe much wider religious phenomena that have clear historical dimensions. In this case, the term is intended not to characterize one phrase or one picture, but to describe the essence of the religious endeavor of a larger group of people and texts, to declare that the main essence of their religious creativity falls within the "mystical" category. In these usages, a large field of religious creative activity acquires the characteristic of "mystical," and a claim is made that this adjective is central and most meaningful to the understanding of that phenomenon. Here the responsibility of suggesting a clear and acceptable meaning for the term "mystical" is much greater, and, to some extent, easier, because of the large number of factors involved. In the first case, the scholar provides a literary-religious characteristic for a textual element; in the second, he offers a historical characterization of a wide phenomenon. Our concern in this study will be exclusively with the second type of adjective usage of "mysticism."

The main difference between the historical and the literary use of this term is that of the centrality of the adjective and the intellectual and spiritual demands that it presents. It is very different when one says that a phrase has a mystical aspect, and when one says that "Sufism is mystical Islam." In the first case, "mystical" is just one adjective among many possible descriptions of the emotional and religious characteristics of the phrase. In the second case, this is a historical statement that places the phenomenon under discussion within a strict type or category, thus excluding many others. When a scholar identifies the Jewish kabbalah or Muslim Sufism as mystical expressions, he makes a far-reaching distinction, creating a large body of associations and connections between these vast religious movements and those of other religions that are also described as mystical. In such cases we do have the right to demand some measure of accuracy and clarity in the use of this adjective, because it involves meaningful scholarly conclusions. The question now is: Can we find a common ground of meaning among scholars of diverse attitudes and backgrounds regarding the use of the term "mysticism" when describing major religious-historical phenomena? It seems that the quest for clarity in such a case is mandatory, and despite our different attitudes we should strive to have a basic, common meaning when we use this loaded adjective.

As a first step in this direction, I think we should give up, from the very beginning, any hope of applying the term to phenomena that are "really" mystical. There are some people—there aren't many, but their presence has to be taken into account—who "really" know what mysticism is. For them, mysticism is so familiar and intuitively clear that they use the term without any element of doubt or hesitation. In most cases, in my experience, such people tend to widen the field in which the use of the term is appropriate; they insist that everything involving anything visionary, anything supernatural, anything apocalyptical, any prophetic phenomenon, is essentially mystical. They believe that mysticism abounds in every spiritual context; sometimes they even tend to identify anything religious as mystical. One cannot argue against such an attitude. How can I prove that prophecy is not mysticism? I am neither a prophet nor a mystic; my only source of knowledge is some acquaintance with prophetic and mystical texts. To me they seem to be different; moreover, I believe that adding the adjective "mystical" to the prophetic phenomenon is not helpful in understanding it. We have enough problems in understanding prophecy; the addition of another confusing term is the opposite of helpful. But can I prove that they are different? I cannot do that, especially when confronted with someone who seems to be certain, experientially and intuitively, that he knows what mysticism "really" is.

In such a case, one can only offer the argument that terminology is the servant of scholarship and should be used in ways that benefit and enhance our understanding of religious phenomena rather than obscure it. The existence of intense religious experiences of various kinds is independent of the observations and categorizations of scholars. Human beings undergo profound spiritual changes and express deep-rooted emotions when confronting the numinous or the transcendent, without necessarily being aware of their typology or classification. Scholarly terminology steps in only later, trying to designate a group of such experiences under a certain typological term.

This attitude is embraced much more easily by a scholar who studies Jewish (or Islamic) mysticism than by a scholar studying Christian mysticism, because of the elementary fact that Hebrew (as well as Arabic) has no term for "mysticism"; thus no Jewish mystic up to the last generation or two ever knew that he was a mystic or what he was supposed to know, see, and feel as a mystic.

A Christian mystic, for whom the term is a traditional one, may feel that he belongs to a certain succession of religious thinkers, and knowingly mold his own expressions according to their earlier terminology and literary genres. The scholar studying Christian mysticism is familiar with the same history of religious expression, and thus is in some kind of harmony with the subject of his research, a harmony that may lead to his overlooking the arbitrary nature of the typological designation of "mystics."

In Judaism (or Islam), a writer may be aware that he is a kabbalist (or a Sufi), and may conform to the traditional ways of expression of this school, but this will not bear directly on his being a mystic or not; for while there are elements in kabbalah (or Sufism) that are close to mysticism, nobody will suggest that they are identical. Both these vast treasuries of religious experiences, texts, and movements include so many variegated expressions, literary genres, scientific attitudes, historical concepts, and other aspects of religious culture that they cannot be described exhaustively by any one term. Thus, while a Christian thinker may define himself as a mystic, and the scholar will in most cases agree with this self-identification, no Jew (or Muslim) ever defined himself as such. The scholar is therefore keenly aware of his outsider's position when he decides that a particular kabbalist is a mystic; he is obviously imposing an external scholarly typology upon the unaware (usually the long-dead) religious thinker, and he is conscious of the need to explain his decision, being unable to say "but he said so himself." [5]

The fact that Judaism does not include an intrinsic distinction between mystics and nonmystics makes the Jewish scholar of mysticism more aware of the arbitrariness of this designation, and of the necessity of constantly checking the appropriateness of this term to the texts or figures studied. This ambiguity, and the inherent hesitation concerning such categorization, is clearly reflected in the history of the study of kabbalah in this century.

For instance, in the early studies of the kabbalah by the great scholar of this subject, Gershom Scholem, the term "mysticism" is almost completely absent. Scholem preferred to describe the great religious figures he was studying as "kabbalists," or to use the traditional term for people who dealt with such subjects, *baaley sod*, that is, those involved in esoterics, a very common self-designation of mystics and esoterics in traditional Judaism.[6] Scholem used the term

---

[5]It should be noted that the number of non-Christian scholars who dedicated their studies to the understanding of mystical phenomena is very small, and most of these few published their works in the last generation or two. Until recently, this field has been almost the sole domain of scholars from a Christian background, and this difference concerning the absence of the term in other religions was not properly realized. A historical attitude is manifest in the works of the Jewish scholars in this field, most notably in the studies of Steven T. Katz (in the opening articles in the three collections of studies he has published: *Mysticism and Religious Traditions*, 1983; *Mysticism and Philosophical Analysis*, 1978; and *Mysticism and Language*, 1992; New York and Oxford: Oxford University Press).
[6]This is characteristic of Scholem's studies, published mainly in Hebrew, between 1924 and 1940. But even in later years, the term "mysticism" is relatively seldom used in his studies written originally in Hebrew. Much more frequent use of the term is found in his works published in German or English. Many of his books and articles in other languages have the word "mysticism" in their titles, while no book and almost no article in Hebrew has such a title.

"mysticism" in a general way only in 1941, twenty years after he
started to study the subject, when he published his first comprehensive presentation of this field in English, *Major Trends in Jewish
Mysticism.*[7] In this book, he accepted and justified the general tendency to see in the kabbalah a Jewish expression of mysticism, but
in several cases he hesitated and explained the difference between
the Jewish phenomenon and mysticism in general. Even concerning the teachings of the greatest work of the kabbalah, the *Zohar*,
written in northern Spain in the last decades of the thirteenth century, he preferred the term "theosophy" to "mysticism.[8]"

The tension between the unique nature of the Jewish religious
phenomena and the accepted meaning of "mysticism" characterizes
the study of the kabbalah and other Jewish esoteric-mystical circles
and movements. The scholar is continuously aware of the necessity
to use from time to time the term "mysticism," and, at the same time,
of the difference between these Jewish expressions of intense religious
experiences and the characteristics of mysticism in general. The
awareness of this tension seems to me to justify the following attempt
by a scholar whose main interest is in the history of Jewish mysticism
to define the characteristics of mysticism as a historical phenomenon.

II

The first and, I believe, the most important aspect of a definition of mysticism as a historical phenomenon is the insistence that
such a definition be qualitative rather than quantitative. This in itself
is a most difficult task, because most of the current definitions of

---

[7]New York: Schocken 1941; many editions, reprintings, and translations followed.
[8]Op. cit., Ch. 6, pp. 205–243. Concerning Scholem's view of the nature of mysticism, see McGinn, *Foundations of Mysticism*, pp. 334–336. It should be noted
that Scholem's evolutionary theory concerning the place of mysticism in the
history of religions was not a central subject in the totality of his work; he seldom referred to it after including it in the opening chapter of his *Major Trends*.
An important key to his concept of mysticism is found in his essay on kabbalistic
symbolism (see note 18). I intend to analyze Scholem's theories about the nature
of mysticism and its place in religion in a separate article.

mysticism tend to stress the quantitative aspect. In almost all descriptions and definitions of mysticism, we repeatedly find terms like adherence and unity with God; constant awareness of divine presence; eternal wish to be in God's proximity; viewing reality as reflecting divine goodness; craving for being in touch with the transcendent; and many similar descriptions.[9] In most cases, these terms reflect elements that are present and central in religion in general, and are not unique to mysticism. Every religion promises, in one way or another, proximity to God, awareness of His presence, and a chance to get closer or even be united with Him.[10] Prayer is described in religion in general as a vehicle for achieving contact, support, and experience of the presence of God.

These definitions, therefore, to a large extent, claim that *mysticism is religion, only a little more so*. This does not mean that there is anything wrong or untrue in such definitions; it seems to me that all such descriptions are accurate and meaningful. Their flaw is that that they are insufficient and do not reflect the sincere feeling of most mystics throughout history that they represent a different quality of religious experience, rather than a more intense and profound variety of the usual claims of religious devotion.

---

[9]The surveys published by McGinn and Waaijman (see note 1) include scores of such formulations. Scholem's basic definition is of the same nature (*Major Trends*, pp. 4–7).

[10]The case of the concept of *unio mystica* is the most typical, and exemplifies the difficulty of this problem. How can one differentiate between "proximity" or "adherence" to God and "union" with Him? Different people, undoubtedly, will characterize an intense relationship with God in one of these terms, depending on their linguistic tendencies and not only on the character of the experience itself. One person's "union" is another person's "adherence." How can a scholar decide who "really" achieved "union" and not just "proximity," when all he has to depend on is the individual style and selection of words of his source? The unavoidable subjective character of the usage of such terms, both by the religious thinker and by the scholar, is clearly evident. A controversy concerning the place of *unio mystica* in the kabbalah became a major subject of discussion in Jerusalem in the 1960s, when I. Tishby and E. Gottlieb severely criticized Scholem's rejection of the centrality of this phenomenon in the kabbalah, and their view dominated among most Jerusalem scholars. Compare M. Idel and B. McGinn, eds., *Mystical Union and Monotheistic Faith*, New York: Macmillan 1989.

This problem is closely connected with one of the most serious aspects of the study of Christian mysticism, namely the relationship between what mysticism is and what mysticism should be. The very common concept, found among both mystics and some scholars (mainly in Catholicism), that mysticism is the supreme pinnacle of religion demands that a discussion of mysticism will often be intermingled with the problem of the final purpose, or the supreme achievement, of religiosity. This problem, despite its great importance, is an unhistorical one, because history is concerned only with what was, not with what should or could have been. A tendency to describe mysticism in the same terms by which religiosity is defined is natural in such a context, but it is not helpful in the attempt to understand mysticism as a historical phenomenon.[11]

In Judaism and Islam, when "mysticism" is applied to separate, relatively well defined groups, like the kabbalists and the Sufis (if their intrinsic diversity is taken into account and the term is not used comprehensively), the distinction between religiosity in general and the phenomena under discussion as candidates for the designation "mystical" is more evident.

In order to understand mysticism in a historical context, we must seek those aspects that are unique to the mystics and are absent from religion in general. Otherwise, mysticism will remain a degree within religion rather than a separate entity. There is nothing wrong with mysticism being a degree within religion; the problem is that in many cases the mystics seem to insist on their own unique position and a distinct attitude, which, while being religious, is of a separate and different quality. The starting point for a definition of

---

[11]This may be why the modern study of gnosticism almost completely neglects the aspect of gnosticism as mysticism. The gnostics separated themselves, socially and religiously, from other Christians, and later Christianity did not view them as Christians; therefore the term "mysticism" did not seem to be relevant to the understanding of this rich and profound group of religious phenomena. In many comprehensive works about gnoticism, the term "mysticism" may not be found even in the index. Important exceptions to this generalization are, however, those of B. Layton, *The Gnostic Scriptures: A New Translation and Introductions*, New York: Doubleday 1987, passim, and B. McGinn, *Foundations of Mysticism*, p. 369, note 21 et passim.

mysticism should be, therefore, an element that is not shared as a rule by religion in general.[12]

Such a starting point can be the claim, characteristic of mystics everywhere, that there is a realm of supernal truth that cannot be achieved by the usual avenues of knowledge, by sensual perception and logical generalization and analysis. Religion in general does not posit itself in opposition to logical analysis or even common sense, and does not claim to be antagonistic to human everyday sensual experience. Many religious teachers insist that human sensual experience and logic do indicate religious truth, at least in part. Theology is saturated with arguments based on common human characteristics. Mysticism, on the other hand, treats them at least with suspicion, if not with complete negation. The way to achieve true, complete knowledge transcends, according to the mystics, these usual means of acquiring knowledge. For the mystic, truth by its nature is hidden, unperceived by the senses or by the laws of logic. The sincere belief in this transcendent realm of unperceived and incomprehensible truth is characteristic of mysticism, and differentiates it from most aspects of religion in general.[13]

The nature of mystical knowledge or mystical truth is qualitatively different from the concept of truth and knowledge in nonmystical religion. In most cases, religious thinkers insist that not all knowledge can be achieved by man; that God's ways cannot be completely explained by human intelligence; that man can never perceive truth as fully and comprehensively as God; that everything known by man, in comparison to God, is partial and incomplete. The knowledge of God Himself, most theologians claim, is beyond

---

[12]Recent usage of the term "spirituality" is extremely helpful in this connection. A separation between "mysticism," which is a separate and different religious experience, and "spirituality," which is the pinnacle of usual religious life, could help in the most meaningful way in clarifying the terminology in this field.

[13]Examples of the concept of mysticism abound; see McGinn, *Foundations of Mysticism*, XI–XX et passim. The best expression of this attitude with which I am familiar is included in a sentence said by the mysterious fox in Antoine de Saint-Exupéry's *The Little Prince*: "This is my secret, and it is very simple. The really important things are those which are hidden from the eyes."

the abilities of the human mind. Many similar formulations separating truth as perceived by man from the complete, divine truth are easily found. Yet all these postulations of relative human ignorance in the face of divine truth are very different from the mystic's view of the relationship between man's faculties of achieving knowledge and divine truth itself.

The difference is twofold: On the one hand, the mystic is more pessimistic than the theologian about the ability of man's logical mind to achieve any part of the truth; on the other, he is much more optimistic. The mystic profoundly doubts whether human senses and logic can lead man to grasping any meaningful part of truth, whereas the theologian, in most cases, insists that these human means do convey some part of universal, if not of the divine, truth. On the other hand, the mystic is a mystic because he believes that there is an alternative nonsensual and nonlogical way of achieving truth, the *via mystica*, which can lead the mystic (though not humanity in general) to embrace some aspects of the hidden divine truth. It should be noted that, whether "pessimistic" or "optimistic," the mystic positions himself in opposition to the normative, accepted concepts of nonmystical religion. The mystic claims, when viewing religious norms and theology, that what his coreligionists think they know they actually do not, and what there is to be known is completely unknown to them.

The basic difference between the mystic and the nonmystic is not one of content, of a separate concept of the nature of God, His providence, or His attitude toward man and the universe; it is the difference in the concept of the means by which truth can be achieved. The theologian believes that the means given to man by God at creation may be inferior and insufficient for the complete understanding of divine truth, but he does believe that as far as they go, they do indicate truth, partial and incomplete as it may be; he does not believe that there are any other means of achieving truth besides the endowments of sight and hearing, syllogism, and mathematics. The mystic denies that these human faculties are related in any way to divine truth; the more they are developed and followed, the farther one is led away from truth.

The only avenue to truth is the forsaking of these human faculties and the adherence to a completely different quest for truth, in nonsensual and supralogical means.

The theologian and the mystic may thus be united in their belief in the inability of man to achieve coherent knowledge of the secrets of the divine realm, but in everything else they are separated. Their concepts of man, of knowledge, and of truth are far apart. The theologian sees human abilities as partial and incomplete but that, as far as they go, they do convey truth. The mystic doubts everything that the senses and the mind indicate, and believes in the existence of another alternative, of a different way of approaching truth, which is completely unknown to the nonmystic.

Since in this study the quest for a definition of mysticism is focused on the historical aspect of mysticism, it is necessary to indicate the difference between the mystic and the nonmystic in historical terms, in their different position concerning basic religious concepts as they operate on the contingent case of established religions. This can be done, I believe, in the clearest and most meaningful way by an analysis of the difference in attitude between the mystic and the nonmystic concerning language, and within that realm the difference concerning the meaning of scriptures.

Scriptural religions are characterized by a basic ambiguity concerning the nature of language.[14] On the one hand, language is the means by which human beings communicate. On the other hand,

---

[14]Much remains to be done in the study of the religious and mystical concepts of language; the great advances in linguistics and semiotics in the last decades have not been fully applied to these fields. See, for instance, S. Katz's collection of papers on the subject (see note 5). I have prepared for publication a comprehensive study titled *The Language of the Mystics*. See also J. Dan, "The Concept of Language in Ashkenazi Hasidism," in L. Glinert (ed.), *Hebrew in Ashkenaz*, New York and Oxford: Oxford University Press 1993, pp. 11–25; idem, "The Concept of Language in Jewish Mysticism," in K. Grözinger (ed.), *Proceedings of the Conference on Jewish Mysticism in Germany*, Frankfurt: Suhrkamp; idem, "Prayer as Text and Prayer as a Mystical Experience," in R. Link-Salinger (ed.), *Torah and Wisdom: Studies in Jewish Philosophy, Kabbalah and Halacha in Honor of A. Hyman*, New York: Shengold 1992, pp. 33–47.

language is a divine entity, preceding man and independent of him, that originated within God and served Him, among other things, in the process of Creation. The Word, the Logos, is beyond human comprehension, at least in its complete meaning;[15] man cannot conceive how, by the utterance of "Let there be light," a universe came into being. Yet language is used every day within the framework of human life, of human devotion, of human adherence to God, as an instrument expressing man's emotions, perceptions, and logical conclusions. This dual nature of language is reflected, in the most forceful way, in the concept of scriptures, which is the most powerful and distinctive element of the three monotheistic religions. I prefer the term "scriptural religions" to "monotheistic religions": It is much more accurate and expressive of the nature of Judaism, Christianity, and Islam.

Scripture expresses God's message to man; the origin of the language it uses is divine, coming directly from the source of language, from God, who devised language and used it long before man was created. Yet scripture speaks in human communicative terms and conveys human meanings. When trying to understand a scriptural word, a person uses the same sensual or logical means that he employs when trying to understand everything else in the surrounding world. Scriptural language is related, therefore, to human experience, not only to its remote and hidden divine source. This, a theologian

---

[15]Concerning the logos and its linguistic meaning, see, among many other recent works, Walter J. Ong, *The Presence of the Word: Some Prolegomena for Cultural and Religious History*, New Haven: Yale University Press 1967; Wilhelm Kleber, *Die Logoslehre: von Heraklit bis Origenes*, Stuttgart: Verlag Urachhaus 1958; Bernard Jendorff, *Der Logosbegriff*, Frankfurt a/M: Peter Lang 1976; J. H. Heiser, *Logos and Language in the Philosophy of Plotinus*, New York: E. Mellen Press 1991; Thomas H. Tobin, "The Prologue of John and Hellenistic Jewish Speculation," in *The Catholic Biblical Quarterly* 52 (1990), pp. 252–269; B. A. Pearson, "Philo, Gnosis and the New Testament," in his *Gnosticism, Judaism and Egyptian Christianity*, Minneapolis: Fortress Press 1990, pp. 165–182. Compare also the Hindu parallel to the concept of the creation by language: André Padoux, *Vâc: The Concept of the World in Selected Hindu Tantras*, trans. Jacques Gontier, Albany, New York: SUNY Press 1990. The hymns to Vâc and to the creation in the tenth book of the *Rgveda* present a most ancient identification of the creative divine power with divine language.

will usually say, is the result of God's benevolence toward the faithful: He gave them His message in terms that they can relate to their human faculties and surroundings, thus conveying that part of the divine truth that can be conceived by human beings in terms that can reach them and be grasped by them. In other words, scripture does have a literal meaning, and this literal meaning is divine truth, even though it may not be the whole divine truth.

This is very similar to the theologian's attitude toward human logic. It is a characteristic of the human mind to agree, in a universal manner, that if A is greater than B and B is greater than C, A is greater than C. How do we know that this elementary syllogism is true? The proof of the veracity of logic is divine benevolence: God is good, God created man and devised the laws of logic that are inherent in human intellect, and therefore these laws reflect truth; God, being good, will not deliberately mislead man and introduce into his mind norms that are false. In the same way, what we see is not a misleading illusion but something that is really there, because God will not devise laws of optics that will deliberately lead His creatures to falsehood.[16] Scripture reflects literal truth because God, in His benevolence, enables man to achieve that part of truth that can be expressed by the adaptation of divine language to human needs.

The mystic does not accept this series of conclusions. Human language, for him, is the embodiment of the physical and logical perceptions he distrusts. He does not accept the notion that divine truth can be expressed in human terms, based on the sensual and intellectual strata of human language. On the other hand, the mystic cannot deny scriptures as a source of truth without forsaking his adherence to the scriptural religion of which he is a loyal and obedient part (otherwise he would not be in such a passionate quest for

---

[16]This belief was stated, in this century, most emphatically and meaningfully by Albert Einstein when he expressed his rejection of quantum mechanics: "God does not play dice with the universe" (thus rejecting quantum mechanics's denial of causality). As of now, it seems that in this scientific-theological statement Einstein was wrong.

contact with the God of this religion). Not accepting the sensual-logical reading of scripture, the mystic, therefore, adheres to a different reading of the divine message, mystical and true, unperceived and unknown to nonmystics. According to the mystics, within the apparent literal, human meaning of the scriptures, God has hidden a different layer of meaning that cannot be reached unless one has an intuitive, extralinguistic glimpse of mystical truth; with the assistance of his mystical faculties, unshared by this coreligionists, the mystic can come into contact with the hidden kernel of divinity within the verses.

Like mysticism itself, this mystical meaning of the divine language of scriptures cannot be explained fully to the nonmystic.[17] It represents a different way of looking at the divine message, in the same way that the mystic differs from the nonmystic in his perception of the universe and the way toward God. The mystical aspect of the scriptures need not be in opposition or contradiction to the accepted sensual-logical reading of the texts by nonmystics; it is just different, another quality, another layer of truth, to which only the mystic has access.

This difference between the mystical and nonmystical perceptions of the meaning of scripture is expressed historically by the fact that groups of mystics, in various places and times, have viewed themselves as qualitatively separate from the established religious tradition to which they are loyal adherents. They read scriptures in a different way than the rest of their coreligionists. In some historical contexts this difference may be hardly noticeable; the mystic will write a commentary on the scriptures that differs in its literary and

---

[17]It should be emphasized that this distinction between the human meaning of scriptural language and the divine meaning hidden within it has nothing to do with the common typology of exegetical norms found in the three scriptural religions, which defines several layers (usually four) of literal, allegorical, esoteric, analogical, etc. ways of understanding each verse. All these—including the "esoteric"—follow the basic belief that scriptural language is open to analysis and to understanding by the use of human sensual and logical faculties. The mystical way of achieving truth regards all these and similar methodologies as belonging to the literal, human aspect of language.

sometimes its ideological character from other commentaries, but the difference is not so meaningful as to arouse suspicion or animosity, and it blends into the various nonmystical trends in that religious culture. In other cases, the difference in the attitude of the mystics toward scriptures will be an irritant; nonmystics may feel that the mystics have a great secret that they believe gives them a separate, higher standing in the religious hierarchy, and this may arouse antagonism and opposition. In extreme cases this difference leads to controversies, arguments, or even a schism and the organization of the mystically inclined into sects or separate monasteries or circles, giving a clear historical expression to their qualitative difference from established, nonmystical organizations. The vast range of possibilities for historical consequences results from the unique attitude of the mystic to his religious heritage and traditions.

In many cases the mystic may insist that the language of scripture should be regarded as symbolic in nature. The term "symbolism" in a mystical context requires clarification, because it is radically different from its use in everyday language and in some other disciplines concerned with the meaning of text and language.[18] The mystical use of the term "symbol" is unique in its insistence that the symbol, which is a linguistic expression—a word, a phrase, a term—is the maximum revelation in language of something that in itself cannot be expressed by language at all. This concept makes it com-

---

[18]The literature on the nature of symbolism as relating to mysticism is vast, yet the approach suggested here, based on the historian's acceptance that he does not know anything beyond the symbol concerning the mystical entity that is presented by it, is rare. G. Scholem dedicated to this subject his enigmatic short treatise, "Zehn unhistorische Sätze über Kabbalah," in *Geist und Werk: Festschrift zum Dr. Daniel Brody*, Zurich 1958, pp. 209–215; reprinted in *Judaica III, Studien zur jüdischen Mystik*, Frankfurt a/M, 1970, pp. 265–271. This has been the subject of discussion in N. Rothenstreich, "Symbolism and Transcendence: On Some Philosophical Aspects of Gershom Scholem's Opus," in *Review of Metaphysics* (1977), pp. 604–614, and in my "From the Symbol to the Symbolized: Gershom Scholem's Ten Unhistorical Theses on the Kabbalah," in *Jerusalem Studies in Jewish Thought* 5 (1985), pp. 363–385 (in Hebrew). Compare also D. Biale, "Gershom Scholem's Ten Unhistorical Aphorisms on Kabbalah: Text and Commentary," in *Modern Judaism* (1985), pp. 67–93, and see the references there, note 3 on p. 91.

pletely impossible to use the term "symbol" in close proximity to the term "symbolized," as we so often do; that is, stating in one and the same sentence both the symbol and what it is supposed to symbolize. From a mystical point of view, the symbol expressed by language is a dead end: Nothing more can be said about the subject designated by the symbol; no more clarifications or explanations by words can be added to it. It is all that linguistic means can attain when confronting a supralinguistic phenomenon.

This concept of the symbol is one typical apology used by the mystic to explain the impossible: namely, that God, the master and source of all truth, chose language in order to express Himself in the scriptures. God should have known (so to speak) what the mystic knows very well, that words designating sensual and logical phenomena cannot in any way denote the divine, esoteric truth. Yet He did use words when addressing the prophets, and did state His demands of man in such terms. Symbolism (of the kind described here) is the answer: God indeed used words—not as words, but as symbols. The words in the scriptures do not relate to earthly, material objects, but to the mystical, celestial truth, and they represent the maximum that even God Himself can express by words from that hidden truth. The words of the scriptures should be read as remote, vague, imprecise hints that have some tenuous and incomplete relationship to the supralinguistic truth, and not as complete, coherent statements of it. God, in His benevolence, supplied the faithful mystics with these vague hints of His esoteric truth, but they should never be accepted as truth itself; the vague symbol should never be confused with the symbolized, which is eternally beyond any linguistic expression, even by God in His scriptures.

The concept of symbolism, understood in this way, creates the basic difference in attitude between the mystic and the nonmystic when reading the scriptures. The nonmystic finds divine truth in scriptures; the mystic finds there only vague and imprecise symbolical hints of it. For the nonmystic, scriptures mean revelation; for the mystic, scriptures denote the impossibility of revelation by language, and its substitution by the remote and opaque series of symbols, the complete meaning of which is not found within the words revealed

by God to man. Both of them read the same texts, but their attitudes toward them diverge completely.

The difference is so vast that no explanations and discussions
are possible. The mystic's disbelief in the ability of language to express truth makes him a person with whom it is impossible to argue. Discussion and dialogue are based on the assumption that some
common ground exists in the understanding of language, that words
denote the same meaning to both participants in the argument. But
when one side in such an argument denies the possibility of language
denoting truth, and the vagueness of symbolic meaning allows no
precise definitions, language loses even its ability to define differences
between opposing views. In some cases, the mystic does not regard
the literal understanding of scriptures, on any level, as "untrue," but
rather as partial, incomplete, and relatively unimportant; such an
attitude does not leave an opening for argument.

It is thus understandable why mystics in all three scriptural religions were often so frustrated when accused of heresy. In order to
be a heretic, a person has to use language fully and accurately, to
make a clear and meaningful statement that is regarded by others
as heretical. The mystic feels that he cannot do even that, because
language does not allow him to present anything that is true in his
eyes (and false or heretical in the eyes of others). Symbols, because
of their vagueness and remoteness from the complete truth, cannot
be the basis of an accusation of heresy. The mystic cannot be ac-
countable for the literal understanding of his symbols by the
nonmystics: He "never meant it this way."

One of the central and most common symbols of the medieval
Jewish kabbalah provides a meaningful example of this attitude. From
its very beginning in the late twelfth century, the kabbalah insisted
that the divine world (or pleroma) is constituted by ten divine, dynamic powers called *sefirot*. Each of these ten *sefirot* represents (symbolically) a definable, unique aspect of the divine world.[19] The

---

[19]Concerning the concept of the *sefirot*, see G. Scholem, *Major Trends in Jewish
Mysticism*, 3rd ed., New York: Schocken 1954, pp. 207–229 et passim; idem,
Kabbalah, Jerusalem: Keter 1974, pp. 88–116; idem, *From the Mystical Shape of*

kabbalists could very well be accused—indeed they were accused—
of believing in ten divine beings, thus being polytheists rather than
the strict monotheists that Judaism demanded.[20]

Despite the centrality of this symbol in the writings of almost
all kabbalists between the twelfth and twentieth centuries, this obvious "heresy" did not become a meaningful subject of argument or
controversy. The kabbalists, when asked about that, "explain" that
"ten" is a symbol, which cannot be regarded as identical to its earthly
arithmetical meaning. In the literal world, ten indeed is more than
one; but in the hidden realm of divine truth, the symbol "ten" does
not necessarily denote this mundane mathematical fact. In the esoteric level of mystical meanings, "ten" could very well be the essence
of "one," the true, sublime expression of "oneness." In the divine
world, where oppositions are united, where earthly and literal distinctions lose their meaning, the apparent contradiction between
"one" and "ten" vanishes. The kabbalist never insists that "indeed,
there are ten divine beings rather than the commonly held belief in
the unity of God," thus becoming a full-fledged heretic. He insists
that what he symbolically means by "ten" in no way contradicts the
basic concept of monotheism. The concept of symbolism leaves no
avenue for controversy or argument on this subject because, in fact,
the mystic has not presented any statement that is open to argument on linguistic levels. All he says is that when he uses the term
"ten" he uses a symbol, the complete meaning of which cannot be

---

the Godhead, New York: Schocken 1991, passim; and I. Tishby, The Wisdom of
the Zohar, Oxford: Oxford University Press 1989. Concerning the Lurianic concept of the sefirot, which includes a pseudoscientific element besides the mythical, see now J. Dan, Lurianic Kabbalah Between Myth and Science, in Proceedings
of the Fourth International Conference on the History of Jewish Mysticism, ed. R. Elior
and Y. Liebes, Jerusalem 1992; pp. 9–36 (in Hebrew).

[20]The long line of such accusations leads from Rabbi Meir ben Shimeon of
Narbonne in the thirteenth century (see G. Scholem, Origins of the Kabbalah,
Princeton, NJ: Princeton University Press and the Jewish Publication Society 1987,
pp. 42–43, 54), up to Solomon Rubin's numerous attacks on the kabbalah as the
reemergence of pagan idolatry in Judaism, expressed in several treatises published
at the end of the last century.

expressed by words, and which does not contradict in any way the basic faith in the unity of God.

Returning to the historical level, this claim by the kabbalist may absolve him of the accusation of heresy, but it cannot deny the existence of a gulf between him and his coreligionists, who may sometimes be horrified by statements describing the ten powers in the Godhead, and by the detailed descriptions of the relationships between them, especially the sexual symbolism used so graphically by some kabbalists when relating the dynamic relationship between the masculine and feminine powers there. The mystic, of course, says that these terms—"sex," "masculine," feminine," etc.—are nothing but symbols, and that their occurrences in the divine world are vastly different from the earthly practices associated with them. The mystic cannot be blamed for the literal-mindedness of his nonmystical coreligionists. Yet the fact remains that the separation between these two groups of people, who worship together, share the same traditions and ways of life, and seemingly use the same language in their expression of religious devotion, is profound. They are separated by the gulf of their attitude toward language: They may use the same words, but with vastly different contexts of meaning.

The difference between the symbolic and literal attitudes toward scripture is the most important aspect of the qualitative separation between mystics and nonmystics, but it is not the only one. It can be said that the attitude toward scripture reflects a more comprehensive attitude toward universal reality. God, after all, not only is present in scriptural revelation; He is also the Creator of the world and of man. The fact that everything originates from within Him necessitates a relationship between Him and His creatures.

Theology formulated, in many different ways, systems to explain this relationship; for the mystic, however, this connection between the divine and the earthly is a clear manifestation of a symbolic bond. Earthly phenomena represent, vaguely and ambiguously, the tenuous relationship with the divine source in a symbolic fashion. Everything on Earth represents in its inexpressible way some contact with its sublime source. The symbolic meaning of language therefore cannot be separated from the symbolic relationship between the sensual meaning of language and its hidden mystical stratum. Thus, "femininity" is a symbol both in its linguistic usage and in its sensual essence. The "right" to use terminology related to sexual relationship in a symbolic way when describing the hidden processes in the divine world is acquired by the mystic both because God had used such language in scriptures—for instance, when describing the relationship between Israel and God in sexual terms—and because of the very existence of sexuality in the universe created by God, creation being a superior expression of revelation of divine powers. The nonmystic regards created reality in a literal fashion; sexuality, for instance, was devised by God in order to enable His creatures to multiply. For the mystic, it is obvious that the literal understanding of created phenomena is, if not radically false, at least incomplete, inaccurate, and insufficient. Sexuality exists in the created world because it reflects some hidden, suprasensual and metalinguistic dynamism within the Godhead, which is expressed symbolically in the language and the phenomenon of sexuality.

What is true concerning sensual phenomena is also true concerning logical and philosophical terminology, in spite of their abstract nature. William Inge long ago noted the close connections in terms and content between Christian mysticism and neo-Platonism, going so far as to say that they are sometimes indistinguishable.[21] This is also true of some central works of Jewish mysticism, especially in the thirteenth century.[22] Apparently, the mystics' suspicion of logic did not create a barrier between them and rational philosophy and basic neo-Platonist terms, and even more concepts of the

----

[21]William Inge, *Christian Mysticism*, considered in eight lectures delivered before the University of Oxford, The Bampton Lectures, 1899; 8th ed., London: Methuen 1948; and compare the earlier treatment of the same subject: Adolf Helfferich, *Die christliche Mystik, in ihrer Entwicklung und ihren Denkmalen*, Gotha: F. Perthes 1842; Joseph von Gorres, *Die christliche Mystik*, Regensburg: Manz 1836–1842; and in a more modern manner: Louis K. Dupré, *The Deeper Life: An Introduction to Christian Mysticism*, New York: Crossroads 1981; compare William Johnston, *Christian Mysticism Today*, San Francisco: Harper & Row 1984.
[22]For example, Rabbi Azriel of Gerona. See Scholem, *The Origins of the Kabbalah*, pp. 370–378, 416–454.

structure and essence of the universe play a prominent part in the vocabulary of the mystics in the Early and High Middle Ages.[23]

The prominence of neo-Platonism in the writings of the mystics should not be confused, however, with their acceptance of the philosophers' statements. A gulf separates them, though it is not always apparent at first glance. Many pages in books written by mystics can be read superficially as neo-Platonist philosophical works, but they are not. The deep dividing line between them is the one separating rational terms from mystical symbols. The same word may be used by both, but its meaning is radically different.

A clear example of this difference is a concept that plays a central role in both Late Antiquity and medieval neo-Platonism, as well as in many schools of mystics in the three scriptural religions: the concept of "emanation." This is a good example for our subject because of the abstract nature of the concept, which is not directly related to any earthly phenomenon, except by analogy, and in both the philosophical and the mystical contexts is used in statements concerning the spiritual world. The neo-Platonist rationalist views the various strata of spiritual entities leading from the supreme Godhead to the celestial realms as emanating from each other, each layer identical in essence with the one above it but slightly less pure and sublime than its source. The process of emanation is one of evolvement of spiritual beings and of their progressive descent toward mundane reality.

Superficially, this same statement can be used to describe the concept of the succession of divine powers in the world view of many mystics, who also conceive such a hierarchy of spiritual powers emanating from one another and constituting the divine realms. But there is a vast difference: The rationalist philosopher states what he

---

[23]Of course, this problem vanishes the moment one identifies neo-Platonism, and especially the works of Plotinus, as mystical. It seems to me a broadening of the boundaries of this field in a way that prevents any meaningful, concentrated analysis. One should be especially careful to distinguish between those who adhere to a scriptural religion and those who do not; otherwise, the confusion becomes intolerable.

believes to be facts, expressed as clearly as possible in precise language—even if that language uses poetic structures and abounds with
metaphors, like that of Plotinus. These statements are, in his eyes,
provable conclusions derived from the analysis of actual phenomena by logical means. When called upon to do so, he will defend
the veracity and accuracy of reality in these statements. In other
words, for the rationalist philosopher, the process of emanation is
what really happens in the spiritual world.

The mystic, while using the same terms—and sometimes even
employing Plotinus's metaphors—does not claim that the process of
emanation is what "really" occurs; for him, "emanation" is a symbol, a human term that is the closest linguistic approximation to
something which in itself is beyond language. If asked whether the
divine powers really emanate from each other, his answer is, "Of
course not." What "really" happens is something completely different, a mystical process that can never be expressed in words and
metaphors; emanation is a convenient approximation giving a vague,
insufficient hint of something that is beyond language, beyond logic,
beyond the imagination.

The rationalist philosopher is a scientist who believes that the
truth, even concerning the innermost processes of spiritual entities,
can be analyzed and explained by precise terminology. The mystic
may use the same terminology, but for him the words represent only
imprecise and partial approximations of a hidden truth that can
never be conveyed by logical and linguistic means.

This difference is also reflected in the very content of the speculation presented by them. The world as described by the neo-
Platonist philosophers tends to be definite and fixed; reality is an
essentially unchanging structure (especially in the spiritual realms).
The imprecise nature of the mystical symbols leads the descriptions
of the mystics to be much more dynamic and flexible. The neo-
Platonist philosopher, for instance, may often use metaphors derived
from anthropomorphic, sexual, or mythical realms when describing
the spiritual world, but they remain metaphors that do not impinge
upon the finality and preciseness of his statements. The mystic uses
terminology derived from the same linguistic realms, but they are

regarded as symbols, equivalent in their veracity to the rationalistic terminology derived from the works of the philosophers. The intrinsic dynamism of anthropomorphic or sexual images that plays no part in the rationalists' metaphorical use of these images will become immanent and meaningful in the usage of the mystics, being no less "true" or "real" than the logical terms.

Thus, for instance, a rationalist may use an image of birth to denote a process of emanation, but the basic meaning remains that of the logical term "emanation"; the mystic, when using these same terms, sees them as equal symbols, denoting in a similar way a hidden dynamic process that can be, at the same time, both the logical one of emanation and the anthropomorphic, dynamic one of birth (thus denoting a mother–son relationship, love and tenderness, etc., elements that play no intrinsic part in the rationalistic structure of existence).[24]

In this way, the use of symbolism enables the mystic to employ all aspects of existence, linguistic and experiental, in his system of symbols, because God is the source of all; everything may be used in order to seek the best possible approximations for describing His secrets, provided that one is always aware that these statements do not denote truth. At best, they serve as vague and remote hints at the realm of truth, which is essentially beyond human experience, logic, and language.

A digression is in order here, to present, by analogy, the relevance of these distinctions to modern experience with language, and to show the historical nature of these conclusions. It seems that a relationship very similar to the one that existed between rationalists and mystics in the Middle Ages did occur in this century within the world of the scientists, especially physicists, when using language to describe scientific reality. Scientists had always been bothered by the problem of expressing their findings in linguistic terms; they often

---

[24]This concept, and its relationship to the problem of linguistic expression of mystical visions and experiences, was explored by Jacques Maritain in his *Distinguish to Unite or the Degrees of Knowledge* (English translation by G. B. Phelan, New York: Scribner 1959).

found it much easier to present their conclusions with mathematical formulas than with coherent sentences using terminology derived from everyday language. Yet, until the last two generations, they did view their efforts as contributing to a more profound understanding of this terminology. The great advances in the understanding of the universe made by Descartes, Newton, and even Einstein were regarded—by them and by others—as opening our eyes to a deeper awareness of the nature of space, time, matter, energy, light, force, velocity, etc. In that, they were not different from rationalist philosophers and scientists throughout history. This is also evident in the terminology they invented to describe the new phenomena they identified. Terms like electron and neutron, subatomic particles, nucleus, etc. are words striving to serve as a coherent bridge between language and the newly discovered world within the atom.

This situation was dramatically changed in the third decade of this century, when quantum mechanics was discovered, and the change has become more and more radical in recent years. Suddenly, many terms that the scientists used, like Heisenberg's uncertainty principle, are negative in nature. They explain not what is, but what is not. Causality has been replaced by probability, which is essentially a negative term, denoting what is not rather than what is. More recently, the terms coined by physicists tend to be ones without any intrinsic meaning of their own—quarks, which retain the intrinsic clarity of their source in a duck's voice in Joyce's *Finnegan's Wake*,[25] "charm," "flavor," "up," and "down." When physicists begin to explain them, they insist that these names have nothing to do with the ordinary meaning of these words. Even in astronomy, terms like

---

[25]This term, so central in contemporary science, was invented by Murray Gell-Man, using the sound mentioned by Joyce. See Gell-Man's recent letter, *Scientific American*, June 1992, p. 10. Another aspect of modern physics attracted a great deal of discussion concerning the relationship between science, mysticism, and magic. This was best expressed in *The Tao of Physics*, and see a thorough examination in Robert K. Clifton and Marylin G. Regher, "Toward a Sound Perspective on Modern Physics: Capra's Popularization of Mysticism and Theological Approaches Reexamined," *Zygon* 25 (1990), pp. 73–104.

"quasar" are actually negative ones—stating that the phenomenon is nonstellar, but saying nothing about what it actually is. This process has culminated in recent years with the discovery of Bell's theorem and the subsequent experiments that proved its correctness, thus validating the concept of "nonlocality"—another negative term that does not hint at its positive meaning. Concepts like "causality," "certainty," and "locality," so basic to human language, are now central to modern physics by the prominence of their denial. Reality, according to contemporary physics, begins by proving the negation of the common linguistic terms previously used to describe it. Obviously, modern physics has moved into a completely new relationship between the contents of its discoveries and human language.

The physicist, in this sense, is today in a position very similar to that of the medieval mystic: He knows the truth, and cannot express it in words. He looks for roundabout ways to present his findings, using arbitrary and negative terms and metaphors, being unable to use the old terms that were so convenient for Newton and Einstein when describing the structure of the universe. In this century we have witnessed a fascinating phenomenon, in which a science that was deeply engaged in the endeavor of deciphering deeper and deeper meanings of linguistic terms broke away from language, expressed despair, and is now proceeding to develop a metalinguistic truth that lies beyond the boundaries of expression by words. Very much like the mystics, modern physicists are deeply suspicious of — if they do not completely negate—sensual perception; the very act of experiment or measurement, they say, changes reality. Senses, even when extended by the most sophisticated and sensitive instruments, cannot achieve truth, because their very interference causes changes that hide reality from us. Forsaking causality and locality, the meaning of logic has completely changed, and has been replaced by the probability laws of quantum mechanics that do not claim to have intrinsic logical truth; their validity is established in different ways. This is a unique phenomenon in which truth is separated increasingly from language and experience.

No meaningful schism developed between physicists and other scientists or society as a whole—though a gulf of non-understanding does exist—because the physicists succeeded in producing actual, tangible proof of their truth, in the form of laser beams and TV sets. More important, despite these drastic processes, physicists did not change the basic philosophy of their methodology; the laboratory and the mathematical formulas are, at least apparently, unchanged, thus moderating the impact of the radical revolution that this science underwent. The analogy to medieval mysticism is not a complete one, yet I believe that it is sufficient to demonstrate the main point of this discussion: The separation between truth and language is a phenomenon that occurs in human culture. It is an integral, though rare, aspect of human creativity, and it can and should be studied in a historical way.

The question of whether the metalinguistic truth is really true is outside the boundaries of the historian's quest. Most historians will say that the physicists do have a "true" truth, while many of them will doubt whether the mystics have such a valid, nonlinguistic truth. From the point of view of historical study, this does not matter. A historian studying the cultural and linguistic developments in contemporary physics does not have to know whether in the next century it will be discovered that Bell's theorem is wrong; what happened in the last twenty years is not changed by that. In the same way, whether or not the mystics' claim of the existence of the symbolic layer of divine truth within scriptures is "true" is immaterial to the understanding of the cultural phenomenon under study.

At this point a rather blunt definition is in order—a definition of the meaning of "history" and "historical" in this context. A scholar asks the questions: Are the mystics speaking the truth? Is there really a *via mystica?* Do mystics really know the secrets of God? The answer the scholar gives to these questions defines whether he is a mystic (if he gives a positive answer) or a nonmystic (if he gives a negative one). But in both cases he is not a historian. A historian is concerned with what really happens in human society and culture, with what people believe and disbelieve; it is not his task to judge the veracity of their claims that rest beyond the boundaries of human culture. If a scholar investigates whether, indeed, there is or is not a God, he is not engaged in a historical quest; when he tries to understand the nature and the depth of people's belief in God, he is. The important point concerning mysticism is that there can be no doubt that the belief in a metalinguistic and extrasensual mystical truth played an important role in shaping the history of human religious culture, and because of this it is an important subject of historical investigation, independent of the question of the veracity of the mystics' claims.

The insistence on this basic characteristic of historical study has another, most meaningful result. If one seeks to study the veracity of mysticism, investigating the subject of the mystics' speculations and descriptions, the subject of study is one: mysticism. For the historian, however, no such subject exists. For him, there are only mystics. He tries to understand the innumerable texts that mystics produced, their terminology and symbols, their visions and their historical impact, defining to the best of his ability the particular, unique nature of each mystic (or each period in a mystic's creativity), each text, each treatise, each symbol, each vision. When mystics use a certain term often, the historian should try to differentiate between that term's various shades of meanings. His quest is for the detail, for the unique. He tries to define in what way each mystic differs from another, or even in what way a mystic himself changes throughout his life. A historical attitude can therefore be defined as the quest for the individual.

The historical characteristics of mysticism as described above are essentially negative ones; this is the result of, on the one hand, the insistence on qualitative rather than quantitative elements of mysticism, and on the other hand, the result of the nature of the historical quest. A positive characterization of mysticism must by nature be quantitative, and depart from the restrictions of historical investigation. For instance, a positive statement that a mystic is one who strives for and achieves a union with the divine world is immediately recognized to be quantitative—every religion offers such a union, in one way or another, to its faithful, and the mystic will be distinguished from other believers only by the amount or proximity or intensity of this union. At the same time, the use of such a definition includes a judgmental element; it postulates the actual existence and achievement of such a process. It is better, therefore, when seeking a historical definition of mysticism to concentrate on negative aspects that, despite this flaw, give a much more accurate and historically valid result. The negative quest, however, need not be the final stage of analysis. It can be the first and basic one, which will be followed by the contingent analysis.

The mystic is characterized by his disbelief in the veracity of information acquired by human senses and logic and expressed by language. For him, senses, logic, and words are not avenues leading to the knowledge of divine truth. He believes in the existence of a nonsensual, nonlogical (i.e., mystical) way of reaching truth that, because of its remoteness from human physical and intellectual experience, cannot be communicated by language. These beliefs separate the mystic from most other currents and components of human culture, and put the mystic in a unique (and lonely) position within the framework of human civilization. His uniqueness is qualitative, representing a different world view and a specific attitude toward existence and communication.

A mystic who does not believe, sincerely and completely, in a scriptural religion may be denied any means of communicating his mystical experiences and attitudes. He may become an artist, a painter, a dancer, a poet, a composer, seeking new ways of communication, beyond words and senses, in order to get in touch with the society around him. But only scriptural religion offers a valid, structured avenue of mystical expression by its insistence that God, the source of all truth, chose human language for His own expression, both when creating the world by the power of language and when revealing His secrets to the prophets and His other messengers. The mystic in a scriptural religion is thus immersed in the paradox of language being inappropriate for the expression of truth on the one hand, and God's insistence on using it for exactly that purpose on the other.[26]

---

[26]In this, the monotheistic, scriptural mystic finds himself in a similar situation to his Hindu brother, who also believes in the divine origin of language, Sanskrit, and in the creation by the Word, Vâc. See note 15.

As a result of this paradox, the mystic is separated in a mean-ingful way from nonmystics: He believes in the existence of a com-pletely esoteric, symbolic layer of meaning to scriptures and to all of God's manifestations in creation and in man. Every detail is viewed by the mystic in a special way, setting him apart—and some-times against—his coreligionists and the hierarchy of the religious organization to which he belongs. This separation is enhanced and emphasized by the mystic's inability to convey the special meaning of his perceptions beyond the symbols, and therefore by the impos-sibility of argument, discussion, and compromise (all based on com-municative language) between mystics and nonmystics.

These qualitative characteristics give the mystic's beliefs their specific historical meaning and dimension, without relating in any way to the question of the transcendent veracity of his claims. Thus, it is possible to describe the parameters of the mystical phenomenon within a scriptural religion without denying the mystic's claim of his own different and unique quality of religious truth, and without passing judgement on the veracity of his beliefs and experiences. The definition of the historical mystical phenomenon that I suggest, there-fore, is: Mysticism is the negation of the veracity of communicative language, and the belief in a noncommunicative truth lying in a symbolic fashion deep within revealed divine language.

III

It is not surprising that an example intended to validate these conclusions is derived from the history of Jewish mysticism; every scholar develops his generalizations from the particular subject with which he deals, and is limited, naturally, by that background. Yet it seems that a crucial phase in the history of Jewish religiosity does have typological meaning and is helpful to an attempt at understand-ing the appearance of mysticism in the history of other scriptural religions.

When did mysticism start in Judaism? If we follow the conclu-sions of the previous discussion, we should exclude from consider-ation as mysticism anything that is satisfactorily identified as proph-

ecy, visions, apocalypticism, etc., because designating them as "mystical" is no more than a semantic exercise that does not add meaningfully to the understanding of these complex and profound religious phenomena. We should also exclude any element of literary
mysticism, that is, an expression, phrase, chapter, or verse in biblical or postbiblical works that tends to be "mystical," or actually is
mystical, but does not conform to the historical concept of mysticism, which demands the existence of a group of people, a library of
texts, a specific terminology, a body of symbols—the necessary elements that combine to present a definable historical phenomenon
occurring in a specific time, place, and social circumstances and with
describable religious and cultural drives. We should also exclude
elements that are a constant aspect of religiosity, like the presence
of magical elements, vigorous expressions by visions, or descriptions
of religious achievements—possibly mystical in character—attributed
to ancient figures like Moses, Isaiah, Enoch, and Abraham;[27] such
descriptions, such as ascending to the divine realm, abounded in
Jewish tradition for many centuries (their authors were very careful

---

[27]This, indeed, is one of the fundamental difficulties in the historical understanding of mysticism, which should be studied in depth in separate frameworks: the
relationship between historical mysticism and what I think should be called
"pseudepigraphic mysticism." The use of pseudepigraphy is, at the same time, both
immediate and remote, both historical and antihistorical. If Moses and Enoch
are described as having achieved mystical perfection, what does it mean for the
contemporary author and reader? It can mean that this perfection is possible and
attainable, or that it can be achieved only by an ancient Moses or Enoch, while
a contemporary religious enthusiast should give up hope of ever achieving it.
Thus, as far as historical mysticism is concerned, pseudepigraphy can be used
sometimes as a means of denial of any possibility of actual mystical achievement,
or at other times as a paradigmatic means of encouraging similar endeavors in
the contemporary world. Very often it is difficult to distinguish between these
two possibilities. The following discussion is intended to postulate that the Enoch
tradition of the Enoch books I and II belongs to the antihistorical category,
praising past achievements and denying the possibility of present similar practices; the Hechalot traditions (like the medieval kabbalistic pseudepigraphy) served
as encouragement for directly following the pseudepigraphic example. In this case,
as in so many others, it is the historical context of a message that is decisive in
the understanding of its position concerning its actual normative meaning.

not to open the possibility of such practices to other people, certainly not to contemporary ones).

If we seek a beginning, we must find it in the context of a distinct group of people who developed new kinds of experiences, wrote
a new type of treatise using a new terminology and symbolism, and
adopted a new relationship with the surrounding, dominant religious
culture of their time. Such a group, I believe, were the Hechalot
mystics between the third and seventh centuries in Palestine and
Babylonia.[28] These mystics relied heavily on traditions that prevailed
in rabbinic Judaism of that time, mainly those pertaining to the
exegesis (homiletical, not mystical) of the first chapter of the book
of Ezekiel, the vision of the celestial chariot,[29] cosmology and cosmogony, magic, and the traditions concerning celestial ascensions
and visits, as found in biblical, apocryphal, apocalyptic, and rabbinic
sources.

The new elements that characterize these people as mystics in
the historical sense are:

1. Their new relationship to the surrounding culture.
2. Their new terminology.
3. Their new attitude to the possibility of a divine ascension.

---

[28]Compare J. Dan, *The Revelation of the Secret of the World: The Beginning of Jewish Mysticism in Late Antiquity*, Brown University, Judaic Studies Series, no. 2,
1992. The literature about this circle is vast, especially in the last fifteen years.
The main texts are included in P. Schäfer, *Synopse zur Hekhalot-Literatur*, Tübingen:
J.C.B. Mohr (Siebeck) 1981; idem, *Concordanz zur Hekhalot-Literatur*, ibid., 1987–
1989; idem, *Übersetzung Hechalot Literatur*, vols. II–IV, ibid., 1986–1991; idem,
Geniza Fragmente Hekhalot-Literatur, ibid., 1986; idem, *Hekhalot Studien*, ibid., 1989;
G. Scholem, *Jewish Gnosticism, Merkabah Mysticism and Talmudic Tradition*, 2nd
ed., New York: The Jewish Theological Seminary 1965; I. Grünwald, *Apocalyptic
and Merkabah Mysticism*, Leiden: Brill 1980; idem, *From Apocalypticism to Gnosticism*, 1990; D. Halperin, *The Merkabah in Rabbinic Literature*, New Haven, CT
1980; idem, *The Faces of the Chariot*, Tübingen: J.C.B. Mohr 1988; J. Dan, *Three
Types of Ancient Jewish Mysticism*, Cincinnati, OH 1984.
[29]*Maaseh Merkavah*, and the *Merkavah* literature, which comprises most of the
treatises included in the "*Hechalot* and *Merkavah* literature"; most of them are
exegetical and homiletical, but there is no reason to regard them as mystical.

4. Their new concept of the divine world and the symbolism that describes it.

5. Their new concept of history, which contradicts both the traditional view and historical reality.

6. Their specific literary expression of those previous elements.

The Jewish culture, which serves as a background for these early mystics, is the rabbinic one, as it was being formulated in the second and third centuries. The most important characteristic of this religious culture was its extreme reliance on textuality and traditionality, as opposed to divine revelation. Rabbinic tradition declared prophecy to be a thing of the past that ceased early in the history of the Second Temple, several centuries before the beginning of the Christian era. According to this concept, repeated strongly several times in tanaitic and amoraic traditions in the Talmud, not only did the phenomenon of prophecy cease, but if it ever occurs again, it is to be ignored: "The Torah had already been given to Israel, and one should not pay attention to heavenly voices."[30] The biblical era, characterized by constant, ever-present contact with God, in which direct divine messages transmitted to the people instructed them concerning every immediate problem, came to an end.

Direct revelation of God is no longer possible. The only source of truth, the only fountain of religious authority, is found in the previous revelations, in the texts that record the ancient word of God. This source, being divine and expressed in the divine language, is infinite in its meaning,[31] and therefore contains all divine wisdom.

---

[30]Bavli *Berachot* 52a.

[31]The concept of language in religion in general and in mysticism in particular has not benefited meaningfully as yet from the great revival of scholarship in this century in the field of the essence and meaning of linguistic communication and semiotics. Some examples are, however, Gerhard Ebeling, *Einführung in theologische Sprachlehre*, Tübingen: J.C.B. Mohr (Siebeck), 1971 (translated into English by R. A. Wilson, *Introduction to a Theological Theory of Language*, Philadelphia: Fortress Press 1973); a collection of studies edited by R. H. Eyers and W. T. Blackstone, *Religious Language and Knowledge*, Athens, GA: University of Georgia Press 1972; a very valuable collection of studies, covering most aspects of the subject, was edited by R. E. Santoni, *Religious Language and The Problem*

From it every scholar in every generation can glean an answer to every contemporary problem.[32] This basic concept of eternal divine revelation within the text is the concept of the inexhaustible truth contained in scriptures, which characterizes Judaism from that period to the present,[33] as well as much of the history of Christianity and Islam. Yet it was not accepted by all segments of ancient Judaism without question or conflict. At least three major rebellions against it can be discerned in the period between the third century B.C. and the third century C.E.: One is the apocryphal, pseudepigraphic literature; the second is Christianity itself; the third is *Hechalot* mysticism.

These three phenomena represent the insistence on immediate, nontextual contact with the divine. The authors of pseudepigraphic literature substituted the "discovery" of additional new texts of ancient revelation for the exegesis of the old ones. They inserted their new religious message into the biblical frameworks of revelations to the patriarchs and prophets, rather than interpreting their existing words in old scriptures. Similarly, though in a completely different way, the early Christians insisted on a direct revelation of the divine, on listening to a contemporary divine revelation, rather than interpreting the old messages.[34] It is not surprising that there could

---

of Religious Knowledge, Bloomington and London: Indiana University Press 1968. Compare B. McGinn, *The Foundations of Mysticism*, pp. 118–124 et passim. The development of a mystical concept of language based on the midrashic concept of the infinity of meanings of a divine language is the subject of a forthcoming book of mine, *The Language of the Mystics*.

[32]See E. E. Urbach, *The Sages: Their Concepts and Beliefs*, vol. I, Jerusalem: Magnes Press 1979, pp. 304–306.

[33]The development of midrashic exegesis has been the subject of several studies in the last few years. See, for instance, J. Kugel, "Two Introductions to the Midrash," in *Prooftexts* 3 (1983), pp. 131–155; B. L. Visotzky, *Reading the Book: Making the Bible a Timeless Text*, New York: Doubleday 1991; M. Fishbane, *Biblical Interpretation in Ancient Israel*, Oxford: Clarendon Press 1985. Recent studies by M. Fishbane, J. Kugel, D. Boyarin, and others continue to contribute to the further understanding of this complex and difficult subject.

[34]It is surprising to see how soon in the history of Christianity this demand for a direct divine revelation was combined with a midrashic interpretation of the old texts. Already in the Gospel of Matthew we find an insistence that the new

be no compromise between rabbinic Judaism, which denied the possibility of immediate, direct revelation of the divine in the present
and relied on old traditions and exegesis, and the demands of apocryphal literature and Christianity for an immediate, direct divine
revelation. *Hechalot* mysticism was more successful in achieving a
compromise, even though its rebellion against rabbinic norms was
no less radical.

The revolutionary character of *Hechalot* mysticism is especially
apparent in the fact it is so closely interwoven with the rabbinic
framework, but still is entirely different in its message from the other
elements within which it is integrated. Most of the material in
Hechalot and *Merkavah* literature—even in the very same treatises
that describe the mystical phenomenon—belongs to the traditional,
exegetical mold.[35] The innovative attitude is most obvious in a section of *Hechalot Rabbati*, the central text of this literature.[36] In this

message is not only a direct one coming from God, but also an old one, incorporated in the old texts if properly interpreted. Matthew's insistence on corrobo-
rating almost every phase in the report of the life, death, and resurrection of
Jesus by Old Testament verses indicates that revelation was not enough; in order to be completely valid and authoritative, it must be supported by textual
exegesis.

[35]*Hechalot* and *Merkavah* literature consists of about twenty-five treatises. Some
of them are dedicated exclusively to cosmogony and cosmology, like the *Baraita
de-Maaseh Bereshit*; others are dedicated almost exclusively to magic, like the *Harba
de-Moshe*; still others are dedicated to an exposition of the first chapter of Ezekiel,
like the *Reuyot Yehezkel*; most are combinations of all three. Only five of these
treatises belong to the specific mystical tradition of the *Hechalot: Hechalot Rabbati,
Hechalot Zutarti, Shiur Komah, Maaseh Merkavah*, and the *Hebrew Apocalypse of
Enoch*, and even they contain much material that belongs to the other three categories. The distinct Hechalot mystical ascension tradition is therefore represented
only as a minor component, quantitatively speaking, of this literature. It seems
that the thorough literary integration of this mystical material within the "legitimate" exegetical-traditional cosmology, magic, and Ezekiel exegesis helped in
sublimating the rebellious, radical meaning of the mystical element, allowing it
to remain on the fringes of rabbinic tradition.

[36]See, concerning this text: Morton Smith, "Observations on Hekhalot Rabbati,"
in A. Altmann (ed.), *Biblical and Other Studies*, Cambridge, MA 1965, pp. 142–
160; I. Grünwald, *Apocalyptic and Merkabah Mysticism*, Leiden: Brill 1980, passim;
P. Schaefer, *Hekhalot Studien* (see note 26), pp. 63–74. A German translation of
this work is vol. II of P. Schaefer's *Übersetzung der Hekhalot-Literatur*, Tübingen:

section, the leader of the group of mystics, the "ascenders to the chariot," declares the "revelation of the secret of the world,"[37] which is a detailed, practical body of directions on how to achieve the ascension to the divine world. One who masters these instructions is described as having "a ladder in his house,"[38] a means that is constantly at his disposal whenever he wishes to perform the rituals that will lead him to a direct contact with the divine world. There is no parallel in rabbinic Judaism—or even in other segments of Judaism in Late Antiquity—of such a revelation, which opens before the mystic a direct avenue to the achievement of contact with the most supreme realms of the celestial worlds, bringing him face to face with divinity. The startling element in this unique description is one of activity: man taking the initiative to elevate himself through many difficulties, passing from one heaven to another, from one *hechal* to another, overcoming one group of guardians after the other, in order to achieve the vision of "the King in His beauty" and stand in front of the throne of glory.[39]

This unique description is part of a complex structure of theology that includes a distinct concept of a divine pleroma, which separates it from all other segments of rabbinic literature and even from all the rest of *Hechalot* and *Merkavah* literature. The *Hechalot* mystics describe in these treatises a group of celestial powers that include the tetragrammaton in their names. Powers called Totrosiel YHVH Lord God of Israel and Zaharriel YHVH Lord God of Israel play a

---

J.C.B. Mohr (Siebeck) 1987; a general description of this work (and others) is found in P. Schaefer's *The Hidden and Manifest God*, Albany, NY: SUNY Press 1992, pp. 11–54.

[37]Schaefer, *Synopse*, pp. 198–205. I dedicated the paper mentioned in the beginning of note 28 to the analysis of this section.

[38]Schaefer, *Synopse*, pp. 199, 237.

[39]Needless to say, talmudic and midrashic literature does not contain such elements of active mystical endeavor. The few examples that can be found there are closely connected with the *Hechalot* tradition. The best-known among these is the story of the "four who entered paradise"; see D. Halperin, *The Merkabah in Rabbinic Literature*, New Haven, CT: American Oriental Society 1980, pp. 86–92 (and detailed literature there).

central part in these treatises, and only in them.[40] According to one source, their number is eight; a larger number is given in others.[41] It is quite clear that a concept of a divine pleroma, very different from the concept of the divine world in rabbinic tradition, was developed by the *Hechalot* mystics. It is possible that the figure of Metatron was integrated into this pleromatic system,[42] though it acquired its place in ancient Jewish traditions as a demiurgic power independent of the speculations of these mystics.

The theology of the *Hechalot* mystics included a radical concept of the figure of the Creator, described in bold anthropomorphic terms and presented as having astronomical, gigantic dimensions.[43] It is probable that this concept developed together with a new mystical understanding of sections of the *Song of Songs*,[44] a

---

[40]Only once is such a power mentioned in talmudic-midrashic literature, in Bavli *Berachot* 7a, *Akhatriel Ya Adonai Zevaot*, who was revealed to Rabbi Ishmael in the Holy of Holies in the Temple. That section is undoubtedly an interpolation from a *Hechalot* text. See Scholem, *Major Trends in Jewish Mysticism*, New York: Schocken 1954, p. 356.

[41]The most detailed description of these powers is found in *The Hebrew Apocalypse of Enoch*; see P. Alexander's introduction and translation in J. H. Charlesworth, *The Old Testament Pseudepigraph*, vol. I, New York: Doubleday 1983, pp. 223–316. The "eight supreme powers that have the name of their Lord in them" are mentioned there, Ch. 10:3, p. 264. The Hebrew text with a detailed introduction and commentary was published by H. Odeberg, *The Third Book of Enoch*, Cambridge 1928 (new ed. with a new introduction by J. Greenfield, New York: Ktav 1973).

[42]Metatron has been the subject of numerous detailed discussions in scholarly literature since Hugo Odeberg's detailed presentation (see note 42). See J. Dan, *Ancient Jewish Mysticism*, pp. 81–93, and P. Schäfer, *The Hidden and Manifest God*, pp. 29–32 et passim.

[43]The texts of the *Shiur Komah* were assembled and presented by M. S. Cohen, *The Shiur Komah Texts*, Tübingen: J.C.B. Mohr 1985; and compare P. Schaefer, *Hekhalot Studien*, pp. 75–83. An analysis of the work is found in Cohen's previous book, *The Shiur Komah*, Latham, MD 1983. Compare J. Dan, "The Concept of Knowledge in the Shiur Komah," in *Studies in Jewish Religious and Intellectual History Presented to Alexander Altmann*, eds. S. Stein and R. Loewe, Alabama 1979, pp. 67–74.

[44]The relationship between the *Shiur Komah* and the *Song of Songs* has been established by G. Scholem in *Jewish Gnosticism* (note 28), pp. 36–42, and supported by S. Lieberman in an appendix in that book, pp. 118–126. The sanctity

scriptural work that had a unique place in the history of Christian mysticism as well.[45] This description of the divine figure is also connected with the concept of the pleroma: It is possible that the anthropomorphic description is that of the demiurge rather than of the supreme Godhead, though this cannot be proved conclusively by the texts before us.[46]

The spiritual independence, bordering on rebelliousness, characterizing the circle of Hechalot mystics is evident in their unique concept of history, which contradicts the rabbinic concept as presented in the Talmud and the Midrash. Hechalot Rabbati describes the congregation of mystics, in which the revelation of the "secret of the world" was announced, as occurring in the Temple in Jerusalem, while the participants, about ten of whom are named, are sages who were born after the destruction of the Temple. The most prominent Hechalot mystic, Rabbi Ishmael, who lived in the first half of the second century, is described as officiating as a High Priest in the Temple before 70 C.E.[47] Numerous other examples demonstrate that this circle developed a concept of mystical metahistory that negates both historical fact and accepted historical tradition as formulated in the talmudic sources.

The Hechalot mystics developed an independent, unique terminology, which is not found anywhere else in rabbinic literature or even in other treatises of the Merkavah literature. Among the key terms, the term Hechalot itself is found only in the mystical works

---

of this book relied, so it seems, on the interpretation of the verses 5:10–16 as a self-portrait of God, Who was the direct author of the song ("Solomon" in 1:1 being interpreted as one of God's appellations).

[45]Concerning the Song of Songs and Christian mysticism, see McGinn, Foundations of Mysticism, pp. 20–22, 117–141, 213–218.

[46]The possibility that the figure of the divine described in the Shiur Komah is that of the demiurge has been suggested by G. Scholem, who noted that it is consistently described as yotzer bereshit, "The Creator," yet he did not reach a final conclusion concerning this suggestion. See Jewish Gnosticism, pp. 36–42. The problem has been under discussion by all scholars in the field, but no final conclusion seems to have been formulated.

[47]See J. Dan, "The Concept of History in Hekhalot and Merkabah Literature," in Binah vol. I, Studies in Jewish History, New York: Praeger 1989, pp. 47–58.

denoting the temple within a temple in the seventh heaven, in the seventh of which God resides.[48] The *Shiur Komah* is not mentioned anywhere else in our sources, nor are the gates of the temples and the horrors at the gate of the sixth temple.[49] The most important term used by them—and only by them—is the one describing their practice as well as their self-awareness: the "descenders to the chariot,"[50] and the many uses of the picture of ascending and descending to the chariot. Some sections of these works, most notably the opening paragraphs of *Hechalot Rabbati*, describe the "descenders" as a distinct group of people with magical powers and a unique relationship with the surrounding society.[51]

The accumulated meaning of these characteristics presents us with a distinct group of people who refused to accept some of the basic religious and social norms of the surrounding religious culture without breaking all contact with it, remaining on its fringe, half in and half out, who developed a distinct body of literature expressed in unique terminology. They developed a unique concept of the divine world comprised of a pleroma of divine powers, and possibly adopted the concept of a separate demiurgic power besides the supreme God.

But the most important element was that they developed an

---

[48]The term *Hechalot* itself is ambiguous. It could mean either "temple," referring to celestial temples, or "palace," referring to King Solomon's palace, which is replicated several times in heaven (a plausible notion, if the "king" in the *Song of Songs* is regarded as being God Himself).

[49]See J. Dan, "The Entrance to the Sixth Gate," in J. Dan (ed.), *Proceedings of the First International Conference on the History of Jewish Mysticism (Jerusalem Studies in Jewish Thought*, vol. VI, 1-2, 1987), pp. 197-220.

[50]Much has been written about the paradox that the *Hechalot* mystics insist on calling their practice "descent to the chariot" and describing themselves as "descenders." Many explanations have been suggested; the most probable one is found in Songs 1:4: "I have descended to the garden of the nut." The "nut" is identified with the chariot in later Hebrew sources (and Latin ones), relying emphatically on "the book of *Hechalot*," yet in the texts no such identification is found.

[51]Schäfer, *Synopse*, pp. 80-93. These sections contain a long list of the intellectual, magical, and social characteristics of the mystics, indicating that they are exceptional—if not actually superhuman—in every way, constantly protected by God.

independent, original way to approach God, a way that can only partly be expressed in language, radically different from the accepted rabbinic ways of attaining that goal. They tried not to replace the rabbinic norms, but to add to them a higher, more adventurous, and ambitious way to be united with "the King in His beauty." These characteristics, I believe, justify our seeing in them a distinct historical phenomenon for which the adjective "mystical" is completely legitimate.

It seems that this group of ancient Jewish mystics presents us with a paradigmatic case for the understanding of the appearance of a mystical phenomenon within an established scriptural religion. There are many parallels between the development briefly sketched here and the emergence of the Jewish mystical circles in the second half of the twelfth century in Europe, the most important among them being the early kabbalists[52] and the mystics-pietists of medieval Germany, the Ashkenazi Hasidim.[53] Many parallels can also be

---

[52]The kabbalah began in Provence and northern Spain in the last decades of the twelfth century, probably in two or three independent circles. One of them is a relatively well-known rabbinic school in southern France; the others are anonymous authors. Their radical departure from accepted Jewish norms is evident, for instance, by the fact that the intense mythological concept of the divine world presented in their works contradicted radically the one found in Maimonides' great philosophical work written at the same time, the *Guide to the Perplexed*. They developed a unique terminology, congregated in esoteric circles, kept their teachings secret, and developed both a new attitude toward personal achievement of proximity to God and a new way of biblical exegesis. The strongest expression of their separation from the rabbinic tradition of their time is their claim (evident even in the term *kabbalah*, "tradition"), that they received a hitherto unknown ancient tradition of mystical truth that was revealed to Moses on Mount Sinai, making them unique among their contemporaries in their possession of this secret avenue to divine truth. See G. Scholem, *The Origins of the Kabbalah*, ed. R. I. Z. Werblowsky, Princeton, NJ: Princeton University Press and Jewish Publication Society 1986, and compare J. Dan, *G. Scholem and the Mystical Dimension in Jewish History*, New York: New York University Press 1987, pp. 186–187.
[53]Esoteric texts of Jewish mystics in late-twelfth-century Germany indicate the existence of at least three independent circles that developed the concept of a pleromatic Godhead, distinguishing between the hidden Creator and the revealed divine glory. Two such circles are anonymous, but the most important one is well known; the Kalonymus family of rabbis, poets, and lawyers in the Rhineland

drawn with the emergence of the Hasidic movement in Eastern Europe in the middle of the eighteenth century.[54] I believe that this historical definition may be helpful in describing the beginnings of mysticism in Islam[55] and in Christianity.[56]

---

in the second half of the twelfth century and the first half of the thirteenth. They claimed to be in possession of ancient esoteric tradition that reached them from the East, developed an innovative mystical concept of the prayers, and presented a radical, spiritualized concept of ethics. See J. Dan, "Das Entstehen der Jüdischen Mystik im mittelalterlichen Deutschland," in K. E. Grözinger (ed.), *Judentum im deutschen Sprachraum*, Frankfurt a/M: Suhrkamp 1991, pp. 127–172.

[54]There is a vast literature on the Besht, the founder of the Hasidic movement, and the beginnings of this modern Jewish mystical phenomenon, which is still a vigorous component of contemporary orthodox Judaism. There are conflicting views among scholars concerning the characteristics of early Hasidism, yet it is evident that they developed a unique kind of mystical, charismatic leadership, and a schism developed in Judaism as a result of their teachings. See G. Scholem, *Major Trends in Jewish Mysticism* (see note 7), pp. 325–350, and idem, "The Righteous One," in *On the Mystical Shape of the Godhead*, New York: Schocken 1991, pp. 88–138. Modern Hasidism could be regarded as a model example of a mystical movement creating a schism within an existing religious structure, establishing its own institutions, dress codes, particular prayerbook and customs, and style of ritual performance, as well as a mystical structure of leadership. The only unusual element in this picture is the fact that the establishment from which this movement separated was (and still is) led by a leadership that is motivated by kabbalistic theology and symbolism.

[55]A new attitude toward the study of mysticism in Islam, in its Sufi, Shiite, and Ismailite forms, has emerged in the last few years. Among the recent works see those included in the volumes of *Islamic Spirituality*, ed. Seyyed Hossein Nasr, New York: Crossroads 1991; Farhad Daftari, *The Isma'ilis: Their History and Doctrines*, Cambridge: Cambridge University Press 1990; as far as I could determine, these descriptions emphasize the particular circumstances and characteristics of mystical phenomena and their relationship to the cultural-religious background. Compare the classic analysis: Annemarie Schimmel, *Mystical Dimensions of Islam*, Chapel Hill, NC: University of North Carolina Press 1973.

[56]The description of the beginning of Latin mysticism in Christianity, as described by B. McGinn in *Foundations of Mysticism*, seems to be in line with the suggested framework. According to his analysis, the background of the appearance of mysticism in Latin Christianity included the new emphasis on virginity (which included, necessarily, criticism of nonvirgin Christian leadership), monasticism (which includes criticism of nonmonastic leadership), and also a new attitude and a new understanding of ancient texts, like the *Song of Songs* (see note 45). Though Prof. McGinn did not emphasize this element, it seems to be the result of his detailed analysis.

The suggested approach, therefore, emphasizes as a first stage of analysis the universal tendencies of mystical phenomena in scriptural religions that can be described only in negative terms—a pessimistic attitude toward the world; denial of the senses and the intellect as sources of truth; denial of human communicative language as expression of truth; and a sense of separation from the established structures, physical and cultural, of the religion to which they belong. This first stage is followed by contingental analysis, in which positive characteristics of the particular mystical phenomenon are studied: How did this particular group of mystics in specific historical and cultural circumstances overcome the barrier of communicative language and create their own means of expression; how did they formulate their own religious-cultural structures to enhance, change, or replace the ones that were the subject of their criticism; what were their religious-mystical goals; and what was the specific, unique terminology they employed to express them?

This contingental study can then proceed to the comparative stage, designating parallels, close and far, in other mystical historical phenomena. Some indications of common attitudes between the group under discussion and others may emerge, but, being loyal to the contingent-historical approach, they should be studied together with the differences separating them. This attitude demands persistent resistance to the temptation (so common among mystics) to unify all known and unknown phenomena into one set of characteristics, so inferring that if something can be found in one historical circumstance it must be present in all others as well. Only the manifestations that can be demonstrated by philological and historical analysis can be assumed to be present in every contingental phenomenon, and when these phenomena are compared, as they should be, differences are no less important and meaningful than similarities. In this way, even when broad outlines are studied, each phenomenon retains its individuality, and each mystic retains his own contingent personal creative and original contribution to mystical experience and expression.

The key to a contingent approach to the study of mysticism is the concept of beginning. The mystical unifying attitude denies this concept: Mystical truth must be universal and comprehensive in the same way throughout history; it is beyond the concept of time and, therefore, that of history. The very quest for a beginning indicates the concept of change, and therefore of the contingencies of time and place, of historical development, and almost always also those of controversy, schism, and differences. The quest for the beginning of a religious or mystical phenomenon characterizes the contingent, historical, and philological approach, which seeks the creative and the individual aspects, as opposed to the eternity of absolute, un-changing truth, which negates all possibility of creativity and anni-hilates the position of the mystic as a unique contributor, as an individual, to the history of human spirituality. There is an intrin-sic identity between a contingental approach and the recognition of the mystic, as a person or as a part of a group or a movement, as an individual participant in original creativity in religion and cul-ture.

SUMMARY

The historical analysis of mystical phenomena is different from the literary one, which seeks to identify mystical elements within a religious text and is actually the employment of the writer's defini-tion of the term. It is also different from the theological approach, which deals more with the question of what mysticism should be, and what its rightful place within a religion should be, than with an analysis of what mysticism actually is.

The contingental approach suggested here assumes that mysti-cism as a historical phenomenon within scriptural religions can be characterized in a generalized way only in *negative terms*: rejection of the senses and logic as denoting divine truth; rejection of accepted exegetical methodologies as providing insights into divine intentions; rejection of communicative language as an instrument of conveying supreme truth; and, usually, a critical attitude, overt or implied, concerning rituals and social norms of the religious culture. In many cases, a rebellious attitude can be discerned.

Beyond these negative universal attitudes, scholarship should search for the *contingent characteristics* of specific mystical phenomena, which can be presented in a *positive manner* only within a specific historical, cultural, and religious context. In the next stage, some of these characteristics can be generalized, but the contingent context should always be the decisive criterion for any analysis.

The last part of this study is dedicated to the presentation of the beginning of Jewish mysticism in Late Antiquity, the mysticism of the "descenders to the chariot," as an example of such an analytical approach.

ENDNOTE

The subject of the nature and meaning of mysticism is one that always draws attention, and during the few years that have passed since the publication of the article that constitutes this chapter, numerous books have been dedicated to it. Two of them represent the prevalent attitude toward mysticism that my article opposed: That by Nelson Pike, *Mystic Union: An Essay in the Phenomenology of Mysticism*, Ithaca and London: Cornell University Press 1992, seeks to characterize and define the ultimate mystical experience, the mystical union, as a universal phenomenon to which all descriptions relate and that can be summarized in a definite, limited, list of typical experiences. Needless to say, the author succeeded in collecting from many sources those characteristics that define his own inclinations (pronouncedly Christian ones), which he presents as the essence of mysticism in general. In a more obvious way, Jess Byron Hollenback, in the book *Mysticism: Experience, Response and Empowerment*, University Park, PA: Pennsylvania State University Press 1996, selected one example of a series of visions, those of the Black Elk in the Oglala Lakota, and wove around them a comprehensive history and psychology of mysticism in general, actually just to justify the application of the term "mysticism" to these visions.

A completely different approach is manifest in the book by Sachiko Murata and William C. Chittik, *The Vision of Islam*, New York: Paragon House 1994. The authors present a coherent and profound exposition of Islamic spirituality, including a detailed discussion of Sufism, without using the term "mysticism," thus refraining from imposing Western cultural terms upon the Islamic material they analyze. In another volume, Michael A. Sells, *Early Islamic Mysticism*, New York: Paulist Press 1995, the early Sufis are described individually, each according to his own particular characteristics, without seeking to conform them to any generalizations, either Eastern ones or Western ones. These studies can be described as demonstrating the contingental approach to research in mysticism. Another important monograph by Michael Sells, *Mystical Languages of Unsaying*, Chicago: Chicago University Press 1994, describes in depth the negative character of the language of the mystics, presenting a series of examples, Christian and Islamic, emphasizing the unique characteristics of each of the major figures discussed, not allowing the generalizations to obscure the individual message of each of them.

Mysticism in Jewish History, Religion, and Literature

I

The last decade or two has witnessed the beginnings of a profound change in the attitude toward Jewish mysticism within the
framework of Jewish studies, a change that follows another even more
revolutionary one that occurred a generation earlier. The revolution
was the result of the impact of Gershom Scholem's studies in the
history of Jewish mysticism, studies that, for the first time, made
kabbalah in particular and Jewish mysticism in general a legitimate
branch of Jewish studies. Thus ended a long period of neglect and
misunderstanding that surrounded this field since the beginning of
scholarly work in Judaism.

The change that we are witnessing now is one more step—probably a crucial one—in the same direction. For even though Scholem's
work was highly regarded and praised by most scholars, with other
scholars joining him in a detailed study of the history of kabbalah,
the study of Jewish mysticism still was not integrated into the main
body of Jewish studies. Only specialists in kabbalah, usually

Scholem's disciples, were regarded as qualified to deal with problems involving a mystical element, and the results of their studies were considered relevant and meaningful only with respect to the specific field of kabbalah. Attempts by other scholars—most notably, the historian Y. F. Baer—to integrate kabbalah into the mainstream of historical and religious studies were few and far between, so that an almost rigid separation between the study of mysticism and the study of Jewish religion, history, and literature prevailed.

Only in the last two decades or so have we been able to discern the sometimes hesitant beginnings of a new attitude. It is realized that the understanding of the development of Jewish mysticism is essential to the study of most major historical, religious, and literary phenomena, and that this study should be carried out by all interested scholars, and not be confined to a small group of experts whose main field is kabbalah. To put it bluntly, one does not have to be a mystic—or even a "mystic" according to his choice of scholarly field—in order to study some aspect or other of the impact of Jewish mysticism on Judaism in general. It is being realized more and more that the study of the Sabbatian movement, for instance, is a part of the history of the Jews in every country, not only a chapter in the history of Jewish messianism or mysticism; that kabbalists who participated in the creation of medieval Jewish literature made no separation between their mystical attitude and their literary work, so that this aspect has to be taken into account when literary study of medieval works is undertaken; that even halachists who were also kabbalists did not always completely separate their legal decisions from their mystical inclinations, and one cannot be understood without the other.

It seems that this realization has had more impact to date in North America than it has had among the community of scholars in the state of Israel. It is more readily accepted here that the study of Jewish mysticism is an integral part of the education of a young scholar in Jewish studies, and that some knowledge of kabbalah is a tool of historical research. In Israel, on the other hand, the division between "kabbalists"—Scholem,s disciples, in most cases—on the one hand, and scholars in the fields of history and literature, on the other, is much more clear-cut. It seems inevitable, however, that these artificial and outdated categories and boundaries will be set aside, and that in the future more and more effort will be concentrated on understanding basic phenomena of Judaism as a whole, using all available and pertinent data and techniques, including the study of the mystical element. The aim should be a better understanding of all aspects of Jewish culture and history, and Jewish mysticism will be integrated within the general framework of Jewish scholarship, completely removing the mantle of esotericism from scholarship in kabbalah.

It is my purpose in the following remarks to point out briefly a few examples of major phenomena in Jewish religion, history, and literature where the necessity of such an integration is acutely felt. There is no doubt that the choice of these examples is completely subjective, pointing at problems of which I am aware and in which I am interested. It is my hope that scholars will find other problems within their own fields of study to which my proposed conclusions will be applicable.

II

The problem of when Jewish mysticism began has been transformed in recent years from a theoretical question of definition and analysis into a major historical and cultural problem that cannot be studied without reference to the basic historical and religious processes of the periods just before and immediately after the beginning of the Common Era. Thus this problem might serve as an example for the need of integration of all the abovementioned scholarly fields and techniques.

While the problem of the mystical nature of some biblical texts, prophetic or poetic, and some parts of apocryphal literature is mainly a problem of definition, there is little doubt that, from a historical point of view, the first major mystical phenomenon in Jewish culture known to us is the appearance of the *Hechalot* and *Merkavah* literature. This literature is the work not of a lonely mystic, but of a historical school, which probably developed throughout a period of several centuries, and had a profound impact upon later Jewish mysticism. Here we have something that approaches, to some extent, the characteristics of a historical movement, even though its main product was the descriptions of the chariot vision in the first chapter of Ezekiel (the *Merkavah*) and the ascent of mystics to the seven heavenly palaces (*hechalot*). This literature is attributed consistently in our sources to a group of *tanaim*, the mishnaic sages, most prominent among them being Rabbi Akia, Rabbi Ishmael ben Elisha, Rabbi Nehunia ben ha-Kanah, and Rabbi Eliezer the Great.

The major step toward understanding the historical background of this movement was made by Gershom Scholem when he established the close links between the text of the *Shiur Komah*, an undoubtedly mystical text, and the anthropomorphic verses in the *Song of Songs* (5:11–16). The text of the *Shiur Komah* is a list of measurements of astronomical magnitudes of the various limbs of God and a list of the names of these limbs. Scholem had shown that this seemingly stark anthropomorphism is a mystical concept based on these verses, and suggested that this attitude was found in Jewish circles no later than the end of the second century C.E. Saul Lieberman developed this idea further and proved that in the circles of the *tanaim*, especially in the circle of Rabbi Akiva, we find a new, unique attitude toward the *Song of Songs* as a book written by God Himself and given to Israel either on Mount Sinai or at the Red Sea, thus explaining the famous saying (Mishnah Yadayim, Chap. 3) by Rabbi Akiva that the *Song of Songs* is the holiest part of the scriptures.

These conclusions established a long-missing link between tanaitic literature and the mystical *Hechalot* literature. One of the most important *Hechalot* texts, the *Hechalot Zutarti* (the Smaller Book of Palaces) describes in detail the ascension of Rabbi Akiva to the seven palaces in the divine world until he comes before the divine throne, on which sits the figure described in the *Shiur Komah* and the *Song of Songs* verses according to this mystical interpretation. This text is related to the talmudic story of the four who entered the *pardes*, celebrating Rabbi Akiva's maximum mystical achievement.

It is very convenient to point out this religious phenomenon and to use it as a starting point for the history of Jewish mysticism in the schools of the *tanaim* immediately before the Bar Kochba rebellion, schools that discovered unimagined mystical depth in the *Song of Songs* and used it in their spiritual endeavor to ascend to the divine realm, thus beginning a long history of Jewish mystical visions and mystical commentaries on the scriptures. It is very comfortable for the historian to pinpoint here the earliest Jewish mystical speculation, and it seems to me that according to our present knowledge nothing better can be suggested. However, from a historical point of view, such a concept raises more questions than it answers.

It is difficult, if not impossible, to reconcile the attribution of a major personal role in the evolution of *Hechalot* mysticism to Rabbi Akiva with an understanding of the sage's double historical role— that of the most important halachist of his age (and of many other ages), the age that contributed more than any other to the creation of the Mishnah, and that of the person who gave a messianic interpretation to the Bar Kochba rebellion, in which he probably participated and in whose aftermath he was martyred. It is almost impossible to imagine that one person could be active in such a prominent way in two major historical processes without this being reflected in his innermost religious attitudes expressed in a mystical way. It is difficult to accept the notion that when Rabbi Akiva ascended to the chariot, he forgot his messianic ideas, his resolution to fight for Jewish independence against the whole Roman Empire, and his enormous legal and aggadic innovative activity. We cannot dissociate mystical speculation from the all-absorbing historical and religious activities of the sage. In later generations, when mystical speculation became a customary part of the Jewish religious and cultural scene, one can assume the practice of "part-time mysticism" routinely followed by leaders whose main contributions were in other fields. But the very beginning of Jewish mysticism cannot be envisioned as a secondary endeavor, almost completely removed from the major historical, religious, and literary achievements of its founders.

All we have, therefore, is the problem; an answer cannot be

given by a study of *Hechalot* literature alone. In order to arrive at an answer, new knowledge and new understanding are necessary concerning the religious drives that produced mishnaic literature and the historical and messianic impulses that produced the Bar Kochba rebellion. Only an integrated study of all these phenomena can solve the problem of the place of early Jewish mysticism in the Rabbi Akiva period and its impact—if any—on the major historical events of those times.

III

The historical background and the historical problems become much more complicated as we try to penetrate deeper into the nature of early Jewish mysticism. Scholem pointed out emphatically the gnostic characteristics of *Hechalot* literature several times. The questions involved in understanding the relationship between *Hechalot* literature and gnosticism have become more and more complex in recent years, as the Nag Hammadi gnostic texts are published and studied, giving a new impetus to further studies and even to a complete reevaluation of the gnostic problem as a whole.

The enormous differences between Hechalot literature and classical gnosticism are obvious, and have been used constantly to criticize Scholem's terminology, especially the complete absence in these texts of any bisexual aspects of God or any dualistic tendencies. But the fact—which emerges more and more clearly from recent studies of Nag Hammadi and other gnostic texts—that there was a non-Christian gnosis that preceded classical gnosticism in the Middle East, probably in Palestine, and that this sect (or, sects) could even have been pre-Christian, with some unclear connections with Judaism, might change our conclusions concerning the relationship between Judaism in general and Jewish mysticism in particular. A negative answer to the question of whether there was any Jewish influence on the evolution of gnosticism is becoming more and more unsatisfactory, and though positive links between them are few, one still cannot separate today the study of the appearance of this major religious and mystical phenomenon—gnosticism—from developments within Judaism. There is little doubt that exhaustive studies of Greek, Coptic, and Mandaic gnostic literature can contribute to our understanding of developments concerning the emergence of Jewish mysticism, and that the study of Hebrew texts contributes enormously to the understanding of the background of the emerging gnostic sects. A balanced, historical picture can be achieved only by an integrated effort to understand all parts of that puzzling creative period, its religious endeavors, and its literary works.

If we pursue, as we should, this avenue of historical and religious research, complexity increases and certainties fade away. The Dead Sea scrolls, which were studied in detail with respect to their relationship to Christianity and to mishnaic Judaism, have to be studied now to discover their relationship to the gnostic texts on the one hand and to *Hechalot* literature on the other. Indeed, we already have some interesting results of such comparative studies. These scrolls cannot be separated from the literature of the Second Commonwealth—apocalyptic and apocryphal literature—especially the Books of Enoch and Jubilees. These works may antedate *Hechalot* literature by several centuries, but there is no lack of proof that some ideas are common to them. The ties between the early Enoch literature and the descriptions of the ascensions to heaven in *Hechalot* literature reflect some basic similarities, not in any general theological attitudes, but in specific details. Was there a common source that is reflected in all these works, in the scrolls, in the *Hechalot* books, and in the Enoch literature (sometimes quite close to some elements in gnostic literature), or was there some sectarian tradition that influenced all these phenomena, a tradition that surfaced in different, unexpected religious and mystical circumstances? Each discovery, each new analysis, pertaining to one part of this enormous whole can change our perception about basic problems like the character and sources of early Christianity, the origins of gnosticism, and the roots of mishnaic Judaism, as well as the beginnings of Jewish mysticism.

An example that might demonstrate the far-reaching implications of such studies is found in the analysis of the pseudohistorical, or even metahistorical, element in some of the major mystical works of the *Hechalot* literature, especially the Greater Book of *Hechalot*

(*Hechalot Rabbati*) and a later work usually titled the Prince of the Torah (*Sar shel Torah*).

The narrative element of the *Hechalot Rabbati* is a story about the martyrdom of ten sages, among them Rabbi Akiva and Rabbi Ishmael, at the hand of the Roman emperor, probably reflecting the persecutions and executions that followed the defeat of the Bar Kochba rebellion. This story became very well known during the Middle Ages, when a novel relating in detail the sufferings of the ten sages became popular and was adapted to *piyyut* form and included in the *machzor*. In *Hechalot Rabbati*, the story describes a heavenly decision to let Satan (called here Samael) have his will with these ten sages, but Rome was to be destroyed in a terrible manner as a consequence. When the sages in Jerusalem heard about the emperor's decision, they sent Rabbi Ishmael to the heavenly palaces to inquire whether this cruel decision was authorized by God. Rabbi Ishmael discovered that it was, but he was meanwhile shown many secrets of the heavenly palaces, and these descriptions constitute the major part of the text of *Hechalot Rabbati*.

One of the striking characteristics of the descriptions of Rabbi Ishmael and his circle, including his teachers Rabbi Akiva and Rabbi Nehunia ben ha-Kanah, is the insistence upon the notion that all this is happening not only in Jerusalem, but also in the Temple itself. Rabbi Ishmael is even described in numerous instances as the High Priest, and a reference to his practice as a High Priest is found in a talmudic passage in Bavli *Berachot*. This is strange indeed if we take into account that Rabbi Ishmael was no more than a young child when the Temple was destroyed in 70 C.E. and that Jerusalem was destroyed and declared a Roman sanctuary at the same time that he was martyred after the Bar Kochba rebellion, in which at least Rabbi Akiva, and probably others of that circle, took an active part.

This metahistorical attitude is reflected also in the *Sar shel Torah* text, which is sometimes erroneously considered to be a supplement to the *Hechalot Rabbati*. In this text, the main purpose of which is a revelation of the ways to perceive the secrets of the Torah, there is a long dialogue between God and the people of Israel, who have just returned from the exile in Babylonia after the destruction of the

First Temple and are busy building the Second Temple. The Second Temple is described here as having a higher spiritual quality and higher divine status than the First Temple. A detailed description of an event not mentioned in any rabbinic text is the core of this mystical dialogue: the descent of the *Shechinah* and its appearance in the Second Temple after its completion. This revelation is regarded by the circle of mystics from which this text originated as the source of true divine revelation, and the mystical knowledge achieved then was preserved, according to them, by Rabbi Ishmael the High Priest. It seems evident from examination of this text that some of the *Hechalot* mystics developed an attitude toward the Second Temple different from that found in midrashic tradition, and this unique concept was part of their unusual attitude toward history and toward Jerusalem.

The centrality of the concepts of history and the Temple in these texts and traditions proves that the new, esoteric mystical interpretation of the *Song of Songs*, as found in *Hechalot Zutarti* and the *Shiur Komah*, is not the only source of the new *Hechalot* mysticism. Some older metahistorical traditions have to be taken into account when we look for the spiritual sources of this new school of mystics.

It is impossible to ignore in this context the fact that we now have before us a major nonmystical religious work that reflects a hitherto unknown concept of the Temple and a unique attitude toward it—namely, the Temple scroll, published recently by Y. Yadin. The scroll, in which God speaks in the first person and Moses is not mentioned (as in the *Sar Torah* text), is closely connected, linguistically and ideologically, with the Dead Sea scrolls and the apocryphal literature, especially the Book of Jubilees. Was there a connection between the *Hechalot* mystics and old traditions that originated in Jewish sects during the Second Commonwealth, and had the later mystics absorbed some attitudes from the sectarians? Or were there historical ties, as well as theological ones, among all these groups who departed to some extent from mainstream mishnaic tradition? It is impossible to give a clear answer to these questions and many similar ones concerning this early period in the development of Jewish mysticism. One thing, however, is quite clear: The study of these problems may help us understand the origins and some characteristics of early Jewish mysticism, but its implications concerning Jewish history during a crucial period, the development of mishnaic Judaism, of early gnosticism and of the background of the beginning of Christianity, of first-century literature and the Dead Sea scrolls, will be enormous. The emergence of Jewish mysticism is one of the many intertwined phenomena that constitute the religious and literary history of this period, and the complex has to be studied in its entirety.

IV

The emergence of the kabbalah in the second half of the twelfth century poses for the scholar serious historical problems, the study of which involves basic questions concerning the development of Jewish religion in the Middle Ages. Our knowledge of the role of mysticism in Judaism during the more than five centuries of the gaonic period is very scanty, and it is impossible to assess the impact that mysticism had—or did not have—on Judaism during that long, formative period. Jewish culture in Europe, as it developed between the tenth and twelfth centuries, reflects very strong rationalistic elements, whereas mysticism seems to appear only as a marginal phenomenon. Its main impact seems to have been felt much later, and this was interpreted as an expression of dissatisfaction with some of the rational, philosophical answers to basic religious problems. Some aspects of the turn to mysticism by small, esoteric circles of rabbis in the main centers of Jewish culture in Europe (Germany, Spain, southern France) can be understood as a reaction against rationalism and Maimonidean ideas. But were these mystical attitudes completely new, or are they signs of the reemergence of mystical texts and symbols that were present before somewhere in the totality of Jewish religious experience throughout the ages? Was mysticism a reaction against twelfth-century rationalism, or was rationalism a new, medieval alternative offered against mystical attitudes that prevailed in groups and circles whose original works are lost to us? The mystics themselves insist that their symbols and texts were ancient. Usually this can be proved to be an unhistorical claim, but was it completely without foundation in fact?

This problem concerns several groups of Jewish mystics in the second half of the twelfth century and the beginning of the thirteenth. The Ashkenazi Hasidim, the founders of the medieval Jewish pietistic movement in the cities of the Rhineland in the twelfth century, reflect a very strong sense of reliance on an ancient tradition, the authors claiming to deal with ideas and practices received in an unbroken chain of tradition from earlier generations. They possessed an impressive library of *Hechalot* texts, probably with a few layers of commentaries, as well as magical and divination traditions and holy names and their interpretations, which they undoubtedly received from the East. They claimed to have an oral tradition concerning the mysteries of the prayers, which they received through southern Italy from gaonic Babylonia. We can assess the impact of these ideas and traditions in twelfth- and thirteenth-century Jewish communities in Germany. But what was their religious role—if any— during the long period of almost subterranean transmission? Can the historian of Jewish religious thought ignore the possible influence of such sources prior to their incorporation in thirteenth-century European mystical literature?

The early kabbalists in Provence in the second half of the twelfth century and the beginning of the thirteenth used a highly developed system of symbols, a system that served as a basis for later kabbalistic works, including the *Zohar*, which was written at the end of the thirteenth century. The same symbols served all later Jewish mystical movements, from Safed in the sixteenth century until the seventeenth-century Sabbatians and the eighteenth-century Hasidim. What are the sources of this symbolism? One major source was clearly the *Bahir*, the earliest kabbalistic work, which was used by the kabbalists in Provence, and most of the basic mythological and gnostic elements in the kabbalah can be traced back to this book. This, however, was not the first source: Scholem's arguments suggesting that there are in the *Bahir* some layers of early Eastern gnostic symbolism are accepted today by all scholars, though we do not know exactly from what place and period these symbols were taken and by whom they were adapted into the form of Hebrew mystical homiletics. The problem of the influence of these elements inside Judaism before the appearance of the *Bahir* remains, therefore, unanswered for the time being.

But was the *Bahir* the only source of symbols used by the early kabbalists? Studying their works, one may get the impression that there were other sets of symbols, no less important than that of the *Bahir*, that served these early mystics. It is possible that some of these non-Bahiric elements were invented by these mystics themselves; yet, knowing the highly traditionalist attitude of the Provençal rabbis, there are serious doubts as to whether this could explain most of the material before us. If there were other sources, where did they originate? And how should one explain the fact that these sources could be integrated so closely into the Bahiric gnostic symbolism?

These are difficult problems, yet the most important one from a historical, religious, and literary point of view is the question of the influence of such texts prior to their appearance in the circles of esoterics in twelfth-century Europe. It is difficult to assume that such ideas and religious attitudes, which produced a radical set of symbols, would have no impact at all until they reached the schools of the early kabbalists in Provence. This proves again that careful historical study should not rely only on a few very well known rationalistic works when describing the development of Jewish religion in Europe up to the twelfth century. Even though Jewish mysticism appeared as a clear religious and literary movement only in the late twelfth century, a historical picture that does not take the mystical element into account concerning even earlier periods will be lacking a basic and vital element.

V

The historical role of Jewish mysticism within the framework of Jewish religion and literature can be divided into two parts: one before 1492 (the expulsion of the Jews from Spain), and the second from that major catastrophe in Jewish history up to the nineteenth century. In the first period, the influence of Jewish mysticism was felt beneath the surface of major cultural phenomena, for the mystics guarded their esoteric tradition and did not appear in public as possessors of divine secrets. There is little doubt, for example, that some mystics, among them Nachmanides, had a major role in the controversy concerning Maimonides' *Guide to the Perplexed* in the thirteenth and fourteenth centuries, but they did not explain their religious positions by using mystical symbols. They appeared as ordinary rabbinic traditionalists, as if they did not have any original religious doctrines of their own. Historical and literary study of this period tends to uncover more and more examples of subterranean, disguised mystical influence on the development of Jewish culture in the Middle Ages.

After 1492, however, a radical change occurred. The crisis of Spanish Jewry caused a basic change of attitude toward Jewish philosophy, which was discredited to a very large extent, and was blamed for the weakness of a large part of the community when facing the demand to convert. Increasing numbers of Jewish intellectuals turned to the kabbalah seeking answers to the questions of the meaning of Jewish existence in exile and a promise of approaching redemption.

The existence of the kabbalah as an esoteric force in Jewish culture for three centuries before it began to appeal to the masses of Jewish scholars and intellectuals shaped its later historical development. Throughout these three centuries, the kabbalah was an accepted fact within the framework of Jewish culture—little known and little understood, but accepted as a part of religious tradition and experience. The fact that many great rabbis, respected by all because of their halachic teachings, were kabbalists (Nachmanides, Rabbi Abraham ben David, Rabbi Solomon ben Adret) added to the legitimacy of the kabbalah. The long period in which the kabbalah flourished without serious opposition or controversy made some issues like the pseudepigraphic nature of many kabbalistic works, among them the *Zohar* itself, an old and irrelevant problem by the time the kabbalah surfaced in the sixteenth century. Though the kabbalists did not intentionally try to influence the masses of the people, the prestige of the kabbalah gradually grew, and its potential impact became greater and greater. It seems as if Jewish history kept the kabbalah in reserve for many generations until the right time came for it to appear and assume its role.

That time came when the national element in Jewish religion became more prominent than the individual one; when the question of redemption of the whole nation became the paramount concern, overshadowing individual salvation and private religious achievement. The kabbalah in the sixteenth century became the main vehicle for messianic expression and messianic endeavor, and sixteenth-century kabbalists interpreted Jewish traditional commandments as symbolic means, endowed by God in order to enable Jews to bring forth their own national redemption. Everyday religious performance of each ritualistic and ethical commandment or precept received cosmic significance in the kabbalah (especially in Lurianic kabbalah, developed in Safed by Isaac Luria) as helping and enhancing the coming of the Messiah. In this kabbalistic system of symbols, Jewish mysticism became future-oriented, and thus it became a creative historical force, shaping national goals and national behavior and giving historical dimensions to everyday religious practices.

This revolution, which began within Jewish mystical thought, became a major transformation of many basic aspects of Jewish culture. Against this background, there developed both the Sabbatian movement and the Hasidic movement, as well as many other schools of thought, from the teachings of the Maharal of Prague to those of Rabbi Kook of Jerusalem in this century. It produced an enormous ethical and homiletical literature, its volumes numbering in the thousands and constituting the main form of literary and religious expression for three centuries of Jewish writers. Some unique literary phenomena are also attributable to this mystical revolution, including the works of Rabbi Moses Hayyim Luzzatto in the eighteenth century and Rabbi Nachman of Bratslav in the nineteenth.

This powerful impact of Jewish mysticism on Jewish culture in the last half-millennium should be taken into account when studying earlier periods in Jewish history. The vast spiritual power hidden *potentially* within Jewish mystical speculation in the period prior to the expulsion from Spain should not be disregarded when studying any literary, religious, or historical phenomenon within Judaism.

END NOTE

This article is based on an opening lecture delivered at McGill University in Montreal in 1978, as part of a conference dedicated to the study of Jewish mysticism, which was convened as a regional conference by the Association of Jewish Studies in North America. The lectures in this conference later appeared as a volume, *Studies in Jewish Mysticism*, published by that organization (Cambridge, MA 1979), edited by the late Prof. Frank Talmage and myself. The study "The Emergence of the Mystical Prayer," included in the volume *Jewish Mysticism: The Middle Ages* in this series, was originally published there.

The question of the role of Jewish mysticism in the history of Jewish culture has been discussed in many contexts since then. Eliezer Schweid criticized Gershom Scholem, claiming that he placed the kabbalah at the heart of Jewish culture as a whole, viewing it as the inner spiritual power that motivated Jewish religiosity throughout the ages. In a detailed response, I analyzed Scholem's position and showed that Scholem attributed a central role to the kabbalah only in a relatively brief period—in the sixteenth to eighteenth centuries—whereas in other periods it played a marginal role, being studied in small, esoteric circles. See the material presented concerning this controversy in the volume *Jewish Mysticism in Modern Times* in this series. These discussions occurred mainly in 1984 to 1985; later, however, the views that Schweid erroneously ascribed to Scholem were presented, in a radical form, by M. Idel in his *Kabbalah: New Perspectives* (New Haven, CT 1988).

These and other arguments during the last two decades strengthened my view that it is wrong to present radical generalizations concerning the role of mysticism in Jewish culture. During the talmudic period, for instance, I believe that mysticism has held a marginal position, significantly more modest than the one ascribed to it by Scholem (a brief discussion is presented in the Introduction to this volume;) in the High Middle Ages it was centered in esoteric circles with little impact on Jewish medieval culture as a whole. It became a major moving power in culture and history only after the expulsion of the Jews from Spain in 1492, and expressed itself within the great movements of the Lurianic kabbalah, the Sabbatian messianic heresy, and modern Hasidism.

THREE

The Paradox of Nothingness in the Kabbalah

In the early thirteenth century, *ayin*, the Hebrew word for "nothingness," became one of the most important and profound symbols of the kabbalah. It appears in the works of the early kabbalists in Provence and in Spain, especially in the treatises written by a Jewish mystical group in the small town of Gerona in Catalonia. Later, this concept was extensively used by Rabbi Moses de Leon, the author of the *Zohar*, the greatest and most influential text of the kabbalah written in northern Spain in the end of the thirteenth century. The *Zohar*'s understanding of symbols became central for later Jewish mystics, including the teachers of Hasidism in the eighteenth and nineteenth centuries.

Most kabbalistic symbols were derived directly from the Bible. Every biblical verse was interpreted by kabbalists in a mystical way, and key words and terms found in them became standard kabbalistic symbols. The history of the term *ayin*, however, is unique. This term was based on a philosophical cosmogonic concept, which the kabbalists adopted, integrated into a biblical verse, and gave a completely new and paradoxical meaning.

When Jewish philosophers in the tenth to twelfth centuries endeavored to harmonize the text of the scriptures describing the creation of the world with the teachings of the Greek classical philosophers concerning the origin of the world, one of the key terms they had to use was creation *ex nihilo*, "out of nothingness," as opposed to creation from primordial matter or the Aristotelian concept of eternal, non-created world. The term they adopted (in the Hebrew works of Rabbi Solomon ibn Gabirol, Rabbi Abraham bar Hijja, Rabbi Abraham ibn Ezra, and others) was creation *yesh me-ayin*, "something out of nothing," thus giving the Hebrew biblical term *ayin* the meaning of complete negation, absolute nothingness. Although they did not mean to do it, they gave this Hebrew word the association of being the first, most ancient, and most fundamental stage in the process of creation. *Ayin* thus became a term loaded with mysterious connotations that enabled the mystics to use it in a completely different manner.

Another text that contributed to the mysterious character of this term was a cryptic passage in the *Sefer Yezirah* (Book of Creation), an ancient cosmogonical work, which probably was written in the fourth century by a Jewish mystic-scientist who used terminology characteristic only of this text. The *Sefer Yezirah* had an enormous influence on the medieval Jewish kabbalists; all of its terms and phrases were closely studied and often used. In the sixth paragraph of the second chapter of this brief work we read: "He (God) created from *tohu* (chaos)—substance, and made *eino yeshno*." This phrase can be interpreted as either "He made from what is not what is," or "He made from His nothingness His substance." The term *eino* can be interpreted as referring to some divine attribute, something that is not just nothingness, but a kind of attribute within the precreation of divine existence.

When the kabbalah emerged in Provence and northern Spain in the last years of the twelfth century and at the beginning of the thirteenth, a new element was added to the Jewish conception of the Godhead: the idea that there are ten divine powers, hypostases of the supreme divine being, which are emanated one from the other. The process of creation in the kabbalah is first and foremost the story of the process of emanation of these ten powers, called *sefirot* (a term also derived from the *Sefer Yezirah*). These ten *sefirot* are the main subject of kabbalistic speculation. In the thirteenth century, the term *ayin* became the appelation of the first and highest divine power, the source of all divine and material existence.

The early kabbalists who used this term relied consistently on one verse, Job 28:12, which reads: "But wisdom, where shall it be found? And where is the place of understanding?" The medieval Jewish mystics found in this verse a description of the emanation of the first three divine powers. According to them, the second *sefirah* is called *chochmath*, wisdom, and the third is called *binah*, understanding. They disregarded the phrasing of the verse as a question, and read it as a statement. Yet as a statement the Hebrew text does not imply a wondering as to where is a place or source of wisdom, but a divine exclamation that the origin of wisdom is in the *ayin* (the Hebrew *mè-ayin* can be read both as a question, "Wherefrom?" and as a statement: from the *ayin*, from nothingness). For them, this verse therefore meant that God Himself declared the origin of the second and third divine hypostases to be the first, which He called *ayin*.

This terminology, found, for instance, in Rabbi Azriel of Gerona's commentary on the talmudic legends (I. Tishby's edition, Jerusalem 1945, pp. 90 and 107) transformed the meaning of the philosophical term "nothingness" to the highest and most divine form of existence. Thus a term that was used to denote negation and non-existence was transformed to mean the first spiritual step that creates a bridge between the completely hidden and inactive Godhead and the emanated divine *sefirot*. Within the realm of this *ayin*, the divine will to create, to form something outside of itself, is being expressed. On the one hand, therefore, the *ayin* is still a symbol of nothingness, because when it was emanated nothing was as yet in actual existence. All that this symbol represents is the first spark of divine will or thought to emanate divine beings of positive existence. On the other hand, this term denotes existence in its most supreme sense. The kabbalists followed in many respects neo-Platonist ideas, and the closer a being is to the divine source, the truer is its existence. The *ayin*, in this sense, exists in a truer manner than everything which is below it, which was emanated from it.

It should be noted that the early kabbalists did not use the same term when they referred to the highest divine realm, the Godhead itself, which is beyond any description, even a symbolic one, and which is eternal and unchanging; they called this realm *ein sof*, meaning "no end." This is a completely negative term that does not convey any specific meaning; any other negative term could be, and sometimes was, used in its place, because *ein sof* refers to the divine realm in which no positive linguistic terms can apply, and therefore all negatives are equally relevant. The *ayin*, the highest *sefirah*, often described by the symbol *keter* (crown), is therefore the first positive divine symbol emerging from the negatively described *ein sof*. The *Zohar*, the most important kabbalistic work of the Middle Ages, even strengthens the paradoxical relationship between *ayin* and *ein sof* by stating: "*Ein sof* cannot be known, it makes neither end nor beginning, but the primordial *ayin* emanated beginning and end" (Zohar vol. II, p. 239b). The author emphasizes here that while the term "end" has no meaning when applied to *ein sof*, it does have a meaning when applied to *ayin*, the first and highest emanation from *ein sof*.

Various kabbalists used this symbolism in different ways, and in the history of the kabbalah no consistency can be found in the detailed use of this terminology. The paradoxical nature of the *ayin*, however, remained constant in almost all medieval mystical speculations, and was integrated, especially in the *Zohar*, within a system of similar paradoxes: Darkness is the supreme light, silence is the supreme sound, and other similar statements. Still, the close relationship between the symbols of existence and nonexistence was used by many mystics as a source for profound speculations and vivid paradoxical descriptions. The relationship between the first *sefirah* and the Godhead itself was always one of the most intriguing subjects of mystical inquiry, and the problem of the eternity of the *ayin* and its relationship to the *ein sof* have often been discussed. Even the *Zohar* itself contains more than one view on this subject.

The paradoxical nature of the term "nothingness" in the kabbalah opened a space for speculations and even had a strong impact on actual religious life, as it became apparent centuries later. Kabbalists followed the philosophers and spoke of a creation *ex nihilo*, although they gave these terms an entirely different meaning. This did not mean the creation of something out of nothing, but the emergence of all existence from the supreme source of existence that is the divine *ayin*. They spoke of the emergence of all existence from its hidden root within the Godhead; for them existence and nonexistence became one and the same in that hidden realm their source, where, as they sometimes said, all the contradictions are united. For these kabbalists, the mystical secret of being and nonbeing became united in the profound and powerful symbol of the *ayin*.

Mystical activity in the kabbalah was used to uplift the human soul from its material surroundings and unite it with the divine powers. The ladder of emanation, leading from the first to the tenth *sefirah*, and then to the material world, was used as a ladder of ascension. Speculation concerning the emergence of the divine hypostases from the Godhead became also a series of directions concerning the way that the mystic's soul has to take in its attempt to ascend and unite itself with the divine realm. Thus, the *ayin*, the first and highest divine emanation, became also the supreme goal of mystical ascension.

The paradox, therefore, acquired a new strength when the unity with nothingness became the supreme achievement of the mystical way toward the mystical union. In most cases kabbalists did not believe that such a union is possible while a man is alive in the material world. With few exceptions, most of them held that the highest stages of communion with the divine powers may occur only after the body's death. Nevertheless, the powerful symbol of a union with "nothingness" did not lose its literal meaning, as it became apparent especially in the last development stages of the mystical schools within Judaism—the Hasidic movement of the second half of the eighteenth century.

Hasidic teachings are based completely on kabbalistic symbolism, but very often the teachers of this modern movement found new meanings in the old symbols and applied them to actual religious life. Hasidism, unlike kabbalism in general, was a popular movement that tried to influence the Jewish public as a whole, and the number of its adherents reached hundreds of thousands and even millions. When paradoxical symbols are transformed into popular teachings for the masses, changes are bound to occur.

In Hasidic teachings we find the term *ayin* in contexts that seem to denote simply its old meaning: nothingness. The faithful are instructed to devote their religious energies to self-negation in a spiritual sense, emptying themselves of all thoughts and feelings of the material world and "becoming nothingness," thus making themselves into vehicles for the pure flow of divine emanation. In some Hasidic schools, the slogan of "turning into nothingness" acquired a central place in the teachings concerning one's attitude during prayer and worship. It is obvious, however, that the whole history of this term and its development through eight centuries of mystical speculation is hidden within these seemingly simplistic religious instructions.

"Becoming nothing" is a religious goal because nothingness is the essential attribute of the divine. This is so only because the paradox "Nothingness is the true existence" has been retained and even strengthened. The denial of the false existence, that is, material existence, is achieved by the unity with nothingness, that is, the supreme divine existence. When becoming "nothing" in comparison to this world, the Hasid achieve "something" in the true, divine world, where true existence (that is, of nothingness) can be found. In Hasidic teaching there are different shades of literal and symbolic meaning of this subject, but in most cases the identity between nothingness and supreme divine existence has been retained and even strengthened.

The popularity of Hasidism, both within Judaism and in modern descriptions of of Jewish mysticism, made the paradoxical meaning of *ayin* well known even among non-orthodox and assimilated Jews. Every Jew who lived in the vicinity of a Hasidic community could be exposed to this idea. Such communities were found, in the period before the Second World War, in almost every town in which Jews lived. After the war, nostalgic descriptions of the destroyed Jewish world often have described Hasidic teachings, and some of them emphasize this element. The studies of Hasidism by Martin Buber and Gershom Scholem invariably dwelled on it. A Jewish intellectual in Europe could hardly escape being aware of it. To what extent Paul Celan was influenced by it is, therefore, a meaningful question to be studied.

ENDNOTE

The article published here was delivered as a lecture in a conference in 1984 at the University of Washington, Seattle, dedicated to the poetry of Paul Celan. It served as a background for other participants' discussions of the motifs of silence, nothingness, and void in Celan's poetry. It was not intended to present the full scope and complexity of the kabbalistic concepts concerning nothingness. This subject was central in several recent studies: Daniel Matt dedicated to it a comprehensive essay, and Rachel Elior put it in the center of her studies of two major chapters in modern Hasidic thought. "Between *Yesh* and *Ayin*: The Doctrine of the Zaddik in the Works of Rabbi Jacob Isaac, the Seer of Lublin," in *Jewish History, Essays in Honor of Chimen Abramsky*, London 1988, pp. 393–455 is a presentation of the dynamics of the concept of the *Tzaddik* in Hasidism by one of its early creators. The second, Elior's monograph *The Paradoxical Ascension to God*, Albany, NY: SUNY Press 1995, deals with the dynamics of the concepts of *yesh* and *ayin* in the theology of Lubavitch Hasidism. Despite the meaningful variations that the concepts underwent throughout the history of Jewish mysticism, the basic notion, which views nothingness as the true essence of being, reflective of the nature of the supreme Godhead itself, remained central to the spiritual world of these mystics.

FOUR

Imago Dei

"And God said: 'Let us make man in our image, after our likeness . . .' " (Genesis 1:26). This verse is one of the most perplexing in the Hebrew Bible; Jewish commentators, from ancient times to the present, did their best to resolve the theological problems it presented. At the same time, it is difficult to find in the Bible a verse more pregnant with profound meaning, serving philosophers, mystics, and theologians as an ancient authority and source for their ideas. The uniqueness of this verse is the result of the unusual way in which it defines the relationship between God and man. It does not deal with a certain group of men or with any religious context dependent on man's deeds; its subject is man in the most general terms, referring to humanity more as a potential than as an actual existence. On the one hand it is vague, and the relationship described in it cannot be precisely defined; on the other hand it is sufficiently clear to denote an absolute intimacy between man and God, to a degree not usually expected in a religious context. Therefore, one is not surprised to find that this verse served as the basis for Jewish understanding of the nature of God and His relationship to man in a variety of ways, reflecting the deepest spiritual drives and religious sensibility of countless generations of Jewish thinkers.

This essay will deal primarily with one aspect of this verse, an aspect that has been central to the development of Jewish concepts of man and God: the transformation of the problem of anthropomorphic descriptions of God into the source of Jewish mystical symbolism concerning the nature of the Godhead itself and the impact of this transformation on human religious behavior.

In ancient Hebrew rabbinic texts, the main problem discussed concerning Genesis 1:26 is the plural language that God used when referring to the creation of man. Most of the sayings that tradition has preserved for us from this period are intended to defend Jewish monotheism from any doubt that may spring from the plural usage of the passage, "Let us create man in our image." Yet there are indications that the anthropomorphic consequences of the literal understanding of this verse were clear to the ancient rabbis, who apparently were not disturbed by them. It seems that ancient Judaism was able to accept an image of God that bore resemblance to the image of man without its basic theological monism being threatened. One may even suspect that this verse facilitated the development of anthropomorphic interpretations of other verses, even when the literal meaning of the biblical passages did not demand it.

The most outstanding example of such a process can be found in a second-century phenomenon that first appeared, in all probability, in the school of Rabbi Akiva: the understanding of the descriptions of the lover in the *Song of Songs* as a divine self-portrait. From this school we have the first observations that disclose that the author of this biblical book was not King Solomon (Shlomo), but rather "the King of Peace (shalom)," God Himself; that the *Song of Songs* is the holiest book in the Bible; and that it was not "written" but "given" to the people of Israel in the same way that the Torah was "given," either when they miraculously crossed the Red Sea or as a part of the theophany on Mount Sinai. This attitude does not appear to be directly connected to the later allegorization of the *Song of Songs* as the story of the relationship between God and *knesset Yisrael*; rather, it should be understood as a stage in the development of the *Shiur Komah*, a mystical text of the talmudic period, and the central part of the ancient *Hechalot* mysticism.

The *Shiur Komah* (literally "the measurement of the height of the Creator," although actually it means *imago Dei*) was regarded in the Middle Ages as the worst and most embarrassing example of ancient Jewish anthropomorphism. Jewish philosophers did everything they could to cast doubt on its authenticity or to explain away its anthropomorphism. Yet if we examine this text in its historical background, it represents a denial of the literal meaning of *imago Dei* and the beginning of the process that turned this concept into a central one in the mystical structure of the relationship between man and God.

The text of the *Shiur Komah* is based on verses 5:10–16 of the *Song of Songs*, which describe the physical appearance of the lover. It includes a list of the divine limbs, a list of their names—which are long series of Hebrew letters, most of them completely unpronounceable and unintelligible—and a list detailing the measurements of each limb. These measurements are given in units of tens of millions of *parasangs*, with a *parasang* explained as consisting of 18,000 *zeratol* (little fingers) of the creator, each as long as the whole world from one end to another. The limbs mentioned are human—eyes, neck, knees, arms, fingers—but their names and their measurements transcend human conception and imagination, and therefore literal anthropomorphism is denied. It is possible that this text is in fact a polemical answer to those who, following the new exegesis of the *Song of Songs* as the self-portrait of God, understood the physical descriptions of the lover literally. The author of the *Shiur Komah* answers them by stating that though God has a neck and arms, they are astronomical in their size—billions of times the length of the Earth—and their essence is hinted at in bizarre, unpronounceable names. Crude anthropomorphism is thus replaced by a sense of mystical awe toward the Creator, Who, though He is so radically different from anything resembling human physique, can still be described by the use of the names of human limbs.

Jewish mysticism prior to the Middle Ages, as far as we know it today, did not define the meaning of this resemblance between man and God in terms applicable to religious life. The early medieval thinkers were more interested in defending rabbinic Judaism from Karaitic charges of anthropomorphic superstition. They explained the *imago Dei* verse, as well as the *Shiur Komah*, as relating to a created angel, a lower divine being, or as an allegory concerning the relationship between man and the world, positing two levels of divine image—one found in the creation of the cosmos, the macrocosmic image, and one found in man, the microcosmic image. Nevertheless, during the early Middle Ages Jewish mystical speculation concerning the *Shiur Komah* and the mystical connection between the divine and human images persisted, to be revealed again in full force in the early works of the medieval kabbalists in the late twelfth and early thirteenth centuries.

In the earliest work of the kabbalah, *Sefer ha-Bahir*, the divine image is presented in symbolical anthropomorphic terms that advanced beyond the *Shiur Komah*: The limbs of this divine image denote not only parts of the image, but also its different functions. The fingers of the divine left hand, for example, bring punishment to the wicked and evil of the world, while the right arm is the origin of divine deliverance and redemption. The main contribution of the kabbalah—up to and including its central work, the *Zohar*, written in Christian Spain at the end of the thirteenth century—to the concept of *imago Dei* in Judaism is the sincere belief in the symbolic connection between human limbs and the elements that constitute the fullness of the divine realm. There is a double layer of symbolism implicit in this connection. Not only is the relationship itself symbolic, but the celestial counterpart to the human image can be known only by its symbols, the full meaning of which remains completely beyond human knowledge and understanding. This double layer of symbolism prevented any anthropomorphic, and thus heretical, use of the *imago Dei* idea by Jewish mystics. Indeed, by the late thirteenth century, Jewish mystics became so used to this symbolism that the human element in expressions like "God's beard" or "His heart" was almost completely lost and forgotten; in kabbalistic literature these symbolic terms referred first and foremost to the divine world.

The *Zohar* and other thirteenth- and fourteenth-century
kabbalistic works introduced a dynamic element into the idea of
imago Dei on two levels. One, begun by the *Sefer ha-Bahir*, was the
equation of the limbs with the divine functions of providence with
respect to creation; the second was the dynamic symbolism describing the interrelationship among the divine powers themselves: a vast
treasury of symbols detailing the sexual relationship between the masculine and feminine parts of the divine world, between God and the
malchut (kingdom) or *Shechinah* (divine presence), as the female element in the hierarchy of divine emanations was often called. Another group of symbols described the mythological struggle between
the elements of good and evil in the divine realm, after that realm
had been conceived of in dualistic terms by Rabbi Isaac ben Jacob
ha-Cohen in the second half of the thirteenth century. Both the
beneficent divine powers and the evil ones were structured according to the same anthropomorphic image, consisting of ten descending emanations corresponding to human limbs.

The most intricate and imaginative Jewish description of the divine figure in anthropomorphic terms is found in the *Zohar*, which
made use of all the images and symbols introduced by previous Jewish mystics and added to it the author's own creative mystical visions. Gershom Scholem dedicated to this portion of the *Zohar*,
known as the *idrol*, a major part of his penetrating essay on the idea
of the *Shiur Komah* in Jewish mysticism.[1] As Scholem pointed out,
the metaphysical element in these descriptions of the various limbs
of the divine figure is interwoven with, and sometimes even over-
powers, the mythical one. The *imago Dei* tradition was used by the
author of the *Zohar* in order to introduce his mystical conceptions
of the processes operating within the Godhead, directing the development in the mystical realm and influencing the divine providence
of the lower worlds. Since the fourteenth century, when the *Zohar*
increasingly became a dominant power in shaping Jewish ideas and

---

[1]Gershom Scholem, "Die mystische Gestalt der Gottheit in der Kabbala," in *Eranos
Jahrbuch* 29 (1960), pp. 139–182.

symbols, the *Shiur Komah* image of the Godhead became an accepted part of Jewish thought; the most orthodox sections of Jewish society used it more often and more profoundly than others.

Later kabbalistic schools, including the Lurianic kabbalah, which appeared in Safed in the last third of the sixteenth century, and the Sabbatian heresy of the seventeenth and eighteenth centuries used this symbolism in a most central manner. The image of *adam kadmon* (primordial man) became almost identical with the concept of the Godhead. The *Shiur Komah* anthropomorphic structure was found by Jewish mystics not only in the image of the divine realm as a whole, but also in the inner structure of every part of that realm. The founder of Hasidism, Israel Baal Shem Tov, is reported by his disciples to have said that every letter of the Jewish prayers consists of *komah shelemah*, that is, an integrally whole *imago Dei* figure. This mystical figure became the building block of every sacred particle of the divine and earthly realms.

The danger of anthropomorphism in a mystical–mythical concept of *imago Dei* can be overcome in one of two ways. It is possible either to downgrade it—that is, to claim, as did Saadia Gaon and most of the Jewish philosophic tradition, that the anthropomorphic descriptions are related to a lower, relatively unimportant spiritual or even material figure—or to uplift it to such mythical heights that the fact that man also has the same physical structure becomes a minor point. The process of the development of this idea in Jewish mysticism, which began in the ancient text of the *Shiur Komah* related to the *Song of Songs*, is a perfect example of the second way. *Imago Dei* in Jewish mysticism is truly the image of God; it represents in a symbolic way the perfect structure of the Godhead and hides within it the secrets of the inner dynamic life of God. The same divine image is reflected in God's creation, both in the divine emanations and the created, physical beings. Man is but one example of the appearance of this perfect structure outside of the divine realm.

Yet Jewish mysticism did not forsake the element of closeness between man and God that is inherent in the *imago Dei* symbolism. The parallel structure of both the human and divine realms enables man, in his religious and ethical deeds, to influence and even shape the divine processes. The *imago Dei* symbolism reflects not only the original structure of the body of Adam, but a continuous, permanent interdependence between God and his creatures. Thus, *imago Dei* in Jewish mysticism became a major force in enabling man to shape history as well as his own personal fate. Some of the divine powers represented in the transcendent *Shiur Komah* reside within man's own humble physical body. Jewish mysticism and the ethical literature that the kabbalah inspired directed man how to use these powers in order to assist God in achieving His mystical purpose in creating the universe.

BIBLIOGRAPHY

Alexander Altmann, "*Homo Imago Dei* in Jewish and Christian Theology," in *The Journal of Religion*, 48 (1968).

Joseph Dan, "The Concept of Knowledge in the *Shiur Komah*," in *Studies in Jewish Religious and Intellectual History in Honor of Alexander Altmann*, Siegiried Stein and Raphael Loew, eds. (1979).

FIVE

Jerusalem in Jewish Spirituality

The components of the spiritual significance of Jerusalem are variegated and deeply embedded in the experience of Western man. Some of them are temporal: Jerusalem signifies the glories of the past, the moments in history in which man and God have become closest. An example can be found in the *Akedah*, the binding, when Abraham was declared God's beloved and Isaac represented the ultimate human sacrifice, the prototype of all martyrs; another is in the building of the Temple, when God descended to Earth to reside among men. Jerusalem also represents the future, the ultimate union between humanity and God, when the ingathering of the exiles will bring the people to the divine fold, to be united forever. A vision of an eternal future utopia is identified with the name of the city, a vision that embodies a craving for eternal life, the overcoming of death, individual and national redemption, the reign of justice, the achievement of happiness, and religious fulfillment. And, finally, Jerusalem expresses the present desire for spiritual uplifting—for a personal, religious, and mystical experience.

For Jews, in addition to its temporal component, Jerusalem's spatial configuration is also significant. Since creation began in Jerusalem, it is the center of the universe, the meeting point between chaos and creation. It is the name of God that blocks the deluge of chaos from engulfing the Earth; it is both the core of the universe, and its point of emergence. It represents the ultimate evidence of God's gift to humanity—earthly existence. Celestial Jerusalem, by contrast, represents the indestructibility of perfection. The constant contrast between physical ruins and spiritual eternal structure, between earthly desolation and sublime perfection, expresses both the hardship and suffering and the opportunity of spiritual unity in the divine abode, into which the mystic is invited to share God's eternal residence. Jerusalem is the supreme expression of exile and destruction, of poverty and suffering, while it also represents eternal spiritual bliss.

THE PLACE WHERE HEAVEN
AND EARTH MEET

The *Sefer Yezira* (Book of Creation), written probably in the third century, described the cosmos as the infinite expansion of ten directions or dimensions,[1] which represent space, time, and ethics: north, south, west, east, up, down, beginning, end, good, and evil. These are described as divine arms expanding and engulfing the universe. The center is "the holy Temple, which is suspended in the middle." This image obviously unites the spiritual and the worldly, the divine and the earthly, with the cosmic concept of Jerusalem as the center of human and divine existence.[2]

---

[1]They are called in this ancient treatise *sefirot*, an original term for numerals; this term was used, a thousand years later, by the kabbalists to indicate their system of divine emanations. In the *Sefer Yezira*, however, this term represents mainly cosmological aspects rather than divine powers. In one section it may have been identified with the holy beasts in Ezekiel's vision (1:7).

[2]On the *Sefer Yezira*, see G. Scholem, *Origins of the Kabbalah*, trans. A. Arkush, ed. R. J. Zwi Werblowsky (Princeton, NJ: Princeton University Press 1986), pp. 24-35; J. Dan, "The Language of Creation and Its Grammar," in *Festschrift für Carsten Colpe* (Berlin: Walter de Gruyter 1994).

The image of Jerusalem as a spiritual symbol appeals to all human faculties. It includes the intellectual craving for knowledge, truth, and wisdom; at the same time, it represents the consummation of justice and purity. And, most of all, it represents the touching point between the divine and the earthly, the place in which heaven and Earth meet, and where a person can stretch his hand and touch the divine. Unlike the concept of afterlife, which became so dominant in religion in the Middle Ages and modern times—a concept that puts death at the center of human life, by making it the touching point between temporality and eternity, between suffering and perfection—Jerusalem represents the achievement of eternity and immortality without the intervention of death. Jerusalem is the place where present and future merge without the traumatic destruction of one's body. Jerusalem negates the separation between soul and limbs that was a major component of the neo-Platonic spirituality that imbues religious concepts but is contrary to both human experience and cravings. In Jerusalem, redemption and perfection are offered as a direct transition into numinous bliss.

The very beginning of Jewish mysticism—and possibly of mystical expression in any religion[3]—is deeply connected, as recent studies demonstrate, with the pilgrimage to Jerusalem. The earliest descriptions of a spiritual ascent to God, found in the Hechalot mystical literature (third to seventh centuries),[4] are among the most intense expressions in religious literature of the uplifting of the mystic's soul stage by stage until, overcoming difficulties and threats, it confronts the throne of glory and faces the King in His glory in an ancient expression of numinous perfection. It has been suggested that the mystical ascent is a pilgrimage, a substitute for the earthly three-times-

---

[3]See J. Dan, *The Revelation of the Secret of the World and the Beginning of Jewish Mysticism in Late Antiquity* (Providence, RI: Brown University Press 1992).
[4]Two general descriptions of this mystical literature have been published recently: P. Schaefer, *The Hidden and Manifest God* (Albany, NY: SUNY 1992); and J. Dan, *The Ancient Jewish Mysticism* (Tel Aviv: Ministry of Defense 1993). Both include detailed bibliographies.

a-year trip to Jerusalem.[5] Ezekiel's vision of the holy chariot, which travels from Earth to the celestial and divine world, has been identified with the Jerusalem Temple, transformed into intense mystical symbolism.[6] It seems, if these conclusions are correct, that the very concept of mystical ascension emerged in scriptural religion as a counterpart to the pilgrimage to Jerusalem, and that the celestial worlds envisioned by the mystic are reflections of the idealized images of Jerusalem and the Temple. Jerusalem is then identified with the Godhead itself, the purpose of the mystical ascent.

Jerusalem as not just a religious and ritualistic entity but also a political entity—the ideal "king's city,"[7] the city of King Solomon's palace and government—is central to the image of the mystical visions of Jerusalem.[8] The most important complex of symbols and pictures, which was fused with that of the Temple and became one of the most potent sources of spiritual and mystical drives in Judaism and Christianity, is the *Song of Songs*. The allegoristic depictions of this work did not erase its literal, monarchic, and sexual descriptions, which became basic metaphors for individual and communal union with God.[9] A mystical text of that period identifies Solomon's

---

[5]See Ira Chernus, "The Pilgrimage to the Merkavah: An Interpretation of Early Jewish Mysticism," in J. Dan, ed., *Proceedings of the First International Conference on the History of Jewish Mysticism: Early Jewish Mysticism, Jerusalem Studies in Jewish Thought 6*, no. 1-2 (Jerusalem: n. p. 1987), pp. 1-36 (English section).
[6]This has been demonstrated in great detail by Rachel Elior in a series of studies. See, for instance, "Mysticism, Magic and Angelology: The Perception of Angels in Hechalot Literature," *Jewish Studies Quarterly* I (1993-1994): pp. 1-53.
[7]Compare Psalms 48:3.
[8]G. Scholem, in his first study of the subject, emphasized the monarchic aspects of the pictures drawn by the *Hechalot* mystics. See his *Major Trends in Jewish Mysticism*, 2nd ed. (New York: Schocken Books 1954), pp. 40-78. This is contrary to the images governing gnostic mysticism; gnostic myths do not include this element, nor do they emphasize the mystic's position as a servant and slave.
[9]Concerning the role of this biblical text in the evolvement of ancient mysticism, see S. Lieberman, "Mishnat Shir ha-Shirim," published as an appendix to G. Scholem, *Jewish Gnosticism, Merkabah Mysticism and Talmudic Tradition*, 2nd ed. (New York: The Jewish Theological Seminary 1965), pp. 118-126; G. Scholem, *On the Mystical Shape of the Godhead: Basic Concepts of the Kabbalah*, trans. Joachim Neugroschel (New York: Schocken Books 1992), pp. 20-37. Scholem and

throne with that of God Himself.[10] R. Elior emphasized the priestly characteristics of the *Hechalot* terminology;[11] Rabbi Ishmael ben Elisha, for example, the central figure in several *Hechalot* texts, is described as a High Priest who is the son of a High Priest, and a mystical paragraph describing his meeting with God when officiating in the Temple is found in the Talmud.[12] Another example is a group of *Hechalot* mystics described as meeting in Jerusalem, in the "third entrance" to the Temple, even though the mystics named in this narrative lived two generations after the destruction of Jerusalem and the Temple.[13] Thus, the first picture of a congregation of mystics, which was destined to play a major role in medieval Jewish mysticism—in the depictions of the *idras* ("sacred conventions") in the medieval *Zohar*—is seen in the destroyed yet mystically alive Jerusalem. One of the most influential Hebrew mystical texts describes in detail the revelation of God in Jerusalem while the Second Temple was being built.[14] Thus, the earliest texts of Jewish mysticism established a vast panorama of symbols, metaphors, and terminology that associated Jerusalem with every vision of God, adding

---

Lieberman discuss mainly the image of God in *Hechalot* mysticism, the *Shiur Komah*, which is based on the *Song of Songs*, but the conclusions relate to other aspects as well. Compare B. McGinn, *The Foundations of Mysticism* (New York: Crossroads 1991), pp. 118–127 et passim.

[10]The text was often quoted in medieval literature in mystical and utopian contexts. See, for instance, ms. Oxford 1567, the Bodleian Library, pp. 114–116. The fact that the *Hechalot* mystics emphasized the Jerusalem-Temple aspect of their experiences is evident from their constant repetition of the formula of the Kedushah, derived from Isaiah's vision (Ch. 6) in the Temple in Jerusalem, whereas the formulas of the regular prayer that are not inherently connected to the experience of the Temple are relatively marginal (compare, for instance, their neglect of the Shema Yisrael prayer).

[11]Compare also I. Gruenwald, *From Apocalypticism to Gnosticism* (Frankfurt: P. Lang 1988), pp. 125–144.

[12]Bavli *Berachot* 7a.

[13]See J. Dan, "The Concept of History in Hechalot Mysticism," in J. Dan, ed., *Binah*, vol. 2, *Studies in Jewish History* (New York: Praeger 1989), pp. 47–58.

[14]This text, known as the *Sar Torah*, often is appended to *Hechalot Rabbati* in manuscripts and printed editions. See J. Dan, "The Theophany of the Prince of the Torah," *Jerusalem Studies in Jewish Folklore* 13–14 (1992), pp. 127–157.

new dimensions to the biblical and talmudic traditions that described the political, ritualistic, and cosmic significance of the city.

The Jerusalem of these early mystics is both destroyed and alive, in ruins and in full splendor. This dual nature of Jerusalem was regarded as expressing the dual state of the human soul, residing in a body and in a world of matter, evil and exiled, yet at the same time a resident of utmost beauty and perfection in the divine city. Two different elements were interwoven in this concept: the utopian-apocalyptic and the individual-mystical. When Rabbi Akiva is depicted in a talmudic story as walking over the ruins of Jerusalem laughing while his colleagues were weeping, because the promise of the rebuilding of Jerusalem would be fulfilled in the same way that the promise of its destruction was,[15] he was expressing the utopian belief in the imminent, worldly salvation of the city. The same Rabbi Akiva is described in the mystical treatise *Hechalot Zutarti* as ascending to the divine palaces and achieving the supreme spiritual proximity to God as an individual.[16] Hebrew apocalypses of Late Antiquity, like the *Sefer Zerubavel*, describe the beginning of cosmic redemption in Jerusalem, which will be destroyed again during the wars of that era, but from one corner of the city the victorious Messiah will emerge and overcome the hosts of the devil.[17] These two aspects of the visionary Jerusalem combine with the duality of dead-yet-alive Jerusalem: It represents the way the individual can escape his imprisonment in the world of matter and suffering within the framework of the present phase in history, and it represents the future, utopian eschatology of the people and the community, in which there will be no more exile and oppression, and in which the two Jerusalems, the ideal and the earthly, will be reunited. The future building of Jerusalem thus becomes the descent of the celestial city

---

[15]Bavli *Makkot* 24a.

[16]P. Schaefer, *Synopse zur Hekhalot-Literatur* (Tübingen: J.C.B. Mohr [Siebeck], 1981), pp. 142–158, 172–182, and R. Elior's edition of the text in *Jerusalem Studies in Jewish Thought*, Supplement 1 (1982). See note 18.

[17]*Sefer Zerubavel* was published in a scholarly edition by Yehudah Even-Samuel Kaufman in his *Midreshey Geulah* (Jerusalem: The Bialik Institute 1954), pp. 55–88; compare Dan, *Ancient Jewish Mysticism*, pp. 134–143.

to Earth (or the elevation of everything earthly to the level of the spiritual entity).[18] The basic duality of eschatology, that of individual fulfillment and national redemption, is clearly reflected in the vision of the spiritual Jerusalem.[19]

We do not know the origins and early development of the concept of a celestial Jerusalem that exists parallel to the earthly one.[20] There is very little doubt, however, that this concept was not the result of the destruction of the city but developed during the Second Commonwealth period. It thus served both talmudic Judaism and early Christianity as a traditional belief, deeply inherent in the concept of Jerusalem; the destruction in 70 C.E. only gave it a new impetus and a new importance. Indeed, it seems that the rabbinic sources emphasize that the celestial temple was created before the creation of the world, and that the earthly Jerusalem and its Temple were built in correspondence to the celestial ideal.[21] Philo of Alex-

---

[18]An unusual structure of this combination is found in the *Sar Torah* narrative, in which individual and communal elements are interwoven together. The divine revelation in the Temple also includes personal advantages to the mystics, and the visionary new era that is beginning with the mystical experience is one in which individual and national aspects are united. The bizarre element in this picture is that this utopian narrative actually relates to the distant past—the building of the Second Temple by Zerubavel; the story is told several centuries after that Temple has been destroyed. The mystical unification of past, present, and future is clearly evident in this text.

[19]Talmudic-midrashic eschatology is almost exclusively national and utopian, relegating salvation to the next world, the world that is to follow after this world has been destroyed. Only in the Middle Ages did the concept of a celestial, parallel world in which the souls of the righteous are rewarded immediately after their death become dominant in Jewish thought, relegating the apocalyptic, messianic salvation to a secondary position. Hebrew mystical speculations during Late Antiquity served as the main expression of the need for immediate spiritual redemption.

[20]A. Aptowitzer, "Beit ha-Mikedash shel Ma'allah al pi ha-Agadah," *Tarbiz* 2 (1931), pp. 137–153, 257–287. The author tried to show that this belief can be found in biblical prophecy, a concept that is very difficult to accept. The detailed study by Avigdor Aptowitzer of this problem, which presented hundreds of Jewish and Christian sources relevant to the development of this idea, has not been updated, and many questions remain unsolved.

[21]*Tanhuma*, Buber ed., *Nassa* par. 19, and see Aptowitzer, "Beit ha-Mikedash," pp. 137–138 and notes there.

andria, who wrote before the destruction of Jerusalem, seems to have been uncomfortable with the national aspect of this tradition, and reinterpreted it in a cosmic, universal manner.[22] According to him, the logos can be conceived as offering homage to the supreme God like a priest praying in the Temple.[23]

THE MESSIANIC ROLE OF JERUSALEM

Jerusalem's messianic role is interwoven with earthly and spiritual elements. The earthly Jerusalem is the constant guardian of the universe from the primeval chaos; and the rock on which God's name is engraved, deep inside the Temple Mount, is the barrier between the waters of a new deluge and the inhabited world. When King David found it and tried to lift it, the waters surged and endangered the whole universe.[24] This legend is repeated constantly in ancient and medieval Hebrew sources, making geographical Jerusalem no less significant than the celestial one.

In apocalyptic visions and speculations, both aspects of Jerusalem play a central role. The concept of the Messiah and Jerusalem are inseparable in Hebrew texts for nearly two millennia. Throughout the Middle Ages and early modern times, Jews were constantly drawn to Jerusalem as the place from which redemption will start and where the Messiah is destined to make his first appearance. This is the place where resurrection will occur, and people who are buried in this city will not have to wander under the earth until they reach the resurrection point.[25] In this way, Jerusalem was not just

---

[22]*De spec. leg.* I, ed. L. Cohen, V 17, par. 66, and see Aptowitzer, "Beit ha-Mikedash," pp. 139–140, notes 1, 6–7.

[23]*De somniis*, Cohen III, p. 251.

[24]Several studies have been dedicated to the history and development of this legend in antiquity and in the Middle Ages. See especially Joseph Heinemann and J. Dan, "The Legend of David and the Rock in the Literature of the Ashkenazi Hasidim," *Sinai* 74 (1974), pp. 239–241.

[25]The concept of *gilgul mehilot*, belief that became universal in Judaism, actually indicates the existence of a network of underground caves leading from every place to Jerusalem; these will allow the dead, in messianic times, to reach Jerusalem and be resurrected there.

an abstract ideal but a constant option in the life of every individual. Each person had to decide whether he was able to immigrate to Jerusalem and be buried there.

Another concept of Jerusalem, of the city as a feminine entity, began to emerge in antiquity, long before it was integrated in kabbalistic symbolism. The apocryphal work Fourth Ezra includes a detailed parable in which Jerusalem is depicted as a grieving woman;[26] this picture is repeated dozens of times in Jewish mystical literature as well as in folklore.[27] But in none of these motifs has the celestial Jerusalem replaced the earthly one. The concept rested completely on these two legs of the earthly and the divine cities, which only together constitute a whole. While Jerusalem is an intensely significant historical entity, and its fate reflects the vagaries of historical change, the duality itself is not subject to history: Jerusalem is equally meaningful in the creation of heaven and of Earth, and continues to retain its dual character in each phase of the universal past, present, and future.

THE HIGH MIDDLE AGES

In the early centuries of the Middle Ages, we find a decline in the centrality of speculations concerning Jerusalem in Jewish culture. The emergence of rationalism and science, and the theologies that emphasized the religious bond between every individual and God, rather than those of the people or the nation and God, limited the scope of such speculations.[28] For several centuries the mystical dimension in Jewish culture was diminished. Even messianic specula-

---

[26]Fourth Ezra, Ch. 10, 29–54, and see Aptowitzer, "Beit ha-Mikedash," pp. 267–268.

[27]Thus, for instance, the sixteenth-century mystic Rabbi Isaac Luria perceived her in a vision. See M. Benayahu, *Toledot ha-Ari* (Jerusalem: Ben Zvi Institute 1971), pp. 129–136.

[28]Despite this, it was Rabbi Judah ha-Levi, a product of Jewish rationalistic culture (though in opposition to various elements in it), who gave the most moving expression of a love of Jerusalem in his poetry, and he died while on his way to the city. See E. Schweid, *Homeland and Promised Land* (Tel Aviv: Am Oved 1979).

tions, like those of Maimonides, were formulated in a rational, political mode, minimizing the place of the city. This was despite the
fact that at the same time, Jerusalem acquired new dimensions of
meaning in Christian theology and history (during the period of the
Crusades) and its important place in Islamic thought and practice
was enhanced. Nevertheless, Nachmanides, the great mystic of the
first half of the thirteenth century, pointed out that no non-Jewish
entity could be established in Jerusalem; even when Jews were absent from the city, nobody else could claim it as his.[29] Yet many other
mystics of the thirteenth century did not develop Nachmanides'
theme beyond the traditions received from Late Antiquity.[30] It was
the new mystical school that emerged in the second half of the twelfth
century and dominated Jewish mysticism for eight hundred years,
the kabbalah, that reformulated the concept of the spiritual Jerusalem within the framework of a new system of symbols and myths,
and reinvigorated the centrality of the celestial Jerusalem in Jewish
spirituality.

JERUSALEM AND THE KABBALAH

In the earliest work of the kabbalah, *Sefer ha-Bahir*, written in
Provence or northern Spain around 1185, the celestial *Eretz Yisrael*
is identified with the supreme divine wisdom, the second divine ema-

---

[29]This was written following the destruction of the Crusader kingdom of Jerusa-
lem in 1187; the short-lived kingdom remains, to this very day, the only case in
three thousand years of history in which Jerusalem served as the capital of a non-
Jewish political entity. Nachmanides expressed his attitude by immigrating to
Jerusalem. See M. Idel, "Some Conceptions of the Land of Israel in Medieval
Jewish Thought," in R. Link-Salinger, ed., *A Straight Path, Studies in Medieval
Philosophy and Culture: Essays in Honor of Arthur Hyman* (Washington, DC: Catholic
University of America Press 1988), pp. 129–133.
[30]The first kabbalistic messianic treatises were written by Rabbi Isaac ben Jacob
ha-Cohen of Castile in the second half of the thirteenth century, and despite
the intense mythical nature of his apocalyptic visions, Jerusalem does not play a
major part. See J. Dan, "The Beginning of Messianic Myth in Thirteenth-Century Kabbalah," in R. Dan, ed., *Occident and Orient: A Tribute to the Memory of
A. Scheiber* (Budapest and Leiden: Brill 1988), pp. 57–68.

nation in the system of the ten divine hypostases, or *sefirot*, which is the core of kabbalistic symbolism.[31] This work is attributed to various sages of the mishnaic period, and was modeled, to some extent, after *Hechalot* mystical literature. Rabbi Nehunia ben ha-Kanah, the head of the mystical circle in *Hechalot Rabbati*, is the speaker in the first paragraph of this work, and the whole book was often attributed to him; Rabbi Akiva is described as the speaker in several key sections of this pseudepigraphical treatise. The same tendency is evident in the most important work of the kabbalah, *Sefer ha-Zohar*, which was written in northern Spain at the end of the thirteenth century.[32] The author of the *Zohar*, Rabbi Moses de Leon, followed the *Hechalot* and the *Bahir*'s literary tradition and described a circle of mystics of the mishnaic period, led by Rabbi Shimon bar Yochai and his son, Rabbi Eleazar. The deliberations of this circle included celestial ascensions and meetings with emissaries from the divine world, as well as homiletical and hermeneutic discussions of biblical verses. The *Zohar* presented a new integration of the concept of the spiritual Jerusalem within Jewish thought and Jewish ritual.

The vast myths and mystical speculations of the *Zohar* employed all the old motifs concerning Jerusalem, but gave them a new meaning and a new complexity. Thus the *Zohar* states, when discussing the term "Zion":

> When the world was created, it was created from that place which is the perfection and completion of the world, for it is the single point of the world and the center of all, and what is it? Zion . . . as it is written [Psalms 50:2]: "Out of Zion, the perfection and the

---

[31]Margaliot ed. (Jerusalem: Rav Kook Institute 1953), par. 143. The ancient traditions usually spoke about the celestial city or the celestial temple; the concept of a celestial country is rare in ancient sources, though it is implied in many contexts.

[32]On the *Zohar* and its author, see Scholem, *Major Trends in Jewish Mysticism*, pp. 156–204; I. Tishby, *The Wisdom of the Zohar*, trans. D. Goldstein, vol. 1 (Oxford: Oxford University Press 1989), pp. 1–96; and compare Y. Liebes, *Studies in the Zohar* (Albany, NY: State University of New York Press 1992).

beauty, God has shined forth," from the place that is the limit
of the perfection of complete faith, as it should be. Zion is the
strength and the point of the whole world, and from that place
the whole world was made and completed, and from it the whole
world is nourished.[33]

This is a restatement of the ancient concept of Jerusalem or Zion
as the center and source of creation. The two names of the city represent a duality within the divine realm, the separation between divine judgement—embodied by the fifth *sefirah*, *din* or *gevurah* (judgment, power), and by the tenth, *Shechinah* or *malchut* (presence, kingdom)—and divine mercy—embodied by the fourth *sefirah*, *chesed*
(mercy), and the ninth, *yesod* (foundation). These two aspects of the
Godhead are connected by the sixth *sefirah*, *tiferet* (glory, here referred by another frequent symbol, voice). Zion is regarded as the
representation of divine mercy, while Jerusalem is identified with
divine judgement, with the *Shechinah*, which is also the divine presence in the universe.[34]

The two aspects of the physical city, the source and foundation of the universe, and the destroyed capital, the expression of
God's punishment, are hypostasized in the *Zohar* as the two aspects
of the unfolding of divine power into the universe, as the power of
creation and the power of destruction and punishment. Thus divine
duality and historical, physical duality are united into one set of
symbols, which are the central aspects of the Godhead itself. The
relationships between God and the universe have been transformed,
in kabbalistic symbolism and experience, into the internal divisions
and dynamics within the Godhead itself. On the other hand, universal phenomena and events have been transformed into the dynamics of the unfolding of the divine aspects and their cosmic mani-

[33]*Zohar*, vol. I, folio 186a. Translation in Tishby, *Wisdom of the Zohar*, vol. 1, p.
362. The *Zohar* was written in Aramaic; Tishby translated a large selection of
zoharic passages into Hebrew in his monumental *Mishnat ha-Zohar* (Jerusalem:
The Bialik Institute 1949–1961); it was translated into English as *The Wisdom of
the Zohar*.
[34]Tishby, *Wisdom of the Zohar*, vol. 1, p. 363.

festations.[35] Jerusalem thus became an expression of the union with God, without departure from the physical city; rather, physical union with the city was identified with the spiritual union with God. Whereas in *Hechalot* mysticism the ascent to God's palaces entailed a departure from the material world, in the zoharic system the physical contact was identified with the spiritual journey.

This is evident in another central theme of the *Zohar*, expressed in the many passages dedicated to the interpretation of the sacrifices and the rituals in the ancient Temple.[36] The new dynamic concept of the inner life within the Godhead that characterizes the *Zohar* has been expressed in the detailed unity depicted in this work between the rituals in the Temple and the process of unification among the divine hypostases of God.[37] In this context, the feminine character of Jerusalem was again enhanced and developed into an intense erotic symbolism. The identification of Jerusalem with the *Shechinah*, which is regarded by the kabbalists as the feminine element within the Godhead, gave an erotic dimension to the relationship between God and His abode in Jerusalem and in the Temple.

---

[35]I am using here the traditional term "symbolism," which has been central in the scholarly study of the kabbalah. But the term does not express the true relationship between the symbol and the symbolized. The earthly Jerusalem, in this case, is not the "symbol" and the definition, and the *Shechinah* the symbolized— or vice versa. The relationship is one of intrinsic unity between these entities, a mystical metalinguistic concept for which the term "symbolism" is manifestly inadequate. See J. Dan, *The Language of the Mystics* (forthcoming). There may be an interesting parallel between the convergence of the physical and the mystical in the zoharic myth and the convergence of Jerusalem as a geographic-political entity and the spiritual concept of the city in Christianity in the crusading movement, which emerged as a political force after a millennium in which the spiritual aspect was dominant. This relationship is the opposite of an allegorical one, in which one level serves as a substitute for another; rather, this kind of symbolism enhances the importance of and the dedication to both levels.

[36]The beginning of this process is found in *Sefer ha-Bahir*. Several passages are dedicated to the discussion of the sacrifice, which is interpreted as the process of uniting the mystic with God.

[37]A comprehensive selection of passages relating to this subject is included in Tishby, *Wisdom of the Zohar*, vol. 3, pp. 867–940. See also R. Patai, *Man and Temple in Ancient Jewish Myth and Ritual* (London 1947).

Several passages in the *Zohar* describe in detail the sexual union experienced there:

> At midnight [the *Shechinah*] enters through the point of Zion, the place of the Holy of Holies and she sees it destroyed, and the place of her dwelling and her couch defiled. . . . She cries bitterly, raises her voice, and says: "My couch, my couch, the place where I used to dwell. . . . My husband would come to me and lie in my arms and all that I asked him, and all my requests he would fulfill, when he came to me and made his home with me and took delight between my breasts. . . . Do you not remember the days of our love, when I would lie in your arms. . . . Do you not remember how you stretched out your left hand beneath my head, and how I rejoiced in the flow of peace, and your right hand embraced [me] with love and kisses . . . ?"[38]

In the passages dedicated to this subject, such descriptions abound not only concerning the lost past, but also as pictures of the future redemption and reestablishment of the Temple ritual. The mystical meaning of the *Song of Songs*, which played a prominent part in *Hechalot* mysticism, has reemerged in the zoharic myth; the erotic element in this biblical text, which was largely ignored in the ancient mystical texts, has become now the central theme, representing the dynamic aspects of the relationships within the Godhead.

Another aspect of the zoharic myths concerning Jerusalem and Zion, God and the *Shechinah*, is its integration with present-day rituals. Jerusalem and the Temple are not only distant memories, paradigms of the creation and the sacrifices at the Temple; they are also represented by the daily prayers, the rituals of the Sabbath and the festivals, and the vast body of Jewish precepts and commandments. When performing the everyday commandments and rituals, the same dynamism is evoked within the divine realms, and the union between the divine male and female may occur, instigated by human religious activity. The identification between the rituals of the ancient Temple and the commandments of present-day Judaism has

---

[38]*Zohar Hadash*, Midrash Echah 92c–92d; Tishby, *Wisdom of the Zohar*, vol. 3, p. 877; and compare Song of Songs 2:6.

turned every person into a participant in the dramatic myth described in the *Zohar*. The erotic symbolism is thus related also to the worshipper, and not only to the divine powers.[39]

This extension of the symbolism concerning Jerusalem had its spiritual price. The identification of Jerusalem with the *Shechinah* and the various myths connected with her in the *Zohar*, which was developed further in subsequent kabbalistic works, made "Jerusalem" one of the hundreds of religious terms, rituals, and concepts that are associated with this central feminine aspect of the divine world, eroding its uniqueness. When "Jerusalem" became one of a series of symbols, which included the Sabbath, *Kneset Yisrael* (the Congregation of Israel), "earth," "night," and dozens of others, the eschatological and utopian element became diminished. The connection between the spiritual concept and the physical, geographic designation was blurred; large segments of the prayers and the rituals were associated with the *Shechinah*, and the specific meaning of "Jerusalem" was merged with the general, mystical craving for union with the divine world. Yet, throughout the Middle Ages we do not find a definite substitution of the spiritual concept of Jerusalem for its unique physical essence. On the contrary, in the late medieval period and the beginnings of modern times, the messianic element in the kabbalah increased, and with it the centrality of the symbol of Jerusalem representing a union between its earthly and its divine aspects. The intensely messianic works of Rabbi Abraham be-Rabi Eliezer ha-Levi,[40] who immigrated to Jerusalem in the beginning of the sixteenth century, are a clear example of this reintensification.

---

[39]This is not just a three-way drama but a four-way one, because the evil powers, especially the figure of Samael, the arch-devil in zoharic mythology, takes part in it. The desolation of Jerusalem and the exile of the people of Israel are often attributed to the machinations of the devil, which are symbolically depicted as the erotic designs of Samael concerning the *Shechinah*. Samael is represented in every individual, in his evil drives and material existence.

[40]A selection of his apocalyptic treatises has been published by G. Scholem, in *Kiryat Sefer* 2 (1925), pp. 101–141, 269–273; and *Kiryat Sefer* 7 (1931), pp. 149–165, 440–456.

During the sixteenth century, the physical focus of kabbalistic ritual became centered in another place in the land of Israel, in the small town of Safed in the Upper Galilee, where a group of kabbalists established a major spiritual center, close to the legendary tomb of the hero of the zoharic legends, Rabbi Simeon bar Yochai.[41] These kabbalists, however, did not see Safed as replacing Jerusalem in any way; it was part of the combination of the spiritual and material land of Israel, the subject of mystical adherence and physical connection.

The messianic movement of Sabbatianism in the last third of the seventeenth century, which flourished in various ways during the eighteenth century as well, reinforced the union between the spiritual symbolism and the actual messianic endeavor of returning to Jerusalem. The two leaders of the movement, Shabbatai Zevi and his "prophet" Nathan of Gaza, frequently visited the city, where they had many adherents from the earliest stages of the development of the movement.[42] In the year 1700 a large group of Sabbatians from Eastern Europe, led by Rabbi Judah the Pious and Rabbi Hayyim Malach, immigrated to Jerusalem to await the return of the Messiah,[43] this being the largest among many groups who settled in the city motivated by messianic expectations. Similarly, several of the leaders of the early Hasidic movement in the second half of the eighteenth century immigrated, or tried to immigrate, to Jerusalem and the Galilee.[44] In this movement, however, we find the clearest sepa-

---

[41]This period in the history of Jewish mysticism has been studied intensively. See, for instance, Scholem, *Major Trends in Jewish Mysticism*, pp. 244–286; R. I. Zwi Werblowsky, *Rabbi Joseph Karo: Lawyer and Mystic* (Philadelphia: Jewish Publication Society 1973); R. Elior and Y. Liebes, eds., *Proceedings of the Fourth International Conference on the History of Jewish Mysticism*, Jerusalem Studies in Jewish Thought, vol. 10 (Jerusalem 1991).

[42]G. Scholem, *Sabbatai Sevi: The Mystical Messiah*, trans. R. J. Zwi Werblowsky (Princeton, NJ: Princeton University Press 1973), index s.v.

[43]Many of them died in the first few months in a plague; see G. Scholem, *Major Trends in Jewish Mysticism*, p. 331.

[44]According to Hasidic legend, the founder of the movement, Rabbi Israel Baal Shem Tov (known by the acronym "Besht"), tried to immigrate to Jerusalem but had to return after reaching Constantinople. Between 1764 and 1777 several groups of his disciples made that journey, and some of them established communities in northern Israel. In 1798 his grandson, Rabbi Nachman of Bratslav, spent

ration between spiritual and physical Jerusalem in the history of Jewish mysticism. Some of the Hasidic leaders who remained in Eastern Europe and established communities of adherents there developed, for the first time, a distinction between Jerusalem as a spiritual symbol and the physical-geographic entity. The subject has been discussed in detail by Rivkah Shatz,[45] who presented the important Hasidic texts relating to this phenomenon, most of them from the school of Rabbi Elimelech of Lizensk in the late eighteenth century. Several statements of these Hasidic leaders express the view that the spiritual land of Israel and Jerusalem are to be found in the proximity to the *Tzaddik*, the divinely endowed mystical leader of a Hasidic sect, rather than in a physical pilgrimage to the earthly city. These authors made use of the kabbalistic identification of Jerusalem with Zion as the ninth divine *sefirah* or the *Shechinah*, the tenth, to deny the spiritual significance of the earthly city and generalize its meaning in a way that could be included in the rituals carried out in exile.[46] Rabbi Nachman of Bratslav formulated this concept in the ambiguous statement "Everywhere I go, I go to the land of Israel," which actually means that geography is meaningless; spiritual significance is found only in the internal intention.[47] This attitude, which was based on some scattered statements in medieval and early modern kabbalistic writings, acquired political significance in the last

---

a year in *Eretz Yisrael*. The Besht's brother-in-law, Rabbi Gershon of Kutow, settled in Jerusalem.

[45]R. Shatz, *Hasidism as Mysticism* (Princeton, NJ: Princeton University Press 1993; original Hebrew ed., Jerusalem: Magnes Press 1964), *passim*. Compare also Idel, "The Land of Israel," pp. 136–141.

[46]The most paradoxical statement is that which turns upside-down the talmudic statement (Bavli *Ketubot* 110b) "He who dwells abroad is like one who has no God, and he who dwells in the land of Israel is like someone who has a God"; the Hasidic text explains (as shown by R. Shatz) that he who dwells abroad looks like someone who has no God, but really he has, while he who dwells in the land of Israel looks like someone who has a God, but really he has not.

[47]This statement has been misunderstood, and was presented as a Zionist slogan in Israel. It was a part of a deliberate attempt carried out by orthodox Zionists in Israel in the middle of this century to portray Hasidism as a Zionist movement.

hundred years, supplying a theological dimension to the fierce opposition of most of the Hasidic leaders to the Zionist movement.

This change in the attitude toward Jerusalem can be explained as the result of a change in the concept of the city as the actual and spiritual center of the universe. The two aspects of the city, the physical and the spiritual, remain united as long as this belief persists. Once a different *axis mundi* replaces Jerusalem, the bond between the two aspects can be broken. The formulation of the Hasidic concept of the *Tzaddik* as the center of the world and the source of present and future redemption created a physical and spiritual substitute for the Holy City: Clinging to the *Tzaddik*, geographically and spiritually, became the main purpose of religious life. The pilgrimage to the *Tzaddik*'s court replaced the pilgrimage to Jerusalem. In the medieval kabbalah, both Zion and *Tzaddik* serve as symbols for the ninth *sefirah*, which is also called *axis mundi*.[48] The ancient *Hechalot* mystics substituted a mystical journey to the celestial temples for the pilgrimage to Jerusalem; modern Hasidim found such a substitute in the mystical adherence to the *Tzaddik* and the physical visits to his court. In contemporary Jerusalem, followers of the Chabad (Lubavitch) Hasidic sect used to travel on the holidays to the court of the late Menachem Mendel Schneersohn in Brooklyn, and when they returned to the city they described their experiences there in terms reminiscent of the pilgrimage to Jerusalem and the Temple in ancient times. They thus expressed the full paradoxical turnabout; in order to be united with the spiritual Jerusalem, one has to leave the physical city and travel to the *Tzaddik*'s dwelling across the ocean, at 770 Eastern Parkway, Brooklyn.[49]

---

[48]Following the verse *Zaddik yesod olam* (the Righteous is an everlasting foundation) in Proverbs 10:25.

[49]It should be noted, however, that the messianic enthusiasm that engulfed Chabad in the last two decades included a reunification of the spiritual and the earthly Jerusalem; the first event that, according to their belief, should mark the beginning of the messianic era was believed to be the *Tzaddik*'s leaving his Brooklyn home and fixing his residence in the land of Israel. Throughout Jewish history, the bond between Jerusalem and messianic redemption has never been broken.

The intensity of Hasidic mysticism, which was renewed in the last few decades despite the catastrophic results of the Holocaust among the Hasidic communities of Eastern Europe, marginalized other contemporary Jewish mystical traditions and directions. Yet, within the vast picture of the history of Jewish spirituality, this separation between earthly Jerusalem and mystical salvation is an exception. The dominant elements described above are present today, even among many Hasidic sects like Belz and Gur, which made Jerusalem their worldly center.

Jerusalem has become, in the last eighty years, the center of fierce political conflict, which marginalized to some extent the contemporary meaningfulness of the heavenly city. Its physical presence has been, and is, so overwhelming that pure spiritual concentration on its numinous significance has been relegated to a secondary place. But for the first time in its long history the city has become, in this century, the meeting place of the three religions that worship it, even though this meeting has been characterized more by conflict than by mutual understanding.

I belong to a generation of Jews, Muslims, and Christians who grew up in this city when it was divided between Jews and Arabs and governed by a Christian empire, Britain. During the long decades of intense Arab-Israeli conflict, the realization of the deep interest of the Christian world in everything that happened in this city has become evident. In this century, more and more people of the three religions have become aware—for the first time—that narrow streets, synagogues, churches, and mosques in the city represent three spiritual geographies, superimposed one above the other in the tiny area of the Old City. The spiritual significance of the Holy Sepulchre and al-Aqsa can no more be ignored by Jews; Muslims and Christians cannot ignore the meaning of the Western Wall and the excavations of the City of David. A process of mutual recognition of the sanctity of the city is going on, even though it is still characterized mainly by hatred and struggle.

In previous generations, the spiritual and mystical literatures of each of the three religions completely ignored the very existence of the "spiritual geography" of the other two. History is relentlessly

pushing the faithful of all three into recognizing the basic similarities in their attitudes toward the city. This is a new experience in
the three thousand years of the history of spiritual and earthly Jerusalem; the hope that it will culminate in peaceful mutual acceptance
may not be completely futile.

ENDNOTE

This article was published in the Harvard University Press volume dedicated to the three thousand years of history of the city of
Jerusalem, *City of the Great King*, edited by Nitza Rosovsky. The
editor asked me to cover the aspect of the place of Jerusalem in the
spirituality and mysticism of the three great religions that see Jerusalem as central to their faith. Prof. Paula Frederiksen of Boston University contributed the study concerning Christian spirituality, and
Prof. Angelika Neuwirth of the Free University of Berlin presented
the Islamic view. A consistent attempt was made to disengage these
studies from contemporary conflicts and controversies; obviously, it
was not completely successful. The present unavoidably casts a
shadow over discussions of the past.

The Language of Mystical Prayer*

I

The most intense meeting point of mysticism and language in religion is the ritual of prayer. Prayer, more than any other aspect of religion, is the expression of the belief in the possibility of constant dialogue between man and God using language as a means of communication. In the life of every worshipper, prayer is the time and context of his closest, most meaningful approach to God. The full dynamism of mysticism's union and divergence with religious ritual is manifest in this practice. Some aspects of the meaning of the language of prayer in mysticism should, therefore, be investigated in the framework of this study.

*This article is based on a lecture delivered at Harvard University in February 1994. My thanks are due to Prof. Ruth Wisse, Head of the Center for Jewish Studies at Harvard, and Prof. John Huenergard, Chairman of the Department of Near Eastern Civilizations and Languages, for this opportunity. I profited very much from the discussions with colleagues in that department before and after this lecture, especially Prof. James Russel.

Mysticism is, essentially, a visionary experience. Most of the descriptions of a mystical event in the writings of almost all mystics are related to light, color, and images.[1] Prayer, on the other hand, is an auditory experience: The terms associated with it are "listening" and "hearing"; the urgent request of the worshipper in prayer is, "God, please hear my voice"; it anticipates a verbal response.[2] In Jewish mysticism, by a rather intricate and complex process, prayer has become a visionary experience.

The ritual of traditional prayer posed serious problems to theologians in the three scriptural religions. An inherent conflict in the very concept of traditional prayer was discussed very early in the history of this ritual. The repetitive element in the ritual and the universality of the text denied, from the very beginning of this religious concept, its semantic character: Prayer as communication between man and God in using meaningful language was in conflict with the insistence on repeating the same linguistic formulas several times every day by every person in every place in every circumstance, with minor variations for festivals and special occasions. The image

---

[1]There are, however, some exceptions. Mystics who "hear voices" are found occasionally. In the history of Jewish mysticism, auditory mystical experiences are often found among mystics to whom a *maggid* was revealed, an emissary from the divine world who discloses to them divine secrets. One of these was the eighteenth-century messianic pretender and mystic of Padua, Rabbi Moses Hayyim Luzzatto. The *maggid* was speaking from Luzzatto's mouth in a loud voice, which could be heard from behind a closed door. See I. Tishby, *Hikrey Kabbalah u-Sheluhoteha*, Jerusalem: Magnes Press 1993, vol. III, passim, and M. Benayahu, "The Maggid of RaMHaL," *Sefunot* vol. 5 (1961), pp. 267–335; English translation in L. Jacobs, *The Jewish Mystics*, London: Kyle Cathie 1990 pp. 136–147.

[2]While there is a vast literature on prayer and its development, these obvious distinctions have not been emphasized in many studies. Much attention has centered around the beginnings of Christian prayer: See, for example, Paul F. Bradshaw, *Daily Prayer in the Early Church: A Study of the Origin and Early Development of the Divine Office*, New York: Oxford University Press 1982; Adalbert-G. Hamman, *La Prière dans l'Eglise ancienne*, New York: Peter Lang 1989. The mystical aspect is more emphasized in Monique Vincent, *Saint Augustine, maître de prière*, Paris: Beauchesne 1989; and compare J. N. Bériou, J. Berlioz, J. Longère, *Prier au Moyen Age*, Turnhout: Brepols 1991. A classic that is still valuable is James M. Campbell, *The Place of Prayer in the Christian Religion*, New York: Methodist Book Concern 1915.

of God "listening" to countless people pronouncing exactly the same words at the same time cannot be regarded as a semantic event. The constant belief that man is not alone in praying (he joins hosts of angels, who praise God before His throne of glory at the same time) increases the departure from the individual dialogue that is the other demand of the nature of prayer. One may say that while prayer is a dialogue between man and God, liturgy has been deprived of this direct, individual semantic context and has transformed the practice into a nonverbal communication.

The insufficiency of liturgy as a semantic meeting between worshipper and God introduced into religious practice a second kind of prayer: silent prayer, the nonliturgical intimate communication between man and God in which language is used in an individual and creative manner. The prayer of Channah in its intense personal nature[3] is a perfect example of such a phenomenon, and despite its prominent place in the biblical narrative it has not been incorporated in established liturgy. This example enabled later teachers of religious devotion to include the silent individual prayer in the accepted, and sometimes encouraged, practice of prayer in the three scriptural religions.

The significance of this conflict between traditional liturgy and mystical aspirations is best demonstrated on the historical level by the place of prayer in ancient gnosticism. The gnostics, as Kurt Rudolph quotes from the writings of the Nicenes, believed that "the worship of the perfect is spiritual, not carnal."[4] Gnostic ritual tended to forsake any traditional format, be it Jewish or Christian, and adopt individual, spiritual ways of expression.[5] The gnostic writings that

---

[3]1 Samuel 2:1-10.

[4]Hippolytus, Refutatio, V 9, 4; see Kurt Rudolph, Gnosis: The Nature and History of Gnosticism, New York: Oxford University Press 1987, p. 220.

[5]The Mandaean sect is an exception: Its works that have reached us contain a wealth of ritualistic material, formulated in fixed behavioral norms. It should be taken into account, however, that the Mandaeans are the only gnostic sect that survived for many centuries, and that their writings (most of which have reached us in late-Middle Ages versions) reflect norms that directed the lives of the believers in an institutionalized structure for many generations. Concerning the

have reached us include scores of hymns and prayers of many literary kinds, but in most cases they were not edited into formal prayer
books, that is, into liturgy. Like the Jewish mystics of that period,
the "descenders to the chariot," whose writings abound with prayers
and hymns that are individual expressions of the mystics or angelic
poetry that the mystics overhear in their ascensions to the divine
rims, the gnostics liberated prayer from the confines of traditional
liturgy and turned it into a living, vibrant expression of intense
mystical experience.[6]

It is an interesting fact that Judaism and Christianity did not
develop a specific terminology to distinguish between ritualistic, traditional liturgy and the silent, individual prayer. Islam did: The distinction between established prayer—the *salaat*—and the personal
silent appeal to God—the *duaa*—is one that is often found even in
nonmystical Arabic literature concerning prayer.[7] In Christianity,

---

place of the Mandaeans in the history of gnosticism and the reliability of their
ancient traditions, see Edwin M. Yamauchi, *Pre-Christian Gnosticism: A Survey of
the Proposed Evidence*, 2nd ed. Grand Rapids, MI: Baker Book House 1983, pp.
117–142 (includes detailed bibliography).

[6]There is a reluctance among scholars to include discussions of gnostic world-
views when describing the meaning and history of mysticism. It is clear that this
radical, often unpleasant group of heretical sects poses some difficulties when one
is inclined to view mysticism as the highest form of religious worship. Yet there
is no escape from the fact that every possible definition of mysticism results in
placing gnosticism as the most definite, clear-cut example of mystical religiosity.
I do not believe that there is a single aspect of mysticism that can be analyzed
without placing gnostic examples at the centre of the discussion. This is easier
for a scholar whose specialty is Jewish mysticism than for a scholar who deals
mainly with Christian or Islamic mysticism, because since the beginning of scholarly work in the history and development of Jewish mysticism the relationship
with gnosticism has been intense. In 1846, when Heinrich Graetz published his
first study of ancient Jewish mysticism, he used the title *Gnosticismus and Judentum*.
More than a century later, in 1960, when Gershom Scholem dedicated a book
to the same subject, the title was: *Jewish Gnosticism, Merkabah Mysticism and
Talmudic Tradition* (New York: The Jewish Theological Seminary).

[7]See especially L. Gardet, *La pensée réligieuse d'Avicenne*, Paris 1951, pp. 135–140
et passim; Annemarie Schimmel, *The Mystical Dimension of Islam*, Chapel Hill,
NC: University of North Carolina Press 1975, pp. 148–185. For a comparison
between Islamic and Christian prayer, see Kenneth Cragg, *Alivè in God: Muslim
and Christian Prayer*, New York: Oxford University Press 1970. One of the great

despite the prominence of the subject of silent prayer, no specific term has developed to indicate it and differentiate it from ritualistic prayer, leading Evelyn Underhill to state:

> The common implications of the word "prayer", with its suggestions of formal devotion, detailed petition—a definite something asked for, and a definite duty done, by means of extemporary or traditional allocutions—do not really suggest the nature of those supersensual activities which the mystics mean to express in their use of the term. Mystical prayer, or "oraison"—the term which I propose for the sake of clearness to use here—has nothing in common with petition. It is not articulate; it has no forms. "It is," says the Mirror of St. Edmund, "naught but yearning of soul." [8]

The Hebrew language—and Judaism—did not reach even this point: There is no term for silent prayer, in the context of mysticism or otherwise. It is hoped that the following discussion may contribute to explaining this intriguing absence.

II

The problem of "silent prayer" and its relationship to mystical experience will be clarified by presenting three different formulations of the question—one Jewish, one Muslim, and one Christian—and

---

theorists of prayer in Islam was Alghazali, who plays a prominent part in many aspects of Islamic spirituality. See, for instance, Kajiro Nakamura, Ghazali on Prayer, Tokyo: University of Tokyo, Institute of Oriental Culture 1973; E. E. Calverley, Worship in Islam; Being a Translation, with Commentary and Introduction, of al-Ghazzali's Book of the Ihya on Worship, London: Luzac and Co. 1957; another translation is Gazzali's Invocations and Supplications, 2nd ed., Cambridge: Islamic Texts Society 1990. On the whole subject see Muhammad Rassoul, As-Salah, Das Gebet im Islam, Köln: Verlag Islamische Bibliothek 1983.
[8]Mysticism: A Study in the Nature and Development of Man's Spiritual Consciousness, 12th ed., New York: World 1965, pp. 306–308, 381–383, and compare Underhill's later work, Concerning the Inner Life, with The House of the Soul, New York: E. P. Dutton 1925. The term has been extensively used in one of the most important discussions of mysticism in France in the first half of this century: Jacques and Raissa Maritain, De la vie d'oraison, Paris: A l'Art Catholique 1947.

a solution, which is a intensely Jewish mystical one, integrating the two kinds of prayer into one whole, combining the auditory with the visual and the public ritual with the individual mystical experience.

Rabbi Bachya ibn Pakuda, the author of the Duties of the Heart, one of the most influential Jewish ethical works, was faced with the full power of the problem when he wrote his book in the eleventh century.[9] The main theme of this work is the distinction between the "duties of the limbs," the practical and ritualistic commandments, and the "duties of the heart," the spiritual ones, which constitute the meaningful part of religious experience. Bachya's book is one of the earliest, and most complete, expressions of the quest of spirituality in medieval Judaism, and it was written under the influence of Sufi thought. Bachya's definition of the "duties of the heart" is a negative one: They are those aspects of worship that are not expressed by any physical or sensual means. The inclusion of a physical element in the performance of a "duty" destroys its status as one of the ten "duties of the heart."[10] This approach practically excludes all the

---

[9]Almost nothing is known about the time and place of Rabbi Bachya's life. The most important study of the author and the book is by D. Kaufman, "Die Theologie des Bachja Ibn Pakuda," in his *Gesammelte Schriften*, ed. M. Brann, Frankfurt a/M.: Komissions Verlag von J. Kauffmann, 1910, pp. 1–98. The best edition of the Hebrew text (trans. Rabbi Judah ibn Tibbon in the twelfth century) is the A. Zifroni edition, Tel Aviv: Mahbarot le-Sifrut 1949, introduction pp. 5–53. The Sufi sources have been pointed out by D. S. Bannet, *Kiryat Sefer* 3 (1926), pp. 135–137; see also A. Lazaroff, "Bachya's Asceticism against its Rabbinic and Islamic Background," *JJS* XXI (1970). pp. 1–38, and especially p. 24, note 99; and the detailed study of G. Vajda, *La Théologie ascétique de Bachya Ibn Pakuda*, Paris 1947. An anthology of his main ideas, with detailed commentary, is found in I. Tishby and J. Dan, *Mivhar Sifrut ha-Musar*, Jerusalem: Newman 1971. See also J. Dan, *Sifrut ha-Musar veha-Derush*, Jerusalem: Keter 1975, pp. 47–68.

[10]It seems that Bachya's ambition was to present a second "ten commandments," spiritual ones, as the new concept of Judaism suggested by him. It is surprising that such a daring, almost heretical, concept could be adopted by medieval and modern Judaism without criticism. The author is a respected figure in Judaism to this day. See J. Dan, *Jewish Mysticism and Jewish Ethics*, Seattle and London: Washington University Press 1987, pp. 22–25 et passim.

traditional precepts of Judaism, replacing them by the abstract demands of the understanding of divine unity faith and trust in God,
spiritual repentance, the love of God, etc. Prayer, despite the fact
that it is described in talmudic sources as "worship of the heart,"[11]
is denied a place among the spiritual "commandments" because its
practice demands the pronunciation of words by the lips, presence
in the synagogue, the participation of nine other worshippers, and
other "physical" aspects. Bachya did not go so far as to dedicate a
specific chapter to silent prayer as a spiritual substitute for the "prayer
of the limbs," but in several parts of his extensive work he emphasizes the value of a prayer said in private, in the worshipper's own
words, addressed directly to God. Bachya's work has some mystical
characteristics,[12] but it cannot be described as an outright demand
for a mystical way of religious life. Bachya did not try to replace the
traditional ritual of prayer by the silent address of God; he suggested
the *kavanah* as a solution to the conflict between the two types of
worship: The physical ritual should be accompanied by an intense
spiritual address within the worshipper's soul.[13] Yet religious value,
according to Bachya, is attached only to the spiritual aspect of wor-

----

[11]Bavli *Taanit* 2a: "What is that worship which is within the heart? It is prayer,"
and see Maimonides, Mishneh Torah, *Tefilah u-Nesiat Kapayim*, Ch. 5.
[12]It can be described as containing all the negative aspects of mysticism, without
presenting any of the positive ones. It clearly negates the senses as a vehicle of
approaching divine truth, and sees in worldly activity destruction of the spirit:
"The more the land is cultivated and built, the more is the destruction of the
spirit," an almost gnostic declaration. The ideal is "to see without eyes, to hear
without ears," which is so common in mystical literature. There is no description in this work of the positive side of the negation of the material and the
sensual. See J. Dan, "In Quest of a Historical Definition of Mysticism: The
Contingental Approach," in *Studies in Spirituality* 3 (1993), pp. 58–90.
[13]Bachya's solution seems to have been inspired by an ancient statement in the
Mishnah concerning "the early Hasidim" who used to "wait" one hour before
prayer, meaning that they used to prepare themselves in a spiritual manner before beginning the ritual of prayer. It is doubtful, however, that this practice
actually refers to a preference for silent prayer; it seems in that context that they
treated the liturgical ritual as an actual meeting with God and participation in
a heavenly ceremony that requires intense spiritual preparation. This is an en-
hancement of the meaning of ritual, opposite to Bachya's conception.

ship; the physical address of a spiritual God is meaningless. The problem of the place of the traditional commandments and rituals in a spiritual way of life has not been answered. Bachya's detailed discussion enhanced the gap between the two modes of worship, without supplying any reason for the liturgical worship of God.

In linguistic terms, Bachya's concept of silent prayer tends to be a metasemantic one, viewing verbal communication as closely related to the inferior—actually, meaningless—physical aspect of religious life. Semantic contact with God is paradoxically conceived as a meaningless approach to Him. The transcendence of the ritual, of social framework of worship, of tradition, and of liturgy is understood as equal to the transcendence of language and communicative meaning.[14] Bachya did not find a way to integrate verbal communication with God in a traditional, liturgical context with the mystical worship he preferred. The divergence between tradition and individual religious expression has increased in his work.

Bachya was influenced by Sufi literature in many of his religious attitudes; he may have known some Muslim mystics and witnessed their behavior. It is interesting, therefore, to compare his conclusion to that of one of the best-known and most influential Sufi teachers. Hadrat Abd al-Qadir al-Jilani, who lived a generation or more after Rabbi Bachya.[15] One of his works, Futuh al-ghayb, translated into English under the title The Secret of Secrets, is dedicated to the detailed description of the mystic's way of life and worship.[16] Several chapters in this work raise the problem of the relationship between spiritual and mystical worship and traditional, physical

---

[14]It should be emphasized that, in several places of the book, Bachya does offer words to be used in a silent prayer. It is only the supreme part of this prayer that is completely nonlinguistic; silent prayer using individual, unuttered words is an acceptable mode of spiritual worship.

[15]On Al-Jilani, see A. Schimmel, The Mystical Dimension of Islam, passim, and see the following note.

[16]The Secret of Secrets by Hadrat Abd al-Qadir al-Jilani, interpreted by Shykh Tosun Bayrak al-Jerrahi al-Halveti, Cambridge: Islamic Texts Society 1992. There is a previous German translation by Alma Giese under the title Enthüllungen des Verborgenen, Köln: Al-Kitab 1985, with a detailed bibliography, pp. 194–200.

ritual. The author interprets the Koran's emphasis of the "middle prayer" as referring to the "prayer in the middle," that is, in the heart, while "ritual worship" consists of standing, reciting from the Koran, bowing, prostrating, kneeling, and audibly repeating certain prayers. These movements and actions involving the members of the body, recitations spelled out and heard involving the senses, are the worship of the material self.[17] Spiritual worship is so described: "Prayer is the supplication of the created to the Creator. It is a meeting of the servant and the Lord. The place of this meeting is the heart." [18] A detailed description of the silent, individual prayer follows, and the whole section could have been found in Bachya's *Hovot ha-Levavot*. Al-Jilani is less emphatic than Bachya in the denial of meaning of traditional, physical ritual, but the supremacy of metasensual worship over the "duties of the limbs" is as intense and complete in Al-Jilani's work as it is in Bachya's. The formulation of the problem can be regarded as identical in these two treatises. Al-Jilani, however, has a different suggestion concerning the integration of the two modes of worship.

A subsequent chapter in the treatise On the Pilgrimage to Mecca and the Inner Pilgrimage to the Essence of the Heart[19] starts with a detailed description of the rituals involved in the performance of Islam's most sacred precept, the visit to Kaaba and the prayers and ceremonies to be performed on this occasion, including the preparations for it and the internal and external purification associated with it. Immediately following the discussion of the physical experience of the pilgrimage, the author turns to the description of the main subject of this chapter: the inner, spiritual pilgrimage that the mystic has to perform within his heart, toward his own innermost heart. The spiritual Kaaba is found deep within one's self, and the pilgrimage to it is an intense religious experience of uniting one's soul with the divine names and attaining one's mystical goal. The physical, external pilgrimage is an allegory of an internal voyage; every detail

---

[17]Ibid., p. 73.
[18]Ibid., p. 74.
[19]Ibid., pp. 84–88.

of the external ceremony has a counterpart in the spiritual process. It is an allegory because the performance of the spiritual voyage does not depend upon a parallel physical one. While a journey to Mecca may occur once in a lifetime, the internal experience is one that can and should be pursued constantly, and can be carried out at any time and in any place. The legal demands concerning the physical pilgrimage are used as a starting point and interpreted to be a minimum, which the spiritual pilgrimage must exceed. If the Koran demands the purification of the area of the Kaaba, the author insists: "Indeed the material Kaaba in the city of Makka is kept clean for the pilgrims. How much cleaner should one keep the inner Kaaba upon which truth will gaze!" [20]

The process of internal pilgrimage is evidently a mystical one, not only a religious or ethical purification and uplifting: "After these preparations the inner pilgrim wraps himself in the light of the holy spirit, transforming his material shape into the inner essence, and circumambulates the Kaaba of the heart." The whole process is identified with the inner, spiritual recitation of the series of names of God. The twelve names of God are described as an ascending ladder,[21] leading the mystic from one stage to a higher one, bringing him into an intimate spiritual contact with God. The final achievement is given in terms that, in a Christian context, could be regarded as a description of a state of *unio mystica*:

> In drinking from this Source[22] one sees all the veils lifting from the eternal face. One looks upon It with the light coming from It.[23] That world has no likeness, no shape, no form. It is inde-

---

[20]Ibid., p. 85.

[21]On the nature and meaning of these names, see below.

[22]The twelfth name, Samad.

[23]It is impossible to resist pointing out the Jewish parallels, even though they are separated from Al-Jilani's world by many centuries and deep cultural differences. The "face" originates, in Hebrew usage, from the verse in Numbers 12:8, "And the similitude of the Lord shall he behold: *u-temunat adonai yabit*." On the meaning of this "picture of the Face" see below. Concerning the source of light, this may be regarded as parallel to the many discussions of the viewing of God through an *ispaklaia meirah*—clear, luminous glass. It should be noted that these Hebrew

scribable, unassociable, that world "which no eyes have seen, no ears have heard its description, that no man's heart remembers." The words of Allah are not heard by sound nor seen as the written word The delight that no man's heart can taste is the delight in seeing the truth of Allah Most High, and hearing Him speak.[24]

Al-Jilani is regarded, in the history of Islamic mysticism, as an orthodox thinker. Unlike Bachya ibn Pakuda in Judaism, he is not a revolutionary, and does not seek change and extremes. His spiritualization of the concept of the Hajj does not mean that the physical pursuance of Islam's religious laws is superfluous or meaningless. Rather, the physical precepts are regarded as paradigmatic, bringing forth the allegory to the inner pilgrimage without negating themselves. Yet there can be no mistake concerning his attitude toward the relationship between the physical and the spiritual. The mystical experience achieved in the inner Hajj is one in which words, as sounds and as pictures of written letters, lose all their meaning and are completely transcended into a new realm of supersensual existence. The inner, or silent, prayer is thus conceived as leading to the maximal religious achievement, that of mystical union, something that the physical recitation of the text can never achieve, even in the exceptionally sacred circumstances of the pilgrimage of Mecca.

Al-Jilani has achieved in this structure an integration of the ritual and the spiritual far exceeding that of Rabbi Bachya. Bachya could not find a role for the language of ritual prayer within the framework of spiritual worship. Al-Jilani did find some role for it, as a paradigm expressing in allegorical language the innermost metalinguistic processes of inner worship and mystic ascension. A completely different presentation of the problem is found in the Christian example selected for this analysis, that of the great Carmelite mystic of the sixteenth century, Saint Teresa of Avila.

---

sources speak about prophetic revelation, when the example discussed is often Moses on Mount Sinai. Medieval mystics however, did use the same terminology to describe the achievement of a mystical experience.
[24]Op. cit., pp. 86–87.

III

Teresa's mysticism has been the subject of detailed study for generations, and her life, especially, is regarded as one of the finest examples of this type religious experience in any language or creed. One of the most prominent characteristics of Teresa's mysticism is its close adherence to the concept of prayer. Her insistence on connecting mystical experience with a liturgical framework is a demonstration that she do not seek to divorce mysticism from liturgical language in a radical manner. Like Al-Jilani, she was essentially a conservative religious teacher, who wished not to break new ground and chart new religious vistas, but rather to strengthen and reinspire existing religious structures.

Teresa's classic work on the subject under discussion here is The Way of Perfection, or *Paternoster*, the manual she wrote for the young nuns under her supervision. This is an early treatise of hers, but it is extant in two versions, the second corrected by the author at a later date.[25] This means that she perceived this treatise as an adequate expression of her attitude to prayer, suitable to be continuously used for instruction. The didactic nature of the work indicates that it can and should be used by beginners, discussing in detail some fundamental concepts. At the same time, Teresa's intense mysticism is clearly apparent in this treatise, and the final goal of mystical union is forcefully presented. This makes The Way of Perfection an excellent example for the investigation of the relationship between ritual, traditional prayer and the silent, metalinguistic one leading to mystical experience. Indeed, the tension between the deep loyalties to both conflicting aspects of worship is the most meaningful characteristic of this work.

A combination of ascetic and mystical motives guides the first chapters of the treatise, when the author directs her listeners and readers away from the demands of the flesh and into immersion in contemplation and denial of worldly values. Worldly intellectual and

---

[25]The two versions are extant in autographs, the first kept now in the Escorial, and the second in Valladolid. It is probable that the title is a later addition, not by the author's hand. The first version was written between 1563–1565.

emotional involvements are rejected together with material needs. Dedication to ritual prayer is suggested as replacement for these, and the importance of adhering to the text of the traditional prayers is stressed repeatedly. People who cannot understand the deeper meaning of prayer should not be discouraged; the attachment to this practice is viewed as universally beneficial.

Teresa identified "mental prayer" with concentration on the meaning and purpose of the prayer, whether or not it is connected with moving lips. The utterance of actual words is secondary or less in importance, compared with the spiritual intention and concentration. But this is only the beginning; as her instructions reach higher and higher levels, the centrality of silent prayer increases, until ritual and language are completely sidetracked in the process of silent contemplation and spiritual uplifting.

Teresa, therefore, establishes the connection between the ritual of traditional prayer and the meaningful silent mental and mystical prayer by the link of interpretation: The text of the traditional prayer, especially the Pater Noster, can be the starting point for contemplation, exegesis, and association, which leads the worshipper away from the ancient text into personal expression in his or her individual words, and from there further into the realm of approaching God and receding from the realm of words and meaning. For Teresa, the ancient text can serve as a first step, or even a springboard, into the textless and wordless experience of mystical union. It seems that she regards this method as not the only one leading to the mystical realm, but one among many. It is important because it gives some meaning to the otherwise meaningless demands of the traditional ritual. Liturgy may have its own meaning in the lowly realm of religious performance; its only link with higher religious strata is through this kind of interpretation.

Compared to Al-Jilani and Bachya, Teresa does find a connection between the ancient traditional text of the liturgy and the mystical surge beyond words that is the perfect prayer according to all three mystics. The kind of interpretation she suggests is purely semantic: The words of the ancient text evoke ideas, emotions, and associations that are also presented on the semantic level and lead the worshipper away from the actual text into the realm of individual semantic expression, and from there onward to the metalinguistic realms. This link between the text and silent mental prayer is purely individual: Her commentary on the traditional text constitutes an example of its use for the purpose of personal expression. It does not constitute an investigation of the "true" meaning of the text or the revelation of hitherto hidden strata of esoteric meaning in it. The quest is not for the meaning of the text, but for the fusion of the individual self with it, bridging the gap between personal religious experience and the dead letter of the universal ritual.

As solutions to the problem of the meaning of the text of the prayers to the mystic, all three are unsatisfactory. In all of them, mystical ascent can be achieved independently of the text of the prayers. If the authorities of each of the three religions were to decide to change completely the texts used in the daily ritual of prayer, these three mystics would not be adversely affected. Their solutions could easily be applied to the new text, because they do not originate from the text itself. Their discussions remove the ancient text from the position of an obstacle to mystical experience to that of a mildly beneficent point of departure. The conflict between traditional prayer and mystical expression is resolved into coexistence, but they remain separate realms of religious expression.

IV

When presenting Judaism's solution to this problem, it is impossible to present one particular thinker as the origin or representative of that solution. It was a long process of intricate spiritual development that led Jewish mysticism to integrate the ancient text of the prayers with mystical ascension, and to unite the auditory and visual elements into one whole. Only brief outlines of this process can be discussed here, and I should start from the end, from the most forceful expression of that union. I find it in one of the sayings attributed to Rabbi Israel Baal Shem Tov, the founder of the Hasidic movement in the middle of the eighteenth century, in a collection of instructions concerning man's behavior and religious practice known as The Testament of Rabbi Israel Baal Shem.[26] Several statements in this brief treatise deal with prayer, and there is no doubt that prayer is conceived in this work as a vehicle for mystical adherence to God. The statement relevant to this discussion is: *ve-da ki kol teva ve-teva [betefilah] yesh bah komah shelemah*, "You should know that every word in the prayers includes a whole [divine] stature." The term "stature" is an abbreviation of the term *shiur komah*, "the measure of the [divine] stature," and it indicates the complete anthropomorphic vision of God, as described in an ancient treatise under this title, the classic *Shiur Komah*.[27]

---

[26]*Zava'at ha-Rivash*. This text is one of the earliest treatises of the Hasidic movement, and was prominent during the early controversies between the Hasidim and their opponents after 1772, especially because of a few statements in it that seem to prefer mystical union (*devekut*) to the study of the Torah. It has been assumed that a major part of it is derived from the teachings of the disciple of the Besht, Rabbi Dov Baer, the Maggid of Mezeritch. On Hasidic concepts of prayer and the place of this text in it, see R. Shatz, *Hasidism as Mysticism*, Princeton NJ: Princeton University Press 1992, pp. 144-188. An analysis of the structure and sources of this brief text was presented by Z. Gries in his *Sifrut ha-Hanahgot*, Jerusalem: The Bialik Institute 1990, pp. 149-230. See also note 56.

[27]On this text and its place in the history of Jewish mysticism, see G. Scholem, *On the Mystical Shape of the Godhead* (actually, the title of this book is the rendering of the term "Shiur Komah" into English), New York: Schocken 1991, pp. 15-54; idem, *Jewish Gnosticism, Merkabah Mysticism and Talmudic Tradition*, 2nd ed. New York: The Jewish Theological Seminary, 1965, pp. 36-42, and S. Lieberman's appendix to this book, pp. 118-126. See also P. Schaefer, *The Hidden and Manifest God: Some Major Themes in Early Jewish Mysticism*, Albany, NY: SUNY Press 1992, pp. 60-62, 99-102 et passim; J. Dan, *Ancient Jewish Mysticism*, Tel Aviv 1989, pp. 48-58; idem, "The concept of Knowledge in the *Shiur Komah*," in *Studies in Jewish Religious and Intellectual History Presented to A. Altmann*, edited by S. Stein and R. Loewe, Alabama: Alabama University Press 1979, pp. 67-74. Compare also the monograph on the subject by M. S. Cohen, *The Shiur Qomah: Liturgy and Theurgy in Pre-Kabbalistic Jewish Mysticism*, Latham, MD: Scholar's Press 1983. A comprehensive collection of early and late *Shiur Komah* texts was presented by Cohen in the volume *The Shiur Qomah: Texts and Recensions*, Tübingen: J.C.B. Mohr (Siebeck) 1985. For an attempt to find a connection between the *Shiur Komah* and talmudic literature see M. Bar-Ilan, "The Hand of God: A Chapter in Rabbinic Anthropomorphism," in G. Sed-Rajna (ed.), *Rashi, Hommage à E. E. Urbach*, Paris: Cerf 1993, pp. 321-335. Compare also A. Farber-Ginat, "Studies in the *Shiur Komah*," in M. Oron, A. Goldreich (eds.), *Massu'ot: Studies in Kabbalistic Literature and Jewish Philosophy in Memory of Prof E. Gottlieb*, Jerusalem: Bialik Institute 1994, pp. 361-393.

The *Shiur Komah* is one of the most potent and central symbols of Jewish mysticism, originating in Late Antiquity (probably second or third century C.E.), and having an impact to this very day. It identifies the image of God in gigantic, anthropomorphic terms, which were later regarded as abstract symbols while retaining the visionary anthropomorphic texture of the ancient text. It is a purely visionary mystical text, based on the graphic description of the lover's limbs in the Song of Songs 5:10–16, which was interpreted as a divine self-portrait when the Song became understood as a divine self-revelation rather than a Solomonic love poem. The kabbalah in the late twelfth century—especially the earliest kabbalistic treatise, the *Bahir*—attributed the images of the *Shiur Komah* to the emerging new kabbalistic symbolism of the divine, emanated *sefirot*. Later kabbalists, especially those of the *Zohar* at the end of the thirteenth century, studied the *Shiur Komah* as the greatest secret of the divine "shape" and essence, and saw in it the boldest linguistic expression of the hidden, mystical essence of God.[28] One of the earliest statements in medieval Jewish mysticism concerning prayer probably makes use of this image.[29] One of the early traditions concerning prayer insists

---

[28]See Y. Liebes, *Studies in the Zohar*, Albany, NY: SUNY Press 1993, pp. 95–98 et passim. Concerning the concept of the letters of the alphabet in the *Zohar* see also E. Wolfson, "The Anthropomorphic and Symbolic Image of the Letters in the Zohar," In J. Dan (ed.), *Proceedings of the Third International Conference on the History of Jewish Mysticism* (*Jerusalem Studies in Jewish Thought*, vol. VIII), 1989, pp. 147–181.

[29]This statement is attributed to Rabbi Abraham ben David of Posquière, the father of the first kabbalist known to us by a kabbalistic treatise, Rabbi Isaac the Blind. It says: "The first three [benedictions] and the last three [benedictions] to *ilat ha-ilot*, and the [twelve] middle ones to *yotzer bereshit*." The term *yotzer bereshit* is the one by which the divine entity described anthropomorphically in the *Shiur Komah* is called. A key phrase in the text seems to differentiate between the supreme God and the Creator: *kol ha-yodea shiur zeh shel yotzrenu ve-shivho shel ha-Kadosh baruch Hu shehu nistar min ha-beriot*. This sentence can be interpreted as regarding the Creator as a revealed divine power, while God Himself is completely hidden, cannot be viewed, and can only receive praise. Scholem presented this possibility and added to it the observation that one of the most important Jewish prayers, which may have originated among the ancient mystics, *Aleynu le-Shabeah*, includes the same distinction in its opening sentence: *Aleynu le-shabeah la-Adon ha-Kol ve-latet gedulah le-yotzer bereshit* ("We have to praise

that the main prayer of the daily service be divided between two aspects of the divine world: Praises should be directed toward the supreme Godhead, while requests should be presented to the Creator—probably referring to the anthropomorphic image described in the *Shiur Komah*.[30]

The emergence of the concepts of prayer among the Jewish mystics and esoterics in Europe in the late twelfth century and the beginning of the thirteenth is very closely related to the text of the *Shiur Komah*. The problem of the relationship between the image of the divine power as described in the ancient text and the ritual of prayer was paramount in the minds of all circles in this period. They welcomed the integration of the *Shiur Komah* in their theologies because of the solution it offered to the problem of prophetic revelation.[31] Concerning prayer, however, there was a problem: Can prayer be directed toward a divine power that has an image? The danger of idolatry led several thinkers in this period to hesitate, and to demand the dedication of prayer to a divine power that does not have any image or dimension.[32]

---

the Lord of All and give greatness to the Creator"). See his *Jewish Gnosticism*, pp. 27–28, 105. Concerning the term *ilat ha-ilot*, see M. Idel, "Kabbalistic Prayer in Provence," *Tarbiz* 62 (1993), pp. 265–286. His attempt to give the statement of the Ravad a purely kabbalistic technical interpretation and to attribute it to Rabbi Jacob ha-Nazir is based mainly on minor corruptions in manuscripts.

[30]Scholem discussed this tradition in detail in *Origins of the Kabbalah*, pp. 208–213. He tends to see in the terminology used in it an early indication of kabbalistic symbolism, rather than a continuation of the *Hechalot* mystical concepts. It seems to me that greater emphasis should be given to the presence of the *Shiur Komah* terminology in the early kabbalistic references to the division of prayers among the divine powers. See also J. Dan, "The Emergence of the Mystical Prayer," in *Studies in Jewish Mysticism*, ed. J. Dan and F. Talmage, Cambridge, MA: Association of Jewish Studies 1979, pp. 85–120.

[31]It seems that Rabbi Abraham ibn Ezra (d. 1167) was the first to associate the *Shiur Komah* as a divine power with the revelation of God to Moses in his commentary on Exodus 33 (before him, the divinity of the revealed power had been denied by Saadia Gaon and his school). His concepts were adopted by the most important school of Ashkenazi Hasidic esoterics, the Kalonymus family. See J. Dan, "The Emergence of Jewish Mysticism in Medieval Germany," in R. A. Herrera (ed.), *Mystics of the Book*, New York: Peter Lang 1993, pp. 57–95.

[32]The clearest example of this process is found in the Unique Cherub circle of mystics, who differentiated between the *Shiur Komah* as the divine power revealed

The kabbalists adopted a radically different view: They integrated the *Shiur Komah* images with their comprehensive symbolism of the divine realms, and identified it with the totality of the divine pleroma.[33] The *Shiur Komah* became a vibrant symbol of the whole system of divine emanated powers.

Kabbalistic instructions concerning prayer, which developed in the first half of the thirteenth century into commentaries on the prayers, utilized the concept of the *Shiur Komah* together with other systems of symbols of the divine pleroma. Their main purpose was to divide the various parts of the prayers between the divine powers responsible for their fulfillment.[34] This became one of the most distinctive aspects of the new kabbalah, noticed by opponents of the new schools of mystics in Spain and Provence.[35] This was the beginning of the development of the kabbalistic *kavanot* of the prayers, a subject that became one of the central concerns of the kabbalah for many centuries.[36]

These early kabbalistic concepts of the mystical meaning of the prayers can be described as developing on the narrow borderline between semantic commentary and independent intention, "silent prayer." The meaning of the words of the traditional prayers was the starting point in deciding the mystical intention attached to them. A layer of "silent" intention was added to the traditional

---

to the prophets, and the divine glory, the object of intention in prayer, who has no image or dimension. See in detail J. Dan, *The Circle of the Unique Cherub*, Tübingen: J.C.B. Mohr (Siebeck) (in press).

[33]This process was described in detail by G. Scholem in his essay on the *Shiur Komah* in the kabbalah; see his *On the Mystical Shape of the Godhead*, New York: Schocken 1991, pp. 15–54.

[34]The most detailed such commentary is that of Rabbi Azriel of Gerona; see G. Sed-Rajna, *Azriel de Gèrone, Commentaire sur la liturgie quotidienne*, Leiden: Brill 1974.

[35]Especially the epistle by Rabbi Meir ben Shimeon of Narbonne; see G. Scholem, *Origins of the Kabbalah*, ed. R. I. Zwi Werblowsky, Princeton, NJ: Princeton University Press 1986, pp. 398–400.

[36]The concepts of prayer and *kavanot* in the early kabbalah was described in detail by I. Tishby, *The Wisdom of the Zohar*, vol. II, Oxford: Oxford University Press 1989, pp. 941–1015. An important aspect of this subject was studied by E. Ginzburg, *The Shabbath in Classical Kabbalah*, Albany, NY: SUNY Press 1990.

prayers, but in most cases it was an elaboration of the semantic message of the ancient texts. In this sense, the kabbalistic intentions were a superimposition of a new set of symbols over the traditional texts and rituals, when the two layers were held together mainly by the meaning of words.

A completely different approach developed by an individual mystic at about the same time represents a radical departure from the semantic layer of the prayers and attaches to them a mystical significance completely independent of the meaning of the words. This phenomenon is found in the extant quotations from the lost commentary on the prayers by Rabbi Judah ben Samuel "the Pious" of Regensburg.[37] Rabbi Judah's commentary on the prayers was the first such work to be written; until then many commentaries had been written on the piyyutim,[38] but none on the ritual prayerbook. Rabbi Judah's motivation in this endeavor was polemical: Its main purpose was to castigate neighboring Jewish communities in France

---

[37]I have written on various aspects of this problem in several recent studies. See "The Historical Position of Rabbi Judah the Pious," in Studies in Memory of H. H. Ben Sasson, ed. by R. Bonfil, M. Ben Sasson, and J. Hacker, Jerusalem: Shazar Center 1989, pp. 389–398; "Prayer as Text and Prayer as Mystical Experience," in Torah and Wisdom, Studies in Jewish Philosophy, Kabbalah and Halacha in Honor of A. Hyman, ed. R. Link-Salinger, New York: Shengold 1992 pp. 33–47; "The Emergence of Jewish Mysticism in Medieval Germany," in R. A. Herrera (ed.), Mystics of the Book, New York: Peter Lang 1993 pp. 57–95; "The Concept of Language in Ashkenazi Hasidism," in Hebrew in Ashkenaz, ed. L. Glinery, New York: Oxford University Press 1993, pp. 11–25; "Ashkenazi Hasidism, 1941–1991: Was There Really a Hasidic Movement in Medieval Germany?" in Gershom Scholem's Major Trends in Jewish Mysticism: 50 Years After, Proceedings of the Sixth Conference on the History of Jewish Mysticism, ed. P. Schaefer and J. Dan, Tübingen: J.C.B. Mohr (Siebeck) 1993, pp. 87–101; "The Concept of Language in Jewish Mysticism in Medieval Germany."

[38]The development of the commentaries on the piyyutim in medieval Germany and the background for the emergence of commentaries on the prayers have been described in detail in E. E. Urbach's Introduction to his edition of Rabbi Abraham ben-Rabbi Azriel's great commentary on the piyyut, Arugat ha-Bosem, vol. IV of the edition, Jerusalem: Mekizey Nirdamim 1963, pp. 3–111; see also A. Grossman, "The Background of the Emergence of Piyyut Commentaries in France and Germany in the Eleventh Century," in Shlomo Simonsohn Jubilee Volume, Tel Aviv: Tel Aviv University 1993, pp. 55–72 (of the Hebrew section).

and England[39] who adhered to a tradition concerning the text of the daily prayers that was slightly different from that of the Kalonymus family. Such minor variations in the text of the prayers are accepted as normal among Jewish communities; lists of differences in the text of the prayers are extant from the gaonic period, concentrating on the differences between the Babylonian and the Palestinian customs. Never before (or after) were they the subject of heated controversy.

The concept introduced by Rabbi Judah is that there is a true version of the text of the prayers, which is the only sacred one and cannot be changed—not even one single letter. In Rabbi Judah's commentary we find the first statement declaring the text of the prayers sacred beyond its semantic message: It does not matter whether or not the meaning of the words and the content of the sentences .is changed. The prayer is sacred as such, as a mystical entity. It is not a collection of sentences by which man presents praise and requests to God. It is a divine whole that, like the text of scriptures, cannot be changed in any way. The uniqueness of Rabbi Judah's concept is expressed by the fact that, when demonstrating this unchangeable character of the text of the prayers, the semantic level is completely neglected and the language of the liturgy is regarded as a deliberate divine structure based mainly on numerical harmony.

Rabbi Judah's lost commentary was a comprehensive work, consisting of six folio volumes.[40] Judging by the extant quotations, these volumes consisted almost exclusively of numerical computations and the presentation of parallel numerical structures. Rabbi Judah presented the numbers of letters, words, and phrases; the numbers of particular letters and words, and especially the numbers of divine names in various sections of the prayers; and occasionally also the computation of the numerical value of words and phrases. These were

---

[39]Rabbi Judah did not refer to England by name. He called his opponents *ha-Zarfatim ve-yoshvey iyey ha-yam*, "the French and the inhabitants of the islands of the sea."

[40]*Mahazik sishah kunteresim gedolim.*

compared to similar counting of letters, words, phrases, and names in particular sections of the Bible, demonstrating the numerical parallelism between them Together they indicated, according to Rabbi Judah, the intrinsic numerical harmony between the various parts of sacred texts.[41] The numerical harmony not only is significant in itself; it is the proof of the existence of divine structure inherent in the text of prayers, a structure that may not be obvious on the semantic level of liturgy. Because of this, the most minute change, affecting even one word or syllable, could destroy the whole harmonious structure and, in his words, "turn the prayers into a kind of song of the Gentiles,"[42] that is, lose their divine character and be turned into human expression. According to Rabbi Judah, the breaking of this hidden divine harmony turns the prayers into a human semantic creation, divorced from divine meaning and purpose, and therefore meaningless as religious ritual. Those who do it, the "Frenchmen and inhabitants of the islands of the sea," bring upon themselves and upon their descendants eternal exile.[43]

Rabbi Judah was a mystic who believed in his own revelation of the intrinsic meaning of the text of the prayers, which is independent of the semantic level of the words and sentences that compose them. In a similar way, he regarded scriptures themselves as representing such a numerical harmony, thus marginalizing the linguistic meaning of the message included in them. As a mystic, he was sure that this revelation of divine structure was the supreme truth, which should dictate the actual religious ritual of everybody. It seems that he was completely isolated in this: While his methodology was universally accepted, its exclusivity was not, and it joined the other numerous midrashic methods of deciphering the infinite meanings within the divine text.

---

[41]Rabbi Judah was aware of the Jewish tradition that the text of the prayers was established by human beings, by the sages of the Second Temple period. This did not deter him from the belief in the divine origin of these texts, which were formulated by divine inspiration. The belief in the complete sanctity of the text of the prayers was almost universal in medieval Jewry.

[42]Ke-min zemer shel ha-goyim ha-arelim.

[43]Gormim galut lahem ve-livneihem ad olam.

The importance of Rabbi Judah's mystical endeavor was in the negation of the semantic element in prayers, at least as a dominant one, and in demonstrating in the most forceful manner that language can be and should be meaningful within religious ritual without concentration on the meaning. When compared to the examples discussed above, this is a partial answer to the problem of the relationship between the text of the prayers and mystical expression. Rabbi Judah undoubtedly believed in the possibility of the text expressing a mystical connection between man and God, enabling man to immerse himself in the intrinsic harmony of the divine world; yet the price was denying the semantic message of the text and turning it into an assembly of syllables and names held together by numerical ties.[44] A more elaborate system was developed by the kabbalists, culminating in the Besht's dictum identifying the *Shiur Komah* with every word in the text of the prayers.

The Besht's concept of the prayers is similar to that of Rabbi Judah's in its mystical belief in the existence of a metasemantic mystical level in the text. It differs from Rabbi Judah's concept in its belief that this level is visionary, rather than numerical. The two concepts agree in the denial of the semantic message; but where Rabbi Judah's mysticism perceives a numerical structure, the Besht perceives an image of the divine world, the various parts of the divine entity that are portrayed, anthropomorphically, as limbs and conceptually they are the totality of the divine pleroma, the ten *sefirot.*

The history of the development of this concept in the kabbalah, between the thirteenth and the eighteenth centuries, is a long and complicated one. It is not the story of the emergence of an idea or the formulation of a doctrine. It is the result of individual mystical attitudes and concepts of hundreds of visionaries, each developing his own system, each contributing another element to the intricate

---

[44]Rabbi Judah used the talmudic expression *bi-kerasim u-ve-lulaot* (see Bavli *Shabbat* 99a) to denote these intrinsic ties. The phrase can appropriately be rendered into English as "by hook or by crook."

concepts of the prayers as mystical expression. The two fundamental concepts that are found in all these formulations are the Hebrew language as divine expression, of which the semantic level is only one, not the dominant one; and the insistence of the kabbalists that traditional ritual is the essence not only of religion, but of mysticism—therefore mystical expression should not be found besides it or instead of it, but deeply embedded in it.

A religion that receives the word of God in translation cannot create a barrier between the language of liturgy and its semantic level. In fact, the linguistic meaning is all it has. Only a religion that views language as divine instrument, independent of the role of human communication, can treat a text in this metasemantic way.

In contemporary terminology, this concept of language can be described as semiotic rather than semantic. The inexhaustible nature of language, which has variegated functions, including the one of creation, makes the communicative aspect a secondary, even marginal one. Kabbalists had long held the notion that language is a collection of pictures, no less than of signs or sounds. One of the classical works of the kabbalah, the anonymous *Sefer ha-Temunah*, probably written in the early fourteenth century, views the "picture of God" as the pictures of the letters of the alphabet. The *Zohar* itself contains an extended commentary on the forms of the letters.[45] These and many similar mystical descriptions made the identification between the letters of the alphabet and the pleroma of divine powers a powerful one, which the Besht received and popularized.

The origins of the pictorial concept of language are found in ancient Jewish traditions, incorporated in works like the Alphabet

---

[45]See M. Oron, "The Narrative of the Letters and Its Source: A Study of a Zoharic Midrash on the Letters of the Alphabet," in J. Dan, J. Hacker (eds.), *Studies in Jewish Mysticism, Philosophy and Ethical Literature Presented to Isaiah Tishby*, Jerusalem: Magnes Press 1986, pp. 97–110; and see note 29. An interesting fact is that in contemporary Jewish art this concept has had a discernible effect. A prominent example is the Ardon vitrages at the Shaarey Zedek hospital in Jerusalem describing the creation by means of the letters of the alphabet in a dramatic visual process based on the zoharic commentary.

of Rabbi Akiva[46] and the *Sefer ha-Tagin*, a work studying the traditional adornments of the letters,[47] which had an impact on medieval Jewish mysticism from its very beginnings The *Bahir*, the earliest work of the kabbalah, includes several sections dealing with the
shapes of the letters, and Rabbi Eleazar of Worms wrote his work
on the creation in the form of a commentary on the letters of the
alphabet.[48] The influence of the *Sefer Yezira* on this development has
been considerable: Although the pictorial element is not a characteristic of the letters and the *sefirot* described in this book,[49] the very
fact that the letters of the alphabet and the *sefirot* are combined in
the description of the process of creation by language made it possible to merge them in medieval Jewish mysticism. When the *Sefer
Yezira* concept of the *sefirot* as cosmic powers was transformed by
the kabbalists into the divine pleroma with its anthropomorphic symbolism, the identification of this image with the letters seemed to be
based on the ancient text attributed to Abraham.

[46]This text is an anthology of midrashic and mystical traditions of Late Antiquity, arranged in the form of a commentary on the letters of the alphabet. It
was edited in the gaonic period and found in many manuscripts, in different
versions. A scholarly edition of this text has not been published; the best one
available is that of S. A. Wertheimer in his *Batey Midrashot* vol. II, Jerusalem:
Rav Kook Institute 1955, pp. 333–417.
[47]*Sefer Tagin*, printed by S. Saks from the manuscript in Paris, 1876.
[48]Rabbi Eleazar's *Sod Ma'aseh Bereshit* is the first part of his major theological-
esoteric work, *Sodey Razaya*. Part of this section was printed in the popular anthology of mystical and magical traditions, the *Sefer Raziel* (Amsterdam 1701).
The complete text was recently published under the title *Sodey Razaya* by Shalom ha-Cohen Weiss, Jerusalem: Shaarey Ziv 1991.
[49]On the *Sefer Yezira* and its cosmogonical conceptions, there is a vast literature; an increasing interest in it has been expressed in the last few years. See
detailed bibliography in my "The Language of Creation and Its Grammar," and
in *Tradition und Translation, Festschrift Carsten Colpe*, ed. R. Haffke, H. M. Haussig
et al., Berlin-New York: Walter de Gruyter 1994, pp. 42–63. It should be emphasized that in this work the *sefirot* are not divine hypostases but numbers,
cosmic directions, and the stages of the evolvement of the elements. One passage, however, does describe the *sefirot* as having a visual aspect (I:6), and they
seem to be identified with the holy beasts of the vision of Ezekiel.

The semiotic concept of language was united, in this process, with the self-image of the kabbalah as the embodiment of tradition. With very few exceptions, medieval Jewish mystics adhered to Jewish tradition in its entirety, and conceived of their mysticism as being completely integrated with the minutest details of Jewish traditional ritual. Ritual, for the kabbalists, was just another way of divine expression. There is no essential difference between scriptures composed of words, ethical behavior based on principles, and the worship of God by the intricate rituals of observance of the commandments. The divine message to man is one whole, and divine language does not have to employ words. The kabbalists, therefore, were extreme traditionalists, and their teachings fortified the orthodox way of life.[50] Prayer, as a central aspect of traditional ritual, could not be neglected or marginalized in their system; it had to be integrated within the mystical experience. The recognition of the divine pleroma in every word of the prayer is the expression of such an integration.

In the three examples put forward in the beginning of this study, the three mystics described conceived of mystical prayer as a parallel avenue of mystical adherence to God, connected but not integrated with the ritual of traditional prayer. The Besht's dictum provides an example of a much deeper integration, where the traditional liturgy and the visionary experience of the mystic become one. Visualization of a divine entity during prayer has always been a troublesome idea in the history of Jewish thought: Visualizing the entity toward whom the prayer is directed was declared by Maimonides to be heresy,[51] a view completely denied by early and late kabbalists.

On the other hand, the concept that prayer is a semantic event also became intensely associated with visual experience in the intricate development of this idea in Judaism. The midrashic statement

---

[50]See G. Scholem, *On the Kabbalah and Its Symbolism*, pp. 118–156. The best example of a kabbalistic treatment of ritual is the *Zohar*'s detailed symbolization of the Sabbath rituals. See I. Tishby, *The Wisdom of the Zohar*, vol. II, pp. 1215–1237, and compare E. Ginsburg on the ritual of the Sabbath (see note 37).

[51]*Mishneh Torah*, *Yesodey ha-Torah* I, 3.

demanding that during prayer one should address the divine as one's counterpart in dialogue[52] should be understood as expressing a clear understanding of prayer as a semantic experience: A man praying to God is like one man talking to another. Prayer is a semantic dialogue between man and God. The formulation of many Jewish prayers and blessings intensifies this dialogical character of the prayer: "Blessed are You" is the usual opening. This would seem to be the exact opposite of a mystical visionary experience associated with the ritual of prayer, but it is not. A statement parallel to the one quoted is: "A person praying should see as if the *Shechinah* is in front of him." The intention behind this formulation may be the same, but the result is the opposite: It is not only conversation that occurs, but also a meeting in the full semiotic sense, including a visionary experience of the divine power. When this statement was used by kabbalists, who viewed the *Shechinah* as a separate power in the divine world, expressing the feminine aspect of the Godhead, it acquired a completely new meaning.[53]

The statement included in The Testament of the Besht is a brief, succinct summary of this basic kabbalistic attitude. It is part of a short treatise that includes many such epigrammatic instructions concerning various aspects of worship. It became notorious during the early controversies between Hasidim and their opponents, when some sections in this treatise were used by the opponents to prove that the Hasidim did not see the study of the Torah as a supreme value,[54]

---

[52]*Seder Eliyahu Rabba*, Parshah 9: *ke-adam shehu medaber im havero.*

[53]Concerning the development of the concept of the *Shechinah* as a feminine aspect, see G. Scholem, *On the Mystical Shape of the Godhead*, New York: Schocken 1991, pp. 140–195. For a brief discussion of this subject, including a survey of several halachic sources, see M. Halamish, "The Problem of Normative Nature of the Kavvanot," in *Rivkah Shatz Memorial Volume (Jerusalem Studies in Jewish Thought* 12 [1994]) ed. R. Elior and J. Dan.

[54]M. Willensky, *Hasidim and Mitnagdim*, vol. I, Jerusalem: The Bialik Institute 1970, pp. 18, 28 et passim; Z. Gries, *Sifrut ha-Hanahgot* (see note 27), pp. 149–150. This accusation was based on the paragraphs in the Testament that clearly prefer communion with God, *devekut*, to the study of the Torah. G. Scholem viewed this emphasis on communion with God in a popular treatise intended to be a manual for everybody as one of the main innovations of Hasidism, whereas

emphasizing instead the value of *devekut* in prayer. The Testament is essentially an anthology, based on the writings of early Hasidim, later attributed to the Besht.[55] In the case of the statement under discussion, however, there can be no doubt that the idea, and probably the language, of this epigram is indeed an authentic view of the founder of Hasidism. An elaborate and detailed presentation of this attitude is found in a paragraph in one of the few—if not the only—authentic letters of the Besht, his epistle to his brother-in-law, Rabbi Gershon of Kutov,[56] who was at the time on a journey to *Eretz Yisrael*. The letter includes an account of an experience the Besht had several years before, in 1747, of an "ascension of the soul" (*aliyat neshama*), during which he met and had a conversation with the Messiah. This is undoubtedly an authentic account of a mystical experience.[57] In the last part of this letter the tone changes, and instead of the personal account of a unique experience, the author instructs Rabbi Gershon in the correct way to pray. The context clearly indicates that this is the right way to perform the ritual if

---

the kabbalists reserved this supreme mystical state as the last achievement for mystics only. Tishby argued against this thesis, proving that earlier kabbalists and ethical teachers in Judaism put forward this concept long before the Besht. See G. Scholem, "Devekuth or Communion with God," *Review of Religion* 14 (1949/1950), pp. 115–139 (reprinted in *The Messianic Idea in Judaism and Other Essays*, New York: Schocken 1971); I. Tishby, *The Wisdom of the Zohar*, vol. II, pp. 990–1015.

[55]The study of the sources of the Testatment by Z. Gries (*Sifrut ha-Hanhagot*, note 27) emphasized the close ties between the various statements and the teachings of the Great Maggid, Rabbi Dov Baer of Mezeritch, the Besht disciple and heir. A different view is presented in a recent Ph.D. thesis on early Hasidism by Mor Altshuler Salay, who identified the teachings of a radical Hasidic sect, headed by the Maggid of Zlotchov, in several statements in this treatise.

[56]The epistle was printed in the end of the second Hasidic book ever printed, Rabbi Jacob Yosef of Polonoy's *Ben Porat Yosef*, printed in Koretz in 1781. This letter was studied intensively by all scholars dealing with early Hasidism, including S. Dubnow, B. Z. Dinur, R. Shatz, A. Rubinstein, and many others. The most important subject discussed in these studies is the messianic element in early Hasidism. The concept of prayer was rarely mentioned by them.

[57]An English translation, with some notes and bibliography, is found in Louis Jacobs's anthology, *The Jewish Mystics*, London: Kyle Cathie 1990 (previously published as *Jewish Mystical Testimonies*, Jerusalem: Keter 1976), pp. 148–155.

one wishes to use it as a vehicle for a mystical experience similar to the one previously described.

The Besht instructs the recipient of the epistle:

> And every utterance and word from your lips you should direct [techaven] to unify a Name [le-yahed shem][58] for in every letter there are worlds and souls and divinity. They ascend and are attached and are united one with another, and the letters are united and become a word, and they are unified in a true union in the Godhead. You should incorporate your own soul with them, in every aspect of those aspects, and all the worlds are united together and become happiness and great pleasure which cannot be measured, in the pleasure of bride and bridegroom, in "smallness" and corporeality and even more so in such a supreme stage.[59]

Whereas in the writings of many kabbalists the connection between *yichud* and sexual union is glossed over or minimized, in this letter of the Besht there is an insistence on the erotic dimension of this experience; it is equated to the immense pleasures of "bride and bridegroom," a phrase used in Hebrew to denote not any sexual in-

---

[58]The term *yichud*, in its various forms, is repeated several times in this paragraph, and is the key term concerning the experience described. The term has a long history in the kabbalah, and its meaning varies in the writings of many kabbalists. It is especially central in the *Zohar*, and even more so in the Lurianic kabbalah and its teachings concerning prayer. It represents a combination of two elements: bringing unity to the divine world and expressing adherence to the unity of the Godhead (following the Arabic, which was introduced into Judaism by the early medieval philosophers), and the sexual union, which this term denotes in Hebrew. The result of this complex combination is a concept of the sexual union within the masculine and feminine elements in the Godhead, with an additional undertone of such union between the worshipper and the divine realm, especially the *Shechinah*. Concerning the concept in early kabbalah, see M. Verman, "The Development of Yihudim in Spanish Kabbalah," in *Proceedings of the Third International Conference* (see note 27), pp. 25–42 in the English section.

[59]*Ben Porat Yosef*, Koretz 1781 (I did not find any explanation of why Jacobs insisted that the text was printed in 1771), 101a–b. I am using the Pieterkow edition, 1883, pp. 254–256. The text is also included in another authentic Hasidic work—Rabbi Ephrayim of Sedlikov's *Degel Mahane Ephrayim*. Rabbi Ephrayim was the grandson of the Besht and retained direct communications from him.

tercourse, but specifically the first sexual union of a just-married couple. There is little doubt that the pleasure described includes that of the worshipper, not only that of the divine powers.[60] This is a mystical union, described as supreme pleasure, expressed in terminology indicating an erotic experience within the divine world and between man and divine powers.[61]

The most important aspect of this text is its expression of the mystical concept of language. The instruction in the Testament of the Besht is presented as commentary on the verse in which God instructs Noah to make a window to the ark *ve-zohar taaseh le-tevah*.[62] The Hebrew term for "ark" is homonym for "word," whereas "tzohar" is a skylight, a small window often directed toward the sky. The verse is interpreted, therefore, as meaning "open up the word [of the prayer] toward heaven." The term "word" thus acquires an abstract aspect, language in general, without losing its specific context of a component of prayer.

---

[60]The early Hasidim were accused by their opponents of indulging in sexual experiences during prayer. The famous notes found in the margins of a halachic work in the house of Leib Melamed served as proof: One of the notes indicated that in prayer one should visualize a naked woman standing in front of him. See Willensky, op. cit. Recent research, especially by Mendel Piekarz, proved that such ideas were prevalent before Hasidism and outside of the Hasidic movement— probably more than among the Hasidim themselves. See M. Piekarz, *Biymey Zemihat ha-Hasidut*, Jerusalem: The Bialik Institute 1980, passim.

[61]An attempt has been made to give this text a magical dimension, because in the continuation of the paragraph the Besht indicates that after achieving this stage God will fulfill the worshipper's wishes. I believe that this is a completely wrong interpretation. The context, after all, is that of prayer, which includes requests from God, so that it is completely natural that as a result of this union these requests will be fulfilled. The picture is one in which the worshipper joins, in this mystical union, the divine family, and therefore everything he wishes will be granted. Compare the description of the love of God in the *Sefer Hasidim*, written five and a half centuries before the Besht, in which such a relationship is described. The erotic element is also present in the writings of these early mystics, describing the relationship with God as the ejaculation by a young man who had not had sex for a long time. The specific context of prayer, and the close relationship with language, is absent in these early descriptions.

[62]Genesis 5:16.

In this presentation, the semantic element in the "word" is almost completely forgotten. The notion of "prayer" in the traditional sense is retained in the context of man's appealing to God in a specific, formal ritual. Yet the nature of the text of the prayers is transformed into an intricate structure of divine powers, which find their expression in the letters and words of the ancient ritual. The Besht's statement seems to indicate that man does not deliver any semantic message to the divine world: He just pronounces letters and sounds that, when they ascend to the divine realm, are assembled, are united, and create words in a process that has sexual characteristics. Thus the abstract formula in the Testament, that every word includes a "whole stature" of the divine world, is developed in the epistle: The letters of the ancient text are the components of which a divine structure is composed.

The idea itself is not new, as we have observed above, but in modern Hasidism it became an integral part of the instruction in mystical prayer directed to the wide public. The concept of language reflected in it has become, in this way, the accepted image of linguistic expression within ritual, no longer enclosed among groups of esoteric mystics. According to this concept, the ritual of prayer is one in which, by the utterance of sounds, man participates in a mystical, visionary process in the divine world that is characterized by sexual symbolism. A rare union is achieved between the visionary and the auditory, between the sensual and the intellectual, between the semantic and the semiotic, between everyday life and supreme mystical experience, all as a result of the development of the concept of divine language in mystical prayer. The paradoxical relationship between unique mystical experience and common traditional ritual is resolved. Silent prayer and the vocal one have been unified within this concept of language.

SUMMARY

Though prayer traditionally served as a vehicle for mystical contact with God in the three scriptural religions, the problem of the relationship between linguistic expression and mystical truth haunts this encounter throughout the history of spirituality. Mysticism often represents the denial of the ability of communicative language to represent divine truth, yet it is the basis of prayer. As a result of this conflict, the concept of language within the context of mystical prayer underwent several transformations. One of the foci of this process is the concept of the "silent prayer," the language-without-language of mystical contemplation. Some examples from the works of Saint Theresa, Bachya ibn Pakuda, and Al-Jilani are examined in this paper. One of the most profound responses to this problem is found in Jewish mysticism, where the visionary element of mysticism united with the linguistic one is the concept that the words and letters of prayer represent the visual image of God. This is presented in the strongest terms in the teachings of Rabbi Israel Baal Shem Tov, the founder of the Hasidic movement, who maintained that "every letter of the prayer includes a full image of God." Relying on the long history of the concept of divine revelation by the shapes of the letters of the alphabet, modern Hasidism created a unity between the linguistic and the metalinguistic in mystical union achieved in prayer.

END NOTE

The subject of the mystical prayer in the history of Jewish mysticism is presented in a series of studies that are included in the volume *Jewish Mysticism: The Middle Ages* in this series. The article presented here is an attempt to analyze some of the basic, abstract characteristics of the subject in comparison to Christian and Islamic examples and viewing the subject throughout Jewish history, including the modern Hasidic movement. It is postulated that this problem is an essential one concerning the understanding of the relationship between mysticism and religion, because prayer is that aspect of normative religion that the mystics found most open to their own particular spiritual attitudes and that was most easily incorporated in their "mystical way"; at the same time, prayer gave the mystics the means for integration and inclusion in their religious communities, despite the deep differences in the attitude toward language, scriptures, and worship.

Discussions of this crucial subject are relatively rare in contemporary studies of mysticism; it has not been thoroughly problematized at this point in time. The study of liturgy, in the three scriptural religions, is concerned with the history of texts, the development of canons, the literary genres employed, and the rituals in which it is integrated, while the basic theoretical questions concerning the role of language in bringing together the worshipper and God in the prayer ritual are still being ignored to a large extent. It is hoped that this essay will contribute to the awakening of interest in pursuing these questions.

SEVEN

The Name of God, the Name of the Rose, and the Concept of Language in Jewish Mysticism

I

The concept of the divine name, its meanings and powers, cannot be separated from the concept of the divine language, which is a basic, nonmystical constituent of Judaism. The world was created by the word of God, by his utterances; therefore language evidently preceded the creation, and certainly existed before human beings and their communicative needs existed. The blueprint for the creation, according to Jewish tradition,[1] was scriptures, the Torah, which existed before the creation, and God "was looking at it and creating the world." Language, formulated into a text, thus guided God in that process. Divine language has been used to give framework to human communication—speech and writing as divine gifts to man; it has been used for communication between man and God in the theophanies and revelations; it has been used to create the concept

---

[1]Bereshit Rabba 1:1; see *Bereschit Rabba mit Kritischen Apparat und Kommentar,* von J. Theodor, Jerusalem: Wahrman 1965, additional corrections by Ch. Albeck, pp. 1–2 and the notes there.

of infinite, eternal meaning incorporated within the sacred text and deciphered by midrashic hermeneutics. On a different level, language as a divine instrument explained the process and nature of creation itself. In all these aspects, divine language retained its communicative and instrumental nature.[2] Language may be divine in all these formulations, but it remains a means. Language embodies within it the infinite wisdom of God and His creative powers, which are revealed, in a limited form, in the created world, serving various functions.

In the concept of the holy name of God, language stops being a means and becomes an independent divine essence, in which language and divinity are united. The holy name of God is not an expression of the divine: It is the essence of divinity itself. It is not revelation, it is the Revealer. It is not the instrument of creation, but the Creator. This is the culmination of the process that began with the appearance of the concept of scriptures: God has become a linguistic entity, His essence incorporated within a linguistic phenomenon. In this concept, indeed, the distinction between religion and mysticism becomes a most tenuous one.

This complex spiritual process is best explained by the juxtaposition of Jewish and Christian attitudes concerning the holy name, which is also the comparison between Hebrew and Greek (or Latin) discussions of the subject. One of the most profound expressions of Christian mysticism in all its long and variegated history is the

---

[2]It seems that today the opposite view, seeing language as an intensely human phenomenon, is increasing in power, and we are actually returning to the ancient Greek scientific view, which identified humanity by the power of speech, which separates humans from animals. Two major books have been recently published, demonstrating the comprehensiveness of this concept and the far reaches of its conclusions. See Steven Pinker, *The Language Instinct: How the Mind Creates Language*, New York: Morrow 1994 (the title is not completely accurate: The mind creates not language, but grammar. Particular languages are the result of the particular developments of different peoples); Ray Jackendoff, *Patterns in the Mind: Language and Human Nature*, New York: Basic Books 1994. These two forceful presentations conclude almost a half-century of development of this school. In the context of this study, one should be reminded of the fact that Noam Chomsky formulated his concepts half a century ago in the context of the study of modern Hebrew, the language in which he was proficient when he started his linguistic work.

pseudo-Dionysian treatise *The Divine Names*. This text, together with other works attributed to Dionysius of Areopagita,[3] had a profound influence on subsequent Christian mysticism. Despite the intense neo-Platonic character of the speculations of this treatise, its adherence to the scriptural texts is deep-rooted, and many sections in it are essentially exegetical. The mystical attitude of the author is almost a textbook one, starting from a radical negation of sensual and intellectual perceptions,[4] and instead using scriptures: "Let us therefore look as far upward as the light of sacred scripture will allow, and, in our reverent awe of what is divine, let us be drawn together toward the divine splendor."[5] The negation of sensual perception and intellectual human faculties is complete and radical: "Just as the senses can neither grasp nor perceive the things of the mind, just as representation and shape cannot take in the simple[6] and the shapeless, just as corporeal form cannot lay hold of the intangible and incor-

---

[3]See Acts 17:31. The mystical works of Pseudo-Dionysius are usually attributed to an anonymous neo-Platonic Christian mystic who flourished in the sixth century. For nearly a millennium, Christian mysticism developed under the impact of this intensely spiritual as well as profoundly philosophical small library, so much so that one of the greatest historians of Christian mysticism declared his inability to distinguish between Christian mystician and mystical neo-Platonism (see W. R. Inge, *Christian Mysticism*, London: Methuen 1899). A vast library of research has developed around these texts. A recent comprehensive presentation of Dionysian mysticism is included in B. McGinn, *The Foundations of Mysticism: Origins to the Fifth Century*, New York: Crossroads 1991, pp. 157–182, and detailed bibliography there. A recent study of the subject of the apophatic language of this and other works is that of Michael A. Sells, *Mystical Languages of Unsaying*, Chicago and London: Chicago University Press 1994 (see especially pp. 14–62)
[4]For a detailed discussion, see J. Dan, "In Quest of a Historical Definition of Mysticism: the Contingental Approach," *Studies in Spirituality* 3 (1993), pp. 58–90.
[5]I am using one of the most recent translations of the text, that of C. E. Rolt and J. Jones, included in *Pseudo-Dionysius, The Complete Works*, New York: Paulist Press 1987. This volume includes translations by Colm Luibheid and Paul Rorem, notes by Paul Rorem, and Introduction by Rene Roques, Jaroslav Pelikan, Jean Leclercq, and Karlfried Froehlich.
[6]"Simple" in this context means the opposite of "complex," something that cannot be divided into its constituent parts. Only the divine, therefore, can be "simple." In medieval Hebrew, the term was translated as פשוט, and was reserved for the descriptions of the unity of God.

poreal, by the same standard of truth beings are surpassed by the infinity beyond being, intelligences by that oneness which is beyond intelligence. Indeed, the inscrutable One is out of the reach of every rational process."[7] Human facilities cannot conceive any part of the mystical truth. It is only scriptures that open a window—if correctly interpreted—to some glimpse of that divine truth:

> We learn of all these mysteries from the divine scriptures and you will find that what the scriptures writers have to say regarding the divine names refers, in revealing praises, to the beneficent processions of God. And so all these scriptural utterances celebrate the supreme Deity by describing it as a monad or henad, because of its supernatural simplicity and indivisible unity.[8]

The author saw in the divine names that part of scriptures which is most revealing concerning the hidden, mystical nature of God. The power of the divine name is demonstrated in the New Testament by the power of the name of Christ,[9] so that the mystic can feel that he is conservatively following ancient concepts when he develops his own mysticism of the divine names.

But what does he mean by the term "names"? On the one hand, the author recognizes that there is a group of names which is beyond revelation, beyond linguistic expression of any kind.[10] But he continues: "And yet on the other hand they give it many names, such as 'I am Being,' 'life,' 'light,' 'God,' the 'truth.' These same wise writers, when praising the Cause of everything that is, use names

---

[7]Pp. 49–50.

[8]P. 51.

[9]For instance, Acts 4:10–12.

[10]"Realizing all this, the theologians praise it by every name—and as the Nameless One. For they call it nameless when they speak of how the Supreme Deity, during a mysterious revelation of the symbolical appearance of God, rebuked the man who asked: 'What is your name?' and led him away from any knowledge of the divine name by countering: 'Why do you ask my name, seeing it is wonderful?'" (p. 54). The biblical scene referred to is that of Genesis 32:25, the struggle between Jacob and the mysterious power on the Yabok. "Wonderful" is the translation of the Hebrew פלא, which in this context actually means "mysterious."

drawn from all the things caused: good, beautiful, wise, beloved, God of gods, Lord of lords, Holy of Holies, eternal, existent, Cause of the ages. They call him source of life, wisdom, mind, word, knower, possessor beforehand of all the treasures of knowledge, power, powerful and King of Kings, ancient of days, the unaging and unchanging," and so on.[11] It is quite clear that this list of appellations of the divine, collected from the Old and New Testaments, is a semantic one: These are terms that convey some meaning on the linguistic level, and their significance can be found in their semantic nature. The author is aware of the partial and incomplete nature of the semantic information given in this way, yet he uses language in the only way he can: with words that convey a specific meaning. The concept of symbolism is the one that enables him to hint at the existence of a mystical, metasemantic significance to these terms.

For the author of the treatise *The Divine Names*, the Greek words collected from the text of the scriptures denote names that are words, despite the deep awareness of the mystic of the vast distance separating the essence of the divine from human linguistic expression. He does not conceive of a name that is not a word on the semantic level, a group of letters and syllables that does not convey meaning as words do. Similar discussions of divine names abound in all three scriptural religions. Thus, for instance, the great twelfth-century Sufi leader, Hadrat Abd al-Qadir al-Jilani, describes in his treatise The Secret of Secrets[12] the twelve divine names that are a part of the "ladder of ascension" of the mystic.[13] In every stage of the spiritual process, the mystic pronounces one of the holy names

---

[11]Pp. 55–56; and see the biblical references there for each of these appellations.
[12]The Secret of Secrets by Hadrat Abd al-Qadir al-Jilani, interpreted by Shykh Tosun Bayrak al-Jerrahi al-Halveti, Cambridge: Islamic Texts Society 1992. See a previous German translation by Alma Giese under the title *Enthullungen des Verborgenen*, Köln: Al-Kitab 1985, and a detailed bibliography there, pp. 194–200.
[13]Pp. 86–87 et passim. The mystical attitude of Al-Jilani toward language is apparent also in his concept of prayer, in which insistence on the semantic message is mixed with the quest for transcending language into the realm of the mystical silent prayer.

of God, and this name both signifies his achievement of this stage
and enables him to proceed to the next:[14]

> After the inner purification, one must recite the Names of the
> attributes of Allah, which will kindle the light of Allah's beauty
> and grace. It is in that light that one hopes to see the Kaaba of
> the secret essence. Allah ordered His prophets Abraham and
> Ishmael to this purification. . . . After these preparations the in-
> ner pilgrim wraps himself in the light of the holy spirit, trans-
> forming his material shape into the inner essence, and
> circumambulates the Kaaba of the heart, inwardly reciting the
> second divine Name—Allah, the proper name of God. . . . There
> he stands reciting the third Name—hu . . . then he recites the
> fourth Name—haqq, the Truth, the name of the light of Allah's
> essence—and then the fifth name, HAYY, the divine life, eter-
> nal from which all temporal life derives. Then he joins the di-
> vine Name of the Everliving with the sixth Name—
> QAYYTUM, the Self-existing one upon whom all existence
> depends.

The position of the semantic element in this system is a lesser
one than in the pseudo-Dionysian text. The first names do not denote any meaning; they are sounds (and, probably, also pictures,
when written), unrelated to a specific linguistic reference. The lower
names, however, are composed of a combination of the semantic and
the nonsemantic: They do convey the meaning of truth, life, or
existence, yet obviously it is not just this meaning that makes them
so powerful in the mystical process. The meaning ascribed to them
is at least partially a negative one—truth that is beyond earthly truth,
life that is beyond human life, existence that is beyond material
existence. It may be surmised that the potency of these names is
derived not from their position in communicative language, but in

---

[14]This process is similar, to some extent, to the ascension of the Hechalot mystic
from one palace to the other, when in each stage he presents the "seals" that are
holy names, probably engraved. Both the oral (auditory) and visual aspects of
the holy name are evoked in this process. See in detail A. Kuyt, "Heavenly Jour-
neys in Hekhalot Literature," Ph.D. thesis, Amsterdam 1992.

their intimate, metalinguistic relationship to the mystical divine being. The significant aspect of this list, from the point of view of this
discussion, is that those names that have a semantic level are described as lower than those that do not. The mystical power of a
name is increased when its linguistic meaning is diminished.

The main thesis of this discussion is that the sanctity of the
name in the mysticisms of the scriptural religions is derived from
the fact that a name, in essence, is that part of language in which
the semantic level is minimal or nonexistent. Meaning, like communication, is an obstacle to the mystic's progress. The perfect mystical language is one that does not have a semantic level at all. The
language of divine names, it is suggested, should be viewed as a
semiotic rather than a semantic one. The following examples and
analysis should elaborate this concept.

II

A quarter-century ago, Gershom Scholem published one of his
most profound studies, dedicated to the holy name and the concept
of language in Jewish mysticism.[15] It is necessary to return to this
subject because of the progress made in the last generation in the
understanding of the nature of language and its place in religion and
mysticism. One of the most important contributions to this renewed
understanding comes, so to speak, from Scholem's own backyard:
The philosophy of language, and especially the philosophy of names
in language, was developed by Scholem's best friend, Walter Benjamin. One of his earliest works, published only after his death, is
most pertinent to this subject: It is one of the very few studies of
language ever written that deal in a profound way in the metahuman

---

[15]G. Scholem, "Der Name Gottes und die Sprachtheorie der Kabbala," *Eranos
Jahrbuch* 39 (1970; actually published in 1973), pp. 243–299; reprinted in *Judaica
III, Studien zur Judische Mystik*, Frankfurt a/M: Suhrkamp 1973; English transla-
tion by Simon Pleasance: "The Name of God and the Linguistic Theory of the
Kabbalah," *Diogenes* 79 (Fall 1972), pp. 59–80; 80 (Winter 1972), pp. 164–169 (also
a French translation in *Diogenes*, same issues).

and metacommunicative nature of language.[16] The last generation saw an increase in the awareness, among linguists, of the intrinsically human nature of language, as a result of the works of Noam Chomsky and his influential school. Benjamin is the representative of the opposite direction in this field. Benjamin's contention that language includes the ability of things—designated by names—to address us, and that things communicate among themselves, has in it the element of a semiotic, rather than semantic, concept of language; this communication, according to Benjamin, includes dancing, mime, painting, sculpting, music, poetry, etc. The meeting point between "language as such" and "language spoken by man" is the name-giving. In Benjamin's complex system, this process is a revelation of the innermost nature of man, as well as the closest touch with the things themselves. I believe that Benjamin (like Scholem) recognized in the process of name-creation a creativity that is not merely facilitation of communication, but also the touching between two different essences, which are both present in this occurrence.

Neither Benjamin nor Scholem used explicit religious terminology when presenting their concept of language. Yet it seems that the closest parallels to their views are found in the works of mystics, describing the semiotic communication between man and God. Thus, for instance, the pseudo-Dionysian treatise on the Divine Names states:

> If God cannot be grasped by mind or sense-perception, if he is not a particular being, how do we know him? This is something we must inquire into. It might be more accurate to say that we cannot know God in his nature, since this is unknowable and is beyond the reach of mind or of reason. But we know him from the arrangement of everything, because everything

---

[16] "Uber Sprache überhaupt und über die Sprache des Menschen," included in the *Gesammelte Schriften*, vol. 1, ed. Rolf Tiedmann and Herman Schweppenhauser, Frankfurt a/M 1972, p. 140. English translation: "On Language as Such and on the Language of Man," in *Reflections*, ed. P. Demetz, New York: Schocken 1986, pp. 314–333. My thanks are due to Dr. Berendan Moran, who gave me an unpublished study of his, "Walter Benjamin's Early Philosophy of Language," which I found most helpful.

is, in a sense, projected out from him, and this order possesses certain images and semblances of his divine paradigms. We therefore approach that which is beyond all as far as our capacities allow us and we pass by way of the denial and the transcendence of all things and by way of the cause of all things. God is therefore known in all things and as distinct from all things. He is known through knowledge and through unknowing. Of him there is conception, reason, understanding, touch, perception, opinion, imagination, name and many other things. On the other hand he cannot be understood, words cannot contain him, and no name can lay hold of him.[17]

This is a description of the semiotic system, in which all things are signs, by which the mystic can know something of God. The mystic "reads" everything in existence as an indication of the existence and nature of God, but he must be aware of the fact that God "speaks" to him in this way also by not presenting, by the absence of signs, by the "unknowing." Actual signs and missing signs play an equal part in this semiotic system, in which language is a small, insignificant part. Even so, "names" are an element selected for emphasis by the author; scriptures are not mentioned, but names are.

It is the nature of a name to refer to the thing designated in its unique individuality, conveying the specific character, and separating it from other beings. What is true about generic names is doubly so concerning personal names. These do not contain a semantic level; they only designate an individual by a sign, on a semiotic level. If this personal name has a meaning (as in calling a girl by the name "Belle"), this meaning is an obstacle separating the sign from the thing designated.[18] The less meaning in a name, the better it can be iden-

---

[17]Pp. 108–109.
[18]In this way, I believe, we can explain the title of Umberto Eco's novel, *The Name of the Rose*. This novel narrates a story told by books, to books, about books. Every passage, every character, every event, is either a direct quotation or a paraphrase of a literary or theological work. The title serves as a warning (usually unheeded, especially by the makers of the movie based on this novel) that the work does not deal with the thing itself, only with its linguistic expression in the Name. The subject of the book is the difference between things and

tified with the individual being. Therefore, the name "Allah" is thus more sacred than the appellation "All-merciful," in which the semantic level has to be ignored so that the concept of the divine can be absorbed. The name YHVH thus can become the supreme divine name, because there is no fixed, necessary semantic level to it, despite the dozens of exegetical attempts.

An example will be useful in clarifying this concept. In the beginning of the second century there seems to have been, among Jewish exegetes, a tendency to forsake the previous understanding of the *Song of Songs* as essentially a secular poem, describing a love affair between King Solomon and a beautiful Jerusalemite shepherdess, and to find new dimensions of allegorical meaning in it. Generations passed until complete allegory came into being, probably in the third century, both in Christianity,s great commentary on this work by Origen of Caesarea, and in Judaism's midrashic compendium, *Shir ha-Shirim Rabba*.

In the early second century, there was only a partial allegorical treatment of specific verses in this work. The earliest of these is probably attested by story of the "four who entered the *pardes*," [19] in which the successful mystical experience of Rabbi Akiva is hinted at by the verse "The king has brought me into his chambers," [20] denoting for the first time that the "king" of this work is not Solomon but God Himself. Similarly, it is reported that Rabbi Akiva declared that the *Song of Songs* is the Holy of Holies of the scriptures, and he claimed that the book was "given" to the people of Israel (in the same terminology denoting the "giving" of the Torah by God), on Mount Sinai, a part of that supreme theophany, many centuries before King Solomon was born. (His colleague, Rabbi Eliezer, maintained that the book was "given" when the Red Sea parted to allow Israel to

---

names, in the same way that Eco's subsequent novel, *Foucault's Pendulum*, deals with the difference (and, later, congruence) between reality and scholarship. See my Introduction to the Hebrew translation of this novel, Tel Aviv: Kineret 1991, pp. 7–13.

[19]Tosefta *Hagiga* 2:4.

[20]Song of Songs 1:4.

cross, based upon the belief that when the sea opened, the heavens opened as well and their secrets were revealed.) This led to the interpretation of the first verse of the Song of Songs, which states that Solomon was its author, as meaning that it was given by "the King of Peace," God Himself.

It seems that this new attitude toward the book was expressed first and foremost by a new understanding of the verses 5:10–16. In these verses, the physical characteristics of the "lover" are described—his head, hair, legs, teeth—in a most sensual manner. If the author of this work was not King Solomon, then the description is related to its true author, God Himself. Understood in this way, these verses become the most anthropomorphic description of God in the Bible, presenting the clearest appearance of God in biblical literature, making the visions of Moses, Isaiah, Ezekiel, and Daniel pale in comparison. Ezekiel can only mumble about "an image like that of a man's above it," whereas the Song describes in detail the various limbs of the divine figure. These verses served to create the image of the Shiur Komah, the gigantic, anthropomorphic figure of God described in detail in a third-century Hebrew mystical treatise, which was used by all subsequent Jewish mystics in the Middle Ages and modern times.[21]

---

[21]On this text and its place in the history of Jewish mysticism, see G. Scholem, On the Mystical Shape of the Godhead (actually, the title of this book is the rendering of the term Shiur Komah into English), New York: Schocken 1991, pp. 15–54; idem, Jewish Gnosticism, Merkabah Mysticism and Talmudic Tradition, 2nd ed., New York: The Jewish Theological Seminary 1965, pp. 36–42, and S. Lieberman's appendix to this book, pp. 118–126. See also P. Schäfer, The Hidden and Manifest God: Some Major Themes in Early Jewish Mysticism, Albany, NY: SUNY Press 1992, pp. 60–62, 99–102 et passim; J. Dan, Ancient Jewish Mysticism, Tel Aviv 1989, pp. 48–58; idem, "The Concept of Knowledge in the Shiur Komah," in Studies in Jewish Religious and Intellectual History Presented to A. Altmann, ed. S. Stein and R. Loewe, University, AL: Alabama University Press 1979, pp. 67–74. Compare also the monograph on the subject, M. S. Cohen, The Shiur Qomah: Liturgy and Theurgy in Pre-Kabbalistic Jewish Mysticism, Latham, MD: Scholar's Press 1983. A comprehensive collection of early and late Shiur Komah texts was presented by Cohen in the volume The Shiur Qomah: Texts and Recensions, Tübingen: J.C.B. Mohr (Siebeck) 1985. For an attempt to find a connection between the Shiur Komah and talmudic literature, see M. Bar-Ilan, "The

The impact of this interpretation of the *Song of Songs* verses was, undoubtedly, a visual one. While its development was textual and exegetical, that is, linguistic, the result carried enormous visual, sensual power, which became a potent element in Jewish metalinguistic expressions of divine revelation. It is no wonder that the people who developed this concept in its initial stages were the *Hechalot* mystics, who rebelled against midrashic hermeneutics, and believed in their ability to face God directly—in His image of the *Shiur Komah*. The anthropomorphic figure of God is the exact opposite of the textual, midrashic God, hiding inside the esoteric layers of biblical language.

Yet, when the most intensely mystical treatise in *Hechalot* literature describes the most celebrated mystical journey in the history of Jewish mysticism—the ascension of Rabbi Akiva to the supreme seventh palace, in which God Himself resides and sits on His throne of glory—something unexpected happened to these verses from the *Song of Songs*. In the pinnacle of the mystical experience, when Rabbi Akiva was facing God directly, the holiest names of God were revealed to him. Many of these names are ones known to us from other *Hechalot* mystical treatises, and some of them have histories of their own (some information concerning their origins and development can be gleaned from the text[22]); others are obscure. But among them, in a most prominent position, we find a completely different sequence of the most secret and most potent names of God. These are none other than the actual verses from the *Song of Songs* 5:10–16, arranged

Hand of God: A Chapter in Rabbinic Anthropomorphism," in G. Sed-Rajna (ed.), *Rashi, Hommage à E. E. Urbach*, Paris: Cerf 1993, pp. 321–335. Compare also A. Farber-Ginat, "Studies in the Shiur Komah," in M. Oron and A. Goldreich (eds.), *Massu'ot: Studies in Kabbalistic Literature and Jewish Philosophy in Memory of Prof. E. Gottlieb*, Jerusalem: Bialik Institute 1994, pp. 361–393.
[22] An example is the "name of eights," Azboga, which is composed of the three pairs of Hebrew letters that together give the number eight. Scholem tended to see a connection between this name and the gnostic *ogdoas*; see J. Dan, "The Name of Eights," in *Minha le-Sarah, Studies in Jewish Philosophy and Kabbalah dedicated to Prof. Sarah Heller-Willensky*, ed. M. Idel, D. Dimant, and S. Rosenberg, Jerusalem: Magnes 1994, pp. 119–134.

in a mysterious rhythm, the title Sabaoth (and Siboth) added to each phrase.[23]

Description had thus been transformed into essence. As long as these verses were read as communicative language, they conveyed the most secret and sublime information about God, but they still dealt with information, revelation, and communication. In this last phase of their development, they no longer describe, but are the subject of description; they do not convey the nature of God, but are the concentration of God's essence. Their linguistic form is retained, but their communicative nature is forsaken. The semantic unit has been transformed into a mystical sign.

Following this example, we can define a sacred name of God as that linguistic expression of the divine that is not communicative; it just *is*, representing in a linguistic form the inexpressible essence of God Himself. Such a concept represents the belief not only that God inspired scriptures and communicated His truth and wisdom to man, but that He Himself actually exists in the scriptures, in those phrases that are noncommunicative and essentially meaningless—יהוה, אדני, צבאות, שדי, אלהים, and all the others. They have no literal meaning (although, throughout history, they accumulated hundreds and thousands of interpretations). They do not convey, inform, or describe; they are the essence of God.

The history of the creation and exegesis of holy names of God in Judaism is characterized by a consistent attempt to divorce language from meaning. The example just presented is an extreme one, because it demonstrates how a passage of meaningful language, probably originally a love song in which the female lover describes the physical beauty of her male beloved, became a sequence of letters signifying the innermost mystery of the Godhead, losing all elements of conveying a message, signs being completely divorced from their signifiers. In most cases the very beginning of such a process is meaningless. The clearest example is found in a much more central name

---

[23]See J. Dan, "The Chambers of the Chariot," *Tarbiz* 46 (1978), pp. 49–56. The text has been published in P. Schäfer, *Synopse zur Hekhalot-Literatur*, Tübingen: J.C.B. Mohr (Siebeck) 1981, p. 419.

than the verses in the *Song of Songs*, a group of three verses in Exodus (14:19–21) describing the safe passage of the Jews through the
Red Sea when fleeing the pursuing Egyptian army. This seems to
me to present a perfect example of the difference between human
and divine language, and the impossibility of conceiving of a divine
language in translation. The verses read:

> 19. And the angel of God, which went before the camp of Is-
> rael, removed and went behind them; and the pillar of the cloud
> went from before their face, and stood behind them. 20. And it
> came between the camp of the Egyptians and the camp of Is-
> rael; and it was a cloud and darkness to them, but it gave light
> by night to these: so that the one came not near the other all
> the night 21. And Moses stretched out his hand over the sea;
> and the Lord caused the sea to go back by a strong east wind
> all that night, and made the sea dry land, and the waters were
> divided.

This is rather straightforward, literal narration. In the Hebrew
original there are some syntactic difficulties, but on the whole this
passage can in no way be described as uniquely obscure or suggestive. There is nothing in the text that can denote that these verses
contain one of the greatest mysteries of God, which Jewish exegetes,
esoterics, and mystics discussed in books not intended for the public for fifteen centuries. These verses constitute the Secret Name of
Seventy-Two Characters, a secret transmitted in whispers from generation to generation. A passage dedicated to its description is included in the first work of the kabbalah, the *Bahir*, and several
Ashkenazi Hasidic commentaries were written on it in the late twelfth
and early thirteenth centuries. People in many generations trembled
at the mention of this secret.

These three verses are unique in the whole Bible in one strange
respect: Each of them contains, in Hebrew, exactly seventy-two letters:

ויסע מלאך האלהים ההלך לפני מחנה ישראל וילך מאחריהם ויסע עמוד הענן
מפניהם ויעמד מאחריהם.
ויבא בין מחנה מצרים ובין מחנה ישראל ויהי הענן והחשך ויאמד את הלילה ולא
קדב זה אל זה כל הלילה.

ויט משה את ידו על הים ויולך יהוה את הים בדרוח קדים עזה כל הלילה וישם את
הים לחרבה ויבקעו המים.

In order to create the holy name, the middle verse has to be written from end to beginning. The source of the idea may have been rooted in the fact that the last word in this verse, "the night," is a word that can be read exactly the same from beginning to end or end to beginning (buxtraphedon); it probably should be translated as "eve" instead of "the night." After writing the middle verse in this way, the text should be read upside-down, forming seventy-two groups of three letters, beginning with והו, that is, the first letter of the first verse, the last letter of the middle verse, the first letter of the third verse; followed by ילי, the second letter of the first verse, the next-to-last of the second verse, and the second letter of the third verse; and so on, seventy-two times.

The result of this process is a meaningless sequence of 216 letters, divided into seventy-two groups of three each, almost none of which constitutes a recognizable word. A series of three relatively comprehensible and communicative sentences has been turned into a heap of gibberish, completely divorced from any kind of meaning, yet containing a strange, suggestive numerical symmetry. We do not know when this name was formed; traditions about its existence are found in Late Antiquity, yet it is not associated with any definite, recognizable school of Jewish esoterics or mystics. Once it was formed, it was used by all Hebrew writers dealing with the secrets of the holiest name of all.

An example of its use in a relatively recent period may indicate its potency. Rabbi Jacob Joseph of Polonoy, the author of the first published work of the Hasidic movement in the eighteenth century, *Toledot Yaakov Yosef*, published in 1780, tells in the name of his teacher, the Besht—the founder of the movement—a detailed, erotic story, derived from a medieval folktale found also in the *Decameron*. This story includes an episode in which a lover, masked as an evil sailor, abducts his beloved, taking her in a ship and raping her on the journey. The Besht offered an allegorical interpretation of this story as a chapter in the history of the intricate relationship between

God and Israel, according to which God sometimes hides His real face and seems to be an evil power torturing Israel, whereas at the end it is revealed that it was all done out of love. The evil sailor is the devil, but, states the Besht, sometimes God Himself assumes the guise of the devil. The frequent name of Satan in kabbalistic tradition is Samael, and this is the one used by the Besht in the interpretation of this story. He then states that the name Samael can be conceived of as the word within which hides the very holy name Sal; when God masquerades as the devil, Sal is transformed to Samael. Sal, of course, is one of the seventy-two groups of letters derived from these verses, and its proximity to the name Samael was already used by thirteenth-century kabbalists in Spain.[24]

This example demonstrates clearly the process in which the holy name of God is first divorced from any linguistic meaning, being presented as a pure linguistic construction expressing only symmetry and form but no content; and then, by the use of simple midrashic exegetical methods, particular meanings are returned to parts of the name, which is then used as a new source of divine truth, a new-old revealed text to be interpreted and utilized in the deciphering of the eternal message of God to man.

Another example—from a completely different field—of this process of the destruction of meaning can be found in the mystical work of early Jewish mysticism, *Hechalot Rabbati*. This work abounds with *nomina barbara*, relating to a wide range of powers of the divine pleroma as seen by those mystics. There are, in this work, several sequences of letters, completely meaningless, presented as the names of God. A classical scholar who studied them discovered, unexpectedly, that many of them are actual words or even sentences in Greek, transliterated into Hebrew characters and thus losing their linguistic message. One of these was proved to be the Greek names of the four elements—air, fire, water, and earth—which became a pile of Hebrew letters, devoid of any meaning, constituting a hidden,

---

[24]An analysis of this story is included in my *The Hasidic Story*, Jerusalem: Keter 1975, pp. 40–46.

mysterious name of God. This attitude was prevalent in Late Antiquity, when Jews seem to have used Greek to lend an air of mystery to the names they employed, whereas Greek-speaking esoterics and magicians seem to have preferred Hebrew sacred names as very potent ones in their pantheon of secret names. This direction was also followed by many gnostic sects, who used, in many ways, Hebrew biblical terms as indicating mysterious, mythological powers in their story of the creation and catastrophe. Their works abound with names like Adonaios, Elohaios, Saddaios, Sabaoth, and the like. One of the most enigmatic names in the gnostic mythology—that of Yaldabaoth, the evil lion-shaped creator—is, most probably, also a Hebrew condensation of the biblical divine names of Ya Elohim Adonai Zevaot, found in several Late Antiquity Hebrew esoteric and mystical texts. The gnostics, presumably, heard these sequences of names and condensed, rather than constructed, a combined name to denote the totality of the God of Israel, the Creator, who embodied worldly evil in their eyes. Suggestions that this name is an artificial gnostic construct from Semitic components do not seem to be well founded, for they have no counterpart in any ancient literature, and there is no proof that the gnostic ever used such constructs from Semitic roots (they certainly did so from Greek components.)

One of the undeciphered mysteries in Hebrew names of God, hitherto unexplained, is the celebrated name of forty-two letters, usually presented as seven groups of six letters: אבניתץ, קדעשטן etc. The name is found in acronymic form in prayers, but it is doubtful whether this is the source: It is more probable that these poetic formulations were made following this name. It seems that it was well known in classical rabbinic Judaism, though the full name is found only in somewhat later sources. Again, the most important aspect of this name is the complete absence of literal meaning, this absence understood as expressing its relation to God's essence rather than His message.

One of the expressions of this attitude is found in Jewish art, in which the tetragrammaton has been stylized in various forms to create a decorative symbol. Some Jewish mystics combined this element with a frequent kabbalistic practice of stylizing artistically the image of the ten *sefirot*, in an anthropomorphic picture or that of a structure or of a tree, and presented the *sefirot* and the name as one symbol, which had a religious, and sometimes mystical, message. It was designed as a fulfillment of the demand presented in verses that attach a visionary element to the divine image, an image one has to contemplate.[25] The word is thus transformed into an intricate visual symbol that can be used for contemplation and mystical absorption.[26]

In the light of these basic attitudes, we can better understand the generalizations presented by medieval kabbalists concerning the relationship between the holy name and the Torah. Nachmanides' statement that the whole Torah is nothing but the names of God, followed by the more extreme statement that the whole Torah is the name of God, achieves one thing: It denies the originality of the divine message cast in language as the original stratum of the Torah, and sees it as a secondary, accidental one. The whole vast body of midrashic hermeneutics is not a decipherment of more and more layers of meaning within the text of a meaningful message, but all these layers are superimposed on a text that is devoid of any original meaning. These statements, before doing anything else, deny the element of communication in any way, on any level, from the Torah. While the Midrash treats the Torah as an inexhaustible text of infinite meanings, the mystic who identifies it with the secret name of God actually treats the text of the Torah as huge blank scroll, as far as meaning is concerned, on which any meaning can be written.

---

[25]Psalms 16:8.

[26]This phenomenon has recently been used (or, actually, misused) in S. Parpola, "The Assyrian Tree of Life: Tracing the Origins of Jewish Monotheism and Greek Philosophy," *JNES* 52 (1993), pp. 161–207. The author maintains that the kabbalistic concept of the ten *sefirot* and their depiction as a tree is found in the second millennium B.C. (when it is actually a product of late-twelfth-century speculation), and he identifies it with the Tree of Life (an identification that is found in Jewish sources only three millennia later). The author relies not on written texts but mainly on various drawings, including that of the tetragrammaton as a tree. He "relies" on some of my papers and books as well as those of Scholem and others, while every sentence in these publications completely negates this arbitrary thesis.

The literal message of the word of God has thus completely disappeared. Instead of a message, the Torah the essence.

Another metaphor, more contemporary in character, that can be used concerning the relationship between the name of God and meaningful, communicative language, is that of the black hole. The name of God is so meaningful, so intensely reflective of the divine wisdom, that nothing can escape from it or can be discerned from it. It is the supreme concentration of divine essence, transcending everything. Yet the mystical attitude toward language is most clearly expressed here: Despite all this, the name is still language. The essence of God, or the best possible approximation of it present in the distant horizon of human conception, is a linguistic structure. It is not a picture, a vision, an emotion, but a text. This text is conceived in a radically different way from that of human language or even of midrashic concept of divine language, but it is still language. The mystical theories of the nature of the Torah and of the name of God strengthen the intrinsic identity between God and language.

One of the most intricate relationships between name and vision is that of the *Shiur Komah*, the central and most potent symbol in Jewish mysticism. On the face of it, this is the supreme expression of visionary mysticism: It embodies the need for a physical, anthropomorphic, visual contact with the Godhead, meeting in it the supreme combination of the familiar and the unknown, the components of humanity and the dimensions of unimaginable myth. On another level, the *Shiur Komah* is the text: It is the intrinsic meaning of the *Song of Songs* verses, a compendium of linguistic symbols exhausting biblical texts. But on yet another level, it is a collection of *nomina barbara*, to sacred names original and traditional, uniting to create the "blank page" on which mystical truth is represented.

The most emphatic statement of this attitude was made in the second decade of the thirteenth century by Rabbi Eleazar of Worms, presenting a tradition that existed for several generations in his family, the Kalonymus family in the Rhineland, and most notably his great teacher, Rabbi Judah ben Kalonymus the Pious. Rabbi Eleazar presented his most esoteric tradition in his extensive work, *Sefer ha-*

Shem, the Book of the Name. This work has never been printed, but it is found in several manuscripts.[27]

Rabbi Eleazar beings his discussion of the holy name by describing a ceremony of "handing over the name" from a rabbi to his disciple, conducted alongside a river or a body of water, in which appropriate verses, mainly from the Psalms, are recited.[28] After the conclusion of the ceremony, a long period of study begins, and *Sefer ha-Shem* seems to be a summary of the esoteric teachings concerning the tetragrammaton and other holy names. In this work, Rabbi Eleazar represents one direction in the mystical concept of the holy name in medieval Judaism—that of the investigation of the comprehensiveness of the spiritual meaning of a group of letters, their inclusion within themselves of all meanings, all phenomena, the inner essence of all existence. This approach expresses the feeling that the physical symbol, the written name, is fused completely with the abstract concept of God as a totality of all spirituality and meaning. Within the name, all differences and contradictions are united, as they are within God, because the name *is* God. Rabbi Eleazar does not even use the Torah as a mediator, as did Nachmanides: The name, the tetragrammaton, is completely identified with the Godhead, a thorough fusion of symbol and the symbolized, between

---

[27]The most important manuscripts are Munich 81 (which is probably a copy of) British Library 737. This manuscript, at the end of the fifteenth century, was in the possession of the Cardinal Edigio de Viterbo, one of the first Catholic Hebraists and the founder of the Christian kabbalah. His notes abound in the margins of the manuscript. The book, *Sefer ha-Shem*, is the third part of Rabbi Eleazar's series of esoteric theological works, called by him *Sodey Razaya* (Secrets of Secrets; the title is numerically equivalent to his name, Eleazar.) The others are The Secret of Genesis, The Secret of the Chariot, The Wisdom of the Soul, and the Commentary on the Sefer Yezira. Several manuscripts in this collection were collected by the great Prague bibliophile of the eighteenth century, Rabbi David Oppenheim, and are housed now at the Bodleian Library, Oxford.
[28]G. Scholem published a translation of this introduction and analyzed it briefly in his study of the transmission of mystical secrets in Judaism. See *On the Kabbalah and Its Symbolism*, translated from the German by Karl Manheim, New York: Schocken 1965, p. 132. I published the Hebrew text in *The Esoteric Theology of the Ashkenazi Hasidim*, Jerusalem: The Bialik Institute 1968, pp. 115–121.

the signifier and the signified. Language is not a means by which God is achieved, because it is God Himself. To the best of my knowledge, such a union of a linguistic element and the essence of the supreme divinity cannot be found elsewhere in Western culture, though some close parallels may be pointed out in Islam and in Eastern mysticism.

The concept of language in ancient Hinduism is essentially similar to that of Judaism: Language, the Word, is the embodiment of divine power of creation, not of communication. The divine power Vâc, which is both a God and the Word, is credited in the *rgveda* as the power of creation.[29] The concept of *tantra*, the holy syllable OM, and many other examples convey the same semiotic attitude and the negation of the semantic level of language as the Hebrew mystical use of the tetragrammaton. This is not the result of any Hindu influence on medieval kabbalah, as some would like to think. This is an expression of the basic diversion between the two irreconcilable concepts of language: the semantic, communicative one, according to which language is a human phenomenon and communication is its essence; and the opposing one, that of the divine language, according to which language is a divine phenomenon of inexhaustible meaning on every semiotic level. The tantric attitude is a vigorous demonstration of the infinity of meaning and power within a word or a syllable, which could not be accepted by cultures based on the Greek, Hellenistic, and Latin concepts of the humanity of language.

This is only one direction in the interpretation and use of the holy name, exemplified forcefully by Rabbi Eleazar's *Sefer ha-Shem*. The opposite direction in Jewish mysticism is also apparent—the process of differentiation, of discovering within the name the various aspects of which the Godhead, and ultimately the whole universe with its infinite number of phenomena, is composed. The theological basis is one and the same: the comprehensiveness of the name, its inclusion within it of all divine and earthly existence. It is a matter

---

[29]Andre Padoux, *Vac: The Concept of the Word in Selected Hindu Tantras*, Albany, NY: SUNY Press 1990.

of emphasis, whether the mystic concentrates on seeing within the name of totality and unity of everything, or whether he dedicates himself to deciphering how all the multiple aspects of the divine are found within the name. Most mystics, and almost all kabbalists, dedicated themselves to the second task.

The origin of this approach precedes mysticism, and is found in talmudic and midrashic literature. The source is found in a hermeneutical question: If God is one, and His name is one, why is it that scriptures use different names for Him? The problem was usually discussed within the framework of the creation story, and was intertwined with the other uncomfortable elements in that biblical narrative that could cast some doubt on the unity of God. The talmudic explanation of the use of the names YHVH and Elohim in the creation story did indeed divide the divine realm into two aspects: The name YHVH indicates God's mercy, whereas the name Elohim indicates the aspect of judgment and severity.[30] This rabbinic distinction does not imply a division within the Godhead.[31] It is a metaphor, denoting two aspects of divine providence for the world. In the same way that when God judges the world He "sits on a throne of justice" while at other times He "sits on a throne of mercy," He metaphorically bears different names when he conducts the universe in these two manners.

An example of the transformation of this concept by medieval mystics is found in the opening section of the treatise *Sod ha-Sodot* by Rabbi Elhanan ben Yakar of London, written about 1225.[32]

---

[30]See E. E. Urbach, *The Sages—Their Concepts and Beliefs*, vol. I, Jerusalem: Magnes Press 1975, pp. 37–40 et passim.

[31]Some recent attempts to see in this explanation an element of a mythical concept of the Godhead in talmudic tradition seem to me to be completely detached from the rabbinic context. See, for instance, Y. Liebes, *Studies in Myth and Messianism*, Albany, NY: SUNY Press 1992, pp. 7–61.

[32]This important theological treatise has not been printed. It is found in two manuscripts at the Jewish Theological Seminary in New York (I published a provisional copy at Academon, Jerusalem 1977, in a collection of Ashkenazi Hasidic esoteric texts). Concerning Rabbi Elhanan and his works, see J. Dan, *The Circle of the Unique Cherub: A Jewish Mystical Group in Medieval Germany*, Tübingen: J.C.B. Mohr (Siebeck), in press. One of Rabbi Elhanan's sources may

According to Rabbi Elhanan, who quotes and develops the rabbinic distinction between mercy and justice concerning the two names of God present in the creation narrative, Elohim is also the name indicating the creative power of God, the eternal Godhead in His capacity as Creator; the name YHVH indicates a secondary divine power, which is more in the nature of an emanated, rather than an eternal, divine entity. The process of creation, according to Rabbi Elhanan, is also the process of the evolvement of YHVH from Elohim; and the Sabbath, which represents the completion of the creation process, is also the celebration of the renewed unity between the supreme Godhead, Elohim, and the emanated divine power YHVH. They come together, he says, like body and soul, and, like them, are inseparable.[33] YHVH is described as identical with the *kavod*, the divine glory, which is the power responsible for divine presence within the universe, of miracles, and for contact between God and man in prayers and in prophetic visions.

The rabbinic metaphor concerning the modes of divine providence has been transformed into a meaningful division within the divine world and the emergence of a pleromatic concept of that realm. The different names indicate different essences, which have divergent positions concerning time, the universe, and man. Elohim is eternal, YHVH is emanated in time; Elohim is the Creator, YHVH functions within the created universe; Elohim is transcendent and present as a "soul" within everything, YHVH communicates with man as an individual, separate entity.[34] The unity between God and His name has been transformed into a number of names expressing the various aspects of the divine pleroma.

The history of mystical speculations in Judaism in the Middle

---

have been the now-lost treatise *Raza Raba*, one of the esoteric works of the early Middle Ages that seems to have reached this circle, and which included discussions of the holy name.

[33]He uses an unusual Hebrew verb, נתאוממו, to express this unity: They "became twins," a term that brings to mind the gnostic use of the Greek term σψξψγψ.

[34]The concept of Elohim as the supreme divine power is derived from the terminology of the *Sefer Yezira*, which viewed the "Spirit of the Living God" (Elohim) of Genesis 1:2 as the first and supreme power.

Ages and early modern times is, to a very large extent, the history of the definitions of the nature of the divine pleroma and the inter-relationship between the various divine names, which have become symbols of the pleromatic powers. The *Bahir*, the earliest work of the kabbalah, is the clearest expression of this attitude, and it in-cludes the most detailed division of divine names and their powers before the kabbalah became established.

It seems that the earliest discussion of the nature of the name of God in a language other than Hebrew is found in the works of Philo of Alexandria. Philo was the first theologian known to us to be confronted with the paradox of dealing with questions concern-ing sanctity in linguistic terms without accepting the dominance of the Hebrew language, in practice if not in principle. A few years af-ter his time, Philo was joined by many other theologians, when the early Christian writers began to interpret the Hebrew scriptures in Greek.[35] Philo followed Plato in his mistrust of spoken language,[36] and preferred the intrinsic, purely spiritual language of the mind, unpronounced and therefore undifferentiated into specific languages. When describing the naming of the animals of Adam, Philo does not elucidate the divine nature of language or the essential connec-tion between a being and its name. He insists, in apparent contro-versy with Epicurus and Lucretius, that Adam's names must have been the most successful, because of his superior wisdom and be-cause of his ability to transmit his wisdom to all humanity, being the father of all. Philo does not indicate that the process of naming involved anything superhuman or divine; it can be described as a

----

[35]Another example is that of Josephus Flavius, who rendered into Greek many Jewish concepts, yet it seems that the more abstract problems of the nature of language and the difference between Hebrew and Greek were not paramount in his thought.
[36]See David Winston, *Aspects of Philo's Linguistic Theory*, The Studia Philonica Annual, vol. III (Festschrift Earle Hilgert), (ed. David T. Runia, Atlanta, GA: Scholars Press 1991, pp. 109–125; compare also: L. L. Grabbe, *Etymology in Early Jewish Interpretation: The Hebrew Names in Philo*, Brown Judaic Series 115 (At-lanta, GA 1988); C. W. Chilton, "The Epicurean Theory of the Origin of Lan-guage: A Study of Diogenes of Oenoanda, Fragments X and XI, *American Jour-nal of Philosophy* 13 (1962), pp. 159–167.

supreme achievement of human wisdom rather than as an expression of a truth beyond man. He insists, however, that Adam could not name himself; naming others does not enable one to understand himself so well as to be able to properly give oneself the correct appellation. This passage seems to touch upon the nature of the name of God: Man, Philo concludes, cannot name anything that he cannot understand; the name of God, therefore, cannot be conceived by man.

III

The distancing of language from the semantic level in the mystical concept of the divine name can be clearly demonstrated by the process in which mystics selected the names to which they attributed the most supreme, secret significance. The name YHVH, which has the least meaning among the biblical names of God, became the most significant name in Jewish esotericism and mysticism. Its designation as the "tetragrammaton" [37] in both Hebrew and Greek indicates the absence of meaning: It can be described only by its external structure, because no synonym for it exists and no semantic definition or description is possible. A more detailed example of this process can be found in thirteenth century kabbalah, concerning the biblical term *amen*.

The absence of a semantic level for this word is evident in the fact that, despite its place in biblical poetry, it could not be translated, and has been included in the Christian scriptures in its Hebrew form (like *halleluja* and a handful of similar terms). In the early kabbalah, this term acquired a unique position as the embodiment of the characteristics of the divine world as a whole. T. Rabbi Azriel of Gerona, in the early thirteenth century, presented this concept in the strongest terms. In his commentary on the talmudic traditions,

---

[37]The Greek term "tetragrammaton" has been used in Hebrew works, mainly as an appellation of celestial and divine powers, like Totrosiai in *Hechalot Rabbati*, and probably the name Metatron, one of the most important powers in ancient and medieval Jewish speculations concerning the divine world, also includes like word "tetra." See J. Dan, *Ancient Jewish Mysticism*, p. 82.

he included a detailed discussion of the talmudic statement that the person answering *amen* after a blessing is greater than the one saying the blessing itself.[38] This paradoxical formulation is explained by the kabbalist as the result of the fact that the letters AMN include in them all the secret names of the emanated divine powers, which do have—at least partially—some meaning, like the terms for "faith" אמונה and "trust" אומן, which refer, according to him, to specific *sefirot*.[39] The hidden divine source is beyond any linguistic meaning; it is just a root, two syllables that do not combine to convey any communicative message. As the divine powers evolve and descend toward the created cosmos, they acquire some elements of specific meaning, as they assume individual characteristics and specific divine functions. The ladder leading from earthly existence to the hidden realms of the divine mystical truth is a ladder leading away from meaning, from semantics to semiotics. The sign is becoming The Sign.[40]

---

[38]גדול העונה אמן יותר מן המברך, Bavli *Berachot* 57b (and compare the end of Bavli *Nazir*).

[39]The text was published by Isaiah Tishby, Jerusalem: Magnes Press 1945 (2nd ed. 1984.) It seems that it was edited into an anonymous tradition attributed to a legendary figure, "Rabbi Yekutiel," at the end of the thirteenth century or the beginning of the fourteenth See J. Dan, "The Worms Epistle and the Problem of Pseudepigraphy in the Early Kabbalah," in J. Dan and J. Hacker (eds.), *Studies in Kabbalah and Ethical Literature in Honor of Isaiah Tishby*, Jerusalem: Magnes Press 1987, pp. 111–138.

[40]This can be compared to the process that transformed the Hebrew name "Jerusalem" into an abstract designation of supreme spirituality in Christianity. The earthly Jerusalem became, in Christian spirituality, a reference to a hidden, unattainable source of divine benevolence. One of the most meaningful levels of the historical controversy within Christianity concerning the Crusades was the clash between the physical and the spiritual significance of this name. Those who viewed it as a purely spiritual term saw no meaning in the actual presence of a Christian kingdom in the earthly place called by that name, while their opponents believed that the acquisition of the earthly Jerusalem brought them closer to the spiritual goal expressed by this term. In Judaism, "Jerusalem" retained its physical designation until the late eighteenth century, when some Hasidic writers began to use it in an abstract, spiritual manner. See, concerning the whole subject, Paula Frederiksen and Joseph Dan, "Jerusalem in Jewish, Christian and Moslem Spirituality," in *City of the Great King: Jerusalem from David to the Present*, ed. Nitya Rosorsky, Cambridge, MA: Harvard University Press 1996, pp. 60–97.

This phenomenon can be exemplified by many characteristics of the use of names in mysticism. Kabbalists and esoterics seemed even to prefer the name MZPZ to YHVH, a name reached by the transmutation of the tetragrammaton by the system of ETBS.[41] The more mysterious nature of this unpronounceable "word" is more satisfying for the mystic who tries to designate the enormous distance between semantic and mystical, metalinguistics and truth. The tendency to create *nomina barbara* is expressed even in the explication of the names of the most supreme realms of the Godhead. The concept of the letters of the alphabet in the *Sefer ha-Temunah* is another example of the rejection of the semantic element in language.[42]

There is an element of similarity between this process in mystical speculations concerning the name of God, and the attitude toward secret names in the various magical traditions. The common characteristics should not hide the vast differences between the two phenomena. In mysticism, as in magic, the name is the essence of an entity and the expression of its power. Both see language as semiotic rather than semantic, and tend to emphasize the mysterious, meaningless names of the powers they address. The difference, however, is that magic creates a language, while mysticism denies it. For the magician, the secret name of a celestial power, the source of its essence and power, is accurate and meaningful. The correct, careful use of this name necessarily results in the achievement of specific, often material, goals. Precision of expression is indispensable for the magician: In order for the formula to work, it must be said (and, sometimes, physical actions also must take place) and performed exactly as instructed. In this sense, the magician is the creator of a system of signs (not symbols) that congregate to create a language

Concerning Jerusalem in Hasidic thought, see Rivka Shatz, *Hasidism as Mysticism*, Princeton, NJ: Princeton University Press 1992.
[41]This is the simplest among the methodologies of *temurah*, in which the first letter of the alphabet is submitted for by the last, the second by the one before the last, and so on.
[42]Concerning this work, see G. Scholem, *The Origins of the Kabbalah*, ed. R. J. Zwi Werblowsky, Princeton, NJ: Princeton University Press 1986, pp. 460–463.

that is used in strictly constructed structures (the "grammar" of magic.)[43] The language of magic cannot tolerate ambiguity of any sort. If the formula is not expressed precisely, it is a meaningless heap of syllables. When correctly employed in a magical procedure, the most bizarre name is nothing but an accurate designation of "the power that governs this realm," which is ordered to perform the requested action. The insistent efforts of magicians to distance their language from common, everyday language is the substitution of an accurate set of semantic signifiers for the inaccurate, ambiguous meanings of communicative language—very much like the use of formulas and signs by scientists to replace the inaccuracy of words.

The mystic, on the other hand, does not deny a particular set of semantic signs. He rejects the very idea that anything linguistic, including magical as well as mathematical formulas, can express divine truth. The infinity of wisdom and knowledge in the divine realm cannot be expressed by any linguistic system. The concepts of truth and accuracy are mutually exclusive: Either you say something precise, or you say something that is true; you cannot do both. In order to approach truth, one has to forsake communicative meanings completely, and use words—if at all—as imprecise, ambiguous, vague symbols.

It seems that the confusion between mysticism and magic in their use of language, especially divine names and *nomina barbara*, contributed more than anything else to the misunderstanding of the role of language in mysticism. Once we disassociate "mysticism" from its common usage as anything supernatural, miraculous, or intensely religious, or even the unknown in general, and accept the specific meaning of the term as designated by the mystics themselves, the separation between magic and mysticism becomes evident. Mystical

---

[43]This is not unlike the system by which mathematics is expressed, when only the precise use of accurately defined signs can produce the desired result. It is very difficult for the modern scholar to overcome prejudices and view magic as it is—a precise science, rather than a vague, confused assemblage of elements resulting from superstition and the belief in the supernatural. Yet it should be recognized that nowhere else in human disciplines did the semantic level of language acquire such complete dominance.

language represents the rejection of magical language together with any other language of communication, replacing them with semiotic signs representing the unknown and the metalinguistic in an imprecise, nonsemantic manner.

The Language of the Mystics in Medieval Germany

I

The emergence of Jewish esoteric and mystical speculation in medieval Germany, especially in the Rhineland, in the middle of the twelfth century signifies a turning point in the history of the Hebrew language. The authors of the treatises written at that time and in the following century had, in many cases, to develop their own language and linguistic norms, having no precedent in the history of Jewish thought for expressing the contents that they wished to present.[1] In many respects, the pietist-mystical circles of that time,

---

[1]The main two avenues of Hebrew expression in the early centuries of the Middle Ages were the tradition of halachic discussion, which developed uninterrupted since talmudic times (with a brief interlude in the tenth and eleventh centuries, when many halachic works were written in Arabic by the Babylonian gaonim), and the homiletical-aggadic, which also continued structures developed in Late Antiquity. These were joined, in a somewhat later development, by the poetical language of the *piyyut*. Theological discourse in Hebrew began mainly in the twelfth century in Spain, under the influence of Arabic and Judeo-Arabic philosophy. In Germany we do not find writings of this nature until the middle of

known as the Ashkenazi Hasidim, were revolutionaries in their attitude toward language more than in any other aspect of their creativity. Some outlines of this revolution will be discussed in the following presentation, serving as a beginning of the study of this subject, in the framework of a more general investigation of the mystical language of the Jewish spiritualists throughout the ages.

It should be stated from the very beginning of this discussion that the analysis we present would have been completely unintelligible to the medieval scholars and writers who participated in this process, for the simple reason that they had neither the concept nor a word for "mysticism," and therefore the subject of "mystical language" would have been extremely mysterious, if not mystical, in their eyes. Mysticism developed in Judaism without any consciousness on the part of its creators as to its meaning and nature. Hebrew, like Arabic, does not have a word equivalent even partially to the Latin-Christian term of "mysticism." Any identification of a certain Jewish religious phenomenon as "mystical" is a modern scholarly decision that relies on the modern scholar's understanding of the term; there is no intrinsic demand in the texts themselves for such a usage. An arbitrary element is always combined, therefore, with any discussion of "Jewish mysticism": The very existence of such a subject is the result of applying terminology and a concept that developed outside Jewish culture into the realm of Jewish phenomena.

The concept of "mysticism" was absent from the world view of the thinkers and writers in Jewish culture in the Middle Ages, but the concept of "language" was very well known to them; yet, their basic attitude toward language was so different from our modern concepts of this subject that the gulf separating them from us is even greater than that concerning the concept of "mysticism." In order to

the twelfth century; the Ashkenazi writers had no example to follow, and, so it seems, they did not seek one. The style and structure of their works is highly original, both in the esoteric, theological, and mystical works and in their ethical writings, like the *Sefer Hasidim*. See, concerning this, C. Rabin, "The Tense and Mood System of the Hebrew Sefer Hasidim," *Papers of the Fourth World Congress of Jewish Studies*, II (Jerusalem 1968), pp. 113–116, and the Ph.D. thesis on the language of *Sefer Hasidim* by Simha Kogut, The Hebrew University, Jerusalem 1966.

make an attempt to understand their use of language, it is necessary to forsake our modern notions and to adapt ourselves to the one governing the thoughts of the medieval writers we are studying.

The attempt to understand the meaning of human language, especially the relationship between a linguistic expression and the reality represented by it (if any, according to some) has been, in the last three generations, one of the most central and important subjects of modern investigation—in philosophy, literary criticism, psychology, and, of course, linguistics.[2] One may even say that this problem united these four fields of scholarship into an inherently unified one. The problem of language often was recast as the problem of a text and its relationship to an existence outside it. The study of language and the study of text can be described as the paramount concern of many modern schools of thought, not the least among them being the now-notorious Deconstruction.[3]

Yet all modern approaches to the problem of language are based on one fundamental assumption: Language is the expression of the human wish to communicate, and it evolved together with the evolvement of the human race and its culture.[4] Following some Greek ideas, language can be regarded, sometimes, as the element defining hu-

---

[2]No attempt should be made here to describe this vast and variegated field of inquiry, to which hundreds of scholars in dozens of schools and directions had contributed and continued to do. The basic questions in a contemporary manner were presented by several schools of linguists and philosophers in France, Germany, England, and the United States; their works are regarded still as relevant in their positioning of the enigma of the relationship between the sign and the signifier. See, especially, the studies collected by C. A. Raschke in *Deconstruction and Theology*, New York: Crossroads, 1982; and compare M. C. Taylor, *De-constructing Theology*, New York: Crossroads and Scholars Press 1982.

[3]Attempts have been going on for nearly a generation to find a way to employ Derrida's methodology, developed mainly for the purpose of the study of literature and philosophy, in the field of religion and theology.

[4]The most famous school in this field, that of Noam Chomsky, presented the most detailed hypothesis concerning the relationship between the development of humanity as a species and the development of language; this thesis was the catalyst of intense linguistic, anthropological, and philosophical study in the last three decades. However, as far as I can see, the possibility of a superhuman origin of language, which will connect these studies with the understanding of scriptural religions, has not been explored.

man beings. The concept of language in Judaism in general, and in
Jewish mysticism and esotericism in particular, is completely different: First and foremost, language is not a human phenomenon.

Jewish tradition states this emphatically and clearly: Before the
creation of the world, God occupied Himself by tying adorning
crowns to the letters of the alphabet.[5] Not only language, but also
the text, existed before the creation; the Torah came into being long
before anything else, cosmos or man, ever existed.[6] Language and
text had their independent, autonomous existence within the divine
world before any kind of human communication could be conceived.
They had—and have had ever since—a meaning unrelated to human
needs. The great discovery of some modern philosophers—the independence of the text and the irrelevance of its context—was made
by the talmudic sages a millennium and a half ago. Language is not
an attempt to describe existing things; rather, existing things are the
unfolding of powers that lie within language.

When language evolved into a means of communication, it did
so in a completely different manner than is conceived in the concepts of language as a human tool. It was language that served God
as the tool of creation. God pronounced the words—or the text—
"Let there be light" and "There was light." There is no mistake, no
place for hesitation, as to which came first, language or reality, or
concerning the nature of the relationship between language and the
subject to which it is related. Language is the source; reality is the
outcome. God's pronouncing of several words, collected in the first
chapter of Genesis, brought forth all existence. Reality is language-
dependent, and it derives its ontology from a force intrinsic to language, a force put into it by God millennia before the actual process of creation. The talmudic sages put this idea into the formula,
that God was looking at the Torah when He created the world;[7]

---

[5]*Hayah kosher ketarim la-'otiyat,* Bavli Menachot 29b, in the description of Moses'
vision.
[6]See *Bereshit Rabba* 1:4 (p. 6, Theodor-Albeck ed.), and compare *Sifrey, Ekev* 37.
[7]*Hayah mistakel ba-torah uvore et ha'olam, Bereshit Rabba* 1:1 (p. 2) and many
parallels listed there by Theodor, and compare especially *Avot de-Rabbi Nathan*
version I, Ch. 31.

that is, the text served as a blueprint for the emergent reality. When God sought an abode within the created world, He instructed the people of Israel to create for Him a tabernacle in the desert. The Talmud explains how this was done: Bezalel, entrusted with the project, "was knowledgeable concerning the letters by which the world was created."[8] The tabernacle was a small replica of the cosmos, and, in order to build it, the secret of creation—the letters of the alphabet—had to be known. The same blueprint was used by Solomon in the building of the Temple in Jerusalem. This concept of the creation was summarized, in a homiletical manner, in one sentence in the Mishnah, *Avot* Ch. 5: "The world was created by ten utterances";[9] ten sentences, a brief text, spoken by God, brought forth all existence.

This basic concept, common to the Bible[10] and the Talmud alike, did not serve as a central element in Jewish religious life during the biblical period. At that time, God was ever-present—to the patriarchs, in the Temple, in the revelation to the people of Israel, to the judges, to the prophets—and constantly gave direct answers to changing needs. This period is described as one in which a direct approach of God to man and of man to God was possible. The central biblical figures are those to whom God spoke, or those who were used by God to address the world. The Bible is a record of the many revelations to individuals and groups, directing their religious life. In this period, therefore, the text did not have a paramount meaning and importance; past revelations paled before God's constant presence and availability.

A radical change in this situation occurred when Judaism adopted the notion that the era of prophecy had ended, early in the history of the Second Temple.[11] From then on, God did not have

---

[8]*Yodea hayah bezalel le-zaref otiyot she-nivre'u bahen shamayim wa-arez*, see Bavli Berachot 55b.

[9]*Be-asarah ma'amarot nivra ha-olam*, Mishnah *Avot* 5:1.

[10]*Bi-devar H'shamayim ne'esu uve-ruah piw kol zeva'am* (Psalms 33:6), and compare *Bereshit Rabba* 4:6 (p. 30).

[11]Concerning this, see especially E. E. Urbach, "Halahkah and Prophecy," *Tarbiz* 18 (1947), pp. 1-27.

a constant presence, living within the people of Israel, guiding and directing them at every stage of history. The only means of knowing God's wishes became the record of the old revelations, the text, the Torah, the scriptures, cast in language. To reach God, one has to study and interpret the old texts and discern from them directions concerning present needs. A revelation originally intended for a specific need at a specific historical juncture became eternal truth, capable of instructing countless generations, if properly exegeted. Exegesis thus became the substitute of revelation; text has become the eternal fountain of divine truth.

At first, this transition from revelation to text was not universally accepted within Judaism. The phenomenon of pseudepigraphic literature demonstrates the adherence of segments of Judaism to the need for constant, direct divine messages. As these could not be contemporary, because of the absence of prophecy in the present, new revelations were ascribed to old biblical figures like Abraham, Isaiah, Ezra, Adam, Enoch—signifying that inspired people could not present their message as directly coming from God, but had to hide behind the curtain of pseudepigraphy, submerging their own individuality and pretending to present divine revelations given long ago to "legitimate" carriers of such messages.[12]

Another result of the absence of prophecy—this one becoming a constant element in Jewish culture—was the claim that ancient divine revelation was not wholly incorporated in the scriptures; parts of it had been transmitted by God orally, and have been preserved as an oral tradition, passing by word of mouth from generation to generation.[13] The concept of the oral law was added to the written law, thus enlarging the body of scriptures, and making the Mishnah—

---

[12]See P. Schäfer, *Synopse zur Hekhalot Literatur*, Tubingen: J.C.B. Mohr (Paul Siebeck) 1981, par. 16, 59; compare the edition of the Hebrew apocalypse of Enoch by Philip Alexander, ed., in *The Old Testament Pseudepigraphia*, vol. I, ed. J. H. Charlesworth, Garden City, NY: Doubleday 1983.

[13]The development of the concept of the Oral Law has been described in detail by E. E. Urbach, *Hazal*, Jerusalem: Magnes Press, pp. 270–278 et passim.

the most important direct presentation of that oral tradition—an integral part of scriptures. The Mishnah thus became a text, to be regarded as encompassing eternal truth, subject to hermeneutical exegesis like the written law itself.

These developments, mainly occurring during the period of the Second Temple and in the first generations after its destruction, marked the increasing centrality of the concepts of text and language in Jewish religious culture. Similar developments occurred in early Christianity: In the first period of its appearance, Christianity represented a direct, revolutionary revelation of God. This, however, was quickly followed by the appearance of scriptures, and, besides it, a body of pseudepigraphic literature and the concept of an oral tradition preserved in the structure of the Church. Soon enough, Christianity came to rely on exegesis of ancient revelation as much as Judaism did, and even the Pope's dicta were supported by exegetical reliance on the old texts.

One peculiar aspect of the emergence of early Christianity was the fact that some of the creators of Christian scriptures did not rely on the living word of God alone, but felt the necessity to couple it with an exegetical reliance on the old revelations as well. The gospel of St. Matthew is the clearest example: Witnessing and testifying to the employs of Christ and presenting his message was not enough for Matthew; he had to show that everything that Christ said and did had its roots in the ancient revelations to Isaiah, Michah, Hosea, and the other Old Testament prophets. The veracity and sanctity of the Christian truth had to be proved not only by the direct appearance of divine presence, but also by proving that it conformed to, and, indeed, revealed the true meaning of, older revelations.[14] This aspect of exegesis became more and more central and dominant in

---

[14]Christianity differed, however, from Judaism in its treatment of the sacred text because of the specific historical circumstances that brought it to sanctify the divine language in translation, in languages that had vast treasures of human creativity cast in them, namely Greek and Latin. I discussed in detail the meaning of this difference in my book *The Mystical Language*.

the development of Christianity; the very concept of the Christian
scriptures, including the Old and New Testament, signifies this unification of new revelation and the new interpretation of the old one.
Those early Christians who refused to accept this unification—
namely, the gnostics[15]—were regarded as heretics and were cast out
of the structure of the young Church.

II

The most important aspect of the concept of a divine language,
encompassing eternal truth, is the infinity of meaning of language.
As long as language is regarded as a human, communicative tool, it
is bound by human abilities in its ranges of meanings. Language
cannot go further than human senses, human emotions, human
intellect. There must be, in one way or another, a human counterpart to every aspect revealed or denoted by language. But if language
is a divine expression, it must represent the infinity of God. As God's
truth is inexhaustible, so is the meaning of language.

The very concept of the components of language is radically
different when it is conceived as a divine attribute. When language
is a human communicative means, it must be directed toward one
goal only: communicating meaning. In order to communicate, meaning should be as clear, precise, and unambiguous as possible. All
the components of which language is constructed—the various
sounds, the letters, their shape, their sequence—are all directed toward conveying meaning. But when language is a divine attribute,
how can man declare some aspects of language more important, more
meaningful than others? If language was revealed by God, first and
foremost, not as a tool of communication but as a tool of creation,
the whole level of meaning cannot be the central one to its essence.

---

[15]The attitude of the gnostics toward scriptures has been studied by several scholars; see, for instance, the editor's detailed notes to the gnostic texts in Bentley
Layton, *The Gnostic Scriptures, A New Translation with Annotations and Introductions*, Garden City, NY: Doubleday 1987.

From the point of view of meaning, for instance, the form of the letters of the alphabet is immaterial; knowledge can be transmitted using any kind of letters—Hebrew, Greek, Latin, Chinese signs or Sumerian cuneiform or ancient Egyptian hieroglyphs. The sounds are also unimportant; the same message can be transmitted whether a table is called *tisch* or *shulhan*. In a divine language, however, nothing can be accidental. Divine truth is conveyed by every aspect of the language—all levels and inflections of sound, shapes of letters, number of letters, and many others to be discussed below.

A language that is used by people for communication purposes does not have to be universal. The Etruscans are entitled to their own language, as are the Japanese. But if language is divine, there can be only one language, the true divine one, as there is only one true and universal God. Other languages, the book of Genesis take pains to demonstrate, are the result of human impertinence and heresy, and the resulting confusion sent by God to prevent the human enterprise of the Tower of Babylon. No Jew throughout history, and almost no Christian,[16] ever doubted that the original, divine language was Hebrew. God created the universe by saying *yehi or*, not by saying "Let there be light." These two statements differ in their sound, shape, length, etc., and only the former can achieve any creative purpose.

Another biblical demonstration of the uniqueness of the divine language is the episode in which Adam names the animals. Later interpretations, which do not diverge meaningfully from the literal text, clearly indicate that the animals had their names from the very beginning, Adam merely recognizing them and pronouncing them.[17] Indeed, the names preceded the actual existence of the animals and

---

[16]The exception is anyone who joins the father in Alabama who stated at a PTA meeting considering the study of a foreign language at school: "If English was good enough for Jesus Christ, it is good enough for me."

[17]Compare the analysis of this episode by Walter Benjamin, "Über Sprache überhaupt und über die Sprache des Menschen," in *Gesammelte Schriften*, ed. R. Tiedemann and H. Schweppenhäuser, Frankfurt a/M 1972, pp. 143-156, who was probably informed about the midrashic treatments of the subject.

are their source of being; Adam understood this and demonstrated his wisdom in front of the angels, but the names themselves were independent of him and of his knowledge.

If Hebrew is the divine language, used by God for creative, communicative, and other purposes (like amusing Himself by adorning them before the creation), then all aspects of the Hebrew language are a part of the divine infinite truth. Hebrew does not have the concept of vowels as Latin languages do, so there are special markings for the sounds, the nekudot. In a communicative language, these marks are relatively unimportant: They assist children when learning to read, but are forgotten when a better knowledge of language is acquired. But if the language is divine, there can be no reason to regard these marks as secondary in any way, and they are an integral, equal part of the means by which divine truth may be discerned within language. In a similar way, the musical signs, the teamim, which denote the melody by which the Torah portions and their accompanying haftarot are to be read in the synagogue, are a part of language equal to any other; the divine message can be found in them like in any other aspect of language. These three elements—the letters, the vowel signs, and the melody signs—all have specific shapes and forms, which cannot be accidental; they were designed by God together with the totality of the linguistic enterprise. A word may derive its meaning from the combination of all these elements. As Hebrew is the only language, at least the only divine one, the shapes of its letters and other signs are intrinsic to it, being a part of its semiotic message. The fact that the sh has three heads and the segol three dots are principal aspects of the language of God.

To these aspects one has to add another, central one in Jewish tradition—the crowns, tagin, adorning the letters. This element, postulated as ancient by talmudic tradition, has been employed by many mystics and nonmystics in their analysis of the divine messages. One of the earliest systematic users was the anonymous (third-century?) author of the Sefer Yezira, who described the process by which God adorned the letters with these crowns as the mystical transition that enabled the letters to become a creative power; the "crowning" of each letter gave it the power and dominance concerning the aspect of creation to which it is responsible.[18]

Another aspect of the divine character of language is the numerical one, often mistakenly understood as "mystical." Hebrew, like Latin, Greek, and other ancient languages, did not have a specific system of signs denoting numbers; only in the last two centuries did Hebrew writers adopt the current numerical signs, which were brought to Europe by the Arabs in the Middle Ages. Before this separation, letters were used to denote numbers, as they did in Greek and Latin. This meant that every Hebrew letter had a numerical meaning, a simple, technical fact carrying no more mystical significance than the use of X for ten in Latin. But if language is divine, the fact that a certain letter denotes a certain number, or that a certain word has a certain numerical value, becomes a part of the divine design of language, and carries a meaning as important as any other segment of language. The analysis of the numerical meaning of letters, words, and sentences is therefore equal to the analysis of shapes of letters or the crowns adorning them.

A more complicated result of the concept of language as divine is the implication concerning the order of the letters of the alphabet within words and sentences. When God selected a certain order of letters in the Torah to convey His message, that order is reflected not only in the sequence of letters combined into words that represent the literal meaning of the message. The fact that He chose a certain letter to begin the whole Torah and another to end it is, of course, meaningful; but this is also true about the beginning of every verse and every word, or the last letter of every verse and every word. Thus, acronyms, creating words from the first letters of a sequence of words, or from the last letters, or from letters in the middle,

---

[18]The author of the *Sefer Yezira* used the literal meaning of *tagin* as crowns to denote not only grandeur and adornment, but also power, mastery, and government. According to him, when God "crowned" a letter, it also gave it dominion on some aspect of creation and existence. The process of "crowning" is thus conceived as one in which the mystical power of creation was inserted into the letters, enabling them to bring forth, and then to nurture and sustain, the various realms of worldly and human existence.

are part of the divine message as much as the ordinary arrangement of the letters. "The signature of God is truth," says the Midrash, following the last three letters of the last three words in the description of the creation in Genesis that combine into the Hebrew term for "truth." [19]

Once the placing of letters becomes a subject for the analysis of the divine message incorporated in language, the number of possibilities increases tremendously. It cannot be an accident that twenty-one letters are used to convey the Ten Commandments and that one, t, is absent. The number of times a certain letter appears in a certain section of the Bible becomes meaningful, as well as the absence of a letter, or even the final form of one of the letters mnzpk. The Ashkenazi Hasidim wrote complete treatise on such subjects.

All these examples refer to the pictures of letters, words, and verses as they are presented in the scriptures, and this alone opens, as we have seen, infinite possibilities of interpretation, never to be exhausted. Yet, all these methods take the picture of scriptures as a frozen one—still photographs, to use a modern metaphor. The situation becomes much more complicated once a dynamic element is introduced, the most potent instrument of the interpreter of a sacred text in a divine language: the concept of the transformation of one letter to another, one word to another—temurah.

This concept, found already in the Bible,[20] is based on another aspect of the sanctity of language: the sanctity of the order of the twenty-two letters of the alphabet. The sequence of letters is an inherent, unchangeable characteristic; every letter has its place in the

---

[19]Bavli Shabbat 55a; Yoma 69b; Sanhedrin 64a. The talmudic sources do not give the obvious reason, which is found in later statements.

[20]See below, bbl-shshk; it seems that the concept of notarikon, in its minimal fashion of writing a poem beginning with the letters of the alphabet in sequence, thus denoting the intrinsic meaningfulness of the order of the letters, is also biblical (psalm 119, etc.). Concerning the numerical value, interestingly enough it is not apparent in the Old Testament, but is present in the New Testament, the famous number of the beast of the Apocalypse, which is a gematria on the Hebrew value of nrwn qsr, neron qesar = 666.

order that reflects its being no less than its shape or sound. *Alef* is meaningfully the first, as *bet* is the second and *tav* the last (it should be noted that the basic order was preserved in most of the alphabet systems that evolved from the Phoenician; the letters *yklmn* are found in the same order in every language—witness *JKLMN*, and, of course, the first ones). This order is therefore divine, and contains divine meaning. But, if so, the letters may be moved one step, or two, or eleven, or twenty-one, and find their equal in another column; that is, one can use the fixed order to substitute another letter for one as long as one retains the correct order. For instance, one can write consistently *tav* instead of *alef*, *bet* instead of *shin*, *gimel* instead of *resh*, and so on, or the reverse, and receive the name of the kingdom of Babylonia, *bbl*, as *shshk*, which was done in the Bible. One can move just one notch, and write *bet* instead of *alef*, *gimel* instead of *bet* (or vice versa), or any other change based on the sequence. In fact, this is very similar to coding made out of numbers, when individual numbers, or groups of them, are substituted systematically for others. It can be done with numbers; because their sequence is both fixed and meaningful, it is no accident that nine follows eight, and therefore the sequence can be tampered with because the fixed order gives it a backbone to return to. *Temurah* thus enables the Hebrew interpreter, assisted by the ancient examples, to substitute any letter for any other, and therefore every word or sentence for every other. Paradoxically, because of the divine nature of language, man has acquired complete mastery of its meanings, and anything he does with these letters reflects divine truth.

Midrashic interpretation, which in classical Judaism, in the talmudic period, utilized only a small fraction of these possibilities, still included all the principles, enabling the medieval homilist and exegete to reach the fullness of the employment of these enormous possibilities. Language, in this sense, contains the *imago Dei* no less than the human form does. And as the human form has infinite variations, contradicting meanings and deeds—although all of them are, in one way or another, a reflection of the divine—so does language: Every aspect of it can be presented and analyzed in infinite ways, retaining within it the kernel of divine truth in all its count-

less metamorphoses. This, it should be emphasized again, has nothing to do with mysticism. It is the nature and the essence of a scriptural religion faced with its own sacred texts in their original, pre-
human and precosmic language.[21]

It should be noted here that the most important Jewish investigation of religious language in antiquity (and probably, in all of
the history of Jewish thought), the Book of Creation (*Sefer Yezira*),
did not utilize most of these possibilities when presenting a system
of scientific thought describing the emergence of the cosmos from
God, using the letters as instruments. The author of this book did
not use one *gematria*, one acronym, or any other of the numerous
possibilities listed above. He did use, in a most central manner, the
temurah, but only one aspect of it—changing the order of letters in
the word to acquire another, but without following the system of
the sequence of the letters "*ng to ng*," to explain the existence of good
and evil in the cosmos. He did not use the shape of the letters, or
the vocalization marks, or the *tagin*, etc. All the systems were offered and remained potential in Jewish thought, to be used, by choice
and following personal taste, by anyone who wished and to the extent
he wished.

III

As stated above, this is not mysticism. The Midrash is a methodology, which can be employed to any purpose. Several great Jewish rationalistic philosophers in the Middle Ages employed such systems for their own purposes, which were scientific and rational.
Where is the borderline? When does Midrash transform into a *via
mystica*?

The key concept in this case is, I believe, the one of freedom.
Gershom Scholem characterized mysticism as an explosion of free-

---

[21]Concerning the position of the *Sefer Yezira* on the subject of sacred language
and its transformation of the laws of language (that is, grammar) into the laws
of nature, engulfing the cosmos, time, and man, see my study in *Jerusalem Studies in Jewish Thought* 11 (1992).

dom of thought and expression within established religion.[22] I believe that he would have hesitated somewhat in his formulation had he considered the enormous amount of freedom of thought and expression that the Midrash itself allows, albeit it is an integral, principal part of established, traditional religion. Yet Scholem is right in his postulation that freedom is one of the most important characteristics of mysticism within a scriptural religion. The ambivalence that I shall try to explain and analyze below is the one of the acquisition of mystical freedom in spite of the fact that mysticism required putting limits upon the infinite freedom of the Midrash.

The earliest example of Jewish mysticism, *Hechalot* visions, should be considered here. There is no deliberate, systematic use in *Hechalot* mysticism of midrashic methodology, One may even suspect that there is an attitude of rejection of it, even though this is not clearly stated. There is no use of letter or language mysticism in any way in this ancient circle of Jewish pneumatics. The reason for that is, I believe, the mystical freedom employed to the utmost by the *Hechalot* mystics: They did not feel it necessary to prove in traditional ways the veracity of their mystical experiences. *Hechalot* mysticism is one of direct revelation: The mystic ascends to the celestial chariot and travels from one divine palace (*hechal*) to the next until he reaches the seventh, where he faces the throne of glory and the figure of the Creator sitting on it. When he returns to this world he recounts his experiences in direct descriptive language, needing no reliance on the old texts of divine revelation; he has seen everything himself, his own experience is the proof of itself, he does not need any exegesis or homiletics to demonstrate that it is indeed divine truth. Implicit here is the rejection of the Midrash and the return to the biblical concept of direct revelation.[23]

---

[22]G. Scholem, *On the Kabbalah and Its Symbolism*, New York: Schocken 1965, pp. 5–31; originally published in German: "Religiöse Autorität und Mystik," in *Zur Kabbala und ihrer Symbolik*, Zürich 1960, pp. 11–48, and *Eranos Jahrbuch* 26 (1957), pp. 243–278.

[23]On *Hechalot* literature, a vast amount of scholarship has been created in the last two decades, but concerning this particular point, it should be stated that most scholars, beginning with Scholem, did not realize the deep division between

The medieval Jewish mystic is characterized by the self-denial of his own experience, by the claim that everything he saw and discovered has been known all along and is hidden within the ancient texts. But that which was hidden in the ancient texts is infinite; the medieval Jewish mystics, especially those in Germany, did more than anyone else in the history of Jewish culture to demonstrate the infinity of possibilities of meaning inherent in the midrashic system, developing it far beyond the boundaries of the midrashic classical exegesis, though without creating any conflict between themselves and the basic norms of the Midrash.

Two main examples of this attitude among the mystics of medieval Germany are clearly illustrated in the works of the Ashkenazi Hasidic circles of the Rhineland in the second half of the twelfth century and the beginning of the thirteenth. One is Rabbi Eleazar of Worms's Commentary on the Creation (*Sod Ma' aseh Bereshit*), which is the opening treatise of the author's magnum opus in esoteric theology, *Sodey Razaya*.[24] In this treatise Rabbi Eleazar analyzes the process of the creation in the format of a commentary on the letters of the alphabet—their shapes, meaning, provenance, and many others.[25] This commentary became very influential in later Jewish mysticism, because it was printed (up to the letter L) as the central part of the popular *Sefer Raziel* in 1701. The second example is the Ashkenazi Hasidic concept of the seventy-three "gates of wisdom," in which the

---

talmudic-midrashic Judaism and the basic concepts of *Hechalot* mysticism; rather, they tended to view the *Hechalot* mystical attitude as the esoteric stratum of mysticism inherent in—and integrated with—talmudic Judaism. I believe this to be erroneous. See in detail J. Dan, *The Revelation of the Secret of the World, The Beginning of Ancient Jewish Mysticism*, Providence, RI: Brown University 1992.

[24]*Sodey Razaya* is a five-part work, that includes the Secret of the Chariot (printed as *Sodey Razayya* by I. Kamelhar, Risha 1930), *Chochmat ha-Nefesh*, *Sefer ha-Shem* and the Commentary on *Sefer Yezira*. The commentary on the alphabet, The Secret of the Creation, is the first part, which is preceded by a short introduction concerning Hasidic ethics. See J. Dan, *The Esoteric Theology of Ashkenazi Hasidism*, Jerusalem: The Bialik Institute 1968, pp. 62–64.

[25]A discussion of the concept of language as revealed in this work is presented in a study of mine published in the book *Hebrew in Ashkenaz*, ed. Lewis Glinert, New York and Oxford: Oxford University Press 1993, pp. 11–250.

Ashkenazi Hasidim concentrated and organized their methods of interpretation of biblical verses.[26] Most of these seventy-three refer to numerical aspects, the occurrences of letters, their absence in certain verses, and the forms of the *temurah*. Others cover all aspects, including the traditional talmudic ones, of interpretation. A special group is one that refers to subjects, some of them literary units— prayer, *Sefer Yezira*, Talmud; others to theological subjects—the divine glory, the unity of God; still others to ethical concepts—humility, love and fear of God, piety. There is no doubt that these "gates" have been utilized by these esoterics and mystics. We have an extensive, anonymous commentary on the Pentateuch, written by an author of this school, each segment of which carries a title that is one of these "gates."[27] In Rabbi Eleazar of Worms's extensive commentary on the prayers there is some use of it. But the main text relating to this system is Rabbi Eleazar of Worms's Book of Wisdom. The largest part of this book is dedicated to a demonstration of the use of these "gates," exemplified by the interpretation of the first verse of Genesis. Rabbi Eleazar explains in detail how to apply these principles to the actual analysis of one verse. While doing so, he actually declares, and demonstrates, the infinity of meaning found in the biblical language. The seventy-three "gates" are, in fact, just examples; five of them, for instance, relate to the number of times that a letter is mentioned in a certain biblical section: *shaar ahadim, shaar ha-mishneh, shaar ha-meshulash, shaar ha-meruba, shaar ha-mehumash*. Of course, one need not stop here, and it is possible to continue and increase the number. In the same way, just a small selection of *temurah* possibilities are included; many others can be added on the same basis. The number seventy-three is an artificial one (it is the numerical value of the term *chochmah*), while the concept itself is clearly one of infinity of meanings. All these methodological discussions do not refer, in any way, to the possibility of contradiction

[26]The list of these gates, from Rabbi Eleazar's *Sefer ha-Hochmah*, was published by me in *Studies in Ashkenazi Hasidic Literature*, pp. 52–57 (Hebrew).
[27]See J. Dan, *The Ashkenazi Hasidic "Gates of Wisdom,"* Hommage à Georges Vajda, ed. G. Nahon and C. Touati, Louvain: Editions Peeters 1980, pp. 184–189.

between meanings. The possibility of a clash between "truths" does not emerge; the belief in the infinity of compatible meanings is absolute.

Another important example of this attitude is found in Rabbi Eleazar's most important theological work, the *Sefer ha-Shem*, which includes dozens of analyses, using many different methods, of the tetragrammaton and other divine names. This work, together with others of the same school, expresses the peak of the medieval development of the midrashic concept, used to the extreme but still adhering to the basic theological and methodological framework created by the ancient Midrash. This process continued to develop during the thirteenth century among kabbalists, most notably in the works of Abraham Abulafia and the early works of Rabbi Joseph Gikatilla.

The problem to be discussed is: When does such a midrashic system, elaborated and developed almost ad absurdum, become a mystical one? The basic concept of the infinity of meanings is not compatible with the basic attitude of mystics, who do believe in a distinction between true and not true, or, at least, between the true and the more true. How does mysticism relate to the Midrash?

Obviously, one should completely deny those popular—even vulgar—tendencies to identify mysticism with any numerical interpretation of verses, or with transmutations of letters, exegesis of the holy name, and similar methodologies. These are external means, their use being dictated by the nonmystical, literal concept of language as divine. Within the framework of such an understanding of language, these methods are actually logical consequences of the basic theology and cosmogony. It is a very poor concept, indeed, that diagnoses mysticism by the use of such methods just because they seem unfamiliar to the reader. The midrashic attitude is inherent in the scriptural concept of cosmogony, and has nothing to do, directly, with mysticism. Mystics may use midrashic methods like many others, but the methodology itself has no mystical element in it.

The problem has some phenomenological similarity to other schools of thought that developed within the framework of the belief in divine language. A traditional Jewish example is that of the law, the *halachah*. The legal aspect of Judaism shares all the theological and linguistic concepts described above, but it cannot sustain the anarchy of infinity of meanings; legal decisions must be clear, unambiguous, and literal so that proper actions can follow and legal definitions between right and wrong can be made. This is impossible within the midrashic structure itself; another dimension of decision making, an external criterion, has to be introduced in order to differentiate between right and wrong from the legal point of view.

In Judaism, this external criterion is tradition. The laws of the *halachah* are not binding because they represent the true interpretation of a biblical verse. The laws differentiating between dairy and meat in kosher food are not binding because they are the correct interpretation of *lo tevashel gedi bahalev immo;*[28] they are binding because they represent the commandments given to Moses on Mount Sinai by God Himself, and transmitted from generation to generation not only orally, but, more important, practically. Even an oral tradition can be interpreted in many ways; practical behavior cannot. The tradition of commandments and their performance is the deciding factor concerning law, and not the interpretation of a biblical verse; this is used almost in an ornamental fashion, to prove that the commandments are also imbedded in the written Torah, but exegesis is not the decisive factor in the creation of the law.

In a similar way, Jewish rationalism in the Middle Ages adopted the external criterion of logic to discern the one true, logical meaning among the infinite midrashic ones. A religious system that is based on logic is not necessarily a completely anthropocentric one. The laws of logic have been implanted in the human mind by the Creator. God, being benevolent and just, will not delude His creatures by making their minds reach untrue conclusions. Strict adherence to human logic, therefore, can be conceived as an adherence to divine truth. The "text of revelation" in such a system can be the rules of logic themselves, as given by God to man when He con-

---

[28]Exodus 23:19, 34:26; Deuteronomy 14:21.

structed his intelligence. Rationalism, therefore, can be regarded as the adherence to one aspect of revealed divine truth, the one implanted in the human mind in the form of reason and logic, in order to discern among the infinite interpretations of linguistic revelation the ones that conform with this "external" yardstick, the laws of logic.

These two examples express the possibility of using one kind of revelation in order to overcome the anarchy of midrashic interpretation of ancient revelation: tradition concerning a legal system or human logic, derived from the divine wisdom, in a rationalistic one. It seems that mysticism reflects a similar phenomenological attitude, though very different in many details of application.

The mystic's avenue to divine truth is metalinguistic. Language, in its sensual and intellectual aspects, reflects, according to him, only the superficial and literal aspects of existence, which are very remote (and, sometimes, even contradictory) from divine truth. Even though language is divine, when it is employed for human and earthly purposes it cannot convey the hidden, mystical divine truth. Language can serve as a means to some remote, partial, and imprecise approach to divine truth only when it is reconnected to its supreme divine source. Such a connection creates the mystical symbol, which is an obscure linguistic approximation of the eternally hidden divine truth. Symbols derive their potency not from their place in language, but from their connection, a mystical undefinable one, to the hidden metalinguistic meaning. That means that the basis for the mystical symbol, and for a linguistic symbolical expression of mystical truth, is the mystical experience, rather than any linguistic exegetical or homiletical enterprise.

The "external" yardstick, by which a mystic distinguishes between mystical truth and literal, earthly untruth is therefore a metalinguistic one of mystical experience. This experience is what enables the mystic to distinguish between the literal, homiletical, logical, and midrashic aspects of language on the one hand, and the symbolic aspect of language, denoting mystical truth, on the other. The mystical symbol can be portrayed as the upper ninth of an iceberg protruding above the sea; truth is the iceberg itself, its totality, whereas the linguistic expression, which is inherently tied to it and is an integral part of it, is the symbol. The symbol can reveal a great deal about the hidden truth, but it is a very great mistake—a titanic one—to see the tip of the iceberg as its totality. The nonmystic cannot differentiate between "tips" that are nothing but that, and "tips" to which an iceberg is connected; this is the unique ability of the mystic in his metalinguistic experience.

This "external" criterion is, on the one hand, very similar to the position of tradition in the quest for legal truth, and of the laws of logic in the quest for rationalistic truth. It differs from them, however, in the fact that while their final achievement is a precise linguistic statement, for the mystic truth will forever be beyond language. Symbolic expression, in language, of mystical truth is anything but precise. The "tip of the iceberg" can be described from various angles and aspects, its characteristics expressed in various linguistic formulations, all of them connected in one way or another to the essence of the hidden truth, but never expressing its entirety.

Rationalism and law put limits, forced by their "external criterion," upon midrashic expression. Mysticism does not necessarily do so. It can adopt all the varieties of midrashic exegesis and incorporate them into its continuous quest for the impossible, for the linguistic expression of metalinguistic truth. There is no inherent contradiction, from a methodological point of view, between midrashic and mystical exegesis. The difference lies much deeper: For the midrashic exegete, midrashic truths are symbols of unknown and inexpressible truth.

This is the reason that Jewish mysticism, throughout the Middle Ages and early modern times, seems to be so close to the world of the Midrash, and why the midrashic format is so central to the literary genres of the medieval mystics. The *Bahir* and the *Zohar* are mystical midrashim. In every external methodological way, they are midrashim, in the full sense of the term. They differ from the classical midrashim in one most meaningful way: Their conclusions are not truth expressed by language, but truth expressed by linguistic symbols, intrinsically supported by the mystical metalinguistic experience of the author.

How does one distinguish between the two? Their appearance
may be not only very similar, but actually identical. This, indeed, is
the· most difficult task facing a scholar who wishes to understand
mysticism within the framework of a divine language, with a rich
midrashic tradition like the Hebrew one. Ashkenazi Hasidism, I
believe, presents in this respect one of the most intriguing and interesting examples.

There are several examples in the history of Jewish mysticism
in which the "external criterion" is clearly expressed. Shem Tov ben
Gaon, in the early fourteenth century, in a kabbalistic treatise completely concerned with linguistic, midrashic study of the kabbalistic
interpretation of biblical verses—some chapters of this work actually read like a mystical-midrashic manual—stops his discussion to
declare that he has seen the heavens open and revealing divine secrets in an immediate, direct manner.[29] The early kabbalists in
Provence expressed this external criterion by the statement that the
prophet Elijah has been revealed to their sages and has disclosed to
them the unique secrets that they describe.[30] Several medieval mystics, in Germany and elsewhere, relied on a "dream question," a
practice of divination assisted by scripture, to reveal to them
metamidrashic truths often related to halachah. Isaac Luria was re-
puted to visit the heavenly academy and study kabbalah with the
prophet Elijah when he seemed to be sleeping. The Besht, the founder
of modern Hasidism, reported his "ascent of the soul" to the palace
of the Messiah, who revealed to him secrets concerning the redemption; there are many, many others. Yet, on the whole, kabbalists
preferred to concentrate on the text, not allowing their readers a
glimpse into their innermost experiences, which gave the basis for

---

[29]See my study of the subject, "The Worms Epistle and the Problem of
Pseudepigraphy in Early Kabbalah," Studies in Kabbalah and Ethical Literature
Presented to Isaiah Tishby, vol. III, part I, eds. J. Dan and J. Hacker, Jerusalem
1984 (Jerusalem Studies in Jewish Thought), pp. 111–138.
[30]G. Scholem, Origins of the Kabbalah, trans. Allan Arkush, ed. R. J. Zwi
Werblowsky, Princeton, NJ: Princeton University Press and the Jewish Publication Society 1987, pp. 35–39, 238–243.

their commentaries and sermons, midrashic in nature, debating various aspects of the divine world.

This fact seemed to create a meaningful difference between Jewish and Christian mysticism. The lingering impression is that while
Christian mysticism is experiental, personal, poetic, and direct, Jewish mysticism is more of a theosophy than "real" mysticism. This
impression, however, is completely wrong, because of several reasons.

First, it is wrong to assume that the mystics who described in
personal, poetic language their mystical experiences, like Saint John
of the Cross and Saint Teresa, "the Carmelite school," represent
Christian mysticism. They are just one segment—in many respects
an exceptional one—in the long history of Christian mysticism. For
a long time Christian mysticism could hardly be separated from neo-
Platonist philosophical treatises;[31] there is no personal word in the
greatest masterpiece of Christian mysticism, the pseudo-Dionysian
writings.[32] Eastern Christian mysticism tends very often toward a
"theosophic" character, much like many kabbalistic treatises. The
fame that the Carmelites acquired should not hide the fact that most
Christian mystics were as reluctant to deal with their personal, direct experiences as were Jewish ones.

The second misconception is to equate mysticism with a particular literary genre, dictating to mystics the means of their expression. The fact is that mystics used (and, sometimes, abused) all literary genres, up to and including the scholarly multinoted "study," as
well as many nonverbal ways of expression. There is no inherent
reason that mysticism should be expressed more in a poetic, personal,
experiental language than by a pseudo-neo-Platonic treatise or a
"scholarly" study. Several well-known biographical studies of central

---

[31]The clearest exposition of this attitude is found in the classical study of William R. Inge, *Christian Mysticism*, London: Methuen 1899. It was followed by many
scholars in the present century. See a detailed analysis of this school, Bernard
McGinn, *The Foundations of Mysticism*, New York: Crossroads 1991, pp. 273–278
et passim.

[32]See the recent essay by Jaroslav Pelikan, "The Odyssey of Dionysian Spirituality," in *Pseudo-Dionisius, The Complete Works*, trans. C. Luibheid, New York:
Paulist Press 1987, pp. 11–25.

mystical figures are, to a large extent, expressions of the "scholar's" sharing of the mystical experience of his hero, actually representing a spiritual experience rather than the results of scholarly research. When we approach the works of the medieval mystics, therefore, the literary presentation should be regarded as an expression of the mystic's relationship to his social and cultural environment, which influenced his choice of means, rather than defining his mystical or nonmystical attitude.

The third element, the most difficult one to grasp and utilize in the study of mysticism, is the question of where is God to be found. We tend to assume that God awaits the mystic in visual, extracosmic circumstances, that meeting God means forsaking the earth and the body and being uplifted outside of the material realm in order to approach the pure spirituality of His essence.

This concept, so deeply ingrained in our culture, is one more result of our existence in the realm dominated by the notion that language is a human phenomenon. As such, it is not in language, while divinity transcends language. This is true concerning secular, Christian-based culture; it is completely untrue when we try to understand the creativeness of mystics who reside in a centuries-old culture that believes that language is divine in origin, that it is employed by God for various purposes far beyond communication, that the essence of creativity resides in it, and that the secrets of God are incorporated within it. In such a culture, the tendency to seek God within a book will be at least as natural as to seek Him in heaven.

The immersion in a text, having it as inspiration and as a revelation, is a basic experience within a religion based on divine revelation in and by language. Psychologically, there is an added dimension of directness when the spiritual qualities of the text meet and merge with the spirituality of the mystic. The mystic, by his basic nature, believes in God's presence within language no less, and in a more fundamental way, in the text than in heaven. Such a meeting is actually skipping the visual stage, the pictures of the ascent and the surroundings of the divine essence, and going directly to the spiritual essence without sensual imagery intervening.

There are, in Jewish medieval mysticism, several types of such a mystical experience through the text. One group, which will not be discussed here despite its centrality to the mystical world of the Ashkenazi Hasidim, is the meeting by means of the text of the prayers. This is an aspect of mystical unity with all existence developed in the school of Rabbi Judah the Pious, which should be addressed extensively in a separate study.[33]

Sometimes the text serves just as a slight, marginal excuse for mystical expression. A classic example of that may be found, for instance, in the *Zohar*'s description of the beginning of the creation, when the biblical text that is interpreted serves in a most minor role; the author, in almost a mystical ecstasy, creates his own terminology, and the enormous vision unfolded is a unique expression of a supreme mystical experience, a mystic actually being present in the moment that everything—including God Himself—was just beginning to unfold, as if in the presence, or even with the participation, of the mystic himself. It seems that this is one of the clearest examples of the irrelevance of the homiletical literary framework, and a demonstration of the mystic's ability to express intense, deeply personal, mystical experience in any literary format he may be dealing with.

In other cases it is the biblical verse, or the talmudic saying, or a paragraph from the *Sefer Yezira*, that serves as the trigger as well as the external structure of the mystical experience. This, probably, is the most common way of expressing mystical experience in kabbalistic literature. The writers of these kabbalistic treatises had deep within themselves the glimpse of supernal mystical truth, and then found a way to integrate a symbolic reflection of this truth within their exegetical works. It seems that one should not be surprised by the fact that mystics, so deeply immersed in the language of divine revelation, will interpret their own mystical experience as a direction toward a new understanding of the words of ancient texts. The divine spark that they have envisioned (not necessarily in any

---

[33]A few remarks on this subject can be found in my study "The Emergence of the Mystical Prayer," *Studies in Jewish Mysticism*, eds. J. Dan and F. Talmage, Cambridge, MA: Association of Jewish Studies 1981, pp. 85–120; a more detailed study on this subject is forthcoming.

visual way) was transformed within their personality into a symbolic statement of a new aspect of meaning in the old, traditional words spoken by God to man in antiquity.

Sometimes this process is even more obvious, especially when the mystic himself feels, from the very beginning of his mystical experience, that his contact with the divine is verbal in nature; God, he feels, speaks to him, or even directs his hand when writing. In such cases, the line between old textual revelation and new mystical experience is really very hard to draw, because God speaking to the mystic in words is bound to use the same linguistic formulations He had used in early revelations. Taken to the extreme, this is a phenomenon in which the mystic believes that God Himself is presenting him with a new exegesis of His own ancient words. Many Jewish mystics (and nonmystics) had the very powerful image of divine activity as being modeled after the textual deliberations of an earthly talmudic academy. God, like everybody else, spends His time studying the Torah, together with the great sages and saints of earlier times. Mystical experience is therefore often clothed in the garb of participation in the deliberations of the heavenly academies. In such cases it is no wonder that the mystical expression will be presented, from the very beginning, in the format of commentaries and homiletics. Sometimes one may surmise that this, indeed, was the intrinsic nature of the mystical experience itself.

A case in point, exemplifying and emphasizing this tendency, is the widespread late medieval and early modern kabbalistic phenomenon of the celestial *maggid*, a divine power revealed to mystics and dictating to them divine secrets. Many detailed descriptions survive of this phenomenon, and it seems that in most cases the experience was entirely an audio-textual one.[34] It may appear to be a paradoxical phenomenon, but it actually expresses the thesis we are trying to establish here: Mystical kabbalistic experience is very often the mystical revelation of the old text of revelation itself. Old

---

[34]One of the most detailed descriptions is that of Rabbi Moses Hayyim Luzzatto, early in the eighteenth century. See M. Benayahu, "The Maggid of Ramhal," *Sefunot* 5 (Jerusalem 1961), pp. 297–336.

theophany is transformed into contemporary mystical revelation. In this way, the gulf between the very essence of the mystical experience and its literary expression in the form of commentaries, exegesis, homiletics, and hermeneutics has become a minimal one.[35]

The century between 1170 and 1270, approximately, is the one in which all the phenomena described above came to a head among the Jewish esoterics and mystics in Germany, especially in the Ashkenazi Hasidic circles. Three processes converged in this period to create one of the most intense and variegated spiritual developments in medieval Judaism. The first process was the development of the midrashic methods to their extreme expression of the infinity of meanings of the scriptural verse, especially in the system of the "seventy-three gates of wisdom." The second process was the intrusion of a mystical element into this structure, the appearance of an "external criterion" that transformed midrashic anarchic deliberations into the discovery of mystical symbolism.[36] The third was the ap-

---

[35]A special example of this process can be found in the case of mystics who tend to express themselves by numerical analyses of texts; some of the Ashkenazi Hasidim had this tendency. We may surmise that mystical experience, for them, also carried a numerical character. A similar phenomenon may possibly be apparent even in scholarship, as Scholem has hinted at in the famous case of the Weinstock-Adiriron identification; see his note in *Tarbiz* 32 (1963), p. 258, note 15.

[36]This subject cannot be explored in this paper, yet it should be emphasized that concerning Ashkenazi Hasidim, and especially concerning Rabbi Judah the Pious, who was undoubtedly the most mystically inclined among these esoterical thinkers, this criterion can be identified rather clearly. The mystical element in Rabbi Judah's thought is concerned with the discovery of an intrinsic harmony, structural and numerical, between all parts of the sacred texts, biblical and prayers, and the divine and earthly world. This seems to have been the subject of Rabbi Judah's now lost vast Commentary on the Prayers. Rabbi Judah set out in this work to demonstrate the comprehensiveness of this harmony, insisting that its veracity is attested by ancient tradition, yet its formulation is obviously a new discovery, probably the result of Rabbi Judah's own mystical inclination. The "external criterion" in this case is this deep confidence that everything in existence, spiritual, textual, and physical, has the same "print" of the divine touch, identified by the numerical-structural harmony. I have pointed out this element briefly in the paper "The Emergence of the Mystical Prayer" (see note 33), and it is a subject of a much more detailed analysis in a forthcoming study.

pearance of the kabbalah, and especially kabbalistic texts, which opened new vistas of mystical symbolic expression for the mystics of medieval Germany. The writings of Rabbi Moses, the great-grandson of Rabbi Judah the Pious, probably around 1270, express the convergence of these three processes into one meaningful mystical experience.[37]

The "external criterion" of mystical truth that characterizes Ashkenazi Hasidism is, I believe, a mystical awareness of the intrinsic unity of all sacred phenomena, and their distance from all earthly, material ones. Unlike the kabbalah, Ashkenazi Hasidism does not introduce a dynamic element, a mythical diversity, into the divine world. Therefore, their theological discussions of the celestial realms are not intended to distinguish and separate, as do the kabbalists, but to unite and identify, to show the intrinsic harmony and identity in everything. In demonstrating that mystical truth, midrashic methodology became their main instrument, and therefore the character of their mysticism is intensely linguistic, probably more than that of any other mystical movement in Jewish history.

The phrase that most expresses the Ashkenazi Hasidic mystical attitude is a simple one: *be kerasim uve-lulaot,* "with hooks and loops," denoting the way that all religious texts and all divine phenomena in the world, past and present, are connected.

Rabbi Moses was familiar with all the methods of the Ashkenazi Hasidic exegesis, and used them in his works. But the distinctive new element in his works is the intrusion of two texts into this world, one an ancient work of *Hechalot* tradition, the *Sod ha-Gadol,* The Great Secret, and the other the kabbalistic text of the *Bahir.* When reading Rabbi Moses's commentary on some prayers of the *Shiur Komah* text,[38] one easily observes the enormous spiritual impact that

---

[37]Rabbi Moses's position in the history of Ashkenazi Hasidism and the kabbalah, and the nature of his works, were first presented and analyzed by G. Scholem in an appendix to his *Reshit ha-Qabbalah,* Tel Aviv and Jerusalem 1948, Schocken 1948, pp. 195–238.

[38]Parts of this commentary were printed by Scholem, ibid., pp. 212–238. There are, however, several manuscripts of this work that were not used by Scholem that assist considerably in establishing the text and the structure of the work. In

these two texts had upon the German-Jewish mystic.

These two works, the *Bahir* and The Great Secret, are closely connected, and Scholem dedicated much effort to the understanding of this connection. The *Sod* was undoubtedly one of the sources of the *Bahir*, and a serious problem, still unsolved, is to what extent the concept of the pleroma in the *Bahir* is derived from the ancient work.[39] The quotations from the *Sod* by Rabbi Moses are the only ones we have; earlier references include only its title, and later writers did not preserve its text. One of the haunting enigmas of this chapter in the history of Jewish mysticism is this almost unbelievable accident, that the first German-Jewish mystic to quote the *Bahir* is the only Jewish writer to preserve portions of this source of the *Bahir*, the *Sod ha-Gadol*; actually, Rabbi Moses quotes the two sources almost as if they were one, usually attaching a quote from one to the other, creating a textual structure that is often rather difficult to comprehend, and to point out, with any certainty, which quotations belong to the *Bahir* and which to the *Sod*.

This is an important philological and historical problem, but our concern here is with Rabbi Moses himself, as an independent mystic, and not with his role in preserving ancient texts. In this respect, the interesting aspect is the treatment of these sources by Rabbi Moses. It seems evident that for him, these two texts represented divine mystical revelation. They were, for him, this "external criterion," clothed in linguistic, symbolic garb, which expresses mystical divine truth and transcends the anarchy of midrashic-Ashkenazi

---

the Hebrew version of this study, to be published elsewhere, I shall include a textual analysis of the work, its recensions, and the conclusions concerning the relationship between the various sources as a result of the comparison between the various texts.

[39]Some hesitation can be discerned in Scholem's analysis of this problem. Answering it conclusively is impossible before much more textual work is done in collecting the manuscripts of this work and editing them with a philological analysis. At this moment, however, it seems to me that there is no clear indication here that the concept of the ten *sefirot*, and the symbols of the *Bahir* describing them, is to be found in the "Great Secret," and it still seems that the *Bahir* is the first expression in our possession of this kabbalistic symbolism.

Hasidic expression. The unification of kabbalah and Ashkenazi Hasidism, evident in the use of the *Bahir*, *Sod ha-Sodot*, and *Hechalot* mystical texts, reflects a deeper unity of mystical perception, imposing a new structure of divine truth and harmonizing around it his diverse sources. This is, I believe, a rather typical process, identifying the development of mystical awareness among Jewish scholars in the High Middle Ages.

NINE

Christian Kabbalah: From Mysticism to Esotericism

I

The Christian kabbalah was one of the most influential schools (or, actually, group of schools) of esoteric lore in Europe between the late fifteenth century and the eighteenth century. Recent scholarly work suggests that its realms of influence were more extended than previously thought, and that its role in shaping the world view of key figures not only in Renaissance humanism but also in seventeenth-century and eighteenth-century philosophy and science was quite meaningful.[1] The understanding of this unique phenomenon is therefore an important component in the understanding of the interrelationship between esotericism, philosophy, science, magic, and

[1] A meaningful recent contribution to this subject is the study by Allison P. Coudert, *Leibniz and the Kabbalah*, Dordrecht, Boston, London: Kluwer Academic Publishers 1995 (*International Archives of the History of Ideas* 142); see also K. Reichert, "Christian Kabbalah and Seventeenth-Century Philosophy," lecture delivered at the Houghton Library, Harvard University, in March 1996 (see note 2).

mysticism in the creation of the most important ideas that emerged in early modern Europe.[2]

One of the key problems that confuse and obscure the study of this subject is an erroneous assumption that whatever characterizes the kabbalah is meaningful in the Christian kabbalah, and that the main concepts of the Christian kabbalah are derived from Hebrew kabbalistic sources. If the two are not separated, it is impossible to assess in a valid, scholarly way the nature and the true drives that created the kabbalistic esotericism within Christianity. It is the purpose of this brief discussion to present both the important similarities and the differences between the kabbalah itself and the Christian kabbalah, highlighting the original contributions of the Christian thinkers and their creative and selective attitudes toward their Hebrew sources.

When the Italian humanists turned their attention to the Hebrew kabbalistic works in the last two decades of the fifteenth century, the kabbalah was a three-hundred-year-old esoteric phenomenon within Judaism. Parallel to the development of the Christian kabbalah, the Hebrew kabbalah was gradually transformed into a mainstream Jewish ideology that was destined to dominate Jewish religiosity in the seventeenth century and later. This, however, was unknown at the time to the Christian kabbalists, as well as to their Jewish teachers. When the first meeting occurred, it was a meeting between central intellectual schools in the Italian renaissance, and a minor, marginal phenomenon within Jewish culture.[3] It is important

---

[2]An expression of the renewed interest in this subject was the exhibition held in 1996 at the Houghton Library, Harvard University, by J. D. Coakley and myself. See the catalogue *The Christian Kabbalah: Jewish Mystical Books and their Christian Interpreters*, Cambridge, MA 1996. The symposium that opened the exhibition and an extended version of the catalogue are to be published by the Houghton Library.

[3]The classical study of the beginnings of the kabbalah is that of Gershom Scholem, *The Origins of the Kabbalah*, translated by A. Arkush and edited and updated by R. J. Zwi Werblowsky, Princeton, NJ: Princeton University Press and the Jewish Publication Society, 1986. This authoritative study was first published as a long article in Hebrew, in *Knesset le-Zecher Bialik* 10 (1947), pp. 179–228. This article was published, with several important appendices, as a small book, *Reshit*

to observe that some of the Jewish scholars who helped to create this cultural bridge between Judaism and Christianity were themselves quite remote from the kabbalah in their world views, and some of them were even opponents of the kabbalah. Flavius Mithridates, who converted to Christianity and translated Hebrew esoteric texts into Latin for Pico della Mirandola, did not use the kabbalah in his own presentation of Jewish esotericism within a Christian context.[4] Eliyahu Levitas, who copied esoteric works for Egidio da Viterbo, was not a kabbalist.[5] And, especially, Rabbi Eliyahu Del Medigo, the author of *Behinat ha-Dat*, was an opponent of the kabbalah and insisted that the *Zohar* was a medieval work written by Moses de Leon; he was one of Pico's Jewish teachers.[6] Besides these, however, there were Jewish scholars who were devoted and creative kabbalists, the most important of whom was Rabbi Yohanan Alimano.[7]

---

ha-Kabbalah, Jerusalem and Tel Aviv: Schocken 1948. The book was soon out of print, but Scholem did not allow a reprinting. An extended, enlarged version was published in 1962 as *Ursprung und Anfange der Kabbala*, Berlin: Walter de Gruyter, from which the French translation (*Les origines de la Kabbale*, Paris: Aubier-Montaigne 1966) was made; translations to many other languages followed. Parallel to the German edition, Scholem gave a four-year lecture series at the Hebrew University on this subject, which was published in four volumes by Academon (Jerusalem 1960-1964), ed. Rivkah Shatz and Yosef ben Shlomo. The English translation was published four years after the author's death.

[4]The works of Mithridates were studied in great detail by H. Wirszubsky; see especially his *Flavius Mithridates Sermo de Passione*, Jerusalem 1963.

[5]He copied, for the Cardinal, the magnum opus of Rabbi Eleazar of Worms (d. 1230), *Sodey Razaya*, now found at the British Library, 737.

[6]See the recent edition of this work (which was written in 1490): Jacob Joshua Ross, *Sefer Behinat Hadat of Elijah del-Medigo, A Critical Edition with Introduction, Notes and Commentary*, Tel Aviv: The Rosenberg School of Jewish Studies, Tel Aviv University 1984; the Introduction includes a detailed discussion of the relationship between Elijah del-Medigo and Pico. See also the recent study by Kalman P. Bland, "Elijah del Medigo's Averroist Response to the Kabbalahs of Fifteenth-Century Jewry and Pico Della Mirandola," *Jewish Thought and Philosophy*, I (1991), pp. 23-53.

[7]Concerning this important personality in the emergence of the Christian kabbalah, see G. Scholem, *Kabbalah*, Jerusalem: Keter 1974, pp. 67-68; H. Wirszubsky, *Pico della Mirandola's Encounter with Jewish Mysticism*, Jerusalem: The Israeli Academy of Sciences and Humanities 1989, pp. 256-257; M. Idel, "The Program of Johanan Alemano" (in Hebrew), *Tarbiz* 48 (1979), pp. 303-330.

An indication of the way Jewish scholars regarded the new phenomenon of the Christian kabbalah can be gleaned from what may be the first Hebrew nonkabbalistic reference to it, found in Solomon ibn Verga's treatise, *Shevet Yehudah*, written in the beginning of the sixteenth century. This unusual work ignores the Hebrew kabbalah almost completely, and a reference to kabbalah that is found in a presentation of Christian theology by a fictional Christian scholar describes the kabbalah as the body of texts that attest to the veracity of the Trinity. This is an early expression of an attitude that was destined to influence the concept of the kabbalah in the eyes of many Jews in future generations.[8]

The Christian kabbalah can be characterized as a Christian acceptance of a Jewish claim that was denied, often vehemently, by ancient and medieval Christian theologians: that Jewish nonbiblical traditions contain ancient, universal truth that, because of its antiquity and divine origin, must contain the essential Christian message. The Hebrew Bible was always regarded as a major source of Christian truth, and some sections of the gospels, most notably Matthew, seem to view the revelation of Christianity as twofold: On the one hand, it is the living word of Jesus Christ; on the other, it is a new meaning found in the ancient verses of the Hebrew prophets.[9] Christianity insisted, however, that what the Jews called their oral law—the Mishnah, the Talmud, the Midrash—was a later fabrication, often motivated by anti-Christian attitudes, and deserved extinction. The Christian kabbalists opposed this view, and accepted the Jewish claim that the nonbiblical traditions are equal in antiquity, sanctity, and veracity with those of the Hebrew Bible. The clash between these two Christian concepts was expressed in the formative years of the Christian kabbalah by the fierce conflict between Johannes Reuchlin and his Dominican opponents, who demanded

---

[8]See Shohet's edition of the work, Jerusalem: The Bialik Institute 1953, pp. 31–32.
[9]This phenomenon was forcefully presented in Paula Fredericksen, *From Jesus to Christ: The Origins of the New Testament Images of Jesus*, New Haven and London: Yale University Press 1988, pp. 36–38 et passim.

the banishment and burning of the Talmud and other sources of the Jewish oral traditions.[10] This seems to be a unique occurrence within the history of the scriptural religions: a group of prominent intellectuals, in the mainstream of one religion, declaring the sacred works of another one as relevant, truthful, and meaningful to its own religiosity. To the best of my knowledge, nothing like that happened in the attitudes of Judaism and Islam toward each other, nor in Judaism toward Christianity. Even within Christianity, this was an exceptional phenomenon that was not repeated later, and is not one of the components of Christian religiosity in modern and contemporary times. Despite the increase in tolerance and openness that we believe to characterize our own age, few, if any, Christians today equal Pico and Reuchlin in their concept of the sanctity of Jewish traditions, even if their main motivation was the affirmation of their own religion.

The claim of antiquity, which was universally accepted in Judaism concerning the Talmud and the Midrash, was the basis of the kabbalistic demand to be recognized as a major component of this ancient tradition, a demand that gave the kabbalah its best-known name.[11] When the kabbalah appeared in medieval Judaism, in the last two decades of the twelfth century, it presented itself as a part of the world of the Midrash, and claimed to be based on traditions known to the ancient *tanaim*, the authors of the Mishnah, and, especially, to the ancient Jewish mystics, the "descenders to the chariot," who flourished in Late Antiquity. The *Bahir*, the first work of the kabbalah, presents in its first paragraph a statement attributed to Rabbi Nehunia ben ha-Kanah, a secondary figure in tanaitic litera-

---

[10]This meaningful chapter in the history of the relationship between Judaism and Christianity was studied in great detail by H. Graetz, in his monumental *Geschichte der Juden*. See also S. Baron, *A Social and Religious History of the Jews*, vol. VIII, New York: Columbia University Press 1969, pp. 182–191; and the volume of studies, *Reuchlin und die Juden*, ed. A. Herzig, J. Schops, and S. Rhode, Sigmaringen 1993.
[11]Concerning the names by which the medieval kabbalists called themselves, see G. Scholem, *Kabbalah*, pp. 6–7. It should be noted that several other appellations also refer to esotericism: *chochmat ha-sod*, *torat ha-nistar*, *yodei hen*, etc.

ture who became central in the pseudepigraphy of the ancient mystics and was portrayed as the leader of this school of mystics in the
central treatise of this group, Hechalot Rabbati, as well as in other
texts.[12]

Not all kabbalists emphasized the esoteric nature of their lore
in the same way. Some of them claimed direct divine experience or
revelations of emissaries from the celestial realms who revealed to
them supernal knowledge. Some even tended to identify kabbalah
and rational philosophy and present their teachings as being in
harmony with the results of logical speculation. A whole layer of
philosophical terminology, taken from the works of the Jewish rationalistic philosophers who flourished between the tenth and the
thirteenth centuries, was incorporated in kabbalistic works (a fact
that facilitated, two centuries later, the acceptance of the kabbalah
by Christian scholars, who recognized the Greek origins of that terminology). Yet the esoteric claim of ancient origins, often culminating in pseudepigraphy, remained central, and reached its peak in the
zoharic literature of the last decades of the thirteenth century and
the beginning of the fourteenth.

In the Zohar, the kabbalah is presented as the exegetical deliberations of a group of second-century mystics, headed by Rabbi
Simeon bar Yochai and his son, Rabbi Eleazar, who are constantly
inspired by divine messengers and stay in close contact with the
celestial deliberations of the secrets inherent in the Torah. Every
definition of esotericism can easily be applied to the way the teachings of the kabbalah are presented in this major mystical work of
the Middle Ages. The concept of the traditional text presented in
the Zohar is one of an entity comprising layer after layer of secrets,
which the sages unravel one after another. The essence of God is

---

[12]See J. Dan, The Revelation of the Secret of the World and the Beginning of Ancient
Jewish Mysticism, Providence, RI: Brown University 1992. Compare P. Schaefer,
The Manifest and Hidden God, Albany, NY: SUNY Press 1993. The element of
esotericism was present in this ancient Jewish mystical phenomenon; the Hebrew
terms sod and raz are prominent in the terminology of these mystics. See R. Elior,
Jewish Studies Quarterly 1 (1994/1995), pp. 1–50.

that of a secret within a secret, and the same is true concerning the universe, human beings, the human soul, and everything else. The *Zohar* itself is presented as a compendium of ancient secret lore, which can be transmitted only to an elitist minority of those whose ears and hearts are attuned to accept supreme secrets. When the *Zohar* became the main normative text of the kabbalah, its identification with esotericism was inevitable.

Yet it is important to emphasize that the kabbalah was not merely an esotericism, and that not everything that is esoteric in Judaism is kabbalah. The most important "secret" of the kabbalah— often called the "secret of genesis" (*sod maaseh bereshit*)—is essentially mystical: It describes the process of emanation of the ten *sefirot*, the divine manifestations, and their dynamic relationships, not for the sake of knowledge alone but in order to instruct the mystic in the way to ascend to the infinite realm of the supreme Godhead. Other Jewish medieval esotericists developed independent systems of tradition; the most important among them were the Kalonymides in twelfth- and thirteenth-century Germany, whose writings are prominent in the library of the early Christian kabbalists.

II

The differences between the Hebrew kabbalah and the Christian kabbalah are most obvious concerning the latter's omissions, rather than its additions. When reading Pico's *Conclusions* or Reuchlin's *De Arte Cabbalistica*, one is faced with a combination of elements that is remarkably different from that of the sources they used and the traditions that they believed to be disseminating. First and foremost among them is the secondary position, or even less than that, allotted by the first Christian kabbalists to the system of the *sefirot*, the ten divine hypostases that constitute the core of the Hebrew kabbalah's terminology and world view. Reuchlin's work, which is the first and most influential systematic presentation of the kabbalah in Latin, includes only brief discussions of this subject, which is not integrated in the main message of the work. In one section, Reuchlin seems to be presenting the ten divine powers as if they were angels, secondary in nature and function within the celestial structure.[13] In another, he presents a list of the *sefirot*, accurately described, but this section is not connected with the main subjects under discussion.[14] It is obvious that the mystical dimension of the kabbalah, as expressed in this ladder leading from the supreme Godhead to the world, was not transmitted in its full power and influence to the readers of this and other early Christian kabbalistic works.

Another remarkable difference, closely connected with the first, is the relative absence of the teachings of the *Zohar* from the works of the early Christian kabbalists. This does not mean that they were not aware of the centrality of the *Zohar* in the kabbalistic tradition: The very fact that Reuchlin's hero, Simon, the Jewish sage who presents the secrets of the kabbalah, is portrayed as a descendant of the traditional author of the *Zohar*, Rabbi Simeon bar Yochai,[15] emphasizes the importance allotted by Reuchlin to the *Zohar* as a supreme, ancient revelation of esoteric truth. Giving the stage to this Simon in his work, Reuchlin may be conceived as presenting a text that is analogical to the Jewish *Zohar*. And yet, despite this, there is hardly a meaningful discussion in the book (as well as in Pico's kabbalistic quotations[16]) that is dependent on the *Zohar* alone and reflects the unique mysticism and dynamic myths characterizing this work. The intense descriptions of the interrelationships between the divine powers, the colorful myth of their evolvement within the framework of the narrative of creation, and most notably the erotic

---

[13]*De Arte Cabbalistica* (*sefirot* as angels).

[14]The most extensive presentation is found in Part III, LXII–LXIII, based on the lists of appellations of the *sefirot* that Reuchlin found in the works of Rabbi Joseph Gikatilla, Gates of Light and Gates of Justice, which were written in Castile at the end of the thirteenth century. Reuchlin made use of the Latin translation of the Gates of Light, by Paul Ricci, *Portae Lucis haec est porta tetragrammton iusti intrabunt peam*, Augsburg 1516.

[15]See, for instance, Part III, LVIa, where a quotation from the *Mechilta* by Rabbi Simeon bar Yochai is presented by the Jewish sage as one said "by a member of my family." The connection is emphasized numerous times in this work.

[16]Concerning Pico's use of the *Zohar*, see Wiszubski, *Pico's Encounter*, pp. 48–50 et passim.

metaphors that dominate zoharic literature are completely absent from Reuchlin's and Pico's works. This is evident by the absence of two further dimensions of the zoharic myth that constitute the heart of post zoharic kabbalah: the femininity of the Shechinah and its erotic relationship with the masculine powers in the divine world.[17]

This marked difference, which separates Christian kabbalah from its Jewish sources, is the result of two parallel phenomena: on the one hand, the nature of the sources the Christian kabbalists possessed, and, on the other, the nature of the theology into which the kabbalistic traditions were integrated. Concerning the sources, it is evident that the early Christian kabbalists had very little access to the text of the Zohar itself, although they had before them much material that was not connected with the kabbalistic tradition of which the Zohar was the center.

It has been noted by scholars that many of the early quotations from the Zohar found in Christian kabbalah were taken from secondary sources, most notably from the quotations included in the works of the Italian fourteenth-century kabbalist, Rabbi Menachem Reccanatti,[18] whose selection and adoption of zoharic sections was not accidental; he himself did not present in his anthological works the full force of zoharic myths. The remoteness from the Zohar is evident by the fact that zoharic translations into Latin were few and late to appear in Christian kabbalah, and the Postel translation has never been printed to this very day. It is possible that the Jewish teachers of the early Christian kabbalists were themselves hesitant to transmit the more radical zoharic terminology and mythology to their Christian colleagues.

In addition, the body of translated works that these scholars possessed included many—probably a majority of—works that were

---

[17]Thus, for instance, the list of titles of the tenth sefirah, the Shechinah, presented in the end of the description of the ten divine powers (Part III, LXIIIa) follows Gikatilla in listing masculine and feminine titles without any emphasis on the particular feminine nature of this power or on its erotic connotations.

[18]See Scholem's detailed discussion in his study "The Beginning of the Christian Kabbalah," in J. Dan (editor), The Christian Kabbalah, Cambridge, MA: Harvard University Press 1998, pp. 17-51.

unrelated to the zoharic kabbalistic context: the writings of the
Ashkenazi Hasidim, Rabbi Eleazar of Worms and Rabbi Judah the
Pious,[19] which do not include the concept of ten divine hypostases,
and those of Abraham Abulafia, who rejected this system and emphasized other elements of Jewish esoteric traditions. Within the library at their disposal, the teachings of the *Zohar* did not have the
same centrality that the zoharic myth had for a reader of the
kabbalistic works in their original language.[20] The main sources for
the sefirotic concept that Pico and Reuchlin had before them were
the works of Rabbi Joseph Gikatilla, who systematized and demy-
thologized the zoharic world. In this, the Christian kabbalists were
separated from the development of the kabbalah by two hundred
years, in which the writings of the Ashkenazi Hasidim and those of
Abulafia were relatively marginalized in the Jewish kabbalistic tradition, while the *Zohar* acquired an increasingly central place. It is as
if Pico and Reuchlin were writing their works at the end of the thirteenth century rather than the end of the fifteenth and the beginning of the sixteenth. Yet the legend of the *Zohar* as an esoteric,
ancient work had its full impact on the early Christian kabbalah, in
disproportion to the adherence to its text, imagery, and terminology.

In addition to these textual considerations, one should take into
account the theological context. The zoharic concept of the ten *sefirot*
introduced into Judaism most forcefully a myth based on the neo-
Platonist world view of the sequence of divine emanations. For later
Jewish writers, this was the most normative presentation of neo-
Platonism in an authentic Jewish context.[21] The Christian kabbalists,

[19]Like ms. Vatican 189, which is the translation of Rabbi Judah the Pious's esoteric works, made by Mithridates; see Wirszubski, *Pico's Encounter*, pp. 11–12 et
passim.
[20]It should, however, be emphasized that the Christian kabbalists were not alone
in this attitude; several sixteenth-century Jewish kabbalists marginalized or ignored these aspects of zoharic mythology.
[21]Thus, for instance, the seventeenth-century scholar Manasseh ben Israel used
the *Zohar* for a neo-Platonistic presentation of the concept of the soul, disregarding
and marginalizing the zoharic mythological aspects, in his treatise on the eternity of the soul, *Nishmat Hayyim*.

who had at their disposal numerous neo-Platonic sources, and for whom the basic concepts of this tradition constituted the starting points of their world view in every aspect of their theology, there was no novelty or particular meaning in kabbalistic neo-Platonism. This aspect was used only occasionally to demonstrate the common ground between the kabbalah and other traditions, both the authentic Christian ones and other Hellenistic and Eastern sources, all deeply integrated in the neo-Platonist world view.[22]

Concerning the *Shechinah* and the inclusion of a feminine element within the divine world, Christian thinkers had no particular interest in the meaningful kabbalistic innovation within the Jewish context: They had their own feminine aspect in the figure of Mary, and, in some cases, the feminine metaphors ascribed to the Holy Spirit. Similarly, the ten *sefirot* held less interest within a theology that already had a concept of multiple elements constituting the divine world in the form of the Trinity; the kabbalah could add further proof and strengthen some aspects of the trinitarian theology, but this was not a dramatic innovation, as it was in Judaism when the kabbalah introduced its concept of the divine pleroma into Jewish religious culture.

III

One of the most intriguing aspects of the relationship between the Jewish kabbalah and the Christian kabbalah concerns the attitude toward the powers of evil and the role of Satan in the cosmos. Pico and Reuchlin wrote their treatises at a time when Christianity as a whole was adopting a dualistic world view, and was recognizing Satan and his adherents as present and working in every corner of

---

[22]Thus, for instance, when Reuchlin's Simon presents an unusual essay on this subject, Philolaus responds by saying, rather rudely: "Everything you are telling us, Simon, is Pythagoreanism and comes in the Italian philosophy we discussed in detail yesterday" (Part III, LIIa). The reference is to the discussion that the two scholars had on the Sabbath when Simon was absent, to which part II of the work is dedicated.

the physical and spiritual universes. The struggle between the powers of good and the powers of evil in human society and within the
human soul was given an increasing place in the age's consciousness,
and the pope's bull concerning witches and the *Malleus Maleficarum*
reflect this dramatic development. The Christian humanists, who
constituted the cultural context of the early Christian kabbalists,
in most cases stood away from this process, so it is no wonder that
they, too, did not emphasize this aspect in their writings. But the
meeting with the kabbalah could have had the opposite effect, for
the kabbalah is characterized within Jewish culture as being the main
source and drive for the development of Jewish dualistic concepts.
From its early beginnings in the *Bahir*, the kabbalah contained an
increased recognition of the powers of Satan, and later kabbalists[23]—
among them Nachmanides,[24] and, most emphatically, Rabbi Isaac
ben Jacob ha-Cohen of Castile—described a universe in which this
constant struggle is going on.[25] The *Zohar*'s adoption of Rabbi Isaac's
concept of the "Emanation on the Left," and the presentation of the
myths centered around the *sitra ahra* (the other, evil, left side of the
divine world),[26] introduced this concept into Judaism forcefully
(though some kabbalists were reluctant to include it in their works).

[23]Concerning the concept of evil in the *Bahir*, see Scholem, *Origins of the Kabbalah*,
pp. 150-151. It should be noted that, in the *Bahir*, evil is subservient to God;
only later kabbalists in the thirteenth century attributed to it an increased independence.

[24]Concerning Nachmanides' role in the development of the concept of evil in
the kabbalah, see J. Dan, "Nahmanides and the Development of the Concept of
Evil in the Kabbalah," in *The Life and Times of Mosse ben Nahman, Simposi
Commemoratiu del Vuite Centenari del seu Naixement*, Girona: Ajuntante de Girona
1995, pp. 161-179.

[25]Rabbi Isaac's main treatise (On the Emanations on the Left) was published by
Scholem in *Madaey ha-Yahdut*, vol. II (1926), pp. 244-264. For an English translation, see J. Dan and R. Keiner, *The Early Kabbalah*, New York: Paulist Press
1987, pp. 165-182.

[26]For a detailed description and discussion of the role of evil in the zoharic myth,
see I. Tishby, *The Wisdom of the Zohar*, vol. II, Oxford: Oxford University Press
1989, pp. 447-508; G. Scholem, "Good and Evil in the Kabbalah," in his *On the
Mystical Shape of the Godhead*, New York: Schocken 1991, pp. 56-86.

In the sixteenth century, and especially in the Lurianic kabbalah, this dualism became more and more central.[27] The kabbalah, one may say, was more in harmony with late-fifteenth- and sixteenth-century developments in Christian theology than were the humanists and the Christian kabbalists. The fact that a dualistic attitude was present in some of their kabbalistic sources—though not in those most frequently used by them—did not make the Christian kabbalists change their attitude toward contemporary developments in their own religion. Here, again, we see a convergence of the nature of the sources and basic theological attitudes that shaped the nature of the kabbalah, which the Christian scholars accepted and integrated in their works, diverging further and further from the original nature of the Jewish kabbalah.

Another aspect of this divergence was the result of the fact that, as stated above, the Christian kabbalists not only accepted the kabbalah as relevant to their spiritual world as an ancient esoteric tradition, but included all the nonbiblical Jewish sources—the Talmud, the Midrash,[28] and even medieval commentaries and treatises, including those written by rationalistic thinkers.[29] It is most meaningful, especially concerning talmudic-midrashic material. Many of the quotations presented in the works of the early Christian

---

[27]See J. Dan, "Kabbalistic and Gnostic Dualism," *Binah*, vol. III: *Jewish Intellectual History in the Middle Ages*, New York: Praeger 1995, pp. 19–33.
[28]Reuchlin did attempt to differentiate between talmudic and midrashic sayings and those of the kabbalists, but it has not been effective throughout his work. See, for instance, the clear attribution of a talmudic statement to a kabbalist (Part III, LIXa).
[29]Quotations from Rabbi David Kimchi (Radak) abound in their writings, as well as quotations from other non kabbalists like Rabbi Judah ha-Levi. The most prominent example is, of course, that of Maimonides, whose *Guide to the Perplexed* is constantly quoted as a work of kabbalah. In this, however, the Christian kabbalists were neither unique nor original. Maimonides was transformed, in the eyes of some thirteenth-century kabbalists, into a mystic, and kabbalistic interpretations of his work were composed. The Christian kabbalists, headed by Pico, had access to such works, especially Abulafia's kabbalistic commentary on the *Guide*. See Wirszubski, *Pico's Encounter*, pp. 84–99, and detailed bibliography there.

kabbalists as kabbalistic principles are actually simple, well-known talmudic and midrashic epigrams and commentaries. Sometimes this is because many such quotations were included in the kabbalistic works, which constantly referred to biblical and talmudic verses and sayings, as is the nature of every medieval Hebrew work. But because of this, the image of the kabbalah and the range of its ideas was completely distorted within the framework of the Christian kabbalah: Concepts, notions, ideas, and terms that within Jewish culture were known as universal were attributed in the Christian context particularly to the kabbalah.

What is true about terms and ideas is even truer concerning methodologies. For many Christian scholars, the first meeting with classical Jewish midrashic methodologies was through the Latin translations of kabbalistic works; they came to identify the methods used there with the kabbalah as such, whereas within a Jewish context these methodologies had a universal relevance unconnected in a particular way with the works of kabbalists. The best-known of these is the *gematria*, the computation of the numerical value of letters, words, and phrases and the use of the number to identify a similar number in another word or phrase. This is a classical Hebrew midrashic method based on the fact that every Hebrew letter has a numerical value—as does every letter in Greek and Arabic, and many of the letters in the Latin alphabet. The difference is only that the Islamic and Christian cultures adopted the use of special markings for numbers—the Arabic numerals—long before Jewish culture did (actually, the use of Arabic numerals spread in Judaism only in the last century, and for many purposes the alphabet is used for numbers to this day). There is nothing "kabbalistic" in the use of *gematria*, and the identification of kabbalah with numerology is wholly erroneous. Some kabbalists liked this methodology; others did not. The *Bahir*, the first kabbalistic work, did not use *gematria* (and neither did the non kabbalistic *Sefer Yezira*); the *Zohar* used it seldom; and the Luria school of kabbalists, as well as other Safed masters in this field, like Moses Cordovero, did not indulge in it. Abraham Abulafia, on the other hand, was an enthusiast of this method, as were the nonkabbalists Rabbi Judah the Pious and Rabbi Eleazar of

Worms. It should be mentioned for curiosity's sake that the earliest use of *gematria* known to us is found in the New Testament, not in the kabbalah: the famous "number of the beast," which is the numerical value of Nero Caesar in Hebrew.[30]

This happened also to other Jewish traditional ways of midrashic exegesis, including the transmutation of letters (*temurah*, the exchange of one letter for the another in a systematic way), the basis of which is actually biblical (the first example is that of the substitution of Sheshach for Bavel in Jeremiah[31]). Reuchlin and other Christian kabbalists made extensive use of this method, which they viewed as one of the essential messages of the kabbalah. Some Jewish esoterics, kabbalists, and nonkabbalists used this methodology in their writings, while others marginalized it; but within a Jewish context it was not necessarily conceived as a component of esoteric lore.

The core difference on the methodological level between Jewish esotericism and Christian kabbalah is the attitude toward biblical hermeneutics. For the Christian scholars, any nonsemantic exegesis of verses was regarded as strange, intriguing, and an indication of a great secret; within the context of Jewish culture, such methods were regarded as everyday homiletical practices that could be used for any purpose, even for humorous or aesthetic presentation. The classical format of the Midrash universalized nonsemantic interpretations and made them available to everyone; the Jewish concept of language made the infinite possibilities of interpretation a mundane, exoteric practice used by preachers every week.

This brief discussion is sufficient, I believe, to establish the concept of the relative and contingent nature of esotericism. Nothing is "naturally" esoteric. Esotericism is a designation of the historical role of certain ideas and methods within a culture rather than a description of their intrinsic characteristics. As an adjective, "esoteric" describes a culture's attitude toward ideas rather than the ideas themselves.

---

[30]Revelations 13:18, and see B. McGinn, *Antichrist: Two Thousand Years of the Human Fascination with Evil*, New York: Harper 1994, pp. 50–54.
[31]Jeremiah 25:26, 51:41.

In the example presented, it is clear that what the Jewish kabbalists perceived as the core of their esotericism—the dynamic inner life of the Godhead and the ways to be integrated in it—was marginalized by the Christian kabbalists, whereas the midrashic methodologies—which to a large extent were part of the exoteric midrashic traditions of Judaism—were regarded by the Latin scholars as the core of the kabbalah. These methodologies actually gave the meaning to the word "kabbalah" in European languages (as the legal, exoteric methods of the *halachah* gave meaning to the term "talmudic" in Europe). There was an area of common ground: The secrets of the divine names and their analysis constituted a central subject in both Jewish esotericism and in the Christian adaptations, though, again, it seems that in the Latin works the methodology often overshadows the theological content.

The subject of esotericism and its meanings has been discussed with renewed intensity in the last few years.[32] It seems to me that a possible contribution of this discussion to the subject of European esotericism in general and to the understanding of the phenomenon as a whole can be made by stressing the nature of language as conceived by most esotericists. The language of the esoterics differs from that of theologians—and from that of many mystics—in its delegating of the semantic level of language to a secondary place, and emphasizing the nonsemantic aspects of language. The alphabet acquires importance as an independent subject, unrelated to the words and sentences that can be constructed from it. Exotic forms of letters—Hebrew, Coptic, Arabic, Ethiopian—become a subject of deliberation and emphasis. Pictures, symbols, and logoi abound, substituting the usual semantic ways of expression. The esoteric expert is a "reader": He can read series of signs that other people cannot, be it

---

[32]One of the most important contributions to the subject is the collection of articles *Hermeticism and the Renaissance: Intellectual History and the Occult in Early Modern Europe*, ed. Ingrid Merkel and Allen G. Debus, Washington, DC: Folger Books 1988. The term "hermeticism" is used in many of the studies in this wide-ranging volume as an equivalent of "esotericism" in the present volume. It should, however, be noted that the Christian kabbalah is absent from this volume, as the linguistic aspect of the subject is marginal in most of the discussions.

an exotic alphabet, a system of astrological or alchemical signs, or any other physical system that acquires semiotic significance. The esoteric sees a language where other people see meaningless scratches and a chaos of signs. Numbers become a main subject in themselves and acquire meaning independent of their arithmetic message.

Christian kabbalah's main contribution to Western esotericism in the centuries following Pico was the recognition of the relevance of Hebrew nonbiblical writings and traditions to the affirmation of Christianity. For this purpose, a selection from Hebrew writings, mystical and nonmystical, kabbalistic and nonkabbalistic, was translated into Latin and utilized by the Christian thinkers. This transition, however, changed in a meaningful way the balance and emphases that prevailed in the Hebrew sources, and created a new phenomenon, marked by its concentration upon methodology rather than theology, a quest for the nonsemantic aspects of language rather than a theological or mystical message.

The Kabbalah of Johannes Reuchlin and Its Historical Significance

RELEVANCE

The attitude of Christian scholars—especially the humanists of the late fifteenth and early sixteenth centuries in Italy, France, and Germany—toward Jewish traditional works in general and the kabbalah in particular[1] can be viewed in two different ways, both of them factual and accurate. One way is to see it as a continuation of the centuries-old quest of Christianity for the verification of its experiences, beliefs, rituals, and dogma by Jewish sources. The focus of this quest, since the Gospels, has been the Hebrew Bible, to which later Jewish works, mainly the Talmud and the Midrash, were added

---

[1]There are a few general surveys of the history of the Christian kabbalah. Among the most important are Joseph L. Blau, *The Christian Interpretation of the Cabala in the Renaissance*, New York: Columbia University Press 1944; and François Secret, *Les kabbalistes chrétiens de la Renaissance*, Paris: Dunod 1964. The subject plays an important part in the studies of Frances Yates as well as in those of Paul O. Kristeller, some of which are mentioned in the following notes. The studies of Gershom Scholem and Chaim Wirszubski are also listed in the following notes.

in the Middle Ages. Several Christian apologists, from Petrus Alfonsi at the beginning of the twelfth century[2] to Flavius Mithridates at the end of the fifteenth,[3] most of them converts from Judaism, lead the process. Similar elements are found in the writings of the Christian kabbalists of the Renaissance. The premise of this attitude is that Christian truth is complete and beyond doubt; the added Jewish sources are needed not in order to strengthen it, but mainly to demonstrate its truth to the Jews and to further demonstrate that only the "unnatural stubbornness" of the Jews blinds them from perceiving the inevitability of the recognition of the mission of Jesus Christ. The scholarly enterprise therefore is directed, first and foremost, toward the Jews. This, essentially, was Gershom Scholem's view, which he presented forcefully in his study of the roots of the Christian kabbalah;[4] he was followed by other scholars.[5] There can, however, be a completely different approach, which recent studies of the subject seem to indicate and which is adopted in this chapter.

---

[2]See Bernard McGinn, "Cabalists and Christians: Reflections on cabala in medieval and Renaissance thought," in *Jewish Christians and Christian Jews*, eds. R. H. Popkin and G. M. Weiner, Dordrecht 1994, pp. 11–34. The author presents the christological interpretation of the tetragrammaton by Petrus Alfonsi, a converted Jew, in his *Dialogi contra Judaeos*, which was written in 1110. Alfonsi quotes a Jewish esoteric work, *Secreta Secretorum*, as his Hebrew source. This book should be identified, I believe, with the Hebrew-Aramaic *Raza Rabba* or *Sod ha-Sodot*, which deals with interpretations of the tetragrammaton and served as a source for the kabbalistic book *Bahir*, the earliest text of the kabbalah (end of the twelfth century). Concerning Alfonsi, see also Anna Sapir Abulafia, *Christians and Jews in the Twelfth-century Renaissance*, London and New York 1995, pp. 91–94 et passim; G. Dahan, *Les intellectuels chrétiens et les Juifs au moyen age*, Paris 1990, pp. 239–270; A. Grabois, "The Historica Veritas and Jewish-Christian Intellectual Relations in the Twelfth Century," *Speculum* 50 (1975), pp. 613–634; J. Tolan, *Petrus Alfonsi and His Medieval Readers*, Gainsville, FL 1993, pp. 37–38 et passim.
[3]Concerning Mithridates, see note 17.
[4]This article is published in an English translation.
[5]See especially the introduction of M. Idel to the Martin and Sarah Goodman translation of *De Arte Cabbalistica*, Lincoln, NE 1983. Quotations in this chapter are from this translation.

The Christian kabbalah, especially the works of Pico della Mirandola and Johannes Reuchlin, represents a different, additional message: The nonbiblical Jewish sources are meaningful and relevant to Christianity itself. There is no doubt that the content of these works strengthens and upholds Christianity; yet their study has an impact on Christianity itself, and offers a deeper, more profound understanding of the nature of Christianity. Not only is it relevant as arguments against stubborn Jews; it also benefits the faith of Christians. The message of this school of thought is not only that the Jews should change, but that Christianity itself has to be revitalized by a renewed understanding of its ancient origins that has become possible by the revelation of new sources. These include, first and foremost, the Hermetic writings, and the kabbalah is regarded as an integral—if not the oldest and most sacred—part of these rediscovered pre-Christian sources of divine truth.

This notion of relevance is very nearly unique in the history of the three scriptural religions. I am not aware of any authentic Jewish or Muslim cultural phenomenon that found Christian sources relevant to the establishment of a more profound and meaningful Judaism or Islam. Nor am I aware of any other Christian phenomenon—including contemporary attempts to bring together Christians and Jews—in which Jewish nonbiblical creativity is regarded by Christians as relevant to their own faith. Nor can one find examples in which Jews or Muslims found each other's religious traditions relevant to the analysis and understanding of their creeds.[6] Such a

---

[6]The interest of Jewish rationalist philosophers in the Middle Ages in the great Arabic philosophical works of the ninth to twelfth centuries cannot be regarded as an expression of such a concept of relevance. The Jewish writers were interested in the Greek philosophical ideas and methods on which these works were based and, to some extent, in the process of adaptation of these theories in a monotheistic, scriptural structure. It should be noted that even that was extremely one-sided. Arab philosophers did not express similar interest in Jewish philosophical works (which were written in Judeo-Arabic in the Hebrew script, and thus closed, in most cases, to non-Jews). Later, Jewish interest in the works of Christian scholastics in the fourteenth century, for instance, is similar in nature, expressing interest in methodology and particular philosophical problems.

concept of relevance necessitates an attitude of respect toward the
source included in the tradition of another religion, without tearing
it out of its original context in that culture; in other words, independent of the primary or ultimate motive for interest in the relevant phenomenon, such relevance denotes the existence of some
degree of tolerance toward the teachings of another faith. This does
not mean that the scholar emphasizing such relevance is in any way
hesitant or incomplete in his own faith; on the contrary, he may
believe in the most sincere manner that the analysis of the relevant
texts fortifies and magnifies the superiority of his own faith, compared to those who ignore it. Relevance of this sort may be described,
in terminology used in other areas of human strife, as the rejection
of the "zero-sum conflict" seen as expressing the relationship between
the two religions. The Christian kabbalist rejects, knowingly or
unknowingly, the concept that Christianity is right exactly inasmuch
as Judaism is wrong, and any diminishment in the rightness or wrong-
ness of the one immediately is transferred to the rightness or wrong-
ness of the other. For him, the statement that there is more truth in
Jewish traditions than was previously supposed does not diminish
Christian truth, but enhances it. As stated, I have not been able to
find a credible, sustained parallel to this attitude in earlier or later
points of contact between Judaism, Christianity, and Islam.[7]

The Christian kabbalah must be regarded, from a historical
point of view, as an unusual chapter in the relationships among scholars from different scriptural religions, which have been both very
close and very far from each other for two millennia. In order to
achieve a historical understanding of this cultural phenomenon, the
two terms that combine in the name "Christian kabbalah" should be

---

[7]It should be noted with some sadness that the situation in scholarship concerning the three religions was not, and is not today, much better than that found
in the writings of theologians and teachers of these religions. It is still a rare
phenomenon to find adequate attention given to Jewish sources of the postbiblical
period in the study of the history of religion and culture, in both Christianity
and Islam. While the situation is somewhat better concerning historical studies
in the narrow sense, histories of culture and spirituality are still confined, in most
cases, to one or another religious framework.

investigated; it should not be taken for granted that the term "kabbalah" as a component of the phrase "Christian kabbalah" has the same meaning that it has in other, mainly Jewish, contexts; nor should it be taken for granted that "Christianity" in this phrase is identical in its meaning to any other of the numerous messages of this term throughout the ages. The main concern of this study is Johannes Reuchlin's *De Arte Cabbalistica*, and the discussion of the meaning of "Christianity" and "kabbalah" is therefore mainly directed at the usages of these terms in that particular context; yet the implications are more general, and have relevance concerning the three centuries in which the Christian kabbalah flourished in early modern Europe.

CHRISTIANITY IN "CHRISTIAN KABBALAH"

When Pico della Mirandola published his controversial theses,[8] including the declaration that the kabbalah (and magic) constitutes the best proof of the veracity of Christianity, he was not pointing out a new and powerful affirmation of Christianity; rather, he was stating that the kabbalah (and magic) was the ultimate proof of his own conception of Christianity. Pico's thesis announces not the strengthening of traditional Christianity, but that Christianity should have a different meaning from the prevailing one, the meaning outlined in his nine hundred theses. The term "Christianity" in the phrase "Christian kabbalah" is a new phenomenon presented by Pico and his followers.[9]

The period in which the Christian kabbalah came into being is characterized by three main historical events that changed the

---

[8]The theses relating to the kabbalah have been analyzed by Chaim Wirszubski, *Pico della Mirandola's Encounter with Jewish Mysticism*, Jerusalem and Cambridge, MA 1989.
[9]Scholem was aware of this fact, and at the beginning of his study he pointed out the opposition of traditional Christians to Pico's assertion. Yet the main thrust of his article is the emphasis on the traditional character of this phenomenon rather than its innovative, or even revolutionary, nature within the framework of Christianity and its attitude toward Jewish sources.

Christian world and had far-reaching influence in bringing the medieval world to its end and in shaping Christianity in the modern period. The first is the culture of the Renaissance, especially the humanist currents in Italy, Germany, France, and England. The second is the Reformation and the religious and political upheavals that the first two-and-a-half centuries of its spread brought to Europe. The third is the witch hunts, which began at almost exactly the same time that the Christian kabbalah appeared, and continued to dominate Europe for nearly the same period as the spread of the Christian kabbalah. The mere listing of these four phenomena suffices to demonstrate clearly that the "Christianity" of the "Christian kabbalah" is completely different from that of the witch hunts, the early Protestant sects, and the Catholic reaction, although it is closely connected with the "Christianity" of the humanists of the Renaissance.[10] Interest in the Christian kabbalah in the late fifteenth, sixteenth, and seventeenth centuries denoted an affiliation with trends within Christianity that continued the humanist tradition, while it expressed a remoteness, at least, from the courts of the Inquisition that judged witches and heretics, and at least some kind of disengagement from the fierce religious conflicts between the Church and the various manifestations of the great Reform movement. Johannes Reuchlin and Martin Luther both were condemned, in the same document, by the pope (in 1517),[11] yet the Judaism presented in

---

[10]Even within the culture of Renaissance humanism, the Christian kabbalists constituted a different and radical element. Frances Yates has pointed out, correctly and vigorously, the difference between the Latin humanists—of whom Erasmus is a prominent example—for whom the main value to be derived from classical antiquity is the perfection of Latin style and the aesthetic rhetorical norms in opposition to medieval scholasticism, and the "Greek" or "magical" schools, including Ficino and Pico, for whom the content of ancient esoteric works was paramount. See F. A. Yates, *Giordano Bruno and the Hermetic Tradition*, Chicago and London 1964, pp. 159–168 et passim. Discussion of this important observation is presented in her other studies as well. The Christian kabbalists should be regarded as the most radical wing among the "Greek-magic-science" schools in Yates's distinction.

[11]Pope Leo X, despite his deep sympathy for Reuchlin, banned the treatise written to defend his views—the *Augenspiegel*—in 1520, together with the writings of Martin Luther.

the writings of Luther is as different as one can imagine from that presented by Reuchlin, and the Christianity of *De Arte Cabbalistica* is remote, in the same measure, from the Christianity of Martin Luther. The theses of Pico della Mirandola and the *Malleus Maleficarum* have little in common, even though they were published at almost the same time. While the differences are obvious, it is necessary to try to formulate the particular points of divergence that are relevant to our subject.

As Reuchlin is our starting point,[12] the main difference can be presented in one word that expresses almost everything: Pythagoras. In 1517, Reuchlin wrote a letter to the pope, Leo X, the son of Lorenzo de Medici. The main purpose of the letter was to declare Reuchlin's innocence of the accusations made by his persecutors from Cologne, and to introduce the numerous documents of support for his position. The letter begins with words of praise for the pope and his family:

> The Italian philosophy of the Christian religion, which was once handed down from Pythagoras, the first parent of its fame, to great men of excellent minds, submitted for many years to the loud barking of the sophists, and lay buried for time in darkness and dense night, until by the favor of the gods there rose the Sun of all the best kinds of studies, your renowned father.

---

[12]It is a long time since Reuchlin's life and work received a comprehensive, new scholarly treatment. The classical biographies are still used—especially Ludwig Geiger's *Johann Reuchlin, sein Leben und seine Werke*, Leipzig 1871. Geiger also published Reuchlin's vast correspondence (see note 13). Compare also Francis Barham, *The Life and Times of John Reuchlin, or Capnion, the Father of the German Reformation*, London 1843. An important contribution to our subject is the bibliography of Reuchlin's Judaica library: Karl Christ, *Die Bibliothek Reuchlins in Pforzheim*, Leipzig 1924, pp. 36–50; and compare *Johannes Reuchlin: Gutachten über das Jüdische Schrifttum*, ed. Antonie Leinz-v. Dessauer, Stuttgart 1965. See also Guido Kisch, *Zasius und Reuchlin; eine rechtsgeschichtlich-vergleichende Studie zum Toleranzproblem im 16. Jahrhundert*, Stuttgart 1961, and Noel L. Brann, "Humanism in Germany," in *Humanism: Foundations, Forms, Legacy*, 2, ed. A. Rabil, Jr., Philadelphia 1988, pp. 123–156. Another aspect is explored in Heiko A. Oberman's monograph *Wurzeln des Antisemitismus: Christenangst und Judenplage im Zietalter von Humanismus und Reformation*, Berlin 1981; a detailed discussion of the attitudes of Reuchlin, Pfefferkorn, Erasmus, and Luther to Judaism.

The essence of the Medici achievement is described as the rediscovery of the "Italian philosophy of the Christian religion," the source of which was Pythagoras, who was persecuted by the "sophists" in the same way that Reuchlin was now being hounded by the Cologne clerics. A more elaborate statement is presented in a following paragraph:

> Considering, therefore, that scholars lacked only the Pythagorean works, which still lay hidden, dispersed here and there in the Laurentian Academy, I believed that you would hardly be displeased if I should make public the doctrines which Pythagoras and the noble Pythagoreans are said to have held, so that these works which up to now have remained unknown to the Latins may be read at your happy command. Marsilio [Ficino] has prepared Plato for Italy, Lefèvre d'Étaples has restored Aristotle for the French, and I, Reuchlin, shall complete the group, and explain to the Germans the Pythagoras who has been reborn through my efforts, in the work which I have dedicated to your name. But this task could not be accomplished without the cabala of the Jews, because the philosophy of Pythagoras had its origins in the precepts of the cabala, and when in the memory of our ancestors it disappeared from Magna Graecia, it lived again in the volumes of the cabalists. Then all these works were almost completely destroyed. I have therefore written On the Cabalistic Art, which is symbolical philosophy, so that the doctrines of the Pythagoreans might be better known to scholars. About these doctrines I affirm nothing, but I simply present a dialogue between Philolaus Junior, a Pythagorean, and Marranus, a Moslem, who came together from their various travels in an inn at Frankfort to listen to Simon the Jew, a man highly trained in the cabala. . . .[13]

The history of Christianity, Judaism, and Pythagoreanism is presented here with unusual clarity. The "Italian philosophy of the

---

[13]*Johann Reuchlins Briefwechsel*, ed. L. Geiger, Tübingen 1875; trans. Mary Martin McLaughlin, reprinted in *The Portable Renaissance Reader*, New York 1968, pp. 409–414. Reuchlin's dedication at the beginning of *De Arte Cabbalistica*, which is presented to Pope Leo, includes paragraphs similar to that letter.

Christian religion" was recorded first in the works of the Jewish kabbalah. It was then absorbed by Pythagoras and his disciples. Their writings have been dispersed, and can be reconstructed now only by assembling the fragments of the Greek school and combining them with the remaining volumes of the Jewish kabbalah. Together, they represent the lost philosophy of Christianity, and this is the essence of Reuchlin's enterprise. There is no boundary separating Pythagoras from the kabbalah, and there is no boundary separating them from the philosophy of the Christian religion. According to Reuchlin, in his treatise on the art of the kabbalah he himself "affirms nothing"; he only presents the dialogue between the kabbalist, Simon, and his Pythagorean and Muslim disciples. Christianity seems not to be present anywhere in this scheme, because it is everywhere. Reuchlin describes himself in this letter as "I who have suffered such great wrongs for our Christ," and the sincere meaning of this statement should not be doubted. Reuchlin, like the other humanists, is not an apologist. He does not seek to reconcile Christianity with other traditions, or to differentiate it from them; he is certain that truth and Christianity are absolutely identical. Therefore any true, ancient tradition, being preserved in Greek, Hebrew, Arabic, or "Chaldean," is a true Christian tradition. According to his own description, he did not have to point out how the doctrines of Pythagoras and the kabbalah strengthen or demonstrate this or that element of Christian philosophy, because of his belief that they *are* Christian philosophy. There can be no knowledge that is not Christian knowledge, nor can there be any ancient, true tradition that is not a Christian tradition. The specific rituals that individuals may follow are immaterial; Simon the Jew may observe the Sabbath and other Jewish precepts, and his way of life is respected by his listeners, yet the doctrines he presents are Christian ones, as are those of the Pythagoreans; no specific proof or analysis is needed concerning their Christian nature once their antiquity and philosophical veracity have been established. Reuchlin believed that by identifying the kabbalah with Pythagoras, whose writings were found in the Laurentian Academy library, the pope would be bound to come to his assistance, because Reuchlin's enterprise was a Medici enterprise.

Reuchlin expresses his concept of his own work by comparing it to Ficino's presentation of Plato to the Italians and Lefèvre's presentation of Aristotle to the French. Pythagoras and the kabbalah are no different from Plato and Aristotle in their inherent Christian nature. Being older than the Greek philosophers, and relying on Jewish traditions that originated in a divine revelation, they are more original; Greek truth is derived from the Jewish one, but both are manifestations of Christianity.

The details of this identification will be discussed further later. Here we should emphasize the main point, which is that Reuchlin's Christianity is different, in almost every way, from that of the Dominican Kramer or of Luther. The previously quoted paragraphs are not taken from one of Reuchlin's many published works; they constitute the most important passages in a letter written to the pope, for the purpose of defending himself against accusations that his Christian credentials are not perfect. Reuchlin seeks the pope's help in this controversy, which actually positions the two sides as competing, before the supreme authority, to decide who is the better Christian. Thus, in a context in which his faith is under judicial review before the pope, Reuchlin does not hesitate to define his beliefs in the framework of the triple identification of kabbalah, Pythagoras, and Christianity. He does so because he is certain that this is the only true way, and is supported by the conviction that this was the Medicis' Christianity, which is also the pope's, and therefore the dominant, normative one. Reuchlin seems not to have realized how marginal his concept of Christianity was in that time, and how precarious his religious position was; even the great Erasmus hesitated to join the controversy and come overtly to his colleague's assistance.

This is just one example among many; it proves that the term "Christian" in the phrase "Christian kabbalah" denotes a very specific, highly unusual meaning shared by very few people before, after, or during the period in which this cultural phenomenon flourished. The most important point, I believe, in Reuchlin's presentation is his sincere belief that his work contributes meaningfully to the wholesomeness of Christianity; it is not intended to prove the veracity of Christianity to the Jews by pointing out the Christian nature of their own traditions. He is a reformer of German Christianity who brings the light of the Pythagorean-kabbalistic philosophy to his brothers. This "Christianity" is not that of Kramer or of Luther, but its intrinsic, sincere Christian orientation cannot be doubted.

THE KABBALAH IN "CHRISTIAN KABBALAH"

There is hardly any definition within Jewish culture of the term "kabbalah" with which the term "Christian kabbalah" can be compared. The word is used in medieval Hebrew for both tradition in general (especially the oral tradition, revealed by God to Moses, which includes the oral law and the meanings of the written Torah), and the esoteric tradition as a particular segment of that vast complex. The kabbalists used this term to denote their insistent claim that the material presented in their works is the result not of new, individual revelation or experience (including mystical experience), but of traditions preserved in old manuscripts and by oral transmission of secrets from generation to generation.

The identification of "kabbalah" with mysticism, so common today, is the result of the adaptation of modern terminology to material that did not include, in an authentic form, the concept or a term for mysticism. Hebrew (like Arabic) does not have a word denoting "mysticism," and no kabbalist in the Middle Ages or early modern times knew that he was supposed to be a mystic. "Kabbalah" and "mysticism" can be regarded as opposites, because the first emphasizes tradition and marginalizes individual experience, whereas the second includes the notion of an original discovery of a truth by an individual.[14]

---

[14]An example expressing this conflict can be found in the history of the most important work of the kabbalah, the *Zohar*. The work was published, in separate treatises, by Rabbi Moses de Leon in Castile at the end of the thirteenth century and in the first years of the fourteenth; he claimed that he was copying these secrets from an old manuscript brought from the Holy Land. When Rabbi Moses died in 1305, he left his wife destitute, and a rich kabbalist offered the widow a large sum of money for the original manuscript. The wife could not

The Christian kabbalah uses the term "kabbalah" in a way that is almost identical to that of the kabbalists themselves. It views the material found in the Hebrew works as ancient, esoteric tradition; the concept of mysticism does not play any meaningful part in the descriptions of the Hebrew sources found in the works of the Christian scholars. They hardly ever relate to a Jewish rabbi having an experience or revelation; they insist that their informants were the guardians of the oldest secrets ever revealed by God to man. The antiquity of the material is the proof of its veracity rather than a direct relationship with God, as is the case among Christian mystics. In this sense, the Christian kabbalah should not be regarded as a phenomenon to be integrated into the history of mysticism. Several great Christian mystics made use of the ideas and terms that the Christian kabbalists introduced to Christian culture, but so, also, did rationalistic philosophers, scientists, magicians, and others. Research concerning the influence of the kabbalah on the spiritual world of Jacob Boheme should be balanced by noting the influence of the same sources on Leibniz and Newton.

The meaning of the word "kabbalah" is, therefore, nearly identical in Jewish and Christian usages. Yet, there is a meaningful difference once we compare the texts denoted by the term. The library

produce the manuscript, and claimed that her late husband was "writing from his mind" (see G. Scholem, *Major Trends in Jewish Mysticism*, New York 1954, pp. 190-191; and I. Tishby, *The Wisdom of the Zohar*, vol. 1, Oxford 1989, pp. 13-17). Rabbi Moses claimed to be a kabbalist, a copyist of traditions, while his wife insisted that he was a mystic who wrote down his own experiences. See Scholem, *Major Trends*, pp. 80-118; idem, *The Origins of the Kabbalah*, Princeton, NJ 1987, pp. 180-198 et passim; I. Marcus, *Piety and Society*, Leiden 1980; J. Dan, *The Esoteric Theology of Ashkenazi Hasidism*, Jerusalem 1968 (in Hebrew); idem, "The Emergence of Jewish Mysticism in Medieval Germany," in *Mystics of the Book*, ed. R. A. Herrera, New York 1993, pp. 57-95. A general survey and bibliography on the subject are included in my article "Ashkenazi Hasidism 1941-1991" in *Gershom Scholem's Major Trends in Jewish Mysticism: Fifty Years After*, eds. P. Schaefer and J. Dan, Tübingen 1993, pp. 87-101. See also A. Epstein, "The Ashkenazi Kabbalah," in the collection of his studies, *Mi-Kadmoniot ha-Yehudim*, Jerusalem 1955, pp. 237-250 (in Hebrew); and J. Dan, "The Ashkenazi kabbalah—a Renewed Discussion," *Jerusalem Studies in Jewish Thought* 6: 3-4 (1987), pp. 125-139 (in Hebrew).

of works translated from the Hebrew for the Christian kabbalists and the Hebrew treatises that they used include books that are not regarded, within the framework of Jewish culture, as kabbalistic ones. The most notable group of writings of this kind are the works of Rabbi Judah ben Samuel of Regensburg and Rabbi Eleazar ben Judah of Worms, the two prominent writers of the Kalonymus school of Jewish esoterics in medieval Germany usually referred to as the "Ashkenazi Hasidim." [15] These writers presented in their works esoteric traditions and their own theological discourses (as well as works in the field of ethics, which are irrelevant to the present context). In modern times they sometimes have been included in the literary tradition of the kabbalah, but despite meaningful similarities, the main ideas of the kabbalah are absent from their works.[16] It seems that Flavius Mithridates, the great translator of Hebrew kabbalistic texts into Latin, was attracted to this material,[17] as was Cardinal Egidio da Viterbo, who had copied for him one great collection by Rabbi Eleazar and read it carefully, adding many marginal notes in Latin.[18]

The most significant aspect of the Christian understanding of the term "kabbalah" is the inclusion of numerous talmudic and midrashic quotations and references within the confines of this term. This does not contradict the Hebrew meaning of the term, which, as pointed out, may refer to the oral tradition as a whole. Christian

---

[15]On this more esoteric literature see J. Dan, "The Emergence of Jewish Mysticism in Medieval Germany," in R. A. Herrera (ed.), *Mystics of the Book*, New York: Peter Lang 1993, pp. 57–95.

[16]A detailed comparison between the kabbalah and the esoteric doctrines of the Ashkenazi Hasidim is presented in my study: "The 'Ashkenazi Kabbalah' Re-examined," *Jerusalem Studies in Jewish Thought* 6 (1987), pp. 125–139 (in Hebrew).

[17]C. Wirszubski, *Pico della Mirandola's Encounter with Jewish Mysticism*, pp. 69–76. The main work translated by Mithridates is the collection of treatises, most of them by Rabbi Judah and two by Rabbi Eleazar, preserved in Hebrew in the Oxford ms. Bodleian Library 1967, Oppenheim collection 540, and in Latin in the Vatican ms. Ebr. 189. It seems that Mithridates used the same, or a very similar, Hebrew source.

[18]Ms. British Library Add. 27, 199; this is the *Sodey Razaya* collection by Rabbi Eleazar of Worms, which includes the extensive commentary on the tetragrammaton, *Sefer ha-Shem*.

kabbalists often quoted talmudic sayings and sections as "kabbalah"; sometimes this was done because they found this material within the kabbalistic texts they were discussing. That is, they were taken not from the Talmud or Midrash directly, but from the works of Recanati, Gikatilla, and others. In other cases, however, talmudic material was directly presented as "kabbalah." I did not find, in the literature that I could survey for this study, a clear distinction between talmudic-midrashic traditions and kabbalistic ones. Such a distinction is rare in the Jewish sources as well; after all, many kabbalistic works, including the *Bahir* and the *Zohar*, were presented by the kabbalists as being an integral part of the talmudic tradition, preserved and presented by talmudic sages. This attitude of the Christian kabbalists reflects loyalty to the nature of the texts that served them as sources. There is, however, a meaningful difference: The Jewish reader of kabbalistic works was aware when a talmudic or midrashic statement was interwoven into the kabbalistic text (and so, obviously, was the author). Christian readers were aware of biblical verses integrated into the text, but in most cases they could not distinguish between kabbalistic statements and talmudic ones. In this sense, even an accurate translation into Latin did not convey the same meaning to Jewish and Christian readers: The Jews were aware of the many layers of the text, whereas the Christians, in most cases, understood all postbiblical statements as if they were on one linguistic-historical level.

However, by doing so, the Christian kabbalists ignored and denied attitudes and concepts that had developed in Christianity for many centuries, which condemned the Talmud as an evil and blasphemous work, one that might include the demand to use the blood of Christian children for Jewish rituals, and that had as its main purpose the denial of Christianity. For many generations the Talmud was the subject of trials, and the demand to burn it was a constant one among various Christian orders. This enmity toward the Talmud serves also as a meaningful component of the controversy around Reuchlin.[19] Quoting talmudic sources as reflections of

---

[19]See section "Reuchlin, Hebrew, and Kabbalah."

ancient truth relevant to Christian faith was an act of courage and determination that separated the Christian kabbalists, especially Pico and Reuchlin, from the Christian mainstream.[20] It was easier to present "kabbalah" as a relevant ancient Jewish source of truth, because this term did not have evil associations in Christian culture. There is no doubt, however, that these scholars were aware of their usage of talmudic material, and sometimes stated this explicitly. Following the Jewish concept of the term "kabbalah" demanded a high price when it was done in a Christian cultural context.

The most complex problem concerning the term "kabbalah" in the usage of the Christian kabbalists concerns the main ideas and symbols that this term denotes. The kabbalah has been identified, both by its practitioners and by scholars, as an esoteric tradition that is centered around a group of symbols representing the ten manifestations of God, the *sefirot*. Though not all kabbalists accepted this system or used it in an identical way (Abraham Abulafia is the best-known opponent of this system in the thirteenth century), it remained the most obvious characteristic distinguishing kabbalistic from nonkabbalistic works. This system also includes the new idea, first presented in the *Bahir*, that the realm of the *sefirot* includes a feminine power, the *Shechinah* or *Malchut*.[21] In the *Zohar*, this concept was developed into an intense sexual depiction of the dynamism in

---

[20]Their attitude should be compared to that of Mithridates, who presented, in the sermon he delivered before the pope, talmudic sayings that he derived from the fiercely anti-talmudic treatise of Raimondus Martini as "hitherto unknown secret tradition of the Jews." See C. Wirszubski, *Flavius Mithridates Sermo de Passione Domini*, Jerusalem: Israel Academy of Sciences and Humanities 1963. Jewish converts to Christianity were in the forefront of the attacks against the Talmud (although they did not participate in the attribution of the blood libel to talmudic sources; the first Jew to do that was Jacob Frank, the Sabbatian "Messiah" of the eighteenth century, who supported this accusation in 1757 and 1760, just before he and his followers converted to Christianity in Poland).
[21]See G. Scholem, *The Mystical Shape of the Godhead*, New York 1991, pp. 56–87; I. Tishby, *Wisdom of the Zohar*, 2, pp. 447–546; J. Dan, "Samael, Lilith and the Concept of Evil in Early Kabbalah," *AJS Review* 5 (1980), pp. 17–40; idem, "Kabbalistic and Gnostic Dualism," in *Jewish Intellectual History in the Middle Ages*, Binah, 3, New York 1994, pp. 19–34.

the divine world. Another important characteristic of this literature is the presence of a second system of *sefirot* on the left (evil) side, creating a dualistic concept of existence in both the divine and the earthly realms.[22] These three elements—the pleroma of ten *sefirot*, the femininity of the *Shechinah*, and the parallel world of evil powers— are the core of the world view presented in the *Zohar* and in the kabbalistic works that followed it.

If the teachings of the kabbalah were reconstructed from the quotations and descriptions presented by the founders of the Christian kabbalah, none of these ideas would hold a central place. If the kabbalah were to be defined as writings that present these concepts as their main ones, the Christian kabbalah could not be regarded as rightfully using that title. It seems that the Christian kabbalists, consciously or unconsciously, rejected or marginalized the symbols that were central to the *Zohar* and most other kabbalistic works. Reuchlin's attitude toward them will be discussed later in some detail. In this general survey, some reasons for this marked difference between the Hebrew kabbalah and the Christian one should be pointed out. They are found, I believe, in three realms.

1. The Hebrew sources available to the Christian kabbalists were less emphatic concerning these symbols than concerning the whole body of kabbalistic literature. The writings of Judah of Regensburg and Eleazar of Worms did not include them because they were not kabbalists in this sense of the term. Abraham Abulafia, one of the main sources for Pico, rejected them. Recanati and Gikatilla did not emphasize them in the same way that the *Zohar* did, though the concepts of the pleroma and the femininity of the *Shechinah* are present in their works. It was easier to reject them when facing the li-

---

[22]The first presentation of a dualistic concept of the realm of the *sefirot*, divided into right (sacred) and left (evil) sides is presented in Rabbi Isaac ha-Cohen's *Treatise on the Emanation on the Left*. The Hebrew text was published by G. Scholem in *Mada'e ha-Yahadut*, 2 (1927), pp. 244–264. An English translation of part of the text is included in J. Dan and R. Kiener, *The Early Kabbalah*, New York 1986, pp. 165–181.

brary of works used by the Christian kabbalists than those by someone familiar with the totality of the Hebrew material. The Christian kabbalah developed in a particular time and context where deemphasizing these elements was more possible than in other times and cultural contexts.

2. In many cases, the Christian kabbalists were more interested in detail than in the general theosophical structure of the material they were using. Pythagoras—as they understood him—and Plato, and, obviously, the Christian tradition, supplied the general systematic structure, to which the kabbalistic texts add verification, elucidation of details, and particular information. They often treated the texts as collections of factual information concerning the nature of the universe, rather than theological treatises presenting a complete theosophical system. This caused them to study sentences and paragraphs, marginalizing the integrated message of complete works.

3. All the kabbalistic ideas were problematic when transformed to a Christian context. It is difficult to harmonize the ten divine hypostases—the *sefirot*—with the Christian concepts of the Trinity. It was not difficult to find kabbalistic structures, in the realm of the *sefirot* as well as in the analysis of the tetragrammaton and other divine names, that support the Trinity, but the concept of the *sefirot* did not lend itself easily to an integration with the Trinity. In a similar way, the feminine elements in the concepts of the divine realm in Christianity, the image of the Mother and sometimes the Holy Spirit, could not be reconciled, without difficulty, with the intense sexuality of the kabbalistic descriptions of the *Shechinah*.

Concerning the dualism of good and evil, it seems that the period in which the Christian kabbalah emerged was the most suitable for the fusion of Christian and kabbalistic concepts of the devil and his realms; the end of the fifteen century and the beginning of the sixteenth were when Christian concepts of such dualism were studied, elaborated on, and put into practice by the Inquisition. Yet such a fusion did not happen, and the reason is rather clear: The humanists who ignored the dualism inherent in some of their kabbalistic sources also ignored, or opposed, the contemporary dualistic tendencies in Christianity.

The combination of these attitudes makes it imperative that we understand the meaning of the term "kabbalah" within the framework of Christian kabbalah as independent of any definition or conception of the term "kabbalah" within Jewish culture. The Christian scholars who read and commented on the Hebrew kabbalistic texts formed their own set of emphases and selections, which created unique compilations of texts and ideas. These combinations differed considerably in the writings of the various Christian kabbalists, and we have no reason to assume that a concept found in the works of one necessarily reflects the views of another. (This, of course, is also true concerning the Jewish kabbalists, each of whom selected from the kabbalistic tradition whatever suited him, and created his own combination of traditional and original concepts.) In many cases, the Hebrew texts were not the only sources used by the early Christian kabbalists. They utilized previous Christian translations and conceptions concerning Jewish esotericism, especially the writings of previous Christian kabbalists: In the case of Reuchlin, for instance, the works of Pico and Ricci exerted considerable influence on his comprehensive presentation of the kabbalah. It should also be noted that the image of the kabbalah in the works of the Christian kabbalists was heavily influenced by the selections made by their translators and teachers of Hebrew texts, and there is a possibility that certain aspects of the texts and their meanings were deliberately misrepresented when transmitted to them. The tension between Judaism and Christianity did not vanish completely when Jews, Jewish converts to Christianity, and Christian scholars were engaged together in the enterprise of presenting the Christian kabbalah.

It is impossible, therefore, to transmit any concept automatically from the Hebrew kabbalah to the Christian one, or vice versa. Some of the characteristics of the Hebrew kabbalah are found in the writings of the Christian kabbalists, while others are absent. Christian works describe as "kabbalistic" concepts that cannot be found in the Hebrew texts. The Hebrew works of kabbalah include many elements that cannot be found in the Christian kabbalistic literature. Concepts and terms that are found in both bodies of texts may have different meanings in each. In addition, there is a vast difference in the concept of language between the two, which will be described in the section "Christian kabbalah and the European Hebraist movement."

THE APOCALYPTIC ELEMENT

Christian humanism in the Renaissance can hardly be described as a chiliastic phenomenon; what is called in a Jewish context the "messianic element" is more remote from it than from most other trends and directions in Christian culture at the time. Yet it is possible to discern some marginal manifestations of messianic expectations in the works of some of the Christian kabbalists. The work of Cardinal Egidio da Viterbo is one example; the theme is more pronounced in the sometimes strange ideas of Guillaume Postel.

It seems that any meeting, in a meaningful religious context, between Jews and Christians raises the expectation of a conversion, even a mass conversion, of the Jews to Christianity; such an event cannot escape chiliastic connotations. The Christian kabbalists came to know on a personal level—sometimes in an intense personal contact—various kinds of Jews, kabbalists and nonkabbalists, copyists and intellectuals, and especially many converted Jews. In a few cases we know about Jews who converted within the context of the Christian kabbalistic enterprise; in others we know about attempts to persuade Jewish scholars to convert.[23] These examples do not combine to create a picture of a concerted effort, and it is certainly wrong to suppose that the Christian kabbalists perceived it as their main mission. However, it should be taken into account as an aspect—admittedly, a marginal one—of the phenomenon as a whole. But

---

[23]G. Scholem, in his studies of the Christian kabbalah, was intensely interested in this subject.

Christian kabbalah is essentially a Christian phenomenon, a discourse between Christians about the nature of Christianity.

A particular aspect of this problem, which is directly related to Reuchlin's work, is the impact on the Christian kabbalah of the chiliastic traditions of the school of Joachim of Fiore. The Joachimite concept of historical evolution, in which each period reflects a different aspect of the Trinity, culminating in the future revelation of the Eternal Testament of the Holy Spirit (following the Old Testament of the Father and the New Testament of the Son), was one of the most potent vehicles of medieval apocalypticism, and its influence was maintained, in various forms, for many generations.[24] Gershom Scholem drew attention to the possibility of Joachimite influence on Reuchlin's concept of spiritual history presented in his early work on kabbalistic tradition, *De Verbo Mirifico*, published in 1494, dealing mainly with the tetragrammaton as the miracle-working name in its various forms—a subject that had a meaningful place in the works of Joachim. In Reuchlin's scheme, history is divided into three parts—the age of the patriarchs, in which the divine name known was the three-letter *Shaddai*; the age of the Old Testament, in which the name was the four-letter tetragrammaton; and the age of the New Testament, in which the name is the five-letter YHSWH, that is, Jesus. Reuchlin derived this sequence from his Jewish sources—purely talmudic ones—which divide the six-thousand-year history of the universe into three parts: the age of *tohu* (chaos), the age of Torah, and the age of the Messiah. These millennia will be followed by a thousand years of destruction, after which the "next world" (*olam haba*) will be created.[25] The Jewish sources do not associate these stages in history with different divine names, although the statement

---

[24]Concerning the whole phenomenon, see B. McGinn, *The Calabrian Abbot: Joachim of Fiore in the History of Western Thought*, New York 1985, pp. 161–203; *Joachim of Fiore in Christian Thought: Essays on the Influence of the Calabrian Prophet*, ed. Delno C. West, New York 1975, especially M. Reeves, "Joachimist Influences on the Idea of a Last World Emperor," 2, pp. 511–558 and B. Hirsch-Reich, "Joachim von Fiore und das Judentum," 2, pp. 473–510. Scholem's comparison with the early kabbalah is presented in *Origins of the Kabbalah*, pp. 463–465.
[25]Bavli *Sanhedrin* 77b.

that the oldest name of God by which He was revealed to the patriarchs was *Shaddai* was made by the talmudic sages to explain the
difference between that time and the revelation of the holy name to
Moses.[26]

Reuchlin's historical description of the evolution of the name
can be regarded as essentially opposite to that of the Joachimite tradition: The final revelation of the complete name occurred, according to Reuchlin, at the beginning of Christianity, while Joachim
maintained that the Eternal Testament will be revealed in the future. Thus, while Joachim's teaching could be used as a vehicle for
historical transformation, Reuchlin's includes no historical directive;
the change has already occurred, and therefore no historical consequences may be derived from this theory. It may explain and justify
the truth of Christianity, but it does not indicate the need for any
present or future change. It does not differ markedly from previous
Christian utilizations of the rabbinic concept of history to demonstrate that the Messiah already came more than a millennium ago
and that the Jews did not listen to the predictions of their own sages.
The Messiah that had to come near the end of the fourth millennium was, according to them, Jesus Christ.

Despite this obviously nonmillennarian concept, doubts may lin-
ger. Is it possible that Reuchlin believed that there is a particular
meaning to the understanding of the development of the holy name
in the original Hebrew? Are his writings on the subject to be regarded as purely exegetical, or does the discovery of the original
alphabet letters that make up the name of Christ and their relationship to previous formulations represent a new age of awareness of
the messianic nature of Jesus and his name? In other words, one may
suspect that the return to Hebrew and the attachment to the Hebrew sacred name was supposed to represent a historical metamor-
phosis, and that the age of the Hebraists would bring forth a new
spiritual epoch. I do not think that Reuchlin's works, in the present

---

[26]This subject is discussed in great detail in Rabbi Eleazar of Worms's treatise on
the holy name (*Sefer ha-Shem*), which is a part of the great collection of his works,
Sodey Razaya, which was copied for Cardinal de Viterbo.

stage of the study of his voluminous writings, warrant such an understanding; yet the possibility exists.[27] The dedication to Hebrew, and to the holy name in Hebrew, may have had a more profound spiritual significance than merely a search for additional information or the deeper understanding of old truths.[28]

CHRISTIAN KABBALAH AND THE EUROPEAN HEBRAIST MOVEMENT

Christian kabbalah can be described as an expression of a new attitude to language. One of its most meaningful manifestations is the rejection of the dominant Christian concept that truth is expressed in Latin and Greek. Almost all Christian kabbalists studied several other languages. Reuchlin studied Arabic, and introduced a Muslim as one of the characters in *De Arte Cabbalistica*. "Chaldean" was one of the most important subjects to which their works were dedicated, and, indeed, Aramaic and Syriac became here, for the first time, legitimate components of European culture. Their writings included assemblages of various alphabets, actual and fictional. The undeciphered Egyptian hieroglyphs played an important role

---

[27]It should be taken into account that a century after the publication of Reuchlin's work such ideas were used by the Rosicrucian "invisible underground" in Germany between 1613 and 1620. See, in detail, the analysis presented by Frances Yates in her *The Rosicrucian Enlightenment*, London and New York 1972. It is most striking that although the tetragrammaton has a central position in many contexts in Christian kabbalah, the drawings of the writers associated with the Rosicrucians are the most emphatic in presenting the four Hebrew letters as the source of all existence, under whose wings the righteous reside.

[28]Within Judaism there occurred a development that led a similar historical concept from the nonhistorical into radical messianic activity. The theory of the *Sefer ha-Temunah* in the fourteenth century, which associated each epoch in the history of the universe with one of the divine *sefirot*, had no direct historical consequences, because it was maintained that between one epoch and an other there was a millennium of destruction. This was changed, in the messianic Sabbatian movement of the seventeenth century, into a potent chiliastic symbol by maintaining that the transition from one stage to the other might occur within history. See G. Scholem, *Sabbatai Sevi; the Mystical Messiah, 1626-1676*, trans. R. J. Zwi Werblowsky, Princeton, NJ 1973, pp. 98-99.

in the writings of several Christian kabbalists, magicians, and alche-mists.[29] The whole phenomenon can be described as the ascent of Greek into the central place among languages, with Hebrew in an equal place and numerous other languages, most of them viewed as ancient, mysterious languages of the East, around them. This intense philological and linguistic awareness resulted in a new world view, free from the confines of the identification of truth with a particular language and alphabet. The visual concept, that truth can be writ-ten using strange signs, and the auditory one, that it can be expressed by bizarre noises, necessitate a more flexible and profound attitude toward different cultures.

One of the most striking characteristics of Hebrew kabbalah, and one that had an effect on the Christian kabbalah, is the exten-sion of meaning to nonsemantic aspects of language. Hebrew exege-sis regarded many components of language as integral parts of di-vine revelation, including the shapes of the Hebrew characters, the vocalization signs (*nekudot*) and the musical signs (*teamim*), the names of the letters and of the signs, the "crowns" (*tagin*) adorning the let-ters in sacred writings, the numerical value of letters (*gematria*), the possibilities of transmuting letters and exchanging them,[30] and many others. These methodologies have nothing to do with the kabbalah or mysticism: They are part of midrashic exegesis, which is based on the belief in language as a divine instrument by which God cre-ated the world.[31] Language is an aspect of divine infinite wisdom, and a human being cannot discern what is important and what is

---

[29]A prominent example is that of John Dee's *Monas Hieroglyphica*, which had an important role in the beginnings of Rosicrucianism; see Yates, *The Rosicrucian Enlightenment*, pp. 50–53 et passim.
[30]The best-known method of transmuting letters is the one called ETBASH, in which the first letter is written instead of the last, the second instead of the next-to-last, etc. This is attested in the Bible itself, when Jeremiah calls Babylonia "Sheshach," using this method. There are scores of similar examples used by medieval exegetes.
[31]See J. Dan, "The Language of the Mystics in Medieval Germany," in *Mysti-cism, Magic and Kabbalah in Ashkenazi Judaism*, eds. K. Groezinger and J. Dan, Berlin and New York 1995, pp. 6–27.

secondary in it; therefore all methods, leading to different or even conflicting conclusions, are equally valid. Kabbalists adopted these methods and utilized them in elucidating ancient texts, though, unlike midrashic exegetes, they believed that they knew the ultimate, metalinguistic divine meaning. For the Christian kabbalists, the midrashic methods seemed to be an integral part of the kabbalistic tradition (as indeed they were, if one understands the term "kabbalah" as including talmudic tradition). In this way, the kabbalah became associated in European thought with numerology, strange alphabets, and other nonsemantic exegetical procedures.[32]

The Christian kabbalah, despite its efforts, could not make the transition from the concept of language as a communicative, semantic, and human entity—as it is conceived in a Christian context—to a divine, creative, and metacommunicative tool by which the world was created—as it is viewed in a Jewish context. The multiplicity of meanings, equal in their veracity despite the differences or even conflicts between them, was not accepted by the Christian scholars. These two dimensions of postbiblical Jewish culture—the midrashic perception of the infinity of meanings, and the mystical metalinguistic experiences hiding behind many kabbalistic texts—were not preserved by the Latin translators. They were not aware of that, because the core of truth that they believed to be hidden within the texts they were studying was known to them beforehand. The combination of Pythagoreanism, neo-Platonism, Hermeticism, and Christianity that constituted their innermost conception of truth was discovered in the texts, which were presented as the proofs of its eternal veracity. It was not doubt that led them to the Hebrew texts, but complete confidence in their mastery of truth, to which the Hebrew words served as further demonstrations, rather than a starting point for a quest.

----

[32]This is most perplexing, especially concerning "numerology," because Hebrew is not different from Greek, Latin, and Arabic, each of which used letters to designate numbers. It should be noted that the first *gematria* to be found in any text is present in the New Testament, in Greek, namely in Revelations 13:18, where the "number of the beast," 666, is the value of "Nero Caesar" in Hebrew. See B. McGinn's discussion in *Antichrist*, pp. 52-53.

The Christian kabbalah served as both a continuation of and a new impetus for the Hebraist movement, which reached its peak in subsequent centuries. But the concept of Hebrew is different in the two closely related groups. For the Hebraists, Hebrew was a communicative language, governed by grammatical laws, that, if mastered, could assist in establishing the "true" meaning of scriptures. For the Christian kabbalists, Hebrew was the instrument by which esoteric texts could be approached—texts that included great nonsemantic mysteries—using a group of methods that could reveal hidden secrets. For the Hebraists, Hebrew might supply a better communication with God using language; for the Christian kabbalists, Hebrew could help in achieving freedom from the confines of communicative language and approaching God by nonsemantic means. Reuchlin's first book, *De Verbo Mirifico*, is centered around the Holy Name as such a non semantic divine revelation,[33] while the second, *De Arte Cabbalistica*, adds to it the whole range of midrashic methods that are based on the concept of Hebrew as a divine language.

REUCHLIN, HEBREW, AND KABBALAH

The life and works of Johannes Reuchlin have been the subject of extensive study, concerning both his role in the humanistic movement in the Renaissance in Germany and his attitudes about Judaism and the kabbalah. One of the most extensive studies is included in the *Geschichte der Juden* by Heinrich Graetz.[34] Salo Baron complained that Graetz allotted too much space and detail to the subject,[35] but this is understandable: An optimistic view about the role

---

[33]Concerning the holy name in the kabbalah, see the references in note 47.

[34]H. Graetz, *Geschichte der Juden*, 4th ed. vol. 9, p. 63ff, 477ff, note 2. See note 35, and compare S. A. Hirsch, *Johann Pfefferkorn and the Battle of the Books* (1892), reprinted in the author's *A Book of Essays*, London 1905, pp. 73–115. For a further bibliography, see Baron (note 35), p. 408, notes 28–29.

[35]S. W. Baron, *A Social and Religious History of the Jews*, 2nd ed. vol. 13, "Inquisition, Renaissance and Reformation," New York and Philadelphia 1969, pp. 184–185. Although the importance of this episode in Jewish and general history of the early sixteenth century cannot easily be overestimated, it was mainly Heinrich

of Jews in German society and culture, and the quest for tolerance of Judaism in Germany, must start with Reuchlin, and he can be understood as representing the beginnings of the integration of Jews in modern German society. Graetz had to overcome his aversion to the kabbalah when he portrayed Reuchlin as the hero of this important chapter in history;[36] it was difficult for him to admit that it was Jewish mysticism, which he regarded as superstitious and irrational, that served as the vehicle for the first meaningful meeting between German culture and Judaism. Gershom Scholem was in a much more comfortable position when he dedicated to Reuchlin a central place in his study of the Christian kabbalah,[37] as well as several specific discussions,[38] though he could not, of course, share Graetz's optimism concerning the place of Judaism in German culture.[39] Baron's complaint is misplaced: Despite the episodic nature

---

Graetz's personal exuberance and Germanocentrism that induced him to devote to this issue fully one-fifth of a volume covering the history of Jews in many lands during a crucial period of a century and a quarter (1492–1618). There is no question, however, that the ensuing litigation drew ever-wider circles, and that, from a local conflict primarily affecting certain Rhineland communities, it ultimately became an international political and religious issue, drawing the attention of leaders of the Holy Roman Empire, France, the papacy, and an ecumenical council. Baron's measured historical assessment neglects the intellectual and spiritual meaning of the conflict; it problematized some of the most cherished concepts of the previous millennium of Christian culture, and its impact on subsequent European thought still remains to be fully described and evaluated.

[36]Concerning Graetz's attitude toward the kabbalah, see G. Scholem, *Origins of the Kabbalah*, pp. 3–12.

[37]G. Scholem, "The Origins of the Christian Kabbalah" (German original 1954). Among recent studies of the subject, see especially K. Reichert, "Pico della Mirandola and the Beginning of the Christian Kabbalah," in *Mysticism, Magic and Kabbalah in Ashkenazi Judaism*, eds. Groezinger and Dan, pp. 195–207.

[38]G. Scholem, *Die Erforschung der Kabbalah, von Reuchlin bis zur Gegenwart: Vortag gehalten anlässlich der Entgegennahme der Reuchlin-Preises der Stadt Pforzheim, 10 Sept. 1969*, Pforzheim: Selbstverlag der Stadt 1970. Compare also idem, *Kabbalah*, Jerusalem 1974, pp. 198–199.

[39]See G. Scholem, *On Jews and Judaism in Crisis*, New York 1976, et passim. Concerning the impact of the Christian kabbalah on subsequent European culture,

of Reuchlin's acceptance of Jewish culture, it is a unique and meaningful chapter in the history of the relationship between Judaism and modern culture in Europe. Recent studies concerning the history of the impact of Christian kabbalah on subsequent generations of major figures in seventeenth-century European philosophy indicate that the meaning of this phenomenon has not been exhaustively described

---

Salo Baron expresses a cautionary note. When assessing J. L. Blau's evaluation of the Christian kabbalah (in the preface to his *The Christian Interpretation of the Cabala*; see note 1) as a "fad" and the responses of several scholars to this attitude (Baron, p. 406, note 23), the great historian writes: "Viewing the modern development of Western culture, with its growing secularization, one may indeed opine that the manifestations of Christian kabbalism, however numerous and fraught with emotion for the individual participants, created only a ripple on the stream of cultural progress; not at all comparable with the impact of modern science. However, there is no question that much of the energy invested in Renaissance mysticism did not vanish from the cultural heritage of later generations." With all due admiration for Salo Baron's historical achievements and intuitions, in this case he seems to be following several premises that are manifestly wrong. The key term in his statement is "mysticism," which is juxtaposed with "modern science." Baron denies the meaningfulness of the impact of the Christian kabbalah because mysticism receded in modern culture, together with religion, to make way for "modern science" and secularization. In so saying, he neglects the cultural and spiritual aspects of modern culture, on the one hand, and the scientific, rationalistic aspect of the Christian kabbalah, on the other. The quest for knowledge, the development of comparative philology, the opening for different cultures, the revival of classical culture, and other important aspects of the humanistic movement in general and the Christian kabbalah in particular cannot be separated from the history of modern culture, whose scientific and "rationalistic" foundations seem today to be less secure than devotees of the Enlightenment supposed. If indeed some elements of this phenomenon can be found in the works of Leibniz and Newton, as postulated in two studies in this volume and several other recent scholarly works, the separation between "mysticism" and "science" is less absolute than expressed in Baron's statement. The discussion above concerning the meaning of "kabbalah" in Christian kabbalah attempted to demonstrate that the mystical aspect of the Hebrew kabbalah has been minimized in the Christian kabbalah. It seems that Baron was not aware of this meaningful difference, and attributed to the Christian kabbalah the same characteristics that he found in the Hebrew one, about which he was not particularly enthusiastic and did not believe had a meaningful place in contemporary Jewish culture. These prejudices, reflecting a contemporary Jewish worldview, seem to have influenced his attitude toward the Christian historical phenomenon.

as yet,[40] and that further study may support Graetz's position rather than Baron's skeptical attitude.

Reuchlin's works clearly exemplify the problem indicated in Chapter 9: the relationship between Hebraism and Christian kabbalah, a relationship that is fully complementary, but also includes undercurrents of tension. Hebraism, to which Reuchlin was dedicated from the beginning to the end of his creative endeavor, is concerned first and foremost with the elucidation of the Hebrew Bible as a source of Christian truth. Reuchlin's study of the kabbalah is directed, like that of Pico, Postel, and Ricci, to the unification of the classical philosophical tradition, the esoteric traditions of the East, and the nonbiblical Jewish traditions into a whole that demonstrates the truth of Christianity. At the same time, it is an achievement in its own right, and should be regarded as the core of human intellectual endeavor directed at producing a perfect scholar-intellectual whose main quest is for the truth. This second aspect is the one that distinguishes Reuchlin from anti-Jewish Christian polemicists and apologists (including Jewish converts to Christianity) in previous centuries and in his own time.[41]

---

[40]The most recent comprehensive study on the subject is Allison P. Coudert, *Leibniz and the Kabbalah*, Dordrecht and Boston 1995; the book includes a detailed bibliography (pp. 203–211). See also her previous studies: "A Cambridge Platonist's Kabbalistic Nightmare," *Journal of the History of Ideas* 35 (1975), pp. 633–652; "Henry More, the Kabbalah and the Quakers," in *Philosophy, Science, and Religion in England, 1640–1700*, ed. R. Kroll, R. Ashcraft, and P. Zagorin, Cambridge and New York 1992, pp. 31–67. Early versions of these two studies were given to G. Scholem and are now in his library; see the forthcoming catalogue of the Gershom Scholem Library, vol. 1, nos. 7129, 7130. These and other studies clearly indicate that the influence of the Christian kabbalah on seventeenth-century European philosophy and its later manifestations far exceeds what earlier scholars supposed.

[41]It should be noted, however, that the emphasis on the study of Hebrew that characterized some cultural trends in New England in the seventeenth and eighteenth centuries—a phenomenon that had a meaningful effect on shaping the cultural character of institutions like Harvard and Yale—was motivated, at least to some extent, by this quest for a whole human being, not only for an accomplished Christian apologist.

DE ARTE CABBALISTICA

The literary format of *De Arte Cabbalistica* represents the main themes of Reuchlin's concept of Judaism and the kabbalah. The presentation of three main characters, each of whom represents one of the three monotheistic religions, is highly unusual in itself; the fact that the representative of Christianity is not the dominant figure is even more unusual. It is doubtful whether there is, in European literature, a figure comparable to that of Simon, the Jewish kabbalist, as portrayed by Reuchlin. Nothing is said in the book concerning the personal background of Marranus, who represents Islam, and Philolaus, the Christian; Simon is described as a descendant of Rabbi Simeon bar Yochai, the author of the *Zohar*. Thus he is not only a scholar, but a physical embodiment of his own teachings.

The respect the author shows Simon is evident in the very structure of the work. The first and third parts are dedicated mainly to presentations by Simon; they occur on Friday and Sunday. The second part, occurring on Saturday, the Jewish Sabbath, is dedicated to a discussion between Marranus and Philolaus, who analyze what they heard on the previous day from Simon. The teacher is absent because of his obligation to perform the Sabbath's rituals. When on Sunday Simon suggests that they postpone their discussions for the Christian day of rest and worship, Philolaus declines, stating that absorbing Simon's teachings is superior to any other kind of worship. In this way, Simon is presented as one who is devoted to the practice of his religion in a much more devout way than the two others. It cannot be doubted that Reuchlin expressed, in this way, his deep respect for and deference to the figure of the Jewish kabbalist. The book was written during the height of Reuchlin's persecution by the Dominicans in Cologne, when his case was submitted to the pope, and some sections of the book (especially the beginning of the third part) refer to that affair. It is evident that the fierce criticism and denunciation to which Reuchlin was subjected in the years preceding the writing of this work did not cause him to hesitate to express clearly his appreciation of the teachings of the kabbalah and the personality of the fictional teacher.

The structure of the book also allows the reader to distinguish between the kabbalistic teachings and the way they were absorbed by the disciples, who represent Reuchlin himself. The second part of the book—the discussion between Marranus and Philolaus in the absence of Simon—gives us an opportunity to check what they derived from Simon's series of presentations in the first part. Simon's lectures include long paraphrases and translations from kabbalistic sources; it is difficult to assess, in the first and third parts, how these quotations were understood and what conclusions were derived from them. This is given in the second part. It is evident in many cases in this part of the work that the more abstract generalizations arrived at by the participants in the discussion are actually independent of the kabbalistic texts presented. The consistent drive to identify the teachings of Simon the kabbalist with the Pythagorean, Zoroastrian, and Hermetic traditions often relegates the kabbalistic reference to a marginal, superficial position. When Reuchlin states a profound truth that is undoubtedly meaningful and central in a kabbalistic worldview, he often uses traditional Christian sources. For instance, Philolaus states that:

> [D]ivine causes do not run parallel with those of nature, nor can a science of nature rule the divine, still less can it demonstrate that knowledge of what rests solely on trust can be acquired by human reasoning. One does not infer that what is just "believed" is "known" in the ordinary course of things. That friend of yours, Dionysius the Areopagite (who has, I think, learned something from the Pythagoreans, or is at least strongly reminiscent of them), says in his book *On Divine Names*, in the passages dealing with theology: "There is no logically necessary relationship between causes and what is caused. What is caused holds the image of its causes. The causes themselves are abstracted from what they cause, and are enthroned above as their inherent nature requires." (Part II, p. 141)

This is a profound statement of a mystical worldview that is, indeed, prevalent among kabbalists, but it is inherent as well in the Christian–neo-Platonic tradition. This principle was used extensively by later writers, especially when expounding the microcosmos-macrocosmos concepts of existence that became very popular in the seventeenth century and were often presented as kabbalistic.[42]

In Reuchlin's letter to the pope, he declared emphatically that *De Arte Cabbalistica* was a factual, informative presentation of the teachings of the kabbalah, without the author's intervention; the book, according to him, did not present any theses or conclusions. This is true concerning many sections of the first an third parts of the work; we can learn from them what Reuchlin read and how he translated the texts at his disposal. The second part includes Reuchlin's analysis of this information and the way in which he integrated it in his own worldview.

A large section of the first half of the third part of the work is dedicated to the analysis of the Hebrew divine names, mainly the tetragrammaton and the holy name of the "seventy-two letters." This discussion is most meaningful for the attitude of Reuchlin, in his sources and his heroes, to language; and in demonstrating his awareness of the nonsemantic aspects of language, in which Hebrew differs significantly from Latin. One might say that Latin, as used by the Church, has only one nonsemantic term, the name Jesus. Other terms referring to the divine realm are words that have a semantic message.[43] In Hebrew, most of the references to the divine realm and to God Himself are nonsemantic.[44] Reuchlin, however, quotes Pico

---

[42]Especially in the works of Robert Fludd and Giordano Bruno, as well as the Rosicrucian writers; see, for instance, F. Yates, *Giordano Bruno and the Hermetic Tradition*, pp. 308–311 et passim; idem, *The Rosicrucian Enlightenment*, pp. 74–80. The statement as presented here by Reuchlin can be read as an antiscientific one, and it may have been treated as such for several centuries. Four centuries later, however, both physicists and historians came to adopt this view.

[43]Other nonsemantic terms in Christian worship are taken from the Hebrew: *amen* (also nonsemantic in Hebrew) and *halleluja* (which is a semantic term in Hebrew: "praise God").

[44]This is partly the result of the astonishing fact that the first translators of the Hebrew Bible into Greek, the authors of the Septuagint in the second century B.C., chose to render the Hebrew names of God in a semantic way, rendering *Adonai* as "the Lord" and *Elohim* as "God" (*theos*), thus creating the illusion that the Hebrew text describes the divine realm using words with specific meanings. The Vulgate followed the same tradition in Latin, and European languages imitated it. In Arabic, only the name Allah itself is nonsemantic, leaving Hebrew as the only language used by the monotheistic religions with many nonsemantic appellations of God.

della Mirandola, who had declared in his nine hundred conclusions that "Meaningless sounds have more magical power than meaningful ones" (III, p. 271). While this seems to be confined to magical formulas, it seems that Reuchlin extended it to the spiritual and religious realms, under the influence of his Jewish esoteric sources.[45]

A case in point is Reuchlin's treatment of the subject of the "name of seventy-two letters," which is quoted and discussed in relatively great detail. This name is derived from three consecutive verses in Exodus (14:19–21), each of which includes, in Hebrew, exactly seventy-two letters. The fact gave rise, long before the kabbalah appeared, to a Jewish esoteric practice of deriving from these verses seventy-two groups of three letters each, which together—and each of them independently—represent the most secret and sublime name of God. This is achieved by writing the seventy-two letters of the first verse in a line, and below it the letters of the second verse in an inverse order, beginning with the last letter.[46] Below these two rows the third verse is written, in the usual order. The name is derived from reading these three rows downward; thus the first element comprises the first letter of the first verse, the last letter of the second verse, and the first letter of the third verse; the second group the second letter of the first verse, the next-to-last from the second verse, and the second letter of the third verse, and so on, seventy-two times. The name, therefore, actually includes 216 letters, in seventy-two groups of three letters each. Reuchlin, following his kabbalistic sources, describes this practice in detail, with complete accuracy, and copies in Hebrew the full name (III, pp. 259–273).

This practice represents a radical destruction of the semantic message of the biblical text. The verses relate the parting of the Red

---

[45]This may be the reason for Egidio de Viterbo's intense interest in Rabbi Eleazar of Worms's Book of the Holy Name, which he read in the copy made for him by Elijah Levitas and on which he commented extensively in the margins. This treatise is the most detailed Hebrew discussion of the nonsemantic names of God.
[46]A possible explanation of this method may be found in the fact that the last word in the second verse, "the night," can be read in Hebrew equally from beginning to end and from end to beginning—HLYLH. This may have suggested that this verse should be read from the end to the beginning.

Sea when the Jews fled from the pursuing Egyptian armies. Instead of the straight narrative, this esoteric rearrangement of the letters produces seventy-two groups of three letters that are completely deprived of any semantic message. Seen in this way, the biblical narrative is but a thin cover of mysterious structures that have no communicative meaning. No wonder, then, that kabbalists posed the question of why only these three verses should represent a hidden divine name, and concluded that all scriptures are the names of God, or even that the whole scriptures are one supreme name of God.[47]

It is evident that Reuchlin understood the procedure, but missed its implications. According to his understanding (which is occasionally found in Hebrew sources), this series of names is actually a list of names of angels. Philolaus responds to this exposition: "Never have I seen these angels or known their names" (III, p. 263). This is in response to Simon's statement: "All these names spring from the quality of forbearance, say the kabbalists. This forbearance comes from the ten numerations. I will outline the tree of numerations, please God" (III, p. 263).[48] Marranus and Philolaus deliberately misunderstand Simon's words. He describes these names as being included in the divine structure of the ten *sefirot*, while they understand them as being a list of names of angels. As these scholars represent Reuchlin himself, this deliberate misunderstanding must be attributed to him. This is continued later, when Simon states:

> So there are seventy-two sacred names. They are (in one word), the Semhamaphores that explain the holy tetragrammaton. They are to be spoken only by men dedicated and devoted to God and must be pronounced thus in fear and trembling through invocations of the angels: Vehuiah, Ieliel, Sitael, Elemiah . . ." (III, p. 273)

---

[47]See J. Dan, "The Name of God, the Name of the Rose and the Concept of Language in Jewish Mysticism," in *Medieval Encounters* (in press). Compare G. Scholem, "The Name of God and the Linguistic Theory of the Kabbalah," *Diogenes* 79 (1972), pp. 59–80; 80 (1972), pp. 164–194.

[48]The next section is dedicated to the detailed description of the tree of the *sefirot*.

This list of seventy-two names, all of them meaningless, are constructs of the three-letter groups, with the addition of *el* and *yah*,
which are the characteristic endings of the names of angels in Hebrew, as Reuchlin correctly explains. By transforming them into
angelic names, the conclusion announced by Simon is:

> Gentlemen, you now have access to words with which you can
> do more than mutter secretly to yourselves in the depth of your
> hearts, for now you can express sounds aloud and in conjunc-
> tion. You can summon whatever angel you like by his own
> symbolic name. (ibid.)

Instead of the secret name of God, connected with the divine structure of the ten *sefirot*, we are presented with a list of meaningless
sounds that can be used to conjure powerful angels. Mystical inquiry
concerning the divine realm has been turned into an exercise in the
acquisition of magical knowledge, empowering the user in achieving
his mundane purposes.

A radically different attitude is found in Reuchlin's discussion
concerning the holy name of forty-two letters. The tradition concerning such a name is ancient, and a reference to it is found in
tanaitic literature of the second century, though it is not certain that
it is related to the same groups of letters that we know from medieval texts.[49] The text of this name, as it was known in the Hebrew
esoteric tradition, is seven groups of six letters each, which do not
produce any semantic message. Medieval scholars associated this
name with the first forty-two letters of the Torah, Genesis 1:1-2.
This connection is described by a radical use of the methodologies
of *temurah*, the permutation of letters and the substitution of a desired letter instead of the written one. In this way the communicative message of the first words of the book of Genesis was completely
destroyed, and a sequence of meaningless letters was substituted for
it, letters that were claimed to be the secret name of God.

---

[49]It has been suggested that this name, like the name of twelve letters, was a
pyramidal arrangement of the letters of the tetragrammaton; this is a distinct
possibility, but nothing concerning this subject has been definitely proved.

Reuchlin uses the discussion of this name in order to introduce, in great detail, the methodology of *temurah* and explain it in an elaborate manner. This subject is very difficult for people who are not familiar with Hebrew exegesis, because more than any other method it denies completely the validity of language as communication of meaning. No word is what it seems; every group of letters can be transformed to any other group; meaning is ephemeral, easily exchanged with another group of letters conveying a completely different meaning or none at all. Reuchlin understood this subject completely; his examples are accurate, and the diverse sources he used in this section are relevant and elucidate the subject in a coherent manner. In this section Reuchlin demonstrated that he had indeed mastered the Hebrew language in a dynamic manner; he not only was able to understand words and translate them, but was familiar with the intrinsic structure of the language and the rabbinic understanding of its infinite possibilities.

There are many interesting elements in Reuchlin's exposition of the name of forty-two letters, but the conclusion is most meaningful. Simon-Reuchlin states:

> There are other Kabbalists who have indulged in higher speculation and transcend creation and the creatures, who stand in the sole emanation of the Deity. In holy manner they bestow that emanation, under a vow of silence and through the holy name of twelve letters and the name of 42 letters, upon those worthy men who are devoted to God. This traditional name is written in the *Book of Secret Letters*,[50] where, in answer to the question of the Roman Antoninus about the holy names, Rabbi Hakados says that from the Tetragrammaton comes the name of 12 letters: *Av Ben veRuakh haKadosh*, meaning: Father, Son and Holy Spirit; and from this is derived the name of 42 letters: *Av Elohim, Ben Elohim, Ruah hakadosh Elohim, Shalosha beehad, ehad besheloshah*, which means: "God the Father, God

---

[50] A better translation of the title *Igeret ha-Sodot* would be The Epistle Concerning Secrets. Concerning the history of this quotation, which Reuchlin received from earlier discussions, see Scholem.

the Son, God the Holy Spirit, Three in One and One in Three."
What heights and what depths in matters understood by faith
alone! (III, p. 339)[51]

This statement is described as the culmination of Simon's presentation. He wished to stop here, but his two disciples requested him to
continue, and he did; but the passage quoted still serves as a climax
of the detailed discussion of the holy names, the main subject of this
part of the book. So indeed it is, by being the most explicit
christological statement in the work. The kabbalistic holy name of
twelve letters is identified as the Trinity, and the name of forty-two
letters is transmuted to declare the divinity and unity of the three
powers of the Trinity. The authority in whose name this statement
is made is not a kabbalist but Rabbenu ha-Kadosh—a usual rabbinic
reference to Rabbi Judah the Prince, the great rabbinic authority to
whom the conclusion of the Mishnah is traditionally attributed, at
the end of the second century. There are several references in tanaitic
literature to discussions between Rabbi Judah and the Roman emperor Antoninus, and this quotation pretends to be a part of the
cycle of questions and answers that were exchanged between the two.
The direct source quoted by Reuchlin is not specific; it is nothing
more than a treatise "on secrets" that does not identify the work.

The question that will remain unanswered is whether Reuchlin
was aware of the fact that his detailed exposition concerning the nature of the Hebrew method of *temurah* rendered his christological
conclusion meaningless. If every letter can be substituted for every
other letter, and every group of words can be transformed into any
other, then the trinitarian formula is just one among an infinite number of possibilities. It is not the hidden secret, the ultimate underlying truth, but one more possible permutation; it is not very difficult
to derive the formula "There is no God besides Allah, and
Muhammad is his prophet" from the same group of letters. It is the

---

[51]It is not surprising that this paragraph was often quoted in the circles of the
Christian kabbalists. See, for instance, Pietro Galatino, *De Arcanis Catholicae
Veritatis*, Ortona 1518, cols. 364–366.

inner conviction, independent of this procedure, concerning the Trinity that makes the derivation of this sentence from the forty-two letters meaningful, rather than the procedure itself, which can tolerate any combination and every meaning. Did Reuchlin's grasp of Hebrew and the midrashic methods of exegesis extend far enough for him to realize that his presentation in this case was self-defeating, making the core of the Christian concept of the Godhead one possible alternative among an infinity of others, most of them meaningless?

Reuchlin's analysis of the divine names includes a magical element, but we do not find the same intense emphasis on the connection between kabbalah and magic that is present in the works of Pico, which reflect to some extent the impact of Ficino's ideas. Yet the association of the kabbalah with magic remained a meaningful characteristic of the Christian kabbalah, especially after a series of more recent works reemphasized it in the second half of the sixteenth century.[52] There can be little doubt that this was the result, to some extent, of the medieval Christian identification of Jewish wisdom and knowledge with magic. The Christian kabbalists in this way expressed not only a change of attitude toward Jewish traditions, but also their renewed interest and appreciation of the subject of magic.[53] How-

---

[52]On this trend, which is present in *De Occulta Philosophia* and is repeated constantly during the seventeenth century, see, for instance, Paola Zambrelli, "Scholastic and Humanist Views of Hermeticism and Witchcraft," in *Hermeticism and the Renaissance*, eds. I. Merkel and A. G. Debus, Washington, DC 1988, pp. 125–153.

[53]As noted above, it is most surprising that this change took place at the same time that the intensified Christian dualism and the enmity toward satanic heresy caused magic to become more feared and hated in many segments of Christian culture than ever before; indeed, it was becoming an offense punishable by the Inquisition, as presented in the works of Springer and Kramer and their like. The seclusion of the Christian kabbalah in small circles of intellectuals, who were remote from the popular culture of their time, is emphasized by this fact. The obvious argument was that this is "white magic," unlike the satanic "black magic." See an example presented by Leland L. Estes, "Good Witches, Wise Men, Astrologers and Scientists: William Perkins and the Limits of the European Witchhunts," in *Hermeticism and the Renaissance* (see note 52), pp. 154–165.

ever, the term "magic" itself represents, in this period, a most complicated concept, often markedly remote from the usual meanings of
this word.[54]

CONCLUSION

When assessing the main contribution of Reuchlin to the concept of the kabbalah among Christians in the sixteenth century and
proceeding into the seventeenth and the eighteenth, it seems to me
that the aspect most in need of emphasis is the establishment of the
essence of the kabbalah as a nonsemantic message. Reading *De Arte
Cabbalistica*, one gets an impression that the kabbalah is mainly an
exegetical phenomenon that employs nonsemantic methodologies to
discover secrets concerning other nonsemantic elements of language,
especially the secret names of God. Such an image does not emerge
from reading Pico della Mirandola's theses concerning the kabbalah.
It is Reuchlin's work that placed the kabbalah within the framework
of the Hermetic-estotericist context as far as language is concerned;
Pico's main message was the recognition of the antiquity and authenticity of the kabbalah. Reuchlin's concepts characterized the kabbalah
for centuries to come as an obscure, mysterious doctrine that departs from the ordinary use of language and inhabits instead a bizarre, illogical realm visited only by magicians, visionaries, and the
superstitious. It came to be regarded as a sister doctrine to alchemy
and astrology, and ultimately was positioned in opposition to science, Enlightenment, and the communicative use of language. This
image of the kabbalah, enhanced by later writers and especially by
the great impact of Agrippa von Nettesheim's *De Occulta Philosophia*
and the many works that followed it, remains dominant to this day.
It has shaped not only the meaning of the term "kabbalah" in European languages, but also the image of this doctrine in the writings

---

[54]This is one of the major subjects discussed in the volumes of Lynn Thorndike's
History of Magic and Experimental Science, New York 1958; see, however,
Thorndike's monograph *The Place of Magic in the Intellectual History of Europe*,
New York 1967.

of Jewish scholars in the nineteenth century and the twentieth who have not bothered to read the original Hebrew sources and have relied instead on the impression derived from Christian descriptions and attitudes. The intense rejection, indeed, the hatred toward the kabbalah among Jewish intellectuals of the Enlightenment, including the fathers of Reform Judaism and the scholars of the *Wissenschaft des Judentums*, is derived at least in part from this image, which seemed to clash with their insisted attempts to present Judaism as a rationalistic-ethical phenomenon worthy of emancipated citizens of an enlightened European culture. The kabbalah, for them, became an embarrassment, and they did not realize that it is the image of the Christian kabbalistic texts, rather than the original Hebrew ones, that served as a basis for this attitude.[55]

Needless to say, this image is contrary to Reuchlin's intention and to the intellectual message of *De Arte Cabbalistica*. For him, the *Zohar*, Gikatilla, and Abulafia were as rational as Plato, Pythagoras, and the Gospels. Esotericism, occultism, and magic were conceived, in his works or the works of those who continued to develop the study of Christian kabbalah, not as inferior, superstitious doctrines, but as the keys to divine truth, inseparable from science and logic. The studies of Lynn Thorndike, Frances Yates, and Antoine Faivre[56]

---

[55]The result of this concept was the neglect of the kabbalah, or enmity toward it, which Gershom Scholem had to face when he started to study the Hebrew texts. It is vividly described in the pages of his autobiography, *From Berlin to Jerusalem: Memories of My Youth*, translated from the German by Harry Zohn, New York 1980. Scholem's work was dedicated to changing this attitude and the establishment of scholarly study of the original texts in their historical context.

[56]It should be noted, however, that for Thorndike and, to some extent, Yates, the hermetic-magical works of the fifteenth to seventeenth centuries were meaningful first and foremost as the origins and background of modern science, philosophy, and (in the case of Yates) Elizabethan theater. The study of esotericism, as formulated in the last few decades by Faivre, is different in its endeavor to investigate these phenomena on their own terms, without apologizing by pointing out their importance to the development of "really meaningful" consequences that are acceptable to contemporary prejudices. See, for instance, Antoine Faivre, *Access to Western Esotericism*, Albany, NY 1994; idem, "The Children of Hermes and the Science of Man," in *Hermeticism and the Renaissance*, eds. Merkel and

have clearly established the intrinsic connections between what was regarded in the Enlightenment as superstitious and illogical and sources of scientific method and the cultural environment that enabled the development of modern science and philosophy. The separation between the two is the result of modern prejudices rather than a historical characterization of cultural phenomena.

It is the suggestion of this study to view the differences between the kabbalah and the Christian kabbalah, and also between the authentic Christian kabbalah and its image in the eighteenth and nineteenth centuries, as resulting from different concepts of language. The nonsemantic methods of exegesis emphasized so prominently by Reuchlin are not essentially kabbalistic, but are based on midrashic concepts that were adopted and developed by the medieval Jewish esoterics, especially the Ashkenazi Hasidim and some kabbalists (like Abraham Abulafia); they are not, within the Hebrew context, specific characteristics of the kabbalah. They were presented in the writings of Reuchlin and others as identical to the message of the kabbalah, whereas in the original sources they were methodologies that can be used for the presentation of any worldview. The great enterprise of the kabbalah of the thirteenth century and the beginning of the fourteenth (a period from which most of the sources used by Pico and Reuchlin were derived) was the exegetical transforma-

---

Debus, pp. 424–435. Many other articles in the volume are important contributions to this subject. See also Wouter J. Hanegraaf, "Empirical Method in the Study of Esotericism," *Method and Theory in the Study of Religion*, 7 (1995), pp. 99–129. A general discussion of the subject is presented by Pamela O. Long, "Humanism and Science," in *Renaissance Humanism: Foundations, Forms and Legacy* (see note 12), 3, pp. 486–512; and see also T. J. Reiss, *The Discourse of Modernism*, Ithaca, NY 1982. It seems that the postmodernist writers in France (especially Michel Foucault) contributed meaningfully to the new appreciation of this field as a result of the increasing criticism of modernity and science as the expressions of eternal cultural values. From the point of view of this study, it is impossible to ignore the connection between the renewed interest in hermetism, Christian kabbalah, and the other disciplines and the disappointment and negation of the communicative power of language, expressed mainly by deconstruction. Both represent a new awareness of the nonsemantic aspects of communication, which is also the root of the contemporary fascination with semiotics.

tion of the Hebrew classical sources—the Bible, Talmud, and Midrash—into revelations of the secret dynamic processes within the divine pleroma. Most of this exegesis was performed by means of midrashic semantic methods, intrinsically supported by an intense mystical sense of spiritual communion with these realms and visionary experiences hidden behind the exegetical and homiletical genres of expression. Neither this exegetical enterprise nor its underlying mystical intensity was rendered into Latin in Reuchlin's monograph, and both remained, to a large extent, unknown to the Christian adherents of the kabbalah. The ancient methods were accepted as if they were the message, and were presented in a disproportionate way, undue emphasis being given to the nonsemantic ones.

This fact should not overshadow the uniqueness of Reuchlin's work within the context of Christian-Jewish cultural relations. During the fifteen centuries of separation between Judaism and Christianity before Reuchlin, no other Christian scholar dedicated so much effort to the study of the Hebrew language and Hebrew nonbiblical texts as did Reuchlin, and no one presented the conclusions of his study in such a spirit of empathy and understanding. There are very few examples to equal Reuchlin's work in the centuries following him. The near monopoly held by Jewish converts to Christianity in medieval times over the presentation of nonbiblical Jewish sources to the Christian world was totally broken by Pico and Reuchlin; the door was opened for Christian scholars to approach this material without intermediaries who might have personal agendas in the presentation of Jewish traditions. The clash between Reuchlin and Pfefferkorn, a convert, is very instructive in this sense, the ex-Jew demanding the burning of books that Reuchlin regarded as including most meaningful human and Christian truth.

As a result of Reuchlin's work, there was a kabbalistic component in many major spiritual developments in European culture. Giordano Bruno and Francis Bacon, Robert Fludd and John Dee, Gottfried Wilhelm Leibniz and Isaac Newton all belong to the history of the Jewish influence on early modern science in Europe. Although there was always strong opposition to this trend from various segments of Christianity, the influence of the Christian kabbalah came to an end in the eighteenth century not because of Christian dogmatism, but as a result of the all-conquering rationalistic Enlightenment that engulfed European thought and science.

ENDNOTE

The subject of the Christian Kabbalah seems to be returning to scholarly attention after several decades in which it was relatively neglected. After the articles included here were written, a translation into Italian of Reuchlin's *De Arte Cabbalistica* was published, and it constitutes today the best scholarly edition of the work: Giulio Busi and Saverio Campanini, *Johannes Reuchlin L'arte kabbalistica*, Milano 1996. This edition includes a detailed introduction, a comprehensive bibliography, and an analysis of Reuchlin's Hebrew sources. A brief history of the Christian kabbalah is included in the volume *Storia d'Italia, Gli eberei in Italia*, ed. Corrado Vivanti, Torino 1996; it includes a comprehensive survey of the Christian kabbalah by Eugenio Garin, "L'umanismo italiano e la cultura ebraica," pp. 361–387.

The scholars in the previous generation who studied the subject from the point of view of the history of Jewish mysticism, Gershom Scholem and Chaim Wirszubski, made no attempt to integrate the phenomenon within the framework of European culture (F. Secret made some remarkable observations in this direction, but on the whole he was working on the history of the relevant texts). This task of integration was assumed by Frances Yates, whose penetrating analyses are remarkably relevant today despite the criticism directed at her, especially in the United States. Yates, however, did not have a direct access to the Hebrew sources, and therefore she could not relate to the most important aspect of the process of the development of the Christian kabbalah, namely, what the Christian scholars chose to adopt and what they discarded from the kabbalistic material that was available to them. Their true agenda, I believe, becomes apparent only when this subject is examined, and I tried to point this out in Chapters 9 and 10. On the whole, this analysis seems to support Yates's conclusions concerning the impact of the

Christian kabbalah on the development of European science, secret societies, and utopianism.

Today, the study of the subject is often integrated in the study of what is known as European esotericism. The center of this school is in Paris, and the dominant figure in the field is Antoine Faivre (see, for instance, his brief introductory volume, *L'esotericism*, Paris: Presses Universitaires de France 1992).

ELEVEN

Samael, Lilith, and the Concept of Evil in Early Kabbalah

I

One of the major problems in the study of early kabbalah is the difficulty in distinguishing between old traditions used by kabbalists and new ideas presented in their writings for the first time. Early kabbalists often pretended to be using books and treatises by ancient authorities, a pretense that is usually characterized as pseudepigraphy; however, there can be little doubt that some kabbalists in the Middle Ages did have access to old traditions, transmitted orally or in writing, which they used to mold their own mystical attitudes, and the attempt to distinguish between the old and the new is, in most cases, very difficult, if not outright impossible. The main problem is that scholarly study can never prove a negative: One can do one's best to prove that a certain writer had such and such a source before him, but one can never conclusively prove that a writer did not know a certain text or idea. Still, it is the duty of scholarship to try to follow the development of ideas, themes, and symbols, and to suggest, with the help of close textual analysis, to what extent a certain writer followed ideas and texts, and to surmise carefully what his original contribution was.

In this study an attempt is made to clarify both the sources and the original contribution to the mythological concept of evil as developed by Rabbi Isaac ben Jacob ha-Cohen in Spain in the second half of the thirteenth century. The major text to be considered is Rabbi Isaac's treatise on evil, "A Treatise on the Left Emanation," published by Gershom Scholem in 1927.[1] In this text a kabbalist, for the first time after three generations of the development of the kabbalah, presented a comprehensive concept of evil, based on extreme dualistic attitudes, characterized by Scholem as "gnostic," which indeed bears close phenomenological resemblance to the ancient systems of the Marcionites, the Ophites, and even the Manichaean gnostics. A significant detail in this system is that here, for the first time in a dated Jewish work, Samael and Lilith are described as husband and wife in the realm of the satanic power, a concept that was later incorporated into the *Zohar* and became one of the most popular and well-known chapters in Jewish myths concerning evil.

The following analysis is divided into two parts: The first is an attempt to discover two types of sources that were used by Rabbi Isaac—mythological sources and theological sources; the second part is an attempt to point out the reasons for Rabbi Isaac's mythological attitude and his relationship to other kabbalists, both earlier and later. In this fashion, a conclusion might be reached concerning the role of mythological elements in the development of early kabbalah.

II

The sixth chapter in Rabbi Isaac's Treatise on the Emanations on the Left[2] is opened by a list of the "princes of jealousy and ha-

---

[1] The text was published by Gershom Scholem, "Qabbalot R. Ya'aqov ve-R. Yishaq benei R. Ya'aqov ha-Kohen," *Madda'ei ha-Yahadut*, 2 (1927), pp. 224–264, as a part of the first study of the kabbalah of Rabbi Jacob and Rabbi Isaac ha-Cohen. (The study was also published as a separate book [Jerusalem 1927], from which it is quoted here; the treatise on the Left Emanations appears on pp. 82–102.)
[2] Scholem, *Qabbalot*, pp. 89–90 (pp. 251–252 in *Madda'ei ha-Yahadut*).

tred," that is, the active powers of evil influencing the world, the first of which is Samael. After describing seven such "princes," Rabbi Isaac states: "Truly I shall give you a hint, that the reason for all the jealousies that exist between the princes mentioned above, and the [other, good] princes that belong to seven classes, the classes of the holy angels that are called 'the guardians of the walls,' the reason that evokes hatred and jealousy between the heavenly powers and the powers of the supreme host, is one form[3] that is destined for Samael, and it is Lilith, and it has the image of a feminine form, and Samael is in the form of Adam and Lilith in the form of Eve. Both of them were born in a spiritual birth as one,[4] similar to the form of Adam and Eve, like two pairs of twins, one above and one below. Samael and the Eve the elder, which is called the northern one,[5] they are emanated from below the throne of glory, and this was caused by the sin."[6]

The author goes on to explain the disaster caused by the sin of Adam and Eve in the Garden of Eden, which, according to his description, caused sexual awakening among the two pairs of "twins," an awakening in which the snake, called here Nahasiel or Gamliel,[7] took part. The result was that the snakes became "biting snakes," that is, evil came into its own, and began to express itself.

Several elements in this myth are new, unknown from any previous Jewish source, especially if other motifs, found in parallel pas-

---

[3]Hebrew: *surah*, here probably meaning "a spiritual being," form as opposed to matter.
[4]Hebrew: *toladah ruhanit du-parsufim*, a creature that is, at first, male and female together (see Genesis Rabbah 8:1), and then is divided into separate beings.
[5]See Scholem's note (*Qabbalot*. p. 89, note 4). Samael is identified with the north not only because of the biblical tradition that evil comes from the north, but also because of the possible reading of his name as "left," which is identical to north (if facing east). His spouse, therefore, receives the feminine form of "north."
[6]My translation was prepared with the assistance of Mr. E. Hanker of Berkeley, California.
[7]These names are, in fact, identical, because the snake (*nahash*) had the form of a camel (*gamal*) before he was cursed; this midrashic tradition was included in the Bahir, sec. 200, based on *Pirkey de-Rabbi Eliezer*, Chap. 13—both serving as the basic source for Rabbi Isaac's description of the story of the Garden of Eden.

sages in this treatise, are used to explain this description.[8] But it seems that the first one to be considered should be the joining of Samael and Lilith as a pair, analogous to Adam and Eve. It is a fact that both Samael and Lilith are major figures in earlier Jewish traditions, but nowhere are they mentioned as a pair in a dated work before this passage in the second half of the thirteenth century.[9] Since talmudic times, Samael was regarded as the archangel in charge of Rome, and therefore a satanic figure—especially in the mystical literature known as the *Hechalot* and *Merkavah* literature[10]—though originally he was one of the fallen angels mentioned in the Book of Enoch.[11] The concept of Samael developed in the early Middle Ages. In the late midrash *Pirkey de-Rabbi Eliezer*, he is one of the participants in the drama of the Garden of Eden, as he is also in the first kabbalistic work known to us—the *Bahir*.[12] But nowhere in these detailed descriptions is there a hint that he has a wife or a feminine counterpart, and Lilith is not to be found.

The history of Lilith is even more complex. She seems to have been an ancient Near Eastern goddess, mentioned in the Bible,[13] and she is characterized several times in talmudic literature as a danger

---

[8]Some further descriptions of Lilith are translated below.

[9]A serious problem concerning the development of this idea is related to a medieval text of magic. *Sidrei de-Shimmusha Rabbah*, published by G. Scholem in *Tarbiz*, 16 (1945), pp. 196–209. It is clear that the author of that text knew that Samael and Lilith were related, and there are several other points that suggest a close relationship between it and Rabbi Isaac's treatise. However, the chronological problem has not yet been solved, and it is impossible to decide with any amount of certainty whether Rabbi Isaac used ideas that were known some time before him and reflected in the *Shimmusha*, or that the author of the *Shimmusha* made use of some motifs he found in Rabbi Isaac's treatise.

[10]Samael's role as a power of evil is especially prominent in the section of *Hechalot Rabbati* (Adolf Jellinek, *Beth ha-Midrash*, 6 vols. [Leipzig 1853–1877], 3:87), which describes the martyrdom of ten of the mishnaic sages, as well as in the separate descriptions of this martyrdom in the treatise on the ten martyrs (see my *The Hebrew Story in the Middle Ages* [Hebrew], Jerusalem 1974, pp. 62–69).

[11]The development of the image of Samael is described in detail by G. Scholem in his *Kabbalah*, Jerusalem 1974, pp. 385–389 (and see the detailed bibliography there).

[12]Sec. 200 (the last section; in Scholem's edition, sec. 140).

[13]See Isaiah 34:14.

to infants.[14] A very unclear tradition in the Midrash hints that Lilith
was Adam's first wife before the creation of Eve, and that from this
union demons were born.[15] In all these sources, however, Samael is
never mentioned. How, then, did Samael and Lilith become husband and wife in the treatise by Rabbi Isaac ha-Cohen?

Part of the answer to this question may be found in the famous
source of most of the legends concerning Lilith—the Alphabeth of
Ben Sira, which should properly be called "Pseudo-Ben Sira," a narrative work in Hebrew written late in the gaonic period. This book
has been studied in detail by Eli Yassif, who prepared a critical edition of the text, using dozens of manuscripts.[16] One of the most
important conclusions reached by Yassif is that two versions of the
work exist, one closer to the original and another, known in Europe since the eleventh century,[17] that was edited and enlarged by a
later compilator. This distinction between the two versions, proved
conclusively by Yassif, can shed some light on the history of Lilith
and how she became Samael's spouse.

The early version of Pseudo-Ben Sira tells the following story:

> When God created His world and created Adam, He saw that
> Adam was alone, and He immediately created a woman from
> earth, like him, for him, and named her Lilith. He brought her
> to Adam, and they immediately began to fight: Adam said, "You
> shall lie below," and Lilith said, "You shall lie below, for we are
> equal and both of us were [created] from earth." They did not
> listen to each other. When Lilith saw the state of things, she
> uttered the Holy Name and flew into the air and fled. Adam
> immediately stood in prayer before God and said: "Master of the

---

[14]See Reuben Margulies's collection of the talmudic and midrashic traditions in his
Malakhei Elyon, Jerusalem 1945, pp. 235-237.
[15]This tradition was preserved in Midrash Avkir and elsewhere; see G. Scholem,
Kabbalah, p. 357 (and the detailed bibliography there concerning Lilith, pp. 360–
361).
[16]Eli Yassif, "Pseudo Ben Sira, The Text, Its Literary Character and Status in the
History of the Hebrew Story in the Middle Ages" [Hebrew], 2 vols., Ph.D. dis-
sertation, Hebrew University, 1977.
[17]The later version is the one found in *Bereshit Rabbati* by Rabbi Moses ha-Darshan.

universe, see that the woman you gave me has already fled away."
God immediately sent three angels and told them: "Go and fetch
Lilith; if she agrees to come, bring her, and if she does not, bring
her by force." The three angels went immediately and caught up
with her in the [Red] Sea, in the place that the Egyptians were
destined to die. They seized her and told her: "If you agree to
come with us, come, and if not, we shall drown you in the sea."
She answered: "Darlings, I know myself that God created me
only to afflict babies with fatal disease when they are eight days
old; I shall have permission to harm them from their birth to
the eight days old; I shall have permission to harm them from
their birth to the eighth day and no longer, when it is a male
baby; but when it is a female baby, I shall have permission for
twelve days." The angels would not leave her alone, until she
swore by God's name that wherever she would see them or their
names in an amulet,[18] she would not possess the baby [bearing
it]. They then left her immediately. This is [the story of] Lilith
who afflicts babies with disease.[19]

It seems that every reader of this story in the Middle Ages was
puzzled by one question: Why did the angels leave Lilith alone? They
were ordered by God to bring her back to Adam, and for an un-
stated reason they were convinced by her speech not to do so. But
it is not just an unclear narrative point: In the story as stated in
this version, one might easily come to the conclusion that these three
exalted angels were bribed by Lilith by the promise that she would
never harm babies protected by them or by their names on amulets—and this may very well have been the author's point.[20] It is not

---

[18]These three angels are Sanoi, Sansanoi, and Samanglof, mentioned in the text
of Pseudo-Ben Sira. Many attempts have been made to explain these names by
the use of several oriental languages. It seems to me that they could have been
created by the author of this work as a parody on the angelology of the Hechalot
literature (which often used names like Sansaniel, etc.).

[19]Yassif, "Pseudo-Ben Sira," pp. 64–65. This version is close to the one published
by David Friedman and S. D. Loewinger in Ve-zot li-Yehudah, Budapest 1926,
pp. 259–260.

[20]The question of the meaning of this story depends on one's attitude toward the
character of the Pseudo-Ben Sira. I maintain that this is a satirical, and somewhat

surprising, therefore, to find that the editor of the later version, the one that became known in Europe, changed this part of the story. When describing the encounter between Lilith and the angels in the Red Sea, he wrote: "They tried to take her back, but she refused. They asked her: 'Why don't you want to go back?' She told them: 'I know that I was created for the sole purpose of making babies ill from their day of birth until the eighth day, when I have permission, and after eight days I have no permission. And if it is a female, [this is so] for twelve days!' They said to her: 'If you do not come back we shall drown you in the sea.' She answered: 'I cannot return because of what is said in the Torah—"Her former husband who sent her away, may not take her again to be his wife, after that she is defiled,"[21] that is, when he was the last to sleep with her. And the Great Demon has already slept with me.' "[22] The author goes on to describe the agreement between Lilith and the angels.

It is obvious that the editor of this version was confronted with the difficulty concerning the behavior of the angels, and supplied a halachic reason for why Lilith could not return to her former husband. For this reason he added a new hero to the story, the Great Demon (ha-Sheyd ha-Gadol), whose sole function is to serve as a pretext for Lilith's being unable to return to Adam, since she was defiled by somebody else. The "Great Demon" is a new term, unknown in previous Hebrew sources, but it is quite natural that he could not remain unnamed for long. Jewish tradition usually named the archdemons, as it did the archangels. There was only one possible

heretical, collection of stories by a religious anarchist (see my Hebrew Story, pp. 69–78), although Yassif regards them as usual folktales. (Compare also S. T. Lachs, "The Alphabet of Ben Sira: A Study in Folk-Literature," Gratz College Annual of Jewish Studies, 2 [1973]; pp. 9–28). It is my intention to analyze the problem in detail elsewhere, but it is necessary to point out here that the whole story makes no sense if it is not understood as an expression of Lilith's bitterness toward God for the role assigned to her (in talmudic literature) of a baby-killer.
[21]Deuteronomy 24:4. Naturally, this whole "halachic" discussion has no basis in actual Jewish law.
[22]Yassif, "Pseudo-Ben Sira," pp. 23–24. This version is similar (but not identical; the "great demon" is missing) to the one published by Moritz Steinschneider in his edition: Alphabetum Siracidis, Berlin 1858, p. 23.

name for this "Great Demon" added to the text of Pseudo-Ben Sira
by the later editor, and that name was Samael. This was the only
demonic name associated with the drama of the Garden of Eden, as
described in the *Pirkey de-Rabbi Eliezer* and strengthened, in the eyes
of the early kabbalists, by the inclusion of that description in the
text of the *Bahir*.[23] It is impossible to decide exactly when and where
Samael was identified with the Great Demon, and whether Rabbi
Isaac ha-Cohen had any part in that process. But there can be no
doubt that it was Rabbi Isaac who gave the story of Samael and Lilith
a new mythological dimension, uplifting it from the level of narrative gossip, as it was in the edited version of Pseudo-Ben Sira, and
made it a part of cosmic, and even divine, history. The following
passage is one example of his treatment of this subject:

And now we shall speak about that third Air.[24] The masters of
tradition[25] said that a tradition was transmitted to their fathers
that this Air is divided into three parts, an upper one, a middle
one, and a lower one. The upper one was given to Asmodeus,[26]
the great king of the demons, and he does not have permission
to accuse or cause harm except on Mondays, as the masters of
the tradition had mentioned. And we, with the help of our
Creator, shall expand in this treatise [on this subject] to the
extent that we can. Now Asmodeus, even though he is called
"the great king," is subservient to Samael, and he is called "the
great prince," when compared with the emanations above him,
and "king of kings" when compared with the emanated powers
below him. And Asmodeus is governed by him and serves him.
The Grand Old Lilith[27] is the mate of Samael, the great prince
and the great king of all demons. Asmodeus, the king of the
demons, has as a mate Younger Lilith. The masters of this tra-

---

[23]*Bahir*, sec. 200 (and *Pirkey de-Rabbi Eliezer*, Chap. 13).
[24]Concerning these "airs," see below.
[25]The author here constantly uses the term "kabbalah," which I translated not as
"mystical," but in the sense that the author seems to try to convey—ancient tradition.
[26]Concerning Ashmedai, see Margulies, *Malakhei Elyon*, pp. 215–221; G. Scholem,
"Yedi'ot hadashot al Ashmedai ve-Lilit," *Tarbiz* 19 (1948); pp. 165–175.
[27]*Lilit sabbeta rabbeta.*

dition discuss and point out many wonderful details concerning the form of Samael and the form of Asmodeus and the image of Lilith, the bride of Samael, and of Lilith, the bride of Asmodeus. Happy is he who merits this knowledge.[28]

The author goes on to describe a lower pair of a demon and his mate, and associates these couples with some of the most cruel afflictions of this world, including leprosy and hydrophobia, in a very detailed description.

The way this myth was constructed is clearer in another chapter of that treatise:

> In answer to your question concerning Lilith, I shall explain to you that most important part. There is a tradition received from the early sages who made use[29] of the *Use of the Lesser Palaces*[30] which is the *Use of Demons*[31] which is like a ladder by which one can transcend to the various degrees of prophecy and their powers.[32] In these sources it is explained that Samael and Lilith were born as a hermaphrodite,[33] just like Adam and Eve, who were also born in this manner, reflecting what is above.[34] This is the account of Lilith which was received by the sages in the *Use of the Palaces*. The Elder Lilith[35] is the wife of Samael. Both of them were born at the same hour, in the image of Adam and Eve, intertwined in each other. And Asmodeus, the great king of the demons, has as a wife the Younger Lilith, the daughter of the

---

[28]Scholem, *Qabbalot*, p. 93 (*Madda'ei ha-Yahadut*, p. 255).

[29]*Shimmusha*, meaning "magical use."

[30]*Shimmusha de-Heichalei Zutarti*.

[31]*Shimmusha de-Shedei*.

[32]Meaning that the "magical use" of the "air of demons" is connected with the process of attaining prophecy; see below.

[33]See note 5.

[34]Meaning that the creation in this way reflects the bisexuality in the structure of the spiritual, or even divine, worlds.

[35]It should be noted that in this section, as in several others in the treatise, the author turns to the Aramaic language to express the great, ancient traditions. He relies here on the ancient mystical text, *Hechalot Zutarti*, which was really written mostly in Aramaic, but of course it does not contain any hint of the material referred to by Rabbi Isaac.

king, whose name is Kafzefoni,[36] and the name of his wife is Mehetabel daughter of Matred,[37] and their daughter is Lilith. This is the exact text of what is written in the chapters of the *Lesser Heikhalot*[38] as we have received it, word for word and letter for letter. And the scholars in this science have a very esoteric tradition from the ancient sages who found it stated in those chapters that Samael, the greatest prince of them all, is very jealous of Asmodeus the king of the demons because of this Lilith who is called Lilith the Maiden,[39] who is in the form of a beautiful woman from her head to her waist, and from the waist down she is burning fire; like mother like daughter.[40]

This paragraph clearly states Rabbi Isaac's sources, connected with the Aramaic mystical text describing Rabbi Akiva's ascent to the heavenly palaces, the *Hechalot Zutarti*.[41] Since this text is known to us in several versions, it is easy to discover that Rabbi Isaac's reliance on it is completely apocryphal. Even if one may suggest that portions of this early mystical work were lost, it is still inconceivable that such a fascinating story was included in it (or anywhere else, for that matter), and no other source bothered to mention it until Rabbi Isaac cited it. There can be little doubt that the language of this paragraph is intended to enhance Rabbi Isaac's credibility concerning the previous descriptions of the Liliths, the mother and the daughter, and their relationships with their husbands, the kings of the demons. A mythological narrative was created here, most probably by Rabbi Isaac himself, who made use of various materials that were before him but changed their character completely. The

---

[36]The element *sefoni* seems to be the meaningful part of this name (i.e., from the north—evil).
[37]See Genesis 36:39. The kings of Edom mentioned in this chapter were interpreted as evil powers in later kabbalah, especially in the *Zohar*.
[38]See note 35 and note 41.
[39]*Lilit ulemta.*
[40]Scholem, *Qabbalot*, pp. 98–99 (*Madda'ei ha-Yahadut*, pp. 260–261).
[41]This work is found in several manuscripts, and was partly published in Solomon Musajoff's *Merkavah Shelemah*, Jerusalem 1926, pp. 6a–8b. Several sections were translated by G. Scholem in his *Jewish Gnosticism, Merkabah Mysticism and Talmudic Tradition*, New York 1960.

ancient story concerning Lilith being Adam's first wife was not suitable for Rabbi Isaac's purposes because Samael did not take any significant part in it. He used the later edition of the Pseudo-Ben Sira to introduce Samael into the story, not as Lilith's second husband but as her original mate, creating a kind of parallelism between Adam and Eve and Lilith and Samael. This principle of parallel pairs was carried both forward and backward—reflecting the bisexual nature of the divine world (God and the *Shechinah*) as well as the lower demonic pairs, like Lilith and Asmodeus or Kafzefoni and Mehetabel.

As Rabbi Isaac's concept of the divine world is mythical and dynamic, so are his views concerning the demonic world; an element of strife is introduced by the fight of Samael and Asmodeus over the Younger Lilith. This myth is carried on in a subsequent description until Rabbi Isaac's main concern—the final battle between good and evil—is reached.[42]

The possibility that further sources of Rabbi Isaac's myth concerning the demons will be discovered has to be taken into account, but even so it is quite clear that it was Rabbi Isaac who molded previous traditions into a new narrative myth, expressing his vision of the world and contributing to his theology.

III

An attempt to clarify Rabbi Isaac's mysterious reference to the "third air" and the "air of the use of the demons"[43] leads us to another group of sources that helped Rabbi Isaac create his mythology of the evil powers—the theological works of the Ashkenazi Hasidim. Rabbi Isaac mentioned in his treatise at least twice that he had connections with the Jewish sages in Germany,[44] and it seems

---

[42]See below.
[43]See above.
[44]Rabbi Isaac stated that he and his brother met in Narbonne with a disciple of Rabbi Eleazar of Worms (see Scholem's introduction to the texts, *Gnosticism*, p. 8); among other things, he tells a hagiographic story about Rabbi Eleazar (Chap. 10, p. 92). This story is told immediately after the statement concerning the use of the "demon's air" for the purpose of prophecy.

that in the second half of the thirteenth century several kabbalists emphasized such a connection as a source of their teachings.[45] This is not surprising, since the masters of this pietistic movement were respected throughout the Jewish world because of their ethical teach-ings, their interpretations of the prayers, their pronouncements on Jewish law, and their direct connection with early traditions received from the East.[46] These traditions had an element of magical knowl-edge and the performance of miracles, associated with several of the ancestors of Ashkenazi Hasidism,[47] and reflected in Rabbi Isaac's treatise in the story about the magical flight of Rabbi Eleazar of Worms riding a cloud.[48] It is no wonder, therefore, that the Ashkenazi Hasidim, especially Rabbi Judah the Pious (d. 1217), and his disciple, Rabbi Eleazar of Worms (d. ca. 1230),[49] were regarded by Rabbi Isaac and by some other kabbalists as an authoritative source for esoteric knowledge, with some emphasis on magical and demonological aspects of that tradition.

While it is quite clear that the concepts of the various "airs" between the Earth and the divine world reflect the influence of terms from the Book of Creation (*Sefer Yezira*) and the commentaries on

---

[45]A clear example of such an attitude toward the Ashkenazi Hasidim is found in the Epistle of Worms, included by Rabbi Shem Tov ibn Gaon in his kabbalistic treatise *Baddei ha-Aron* (written in Palestine early in the fourteenth century), ms. Paris 840. These examples attest to the fact that kabbalists in Spain used the repu-tation of the Ashkenazi Hasidim as great mystics and recipients of ancient tradi-tions to enhance their own credibility.

[46]Especially by way of southern Italy; the arrival of Rabbi Aaron ben Samuel of Baghdad in Italy in the eighth century is regarded as the source of Ashkenazi Hasidic prayer mysticism. See my *The Esoteric Theology of the Ashkenazi Hasidim* (Hebrew), Jerusalem 1968, pp. 13–20.

[47]Rabbi Aaron of Baghdad is presented in the *Megillat Ahimaas* as a magician as well as a mystic. A summary of these traditions is found in my paper "The Begin-nings of Jewish Mysticism in Europe," *The World History of the Jewish People: The Dark Ages*, ed. Cecil Roth, Tel Aviv 1969, pp. 282–290.

[48]Scholem, *Qabbalot*, p. 92. It should be noted that this story not only praises Rabbi Eleazar for his piety and his supernatural knowledge, but also states that he failed once in reciting the right formula, fell off the cloud, suffered injury, and remained crippled until his last day.

[49]Concerning the date of his death, see my *Studies in Ashkenazi Hasidic Literature* (Hebrew), Tel Aviv and Ramat Gan 1975, p. 69.

that book, especially that of Rav Saadia Gaon,[50] upon Rabbi Isaac ha-Cohen, the connection between the "third air" and both prophecy and demonology poses a serious problem. In Rabbi Isaac's work, the demons represent cosmic and divine elements of evil, while in the sizable literature of the Ashkenazi Hasidim on this subject one cannot find any dualistic element: The demons represent a natural power that is an integral part of the created world, and their actions conform to the decrees of God exactly as do those of angels.[51] Still, there is a connection between Rabbi Isaac's myth and the Ashkenazi Hasidic speculations, for it was the pietists in the late twelfth century and the early thirteenth who stressed the link between visions of demons and the phenomenon of prophecy.

Several discussions of problems concerning prophecy in Ashkenazi Hasidic esoteric literature deal with a phenomenon traditionally called in Hebrew *sarei kos ve-sarei bohen*,[52] "the princes of the glass and the princes of the thumb." The term refers to a universal practice of divination, using a thin layer of oil spread upon a bright surface, which may be a piece of glass, a sword, a mirror, or even a fingernail—all materials often mentioned in this connection in Hebrew descriptions. The belief was that demons can be compelled to reveal themselves on such surfaces, and when they are asked questions by a professional sorcerer (usually a non-Jew) they must reveal secrets. This practice was used to solve many everyday problems, most often to find lost articles or to catch a thief (generally to reveal where stolen goods were hidden).[53] The sorcerer or the witch

---

[50]This stratification of "airs" or "winds" is based on *Sefer Yeẓira*, Chap. 1, secs. 9-10. Following Rav Saadia, Rabbi Eleazar of Worms in his commentary (Przemysl 1883) described this hierarchy in detail (see especially p. 3c).

[51]See my *Esoteric Theology*, pp. 184-190.

[52]See Samuel Daiches, *Babylonian Oil Magic in the Talmud and Later Jewish Literature*, London 1913; Joshua Trachtenberg, *Jewish Magic and Superstition*, New York 1939, pp. 219-222, 307-308; and my study "Sarei kos ve-sarei bohen," *Tarbiẓ* 32 (1963), pp. 359-369 (reprinted in *Studies in Ashkenazi Hasidic Literature*, pp. 34-43).

[53]The Ashkenazi Hasidim also used some more "prophetic" means to achieve this; compare the story told by Rabbi Judah the Pious concerning the discovery of a thief in *Studies in Ashkenazi Hasidic Literature*, pp. 10-12.

would receive a request, the owner of the lost goods would usually participate in the ceremony, and when the right demon, who was reponsible for that area, was brought by the force of incantations, an answer would be revealed.

This common practice seems to have been very well known in medieval Germany,[54] probably after it had been brought from the east to Europe by the Arabs. The Ashkenazi Hasidim refer to it as a commonplace occurrence that does not have to be described and discussed in detail; no doubt the readers were familiar with it. The problem, however, is that of the relationship between this elementary form of magic and prophecy. It seems that here the Ashkenazi Hasidim found an unnoticed element in this practice that conformed easily to their theology.

The key detail in this magical practice was that neither the sorcerer nor the person requesting the practice could see the demons in the thin layer of oil. The demon could be seen only by a child, a small boy or a virgin girl. The adults surrounding the bright surface did not see anything, but the child would describe in great detail what he saw in the oil—a demon dressed in a certain manner having a certain identifying mark. Often the sorcerer would instruct the child to send that demon back and ask another one to come, until the right demon appeared. The ability of the child to perceive things hidden even from professional magicians was the key to the success of the whole practice.

This detail was the cause for the intensive interest of the Ashkenazi Hasidim in this practice, because it seemed to illustrate the central problem in their concept of prophecy. The pietists relied upon the famous dictum of Rav Saadia Gaon, who stated that what the prophets had seen was a created angel, called the divine glory (kavod).[55] But only one faction among the medieval esotericists accepted Saadia's view; others held different opinions. Some claimed

---

[54]Lynn Thorndike, History of Magic and Experimental Science, 8 vols, New York 1923, 2: 161, 168, 320, 354, 364–365, and 1:774. Compare Rashi to Sanhedrin 67b and 101a.
[55]Dan, Esoteric Theology, pp. 104–118.

that the whole process of prophecy is an internal, psychological one, and no element of external revelation is involved; the prophets described their dreams and their inner thoughts when they described divine revelation. Others—including the main teachers of the Ashkenazi Hasidic school, like Rabbi Judah the Pious and Rabbi Eleazar of Worms—held, following Rabbi Abraham ibn Ezra's interpretation of prophecy,[56] that the prophets did indeed see a divine revelation, and the revealed power is called the divine glory. But this glory is not a created angel, but a divine power, emanated from God, a spiritual being that is not bound by the laws of creation.

This controversy, which holds a central place in the esoteric theology of the Ashkenazi Hasidic movement,[57] brought into discussion as a central theme the magical practice of *sarei kos* and *sarei bohen*, because at least two views could be supported by the procedure of this divinatory practice. Those who believed prophecy to be an internal, psychological process claimed that the demons invoked in this way have no real existence, that they are nothing but dreams and imaginary visions, even though many people believe in their material existence. Others, like Rabbi Judah and Rabbi Eleazar, claimed that this practice proves conclusively that prophecy is a real phenomenon, but that the revealed power is divine and not created. In biblical descriptions of prophetic visions there are some occurrences in which one person—the prophet himself—did see something, while other people standing beside him did not see anything, as in the case of Elisha and his servant when the city was surrounded by chariots of fire.[58] This proves, according to them, that the vision could not be natural, because natural phenomena can be seen either by all or by no one, being subservient to natural law; divine powers can have supernatural revelation of a selective kind, reveal-

---

[56]In the twelfth chapter of his *Yesod Mora*, as well as in his commentary to Exodus 33; see J. Dan, *Esoteric Theology*, pp. 113-116.

[57]J. Dan, *Esoteric Theology*, pp. 129-143, based on the detailed discussion in the first part of Bodleian ms. Opp. 540, part of which was published in Dan, *Studies in Ashkenazi Hasidic Literature*, pp. 148-187.

[58]Dan, *Studies in Ashkenazi Hasidic Literature*, pp. 165-166; 2 Kings 6:15-17.

ing themselves to a certain person while remaining hidden from others. Thus Rabbi Judah and Rabbi Eleazar proved that Rav Saadia's concept of created glory was insufficient in explaining the process of prophecy, and only Ibn Ezra's description of the divine, emanated glory can explain the facts. To this they added the fact that God implanted a miracle within the created world that can serve as a proof of this concept,[59] namely, the fact that only a child can see the demons when divination is practiced, while all others standing around see nothing; what can be done by every common witch can also be performed by the divine glory, and therefore neither those who claim that prophecy is an imaginary process nor those who claim that a created angel is revealed can be right.

When Rabbi Eleazar explained the creation of the throne of glory, he wrote:[60] "Another reason for its creation is for visions, for it is seen by the prophets in visions which include a divine message . . . and the Creator changes the visions according to His will.[61] I shall give you an example, as they evoke *sarei bohen* with a child and he sees in them what his master wishes. The Creator created visions, to teach the prophets the content of His decrees. . . . And among the philosophers[62] there was a controversy about *sarei bohen* and *sarei kos*. Some of them said that the supervising angel[63] enters

---

[59]This is one example for the use of a basic Ashkenazi Hasidic theological idea— that God's miraeles were planted in the world to teach the righteous God's ways; see Dan, *Esoteric Theology*, pp. 88–93.

[60]*Chochmat ha-Nefesh* (Lemberg 1876), p. 18c–d. (The pagination in this edition is completely arbitrary and wrong; this page is marked as p. 20. In the Safed edition, reprinted exactly word for word and line for line, the pagination has been corrected, and this is the pagination used here.) See Dan, *Studies in Ashkenazi Hasidic Literature*, pp. 39–41.

[61]According to the author, the changes in the visions are supernatural and therefore reflect divine characteristics.

[62]"Philosophers" in this text means "sages," including Jews, and has nothing to do with Greek, Arabic, or even Jewish philosophy, to which the Ashkenazi Hasidim were in fierce opposition. See Dan, *Studies in Ashkenazi Hasidic Literature*, pp. 31–33.

[63]According to their concept of divine providence, there is a supervising angel (*memunneh*), who directs the fate of each person; see Dan, *Esoteric Theology*, pp. 235–240.

into the heart and creates thoughts in a person's heart and the child's, and changes his thoughts and gives him knowledge[64] which takes form in his mind like a thief and the stolen goods, and he sees everything, but he really does not see anything."

After reviewing this attitude, Rabbi Eleazar goes on to compare other interpretations, as does Rabbi Judah the Pious several times in his theological works.[65] In one place Rabbi Judah brings out this practice as one example of the principle of *zecher asah le-nifle otav*, the principle that states that every miraculous power of God has a "sign" or "remnant" in the world to prove God's powers,[66] and concludes: "Do not be surprised because God's voice enters the prophet's ears and is not heard by others around him, for it is like a person talking into a tube, the other end of which is in someone else's ear, and, when he talks into it, one hears and the others do not hear. In the same way one sees divine visions and others do not. Is it not true that some people see in the fingernail and in the *sarei kos* and others do not see? In the same way do not be surprised about the visions of the prophets. For it is like a mirror, one can look into one and see everything that is in the opposite direction; so it is with *sarei kos* and *sarei bohen*—everything they see they see like a person looking into a mirror seeing a reverse image."[67]

The Ashkenazi Hasidim used the analogy of this magical practice concerning several theological problems, but the comparison to prophecy is the most frequent and insistent one. It is quite clear in the writings of these pietists that they never imagined an actual connection existing between the realms of demons and magic and the prophetic phenomenon; all their efforts were directed at analyzing the analogy between this practice and prophecy, based upon their monistic concept that the world of demons is an integral part of the world created by God, refuting any possibility of a dualistic attitude.

---

[64]The reading of this sentence in the manuscript is doubtful.
[65]See Dan, *Studies in Ashkenazi Hasidic Literature*, pp. 41–43.
[66]Dan, *Esoteric Theology*, pp. 88–93.
[67]Dan, *Studies in Ashkenazi Hasidic Literature*, pp. 171–172.

When seeking a source for Rabbi Isaac ha-Cohen's description of the "demonic air" that is described as the "air of prophecy," one cannot neglect the possibility that the Ashkenazi Hasidim's analogy somehow turned into fact in Spain, two generations after Rabbi Judah's and Rabbi Eleazar's works were written. It is quite clear from Rabbi Isaac's references to the Ashkenazi Hasidim that he was not a direct disciple of their school, and that those ideas of theirs that reached him did so through intermediaries, about whom we have no definite knowledge whether they really knew this esoteric doctrine from a firsthand source. It seems probable, therefore, that the information that reached the Spanish kabbalist was far from accurate, and Rabbi Isaac could interpret it to mean that there is an actual connection between the process of prophecy and magical divination by the revelation of demons. If this was so, it was possible to conclude that the prophetic vision and the "use" (*shimmusha*) of demons originate from the same cosmic source, the "third air" in his mythical description.

It should be noted that the difference between *sarei bohen* and *shimmusha de-sheydey* could be much smaller than it seems if we take into account the possibility that Rabbi Judah the Pious and his disciples spoke not about *sarei bohen* but about *sheydey bohen*, that is, not "princes of the thumb" but "demons of the thumb." The Hebrew letters can easily be confused, and in one homiletical discussion by Rabbi Judah of the talmudic section referring to these powers it is evident that he read "demons," not "princes." [68]

It is probable, therefore, that Rabbi Isaac used inaccurate traditions originating in the schools of the Ashkenazi Hasidim to describe his concept of the world and the place of demons in it. It is possible, therefore, that he used the same sources, in a similar cre-

---

[68]A homily by Rabbi Judah the Pious (Bodleian ms. Opp. 540, fol. 84v) explains the *leshad ha-shemen* ("a cake baked in oil") in Numbers 11:8 as referring to these "princes," so that it is clear that he called them *sheydim*, not *sarim*. Prof. E. E. Urbah kindly informed me that in the commentaries in medieval halachic literature concerning the relevant passages in *Sanhedrin* (note 54), the halachists often refer to *sheydim*.

ative way, to devise his myth of the "destroyed worlds," which, unlike the "air of the use of demons," has a crucial place in his concept of evil and the creation of a mythological demonlogy.

IV

Rabbi Isaac ha-Cohen began his story of the origins of evil by describing a detailed myth concerning the "destroyed worlds," worlds that were created before our world but could not exist. The importance he attributes to this myth is clear from the long opening statement, telling how this tradition had reached him: "Now we shall turn to speak about the system of the evil powers which are in heaven, of those which were created and then annihilated suddenly. When I was in the great city of Arles, masters of this tradition showed me a booklet, a very old one, the writing in it being rough and different from our writing. It was transmitted in the name of a great rabbi and a gaon called Rabbi Masliah, for the old gaon, our Rabbi Pelatiah, was from the holy city of Jerusalem, and it was brought by a great scholar and Hasid called Rabbi Gershom of Damascus. He was from the city of Damascus and lived in Arles about two years, and people there told stories about his great wisdom and wealth. He showed that booklet to the great sages of that age, and I copied some things from it—things which the sages of that generation had understood, for they were not familiar with that particular writing like those earlier sages who learned it from that scholar and Hasid."[69]

After this story, which includes not even one name or fact that can be verified by any other source, Rabbi Isaac describes the emanation of the first evil powers from a curtain below the third *sefirah* in the kabbalistic system, which he calls, like many early kabbalists before him, *teshuvah* (repentance). The first three evil worlds to be emanated were destroyed, and Rabbi Isaac's discussion of this is based on the talmudic and midrashic traditions about the earlier worlds— the one in the Midrash stating that before God created this world

---

[69]Scholem, *Qabbalot*, pp. 86–87.

He used to create other worlds and destroy them,[70] and the talmudic tradition about the generations that were annihilated, 974 in number.[71] Rabbi Isaac goes even further in homiletical treatment of the subject, by ascribing names to the princes ruling these lost worlds— Kamtiel, Beliel, and Ittiel, names derived from the verse in Job that served as a basis for the talmudic homily.[72]

The basic elements of this myth were taken, therefore, from well-known Hebrew homilies in popular sources. The major new twist given to the myth by Rabbi Isaac is centered on one element, which is completely new here: Those previous worlds or generations were evil, and they were destroyed (nimhu, kummetu—the terms used by the Midrash, which seem to be used by Rabbi Isaac in the sense of "inverse emanation"; their emanation was reversed[73]) because they were much too evil. It is impossible to state that they were destroyed because they contained a satanic element, for Rabbi Isaac's description of our world stresses the existence and the power of the satanic element in it; the destruction was caused by their being totally evil, whereas when our world was created some angelic and good powers were emanated as well.

When seeking Rabbi Isaac's sources for this myth, we must concentrate on these two motifs: The identification of the destroyed worlds and generations as evil, and this evil as the cause of their destruction, while the existing world contains some good beside the evil element. Such a homily, containing exactly these motifs, is contained in Rabbi Eleazar of Worms's Chochmat ha-Nefesh.[74]

The subject discussed by Rabbi Eleazar is the purpose of the creation of the world:

---

[70]Genesis Rabbah 9:2, ed. Julius Theodor and Chanoch Albeck, Berlin and Jerusalem 1903, p. 68, and compare Ecclesiastes Rabbah 3:11.
[71]Hagiga 13b-14a.
[72]Job 22:16.
[73]According to Rabbi Isaac (Scholem, Qabbalot, p. 88), they were emanated as spiritual worlds, and their end came in a spiritual manner, like the burning tip in an oil lamp that is plunged into the oil in order to stop its burning.
[74]Chochmat ha-Nefesh, p. 10c-d.

Why did He create the world, for the Creator does not need the created and has no benefit from them, so why did He create the world? Before anything was created there were only He and His name alone, and He existed without any created being, so why did He need His creatures? Before the creation He did not need them [and he does not need them now]?

The truth is that God did not create the world for His own sake, for He has no benefit from a worthless world, but He said: "If I should create a world without the Evil Yeser[75] there will be no wonder if the creatures will be as good as the Ministering Angels;[76] and if I put into them a strong Evil Yeser, they might be unable to overcome this Yeser. Still, I might find two righteous people among them, like David." He thus created worlds and destroyed them, for He did not find righteous people like David . . . and when He saw that there were no such righteous as David, He destroyed them.

He said: "The fact that there is not even one good person among all these is because I created the Evil Yeser too strong in them . . ." and the Creator said: "The reason why I created such a strong Yeser in them is, that if two [righteous] are found, He would be ungrateful if He did not create them. But He said: I created it too strong, therefore there is no good in them; I shall now create human beings with another Yeser, the Good Yeser.

Rabbi Eleazar's extensive homily includes references to many verses that he interprets as describing the destroyed worlds, and he goes on to analyze the destroyed generations, and the evildoers of the period of the deluge. His main argument is quite clear, relying to a certain extent on the midrashic treatment of the subject, but expressing some of the most important theological concepts of the Ashkenazi Hasidic movement. Righteousness, according to these pietists, can be measured only by means of the opposition that one has to overcome; there can be no righteousness where the only drive is a good one. For this reason, the angels are not regarded as righ-

---

[75]That is, in a perfect way.
[76]This is based on the text in Genesis Rabbah, Chap. 3, sec. 9.

teous. If so, ideal righteousness, the highest possible religious achievement, is one that is demonstrated against impossible odds, without
any divine help, like a created person who has only an Evil Yeser
in him and still succeeds, to some extent, to overcome it and be
righteous (this may be the reason that the example of righteousness
given is David; it cannot be doubted that he had a very strong evil
inclination). The fact is that creation by Evil Yeser alone did not
produce even one such person; still, God had to create these unsuc-
cessful worlds, for He could not damn them into nonexistence before the evil was performed. If even two righteous persons were to
overcome all the obstacles and do some good in those evil worlds,
God would have been ungrateful if He did not create them.[77]

The creation of our world is therefore described as a compromise, a reluctant one, by God. He decided to add a Good Yeser to
help human beings become righteous. This, of course, degrades their
righteousness, for it is now achieved with divine help, not by overcoming maximum difficulties. Still, this compromise is the only way
to create a world that could exist, after the repeated failures of the
previous period. Obviously, according to Rabbi Eleazar a world
cannot exist unless there are in it at least two righteous persons. (It
is possible to surmise that such existence is dependent also on the
extent of their righteousness, which is smaller in our world than it
could have been in the Evil Yeser worlds; it means, paradoxically
enough, that the powers of existence of this world are lesser than in
the ancient destroyed ones; if one of those could exist, it would have
been much more valid than our own.)

Rabbi Eleazar's intepretation of the myth of the destroyed
worlds is one according to which God tried at first to create "ideal"
worlds that would be completely evil, and thus would be able to
produce ideal, complete righteousness. Failing in that, He created a
mixed world in which good and evil are combined, and that successfully produces from time to time righteous persons that justify

[77]Similar ideas were expressed elsewhere in the thirteenth century, as in the mystical *Sefer ha-Hayyim* (mss. British Library Or. 1055, Munich 209). See Dan, *Esoteric Theology*, pp. 230–235 and compare *Sefer ha-Yashar* (Venice 1544), Chap. 1.

its existence. It is clear that there is no trace of a dualistic attitude in Rabbi Eleazar's theology. Evil comes from God directly, and it fulfills a divine function. The extent of evil in every phase of the creation is decided by God, according to His divine plan, which is a perfectly good one—to produce righteousness. Evil is a necessary means to bring righteousness forward, to test it in the most difficult circumstances,[78] and to justify the existence of the world by it. Rabbi Eleazar's achievement in this formulation includes an explanation of the evil character of this world: It is necessary for the sake of the righteous, who could not otherwise show their true nature. But this explanation of the meaning of evil includes no dualistic or gnostic inclination.

This theology includes the basic elements of Rabbi Issac ha-Cohen's myth of the destroyed worlds: The previous worlds were completely evil—they were destroyed because of their completely evil nature. The theology is radically different from Rabbi Eleazar's, for Rabbi Isaac does not offer an explanation as to why these worlds should have been evil according to the divine plan, but it seems that one can safely surmise that Rabbi Isaac's myth was produced under the influence of Rabbi Eleazar's radical theology, which was given a completely new twist in the framework of Rabbi Isaac's mythological concept of evil, which is so different from Rabbi Eleazar's instrumental one.

Rabbi Eleazar's system does not include an element of strife, except the struggle within the soul of the Hasid who is trying to become righteous. Rabbi Isaac's myth is based to a very large extent on descriptions of mythical struggle:

These souls,[79] which are angelic emanations, existed potentially within the depth of the Emanator, hidden from everything, but before they could come out of their potential existence into reality, another world was emanated, from strange forms and destructive appearances. The name of the ruler of this emanation,

---

[78]See my discussion of their ethical attitude in *Hebrew Ethical and Homiletical Literature* (Hebrew), Jerusalem 1975, pp. 121–145.
[79]Meaning "spiritual emanations."

a prince over all its forces, is Qamtiel. These are the Cruel Ones, who began to rebuke and to disrupt the emanation. Immediately there exuded a decree from the Prince of Repentance, who is called Karoziel,[80] who is also called the Echo of Repentance, and said: "Masokhiel, Masokhiel,[81] destroy what you have created and collect your emanations back to you, for it is not the wish of the King of Kings, blessed be He, that these emanations will exist in the worlds." They returned and were annihilated; in the same way that they were emanated they atrophied. Scholars explained this process by an example—like a string saturated in oil which is burning by the oil it constantly absorbs; when you wish to turn it off, you sink it into the oil which makes it burn; the same oil which makes it give light turns it back to nothing.

After this, another world was emanated, from strange forms and foreign appearances; the name of the ruler of their emanation and the prince of their forces is Beliel. These were worse than the first ones in rebuking and disrupting all kinds of emanation, until a decree came forth from the King of Kings, and they were annulled in a moment like the first ones. After that a third world was emanated from strange forms, stranger than the first and the second; the name of its ruler and prince of their forces is Ittiel. These are worst of all. It is their wish and ambition to be on top of the divine, to distort and cut the divine tree with all its branches, until there came a decree from the divine Will that it will be annihilated like the first and second ones, and it was decreed and decided that such an emanation will never again come to the world's air, will never be remembered or mentioned. These are the worlds about which the ancient sages said that God was creating worlds and destroying them.[82]

The difference between this mythical description and Rabbi Eleazar's homily is as clear as the similarities. Rabbi Eleazar's monism is replaced by a stark dualism in this realm, and the relatively

---

[80]From the Hebrew karoz (crier).
[81]From the Hebrew masacch (curtain).
[82]Scholem, Qabbalot, pp. 87–88.

systematic inquiry into the problems of the creation and divine providence is replaced by an unexplained myth, visionary rather than ex-
planatory. Still, the idea that the destroyed worlds were ones of un-
mitigated evil, which caused their destruction, to be replaced by a
world in which good and evil are combined, is based on Rabbi
Eleazar's speculation.

V

The comparison between Rabbi Isaac ha-Cohen's treatise on the
Left Emanations and those sources that we can identify with some
extent of certainty does not diminish the impact of Rabbi Isaac's
original concepts, but rather enhances it. These sources constitute
not basic elements of his mythological worldview, but only materials used when building the innovative kabbalistic system that was
destined to have a major impact upon later kabbalists, especially the
author of the *Zohar*. Though one can never be certain that most of
the relevant sources have been found and properly analyzed, the
three clear examples described above can at least offer the major
outlines of the structure of Rabbi Isaac's use of previous sources.
These outlines seem to suggest that Rabbi Isaac did rely on previous material in secondary motifs, whereas his basic attitudes cannot
be found to date in any known Hebrew work.

If this is the situation at the present stage of the study of Rabbi
Isaac's theology, the main questions remain: What drove Rabbi Isaac
to create this novel attitude toward the world, creation, Satan,
Samael, Lilith, demons, divination, and the destroyed worlds? What
is the underlying mythical or mystical vision that brought forth this
new combination of older material, painted in daring new colors?
In other words: What is the basic difference between Rabbi Isaac's
concept of evil and that of all other Jewish writers before him?

In Chapter 19 of his treatise, after the detailed description of
Samael and Lilith and the fight between Asmodeus and Samael over
the "Younger Lilith," Rabbi Isaac states:

It is said that from Asmodeus and his wife Lilith a great prince
was born in heaven, the ruler of eighty thousand destructive

demons, and he is called Harba de-Ashmedai Malka ("The Sword
of the King Asmodeus"), and his name is Alpafonias,[83] and his
face burns like fire. He is also called Gorigor,[84] [for] he antago-
nizes and fights the princes[85] of Judah, who is called Gur Aryeh
Yehudah. And from the same form from which that destroyer
was born, another prince was born in heaven,[86] from the source
of Malkhut,[87] who is called Harba di-Meshiha ("The Sword of
the Messiah"), and he too has two names, Meshihiel and
Kokhviel.[88] When the time comes, and God wishes it, this sword
will come out of its sheath, and the prophecies will come true:
"For My sword hath drunk its fill in heaven; behold, it shall come
down upon Edom."[89] "There shall step forth a star out of Jacob,"[90]
amen. Soon in our time we shall have the privilege of seeing the
face of the righteous messiah, we and all our people.[91]

In the last paragraph where the myth of Samael and Lilith is
developed, Rabbi Isaac states:

> I shall now teach you a wonderful, unknown thing. You already
> know that Evil Samael and Wicked Lilith are like a sexual pair,
> who by means of an intermediary[92] receive an emanation of evil
> and wickedness, one from the other, and emanate it onwards. I
> shall explain this relying on the esoteric meaning of the verse:
> "In that day the Lord with His sore and great and strong sword

---

[83]The form of this name is quite mysterious, but it seems that it might contain the
Hebrew element *peney esh* (fiery face), which is included in the description of this
power.
[84]The Hebrew element *gur* (cub) is evident here as a scion of Judah.
[85]It should be "prince," in the singular.
[86]The author follows the same structure of parallel births, as he had stated concerning Adam and Eve and Samael and Lilith.
[87]*Malchut*, kingdom, has here a double meaning, both as the tenth *sefirah* in the
kabbalistic system and as a symbol of the kingdom of Judah.
[88]Based on the verse in Numbers 24:17, which was interpreted as referring to the
Messiah.
[89]Isaiah 34:5.
[90]Numbers 24:17.
[91]Scholem, *Qabbalot*, p. 99.
[92]This term is used here in a derogatory sense—an intermediary who leads one to
sin.

will punish leviathan the slant serpent and leviathan the tortu-
ous serpent"—meaning Lilith—"and He will slay the dragon that
is in the sea."[93] As there is a pure leviathan in the sea and he
is called a serpent, so there is a great impure serpent in the sea,
in the usual sense of the term. And it is the same above [in
the divine world], in a secret way. And the heavenly serpent is
a blind prince,[94] who is like an intermediary between Samael
and Lilith and his name is Tanin'iver (Blind Serpent) . . . and
he is the one who brings about the union between Samael and
Lilith. If he were created in the fullness of his emanation he
would have destroyed the whole world in one moment. . . .
When there is a divine wish, and the emanation of Samael and
Lilith diminishes somewhat the emanation achieved by the Blind
Prince, they will be completely annihilated by Gabriel, the
prince of power, who invokes war against them with the help
of the prince of mercy, then the esoteric meaning of the verse
we have quoted will come true.[95]

The concluding paragraphs of the treatise deal exclusively with
this same subject. The final destruction of the powers of evil—Samael,
Lilith, and the serpent—by messianic powers, and a glowing description of messianic times after evil has been overcome, conclude the
treatise.

If we try now to answer the questions posed at the beginning
of this section, we have to take into account the full scope of the
myth told by Rabbi Isaac. In this way it will become evident that
Rabbi Isaac did not combine the motifs he borrowed from earlier
sources to produce a new description of the creation, or even to
explain the existence of evil in the world in the past and in the
present. The myth he presented in this treatise is a coherent one,
starting with the powers of evil that preceded the creation and concluding with the description of the messianic victory over evil.

---

[93]Isaiah 27:1, and compare Bava Batra 74b. See Scholem's note, Qabbalot, p. 100,
note 5.
[94]Samael's name is obviously interpreted here by Rabbi Isaac as derived from suma
(blind).
[95]Scholem, Qabbalot, pp. 101-102.

One of the basic characteristics of this myth is the consistent attempt to produce parallelisms, to describe all existence in terms of two similar antagonistic powers. This is evident both within the realm of evil—Asmodeus and Samael, the Older Lilith and the Younger Lilith—and in the relations between the evil powers and the good. The sword of Asmodeus is reflected in the sword of the Messiah; the pure leviathan is reflected in the evil leviathan, and so forth. Even the creation of Samael and Lilith is a parallel to the creation of Adam and Eve. Rabbi Isaac did not hesitate to depart radically from the content of his sources in order to achieve this, as he did in this last detail, forsaking the myth of Lilith as Adam's first wife in order to be able to present a complete parallel between the two pairs.

This basic attitude brings into focus the meaning of the title of the treatise, a meaning easily neglected because this idea became, after Rabbi Isaac, one of the most famous characteristics of kabbalistic thought—Left Emanation, called by the *Zohar sitra ahra* ("the other side," meaning evil).[96] Rabbi Isaac's concept of two systems of divine emanations, similar in many details but one good and one evil, was not an idea standing alone, but an integral part of a mythological worldview that believed that all existence is governed by the antagonism between pairs of similar structure and conflicting content. This attitude can be found in almost every paragraph of this treatise.

As the examples translated above show, these pairs are in continuous conflict, both within the realm of evil and between the evil system and the good one. It seems that in this mythology the parallel pairs should by nature fight each other, and that this struggle will not cease until one side is completely annihilated and true unity will reign in the divine and earthly worlds. Thus, it is not just a dualistic mythology, but one that is marked by an internal structure that necessitates continuous struggle.

---

[96]"Other," in the zoharic terminology concerning evil, means both "left" and "evil," while *sitra*, "side," refers to the system of emanations. See G. Scholem, *Kabbalah*, pp. 122–127, and I. Tishby, *Mishnat ha-Zohar*, 2 vols. (Jerusalem 1949), 1: 288–292.

It seems that the outcome of this struggle may be the key to the main drive behind the creation of this myth, namely, the messianic victory and the annihilation of evil. It should be stressed that this treatise by Rabbi Isaac can be regarded as the first Hebrew apocalypse to be written in medieval Europe, and certainly it is the first treatment by a kabbalist of the messianic motif in any detail. The dualistic character of the work, its gnostic undertones, and its stark demonological mythology are means to express the basic apocalyptic theme: The struggle between good and evil will come to its conclusion when the messianic sword is raised and destroys the powers of evil. The history of these powers is told in detail in order to lay the foundations of the story of the final victory over those powers.

Messianism was not the main subject, or the main concern, of kabbalistic writers in the first hundred years of the kabbalah, or even in the writings of nonkabbalistic authors of that period. The original vision of Rabbi Isaac should be seen against this background, and his main innovation should be seen as a whole: a mythology of evil expressing a messianic apocalypse.[97]

ENDNOTE

It is a most surprising fact that while studies concerning most aspects of Jewish mysticism have proliferated most meaningfully in the last few decades, the subject of the concept of evil has been conspicuously absent among the titles of recent books and articles. In the last decade, two important studies of this subject have been made

---

[97]It is possible to compare this process to a somewhat similar one that occurred several centuries before Rabbi Isaac, namely, the description of the evil power, Armilos, in the book of Zerubavel (see Yehudah Even-Shmuel, *Midreshei Geulah*, Jerusalem and Tel Aviv 1954, pp. 56–88, and compare my discussion in *The Hebrew Story in the Middle Ages*, pp. 33–46). In this case, too, we have a mythical description of an evil power, the son of Satan and a beautiful stone statute in Rome, who became the spiritual as well as political leader of the world and threatened to destroy the people of Israel. The original mythology of the power of evil is closely connected with the emergence of a new mythology of the Messiah and a detailed description of messianic victories.

available to English readers: Gershom Scholem's study of "evil in the kabbalah," included in the volume of his thematic monographs, *The Mystical Shape of the Godhead*, New York: Schocken 1991, pp. 56–86; and I. Tishby's detailed study of the concept of evil in the *Zohar*, included in his *The Wisdom of the Zohar*, vol. II, Oxford: Oxford University Press 1989, pp. 447–546. To these one should add the discussion of the concept of evil in the *Bahir* and in the early kabbalah, in general, in Scholem's *Origins of the Kabbalah*, trans. A. Arkush and ed. R. J. Zwi Werblowsky, Princeton, NJ: Princeton University Press and the Jewish Publications Society 1986, pp. 292–298 et passim. All these, however, are translations of studies published about forty years ago. Recent publications seem to ignore the subject, probably expressing the reluctance to discuss the deep dualistic tendencies in many central works of Jewish mysticism.

Since I began my scholarly work in this field, nearly forty years ago, I have tried to follow the two parallel lines of the concept of evil in Jewish mysticism. One is the absorption and utilization of popular narratives concerning demons and other powers associated with evil in the works of Jewish medieval theologians; and the theoretical, theological stuggle with the subject of theodicy, explaining on a theological—and often mythological—level the existence of evil in the world. My first scholarly article, which was printed in 1960, included a publication of demonological stories by Rabbi Judah the Pious and their theological background; the article in this collection, comparing Rabbi Judah's stories with those of Caesarius of Heisterbach, is a continuation of the analysis of those texts. Two of the articles included here, concerning the concept of evil in Nachmanides and concerning Samael and gnosticism, are intended to serve as a beginning of a detailed study of the figure of Samael.

TWELVE

Five Versions of the Story
of the Jerusalemite

I

The old Hebrew fairytale, the Story of the Jerusalemite, is one of the few stories in Hebrew literature in the Middle Ages that have been extensively studied, translated to other languages, and commented upon by scholars. Yet, its history is practically unknown, and therefore some of its main characteristics have escaped the attention of the scholars. It is hoped that the new versions that will be discussed here may shed some new light on the history and development of this unique story.

The Story of the Jerusalemite has been translated from the Hebrew into Arabic,[1] Latin,[2] Yiddish,[3] German,[4] and other languages,

---

[1]The translation was published from a manuscript by N. Allony, Jerusalem 1946 (see note 11). The translator was an Eastern Jew of the eighteenth century.
[2]J. Christoph Wagenseil, *Exercitationes sex varii argumenti*, Altorf 1687, pp. 214–240.
[3]Many times; see M. Steinschneider, *Catalogue of the Hebrew Books in the Bodleian Library*, no. 4266[4].
[4]Korn Selig, *Der Sabbathianer*, Leipzig 1835, pp. 91–107 (the book was published under Selig's pseudonym, Gil Blas).

and in 1931 it was rendered into English by Dr. M. Gaster,[5] who
also analyzed its meaning in his introduction to the translation.[6]
Gaster described the story as a Jewish literary compilation, which
was written in the thirteenth century and only later became a folk
story. He believed this story to be a fairytale, and concluded: "I
believe it to be one of the oldest fairy-tales,"[7] or even: "We have
now, in the story which I have translated here, the oldest fairy-tale."[8]
As to the question of its origin, Gaster stated: "Throughout it is so
thoroughly Jewish, that only a Jew could have compiled it."[9] He
proceeded to analyze some of the motifs of the story, and concluded
that they were not found anywhere before the thirteenth century,
when the Hebrew story was written down.

Gaster's conclusions did not remain unchallenged,[10] but even
though in 1947 a critical edition of three versions of the story—two
in Hebrew and one in Arabic—was published,[11] no new material was
discovered that could change Gaster's main thesis—that the story was
a thirteenth-century Jewish compilation, and that the known Hebrew
versions constituted the earliest story of its kind. Furthermore, all the
known versions came from Eastern Jewry, from Egypt and the Near
East; no European version has been found. This fact led scholars to
believe that the main influences that shaped the story were Eastern,
and they searched for Arabic and Muslim elements in it. There have
been attempts to compare its motifs with various tales of the Thou-

---

[5]M. Gaster, "The Story of the Jerusalemitan," *Folk-Lore*, XLIII (1931), pp. 161–178.
[6]Ibid., pp. 156–161.
[7]Ibid., p. 157.
[8]Ibid., p. 158.
[9]Ibid., p. 179.
[10]See Bernard Heller, *Monatschrift für Geschichte and Wissenschaft des Judenturs*,
vol. LXXX (1936), p. 476.
[11]*The Story of the Jerusalemite*, the Hebrew versions of the Constantinople edition and a Yemenite manuscript, with an introduction and notes by Jehudah L.
Zlotnik, Jerusalem 1946. In this book N. Allony published the translation into
Arabic, and R. Patai added a preface and some notes. The book itself is in Hebrew, but Patai's preface also appears in English. The book contains a detailed
bibliography of the story, its editions, manuscript, translations, and studies relating to it.

sand and One Nights.[12] We shall try to prove that in looking for the early history of this story we have to look West, not East.

II

The main versions of the Story of the Jerusalemite constitute a long and detailed story that can almost be described as a novel. It tells the adventures of the Jerusalemite, Dihon son of Salmon, who swore to his father on the latter's deathbed that he would never set out to sea in a ship. However, after his father's death, the Jerusalemite broke his vow, and, hoping to find great riches, embarked on a ship, which, of course, was immediately lost in a storm, and the hero was thrown onto an unknown island. After various adventures in encountering mythological animals, he was carried by a giant bird across the sea and thrown down into the land of the demons. The demons, who are described in the story as law-abiding and pious Jews, were about to kill him for trespassing their land, forbidden to human beings; he succeeded in saving his life only after he married the demon king's (Asmodeus) daughter. After some time he was granted permission to visit his human family, but when he was brought by the demons to his home, he refused to return to his demon-wife. When all attempts to persuade him to return to the kingdom of the demons had failed, his demon-wife killed him, choking him with her kiss. The story is full of descriptions of Jewish customs and beliefs, quotations from Jewish sacred books, descriptions of Jewish rituals, etc. There seemed to be no doubt that this was an original Eastern-Jewish compilation.

However, I have found in a manuscript in the Bodleian Library at Oxford, Oppenheim 540,[13] a Western version of the story that tends to change these conclusions.

Ms. Oppenheim 540 consists of nine theological treatises, written by one of the Jewish pietists in Germany early in the thirteenth

---

[12]Patai, ibid., p. 111; Heller, ibid.
[13]No. 1567 in Neubauer's *Catalogue of the Hebrew Manuscripts in the Bodleian Library*. Ms. no. 1566 (Mich. 111) is another copy of the same work.

century;[14] most probably the author was Rabbi Judah the Pious, the leader of this pietistic movement, who died in 1217.[15] This work was used and quoted by writers early in the thirteenth century, so that it is safe to assume that the book was written about or before the year 1210, which gives us a date somewhat earlier than the time the Eastern version was first written.[16]

This manuscript contains many stories, most of them dealing with the supernatural and describing various kinds of devils, demons, and witches. Some of them resemble quite closely stories told by Caesarius of Heisterbach, the thirteenth-century preacher and moralist, who collected hundreds of stories dealing with the supernatural in his Dialogue on Miracles.[17] This resemblance between the stories of the Christian and the Jewish moralists is quite natural; both lived at about the same time (Rabbi Judah the Pious was Caesarius's senior by a decade or two) and in the same places, and both tried to preach moral education to their communities.

Among the stories in the Hebrew manuscript we find the one in the following section, translated here from the Hebrew.

---

[14]On this movement and its ideas, see G. Scholem, *Major Trends in Jewish Mysticism*, New York 1941, pp. 80–118; S. Spencer, *Mysticism in World Religion*, Baltimore 1963, pp. 181–186; S. Baron, *Social and Religious History of the Jews*, vol. VIII, Philadelphia 1958, pp. 43–53.

[15]I gave a short description of this manuscript and published some stories from it in *Tarbiz*, vol. XXX (1960/1961), pp. 273–289. On the date of Rabbi Judah's death, see *Zion*, vol. XXIX (1964), p. 169.

[16]It is impossible to give the exact date of the composition of the Eastern version. In many manuscripts and editions the story was attributed to Rabbi Abraham Maimoni, the son of Maimonides, who lived in Egypt in the first half of the thirteenth century. These sources go on to claim that Rabbi Abraham translated the story from the Arabic. However, as Zlotnik and others pointed out, the story obviously is no translation, but an original work, and we have no basis to connect this story with Abraham Maimoni in any way. His many writings reveal no interest in either stories or demonology. It is probable that the Eastern version was written by a certain Abraham Maimon who was confused, decades later, with the son of Maimonides. Anyway, it is safe to assume that the story was written in the first half of the thirteenth century. See Zlotnik, pp. 20–21.

[17]The close similarities between the stories of Rabbi Judah and Caesarius constitute the material for another study, which will be published elsewhere.

III

There was a man who used to write amulets. Once he went on his way, and strayed into a forest to answer a call of nature. He was then caught by a demon, who brought him to a faraway place.

The demon told the Jew: "You used to call me from afar and to make me come to you (by magic). I shall now repay you for the trouble you have caused me by that."

The Jew begged of him not to do to him any harm, and the demon answered: "If you marry my daughter, I shall not kill you." The Jew replied: "I shall take her (in matrimony)."

So the demon brought him to his daughter's place, and gave her to him. She gave birth to three sons, whose father was the Jew, and they died (immediately after their birth).

The demon's daughter was crying. Her father told her: "The children died because of the Jew's family. I was in his city, in his home, and I saw his wife and children in deep sorrow and crying, because they did not know where he (the Jew) was." So she told her father: "I shall do whatever you order me to do, so that my sons who will be born from now on shall live."

The demon then told the Jew: "If I bring you back to your home, will you do what I tell you to?" The Jew asked: Tell me what (you will ask me to do)?" The demon told him: "You shall swear to me that you will never write amulets, and you will never use magic and incantations. And when I bring you back to your home, you shall have a special room for my daughter; when you hear a sound coming from that room you will immediately go there and do whatever she will want you to do." The Jew agreed and promised to comply with these instructions.

The demon brought him to his home very quickly, and he arranged a nice room (for his demon-wife), and his wife put a beautiful cover on the bed. Whenever her husband entered that room she took her children away to another part of the house, to give privacy to her husband and the demon, because she was very frightened.

After many days the demon-wife came to the Jew, dressed in black, and told him: "Do not touch me, for my time to die has arrived, and I beseech you to take my sister (for a wife)."

The Jew replied: "What I promised your father that I would do—I did, and I do not want to take your sister; your father did not include this in our agreement."

Then the demon-wife said: "As you have fulfilled all that was in the agreement between you and my father, and your wife treated me with honor, and kept our privacy whenever I came to you (I shall give you good advice): Tomorrow, at such and such an hour, you should go to a certain place, where you will find a small island surrounded by water. You should wear black and walk bare-footed, and you will see there the three children that were born to me since my father brought you back here, so that they lived. You will see them carrying my body for burial." Then she added: "I know that you are happy that I am going to die; nevertheless, you have to pretend to be crying and lamenting me, because only in this way can you save your (human) children from my sons, who otherwise will harm them, for they probably drank water in your house." [18]

The Jew did all this; he went to the place, and when he saw the demons carrying their mother he pretended to be weeping and crying for her and lamenting her. And he heard his demon-sons saying; "He is in sorrow for our mother; we shall do good to his sons and bring him wealth, and we shall not let other demons bring any harm unto him or his sons." And they did so. [19]

IV

The hero of this story is constantly referred to as "the Jew," yet there is no other indication in the story that might convince us that this is, in fact, a Jewish story. The author of this manuscript used

---

[18]Drinking water that was exposed during the night that demons might have drunk from was regarded as very dangerous since ancient times. Here it seems that drinking the same water that demons drank from might give the demons some power over the person who drinks from that water.

[19]Ms. Oxford Heb. 1567, 140b. See Tarbiz, XXX, p. 284, and note 59 there. It was Dr. Dov Noy of Jerusalem who first directed my attention to the problems raised by this story, and I thank him for his advice and help.

many non-Jewish stories in his work,[20] as did other writers from the same movement;[21] there is no definite indication within the story that it was compiled by Jews or that it originated within Jewish society.

Rabbi Judah the Pious, who is probably the author of the work in which this story is included, was not the author of this story, nor did he edit the story or add anything to it. Rabbi Judah used the stories he retold in his theological writings to prove or demonstrate some theological idea; he developed a highly complicated theory that allowed him to use stories to discover theological and ethical truth, which would not stand proved if the story were false, that is, fictitious.[22] All the stories in his writings were written with absolute belief that they represent pure fact; Rabbi Judah did not consciously change them in any way.

This can be demonstrated even by this story, if we consider its context and moral. Immediately before the one translated above the author included another tale, a much shorter one: "There was a man who used to write amulets. A demon came and copulated with his wife in front of him, but only the wife saw it; he knew nothing."[23] This is clearly an incident of the "crime and punishment" sort, and both these stories were included in the book as a warning. Rabbi Judah emphatically forbade his readers to deal with magic (though he and his disciples did), and the accounts were intended to demonstrate the fate of those who disobey. However, the long tale has a happy ending. After all the troubles described in it, the hero returned to his home, the demon died, and the demon-sons promised to protect him and his family from all harm and make them rich, so that they lived happily ever after. Rabbi Judah certainly did not invent,

---

[20]M. Guedemann, *Geschichte des Erziehungswesens und der Kultur der abendländischen Juden während des Mittelalters*, I, Ch. 7.

[21]J. Trachtenberg, *Jewish Magic and Superstition*, New York 1939; I. Baer, *Zion*, vol. 3, pp. 2–7.

[22]I discussed this theological problem briefly in *Tarbiz*, vol. XXX, pp. 276–278; a detailed discussion is included in my *The Esoteric Doctrine of Ashkenazi Hasidism*, Jerusalem: Mosad Bialik 1968, pp. 88–93.

[23]Ms. Oxford 1567, 140b; see *Tarbiz*, op. cit., p. 283.

or edit, a story that ends in this way in order to warn his readers
against any dealings with demons, for it is at least partially in dis-
agreement with this purpose. It would have been quite easy for Rabbi
Judah to change the ending of the story, if only he had treated it as
fiction; but he saw in this tale a factual narrative, and these facts
should not be changed; his theology forbade that. We can be quite
certain, therefore, that Rabbi Judah wrote his account exactly the
way he had read or heard it. If so, the history of this tale does not
begin with Rabbi Judah, early in the thirteenth century; we can safely
assume that this narrative was known by the end of the twelfth century, and probably even earlier.

This tale is a distant variant of the Story of the Jerusalemite.
The variations are mainly two: First, the sin, which caused all that
happened to the heroes of these events, is described in the Eastern
version as the son's noncompliance with his vow to his father;
whereas in the Western version the sin was the use of black magic.
It may be significant to note that the names of these two sins in
Hebrew come from the same root.[24] The second major difference is
that the tragic ending of the Eastern version is lacking in the Western one, which ends happily. The reason for this second difference
is evident: The Eastern version regards the demons as Jews by religion, therefore the Jerusalemite's marriage to the demon is valid, so
that when he breaks his vow to his demon-wife he should be punished. In the Western version no sanctity is attached to the marriage, and when the demon-wife died the Jew was free from his ob-
ligations to the demons. It is interesting to note that Rabbi Judah
the Pious was one of the first to introduce into Western medieval
Hebrew literature the idea that the demons were Jews,[25] but he did
not use this idea in his version—one more proof of the fact that he
did not invent or edit the story.

Though the differences are considerable, it is clear that the narrative translated above is basically the same as the Story of the
Jerusalemite. Both tell the tale of a man whose sins brought him into

---

[24] שבועה and השבעה.
[25] See Zlotnik, op. cit., pp. 27-29.

the power of the demons, and he had to marry a demon in order to save his life. In both versions the hero is brought back to his human wife and children, and for some time he has two wives, a demon and a woman, though the conflict is resolved in different ways.[26] If we accept the thesis that these stories constitute Eastern and Western versions of the same original, we have to assume that their common origin is considerably earlier than the end of the twelfth century. Not only that, but under these circumstances we have no positive proof that the source of both formulations lies within Jewish society. The Eastern version was heavily Judaized, whereas in the Western one no Jewish elements were introduced into the body of the story.

V

I have not been able to discover a clear parallel to this tale in Latin literature of the Middle Ages, and the scholars who searched for an Arab parallel did not find one either.[27] However, it is possible to prove that some form of this story was known in Germany in the thirteenth century, and had left some trace in Latin literature. One report, told by Caesarius of Heisterbach in his Dialogue of Miracles, may prove this point.

In the beginning of his fifth book, On Demons, the Christian preacher tells a few incidents about people who did not believe in the existence of demons, and how this fact was demonstrated to them. One of these, told in Chapter 4,[28] is a yarn about a group of monks who were put into magic circle by their master in order to demonstrate to them the existence of demons. Then Caesarius says that "immediately they (the demons) showed themselves under the appearance of well-armed soldiers, practicing their military games around

---

[26]The Eastern one, however, is the only version of this story in which the hero dies at the end.

[27]See Patai, op. cit., p. 111; B. Heller, *Monaschrift für Geschichte und Wissenschaft des Judenturs*, 80 (1936), p. 476.

[28]*Caesarii Heisterbacensis Monachi, Dialogus Miraculorum*, vol. I, ed. J. Strange, 1851, pp. 279–281 (De Daemonibus, Capitulum IV). English Translation by H. von E. Scott and C. C. Swinton Bland, New York 1929, vol. I, pp. 318–320.

the youths . . . trying in every way to induce them to leave the circle. When they found that this was of no avail, they changed themselves into very beautiful girls, and danced about them, inviting the young men with every kind of alluring movement. One of them, more beautiful than the rest, chose one of the scholars, and, as often as she danced up to him, held out a gold ring, inflaming him to love both by inward suggestion, and by the outward motion of the body. When she had done this over and over again, the youth was at last overcome, and put his finger outside the circle to receive the ring, and immediately she drew him out by that finger, and disappeared with him." The master of these monks, threatened by the youth's friends, later summoned the chief of the band of demons, and, after a long argument during which the master insisted that the youth be released, the demons put the question of his release to a vote, and finally agreed to bring him back. The youth returned to his friends; at first he was weak and haggard because of his experience, but later he joined the order and lived a long life.

It seems that the ring mentioned in this account is the only remnant of what may be assumed to have been the original story: a marriage between a young man and a demon. Caesarius covers up this motif, but the ring could not have had any other meaning in this context. The ending, in which the hero was eventually returned to his place unharmed, forms another link between Caesarius's story and the Hebrew Western version. The demons' court, voting on the fate of the hero in Caesarius's tale, has its parallel in the Hebrew Eastern version.[29] It is understandable that nothing in Caesarius's story hints at the hero's having a human wife, as he is a monk. The place of the human family in his narrative was taken by his friends, who insisted on his release. The whole adventure, in the Latin work, was the result of an attempt to form some contact with demons, and the event demonstrates how dangerous such an attempt can be. This is quite close to the characteristics of the story in Rabbi Judah the Pious's work; in both the moral is not completely convincing, for the heroes emerged from their experiences unscathed.

---

[29]Zlotnik, op. cit., pp. 52-54.

VI

The missing link, which could form a clear connection between Caesarius's account and the Western version of the Story of the Jerusalemite may perhaps be found in a Yiddish tale, which was discovered in a sixteenth-century Yiddish manuscript in Cambridge.[30] It is known as the Story of Worms, and its hero is a rabbi's son from that German town, which earlier in the Middle Ages was one of the centers of the Ashkenazi Hasidim. One day the young men of the town were playing, and the rabbi's son was looking for a friend who had hidden himself in a tree's trunk. Suddenly he saw a hand coming toward him from the hiding place. Mistaking it for his friend's hand, he playfully put a wedding ring on one of the fingers. Years later, when the rabbi's son was married, a demon came and killed his wife. When he married another girl, the demon again came and killed her. His third wife, however, succeeded in rousing the demon's pity, and it was agreed that every day the rabbi's son would spend one hour with his demon-wife, whom he married that day in the tree trunk. After some time, when the demon found the human wife to be considerate and gentle, she left the man who married her and returned the wedding ring.

This story has all the essential motifs of the Western version— the marriage to a demon, the cohabitation with two wives, and the happy ending. At the same time it is a close parallel to Caesarius's account—the finger and the ring being the central motifs, which are lacking in Rabbi Judah the Pious's version. A motif from the Tobit legend was added as well. This yarn, therefore, brings the stories told by Rabbi Judah and Caesarius close together; they seem to be three different versions of one tale, which circulated in central Europe and was well rooted in German folklore. This Yiddish form, like the Western version, does not carry any especially Jewish characteristics that would convince us of its Jewish origin.

---

[30]See M. Weinreich, A History of Yiddish Literature (in Yiddish), 1928, pp. 143–144; I. Zinberg, A History of Jewish Literature (Hebrew translation from the Yiddish), vol. 4, Tel Aviv 1958, p. 90.

It is safe to assume, therefore, that long before the beginning of the thirteenth century various versions of an incident describing a marriage between a man and a demon, a story that had a happy conclusion, were known in both Jewish and Christian circles. There was a parallel to this story that developed in the East, and the Story of the Jerusalemite in its Jewish or Judaized version. There is no reason that we should assume that the original, which was the basis for all these versions, was Muslim, Christian, or Jewish; most probably it was a folktale without any particular religious background.

VII

An interesting sequel to the Western version of the Story of the Jerusalemite is found many centuries later, in both Hebrew and Yiddish, included in the famous ethical book *Kav ha-Yashar*, which was written by a Jewish kabbalist, Rabbi Zvi Hirsch Kaidanover, in Poland early in the eighteenth century.[31] The work was written in Hebrew and immediately translated into Yiddish, and it became one of the most popular Jewish books in Eastern Europe. This story, which is included in the sixty-eighth chapter of the back, came to be known as the Story of the Posen Trial; it was translated into English by J. Trachtenberg in his *Jewish Magic and Superstition*.[32] Trachtenberg, however, did not analyze its antecedents, and it was used by other scholars as an eighteenth-century tale.[33]

The story is centered around a house in the Jewish community in Posen, in which demons dwelled and killed every human being who tried to inhabit it. The demons were brought to trial and were charged with trespassing, for their allotted dwelling places should have been deserts and ruins, not cities. The demons argued before the rabbis of the court that the house belonged to them, because

---

[31]First printed in Frankfurt, 1705.
[32]Pp. 52–54.
[33]See S. Dubnow, *History of the Jews in Russia and Poland*, vol. 1, Philadelphia 1916, p. 213; idem, *A History of Hasidism* (Hebrew), Tel Aviv 1930, pp. 30–31.

they were the sons of a Jew who had married a demon wife while he had also a human wife. Now, the demons claimed, all of the Jew's human family had died in the holocaust of the Khmelnitzki rebellion of 1648, so that the demons were the only heirs to his property, that is, the house. In their argument the demons told of the relationship between the Jew and his two wives who lived in that house. This report is similar to the Western version of the story of the Jerusalemite, though different in many details. The eighteenth-century account concluded when the demons were forced to leave the house by a famous Jewish magician.

This seems to be another version of the Story of the Jerusalemite, though this time it is told in flashback. The situation that caused the trial in Posen seems to be the logical consequence to the situation in which the Western form of the story is concluded. The version told by Rabbi Judah the Pious is the only one in which the Jew has both human sons and demon sons who live after him. As the demons are believed to live longer than human beings, and as they are free of persecution by the Christians, some legalistic problems regarding inheritance of their mutual father's property are bound to arise.

It is clear that the author of the incident of the Posen Trial did not know, or did not use, the Eastern version of the Story of the Jerusalemite, in which the demons are described as living in another country and having no contact with human beings. The conception of the character of the demons in the *Kav ha-Yashar* version is based on the teachings of the kabbalah, which saw in the demons evil powers bent on harming the soul and the body of Jews, an idea that is absolutely lacking in the two earlier versions and that is not clearly demonstrated in the stories of Caesarius and the Worms Yiddish, though the similarity of plot is clear.[34]

Each version is a product of its own time, of its own cultural atmosphere, religious beliefs, and varieties of superstition, yet the basic content, which spread to various countries and cultures, re-

---

[34]Zinberg had noted the similarity between the *Kav ha-Yashar* story and the Yiddish Worms story; op. cit., p. 90.

mained the same. The history of the Story of the Jerusalemite is a very good example of the different ways in which authors in various places and times made use of folktales.

THIRTEEN

Rabbi Judah the Pious and Caesarius of Heisterbach: Common Motifs in Their Stories

I

One of the main subjects that interested scholars who studied the history and literature of the Ashkenazi Hasidic movement in the twelfth and thirteenth centuries was the nature and the degree of outside Christian influences upon this movement.[1] It is the purpose of this discussion to add some material to the inquiry into this problem by comparing supernatural stories contained in the writings of Rabbi Judah the Pious of Regensburg and his Christian contemporary, the preacher Caesarius of Heisterbach.

Rabbi Judah the Pious, the son of Rabbi Samuel the Pious, was the main leader of the Ashkenazi Hasidic movement at the end of the twelfth and the beginning of the thirteenth century. In his own

---

[1] I. Baer, *Zion* III (1938), pp. 1-50; M. Güdemann, *Geschichte des Erziehungswesens und der Kultur der abendländischen Juden*, vol. I, Vienna 1880; J. Trachtenberg, *Jewish Magic and Superstition*, Philadelphia 1939; G. Vajda, "De quelques infiltrations chrétiennes dans l'oeuvre d'un auteur anglo-juif du XIIIe siècle," *Archives d'histoire et litérature du Moyen Age* XXVIII (1961), pp. 15-34.

time and later, he was regarded as one of the outstanding spiritual leaders of the Jews in Germany, his name being mentioned with reverence in later Hebrew literature, in the East and the West alike. Rabbi Judah wrote many books, but his very strict moral code forbade an author to write his name on his work, because his children and grandchildren might sin in pride on account of their famous father.[2] Rabbi Judah's writings were, therefore, circulated and transmitted from generation to generation as anonymous books, and only complicated and laborious bibliographical studies can establish his authorship of those of his works that were preserved.

His writings can be divided into two main categories: first, ethical works, of which the major book is the famous *Sefer Hasidim*,[3] probably the most influential work on ethics to be produced by German Jewry. The second category consists of theological and mystical works, many of them now lost. However, a collection of nine theological treatises, found in two manuscripts in the Bodleian Library at Oxford, was very probably written by Rabbi Judah.[4] These two books, *Sefer Hasidim* and the Oxford manuscripts, will form the basis of this study.

Rabbi Judah the Pious was unique among Jewish scholars in Germany in the Middle Ages for the deep interest he took in stories. In most of his writings he makes extensive use of various kinds of stories, whereas even his direct disciples, such as Rabbi Eleazar of Worms, seldom use stories in their theological and ethical works. *Sefer Hasidim* contains hundreds of stories, short and long, exempla and demonological tales, parables and myths; some of them are well-known early stories, like the famous story of the birth of Alexander the Great as described in *The Gests of Alexander;*[5] others are chronicles of recent events in Germany, especially descriptions of the persecutions and massacres of the Jews in Germany at the time of the Crusades. Some of the stories were used to demonstrate an ethical idea,

---

[2]*Sefer Hasidim*, Frankfurt 1924, Sec. 1528, p. 374; Sec. 1620, p. 395.
[3]First printed in Bologna in 1538; critical ed. of the Parma ms., Berlin 1891–1894, with a preface by A. Freimann, Frankfurt 1924.
[4]Mss. Oxford 1566–1567. See *Tarbiz* XXX (1961), p. 273, note 2.
[5]*Tarbiz* XXX (1961), p. 276.

and are incorporated into the ideological fabric of the book as a whole, whereas other stories have no moral and were included only in order to supply the reader with information about the world and its nature or to point out some theological doctrine. It is evident, especially when compared to other Hebrew writers of the same period, that Rabbi Judah had some personal interest in using narrative forms for expressing his views and instructing his readers.

Dozens of stories are found also in his theological writings. These stories usually serve to illustrate some theological point, and most of them contain descriptions of supernatural and demonological phenomena. Rabbi Judah sincerely believed that stories are manifestations, or even revelations, of divine truth, which, according to his theology, is not manifested in usual, natural phenomena. This idea made him regard stories of the supernatural as legitimate evidence of theosophic, psychological, or eschatological ideas. According to this theology, a necessary requirement of any story to be used for furthering our understanding of the ways of God is that the story must be true. Falsehood and fiction are useless; they cannot be regarded as manifestations of divine truth. Because of this, Rabbi Judah the Pious wrote many stories, but did not invent—or even edit or change—a single one of them. He wrote them as he heard or read them, and had reason to believe, whether correctly or not, that what they described really had happened at some time and some place. This is proved by the simple fact that we frequently find stories that are not in harmony with the theological or ethical argument into which they are incorporated. Rabbi Judah could not bring himself to edit or change them so that they would exactly express his own views, because the truthfulness of the stories was the only justification of their being used in a theological discussion.[6] Needless to say, Rabbi Judah's theology is based upon absolute belief in the existence of powers of evil, demons, and witches and in the power of amulets, incantations, etc. His world was populated by werewolves, vampires, and other kinds of monsters, who play a prominent role in the stories he wrote.

[6]Ibid., pp. 276-278.

Caesarius of Heisterbach was a monk who later became a prior to novices and then prior of the monastery at Heisterbach. He lived at about the same time as Rabbi Judah the Pious, who was probably his senior by about twenty years. Rabbi Judah, who died in 1217,[7] wrote most of his works between the years 1190 to 1215, whereas Caesarius wrote mainly between 1220 to 1235. Both of them lived in the cultural and geographical realm of west and central Germany (Rabbi Judah died in Regensburg, having lived a long time in Speyer).

Caesarius, like Rabbi Judah, was mainly interested in ethics, and, like Rabbi Judah, his interest was not merely scholarly or academic—his aim was to teach and to educate. He was an able preacher, and many of his sermons were later printed. In his sermons Caesarius extensively used stories of many kinds, but mainly of the supernatural. These stories he collected and edited in the twelve books of his *Dialogus Miraculorum*.[8] In this work, a monk, who is the author, tells stories about many subjects, and after a story is told the monk and a novice discuss its moral. Nearly a thousand stories were included in this work, which is one of the most important of its kind in medieval Europe. There can be little doubt that *Sefer Hasidim* and Rabbi Judah's other writings are the closest parallel in medieval Hebrew literature to Caesarius's *Dialogus*.[9]

Though Rabbi Judah and Caesarius were similar in many respects, it is necessary to emphasize an important difference in their relationship to, and status in, their respective communities. Rabbi Judah was the leader of the Jews in Germany; he was a scion of the Kalonymus family, the most important and influential family in

---

[7]See *Zion* XXIX (1964), p. 169, note 4.
[8]*Caesarius Heisterbacensis Monachi Dialogus Miraculorum*, ed. J. Strange, 1851. The quotations in English are from the translation by H. von E. Scott and C. C. Swinton Bland, New York 1929. I wish to thank Prof. H. H. Ben-Sasson for drawing my attention to the importance of this work.
[9]I have analyzed the relationship between a story used by Rabbi Judah the Pious and a similar one related by Caesarius in a study on "The Story of the Jerusalemite," *Proceedings of the American Academy for Jewish Research*, vol. XXXV (1967), pp. 104–108.

German Jewry. His father and grandfather were prominent scholars and teachers. Even more important is the fact that Rabbi Judah
was an original thinker, whose teachings made a great impression
both upon his own generation and on the future development of
Jewish thought and ethics.[10] Caesarius, on the other hand, belonged
to the second, if not the third, echelon of Church leaders in Germany in his time. His writings may interest us because of their unusual literary form, but one can hardly find an original idea in them.
His aim was only to illustrate and teach the commonplace dogma of
the Church, pointing the way toward fulfillment of the regular re-
quirements of monastic life. The unusual and supernatural material
that Rabbi Judah used led him, to some extent, to fresh and new
conclusions in his teachings of ethics and theology; Caesarius used
highly unusual material to demonstrate accepted beliefs.

One more point of difference between these two scholars should
be mentioned. Among the hundreds of stories included in Rabbi
Judah's writings, we hardly find half a dozen in which the name of
the hero of the story is mentioned. The principle that a person's
achievements should remain anonymous seems to have applied also
in the telling of stories. Caesarius, however, not only gave the names
of the heroes of his stories, but supplied all the details he could discover about their lives prior to the supernatural event described, and
usually also told the reader where these people were at the time, and
any other biographical material he knew or invented. This attitude
is understandable: Any supernatural vision or event was regarded as
a step toward sainthood, and should, therefore, be recorded in detail and related to the persons who saw or took part in it. All such
events became part of the history of the monastery or the town where
they happened, and were repeated frequently, to add to the glory of
the Church. It is natural, for these reasons, that Rabbi Judah's stories incline toward descriptions of isolated events, whereas Caesarius's
stories tend to become short biographies of people and institutions,
the supernatural event being the climax of the story as well as the
climax of the hero's life.

---

[10]See G. Scholem, *Major Trends in Jewish Mysticism*, New York 1954, pp. 80–118.

II

The following is the historical problem that needs to be analyzed: If we find similar, or even identical, stories in the writings of Caesarius and Rabbi Judah, we have to establish what was the nature of their common source. The usual source material that these two scholars used had little in common; both relied almost exclusively on the sacred and traditional literature of their respective religions and on Latin or Hebrew literature—Caesarius not knowing any Hebrew, and Rabbi Judah, as far as we know, knowing no Latin. There is no indication in Caesarius's writings that he met with Jews and discussed ethical questions with them; neither did Rabbi Judah come into close contact with Christian thinkers. Though they lived at almost the same time and place, they were as far apart culturally as if they had lived in different countries and centuries. We therefore have to make a close analysis of the parallels that exist between the stories they told in order to find the common cultural source that produced this similarity.

In his theological work, ms. Oppenheim 1567, Rabbi Judah relates the following story, which is one of the very few in the whole collection told with a smile:

> A man asked how many years he would live, and received the answer—MILANT—in a foreign language.[11] The man explained this to himself: MIL means a thousand, and ANT means years, so he thought that he was going to live a thousand years. In fact he lived eighty years, for MIL in *gematria* is eighty.[12]

This anecdote is one in a series of short exempla describing the ways predictions are made by arbitrarily choosing a few letters and analyzing the word or words received. Rabbi Judah, in telling this story, is not surprised by the fact that the Bible gives its prediction

---

[11]ואמרו לו בלעז: מילאנט. The method was to open the Bible arbitrarily, and to use the letters or words found in this way as a sign of future events.

[12]The numerical value of the Hebrew letters מיל is 80. Ms. Oxford 1567, fol. 151b. See Güdemann, op. cit., p. 166, note 1; *Tarbiẓ*, ibid., p. 285.

in a foreign language; even the correct interpretation, according to this story, had the word "years" in a foreign language.

Caesarius tells a more elaborate story in Chapter XVII of his Book of Demons:

> Theobald, of blessed memory, the abbot of Eberbach, told us last year how a certain lay brother, when on a journey, heard the frequent call of the bird, which gets its name of cuckoo from its call, and counted the number of times it was repeated; finding this to be twenty-two, he took it for an omen, and reckoned that his life would be prolonged for as many more years.

Upon this conclusion he left his order and indulged in the pleasures of this world, thinking that he would be able to repent twenty years later, live two more years as a penitent, and inherit everlasting life in the hereafter. In fact, so Caesarius tells us, he died two years later—the same two years that he intended to devote to a religious life; of a course, he died as a sinner. Caesarius explains the prophecy, which is not necessarily false, as an instrument of the devil to mislead men like this lay brother.[13]

The common basis of these two stories is the belief in omens by means of which persons try to determine the time of their death; in both cases, Rabbi Judah and Caesarius oppose these practices, not because they are untrue—the prophecies were correct in both instances—but because they tend to be misunderstood by the recipients. In Rabbi Judah's story it is a simple, technical misunderstanding; in that of Caesarius it is a religious misunderstanding that caused the hero of the story to die as a sinner. The difference is a theological one: Rabbi Judah does not believe, or at least does not state here, that the devil uses natural or supernatural phenomena in order to mislead the faithful.[14]

When no theological problems are involved, the similarity between the two writers becomes even more striking. Rabbi Judah, in

---

[13]Caesarius, Book IV, Ch. XVII.
[14]See *Tarbiz*, ibid., p. 277.

the same manuscript, tells the following story:

> At a certain place smoke was rising from the mountains, and
> passers by heard a voice saying: "Someone[15] has to come to this
> place." Some people heard this voice coming from the smoking
> mountain and after some time they heard the voice say: "He
> has arrived." They investigated who that person was, and were
> told: "He is already dead." On further investigation they found
> out that the man had died at the precise moment when the
> voice said: "He is dead." There were birds on that mountain,
> and the birds were ravens; on the Sabbath they used to leave
> the mountain, and on Saturday evening they used to bathe in
> water and go back to the mountain.[16]

Caesarius, in Book XII, tells practically the same story:

> Once upon a time when some Swedes, on their return from a
> pilgrimage to Jerusalem, were sailing near Stromboli, whose fires
> are ever burning, these words sounded from it: "Welcome,
> welcome our friend, the steward of Kolmere, it is cold, prepare
> a blazing fire for him." Knowing the person, they noted the
> day and the hour, and when they had returned to their own
> land, they found that the same steward had died on that day
> and at that hour.[17]

Caesarius follows this up with two more—essentially similar—
stories about this wonderful mountain.[18]

Though the story itself is identical in both Hebrew and Latin,
its moral is different: Rabbi Judah uses this story to prove that God
knows everything that happens on Earth,[19] whereas Caesarius draws
the moral that sinners should repent unless they wished to be drawn
into the fires of the famous volcano, and that relatives should pray
for the poor souls cast into its flames.

---

[15]פלוני

[16]Ms. Oxford 1567, fol. 146b. See *Tarbiz*, ibid., p. 285.

[17]Book XII, Ch. VII.

[18]Book XII, Chs. VIII, IX, and XIII.

[19]הרי אין דבר מה בעולם [הזה], אם לא ידעו באותו עולם [העליון].

III

Many similarities can be found in the writings of these two scholars in their descriptions of death. Rabbi Judah's manuscript in-cludes two descriptions of events taking place at the deathbed of a sick person:

> Here is the story about a very sick man who was dying. He said: "I see a white dove coming through the window in the corner of the house, and she has a knife under her wings." Then he saw her coming towards him, she arrived first at his feet, then approached his heart, and he could speak no more and died.
>
> A man was dying, and people came to visit him. One of the visitors saw the Angel of Death washing his sword in a glass of water. The Angel was carrying the glass of water towards someone who just then entered the house. He cried out to the person who entered: "Do not drink," but everybody thought that he had lost his mind, for they saw nothing of all this. This person drank and immediately he became sick and died in that same week.[20]

The motifs of these stories are scattered throughout Caesarius's eleventh book. For instance, in Chapter XVI of that book he tells a story about a lay brother who lay dying:

> Two crows suddenly flew up, circled round him and at last perched on the beam which was above his head. . . . And when the cross was carried in, a snow-white dove entered the door of the infirmary in front of it, and flying over the above men-tioned beam, alighted in the midst of those crows.[21]

Caesarius goes on to describe the fight between the dove and the crows, in which the dove won. There is a clear difference between Caesarius's dualistic conception of death as a fight between good and evil forces for the soul of the dying person, and Rabbi Judah's

---

[20]Ms. Oxford 1567, fol. 114a; *Tarbiz*, ibid., p. 283.
[21]Book XI, Ch. XVI.

monistic symbolism, in which the dove symbolizes the Angel of Death, who is a messenger of God.

In another story, Caesarius describes a dying man, around whom demons in the shape of various animals assembled, and how a friend of the dying man overcame them after a long fight.[22] In another story, a dying man who miraculously returned to life after he had been dead for a short time gave the following description of the way death and had reached him:

> Recently when I was sick and in great pain, something came to my bed; and having touched first my feet, ascended step by step, touching my belly and then my breast, and yet I felt no harm from that touch. But when my head was touched, at once I expired.[23]

Rabbi Judah believed that the heart is the place where death sets in, whereas Caesarius believed it to be the head.

Caesarius, like Rabbi Judah, believed that death can be passed on from one person to another, especially near a deathbed. He tells such a story in Chapter LXII of the eleventh book:

> I have been credibly informed that a certain noble matron in the diocese of Cologne fell ill a year ago, and as she appeared to be at death's door, she was anointed. Many matrons of noble degree as well as servants stood round her. At last, calling her sister to her, although hardly able to speak, she said: "Fear not, I shall not die now, for I have seen death retreating from me and casting his eye on that cleric," pointing her finger. Wonderful to say, that very moment the woman whose life had been despaired of began to get better, and the cleric [began] to fall ill and died eight days later.[24]

This motif, of death passing by mistake or otherwise from person to person, is prominent in the stories included in the *Sefer Hasidim*. It tells of a dying man whose friend, as a joke, suggested

---

[22]Book XI, Ch. XV.
[23]Book XI, Ch. XII.
[24]Book XI, Ch. LXII.

that he would buy the illness from him; when the friend promised to pay him, the sick man recovered, and the friend, whose name was the same as the sick man's, died.[25] In the same chapter, Rabbi Judah tells of a man who bought a bad dream from his friend and later died instead of the dreamer. In another section *Sefer Hasidim* relates a story, very similar to the one told by Caesarius, about illness passing from a dying man to a visitor; *Sefer Hasidim* adds, however, that the sick man whose life was saved by the death of the visitor made it a habit to fast every year on the day that the visitor had died.[26] Another section in *Sefer Hasidim* describes the death of a pupil, whom the Angel of Death took instead of his teacher, who bore the same name.[27]

It is obvious that while we may find a few almost identical stories in the works of Caesarius and Rabbi Judah, it is more common to find these two contemporary writers using the same motifs in similar, but not identical, stories. Only a few examples of many such similarities can be given here.

In his famous *Testament*, which was usually printed together with *Sefer Hasidim*, Rabbi Judah has forbidden the burying of two enemies near each other in the cemetery.[28] Caesarius tells a story about two dead men who continued to fight each other from their graves, which were situated close to each other.[29] Two stories in Rabbi Judah's manuscript are intended to point out that demons do not attack or harm anybody unless he has provoked them first;[30] we find the same idea presented in Caesarius's collection of stories.[31]

Among the motifs that are used both in *Sefer Hasidim* and the Book of Miracles, we find stories about dead men who come back to life and describe the sufferings of another person because of a sin

---

[25]*Sefer Hasidim*, Sec. 1523.
[26]Ibid., Sec. 1552.
[27]Ibid., Sec. 375.
[28]Ed. R. Margalioth, Jerusalem 1957, Sec. 1, p. 10.
[29]Book XI, Ch. LVI.
[30]Ms. Oxford 1567, fol. 146b; *Tarbiz*, ibid., pp. 283–284.
[31]Book IV, Ch. II.

he had committed[32] or about dead men returning to life in order to pay a debt that nobody knew about.[33] There are similar stories about a pact between a dying man and his friend, according to which the dying man promises to visit his living friend in a dream after his death and reveal to him some detail or other about the world of the dead.[34] Both Caesarius and Rabbi Judah demonstrate their belief in the omen of a big fire seen from afar, which signifies war or destruction, by an actual story that occurred in a certain place.[35]

We know that Rabbi Judah and his disciples believed that the Messiah was about to come, and they probably awaited his arrival in the year 1240, which is the year 5000 according to the Jewish calendar.[36] It is interesting, therefore, to note that Caesarius, who lived nearer to that year than Rabbi Judah, tells us—among the few things he relates concerning the Jews—that when a very bright star appeared in the sky and produced a red light, the Jews saw in it a sign that the arrival of their Messiah was near.[37]

IV

There are sufficient such examples on which to base the conclusion that a literary connection existed between these two scholars. The question is, what was the nature of that connecting link?

This is not the place to analyze the theological and ethical conclusions that these two scholars derive from the stories they relate. However, I have been unable to find in all these stories even one real connection that might prove the existence of a common theological or ethical written source that served both scholars. There is no similarity whatsoever beyond that of the actual facts and super-

---

[32]Book XI, Ch. XI.
[33]Book XII, Ch. XVIII.
[34]Sefer Hasidim, Sec. 272; Caesarius, Book XII, Ch. XXXI.
[35]Sefer Hasidim, Sec. 35; Caesarius, Book X, Ch. LI.
[36]See Tarbiz, ibid., p. 280, note 20; S. Assaf, Zion V (1940), pp. 116-118, 123-124; G. Scholem, Major Trends, pp. 88-91.
[37]Book X, Ch. XXVI.

stitions that form the stories themselves. These two writers undoubt-edly used the same materials in their examples, but for totally dif-ferent ends. This fact absolutely rules out the possibility that Rabbi Judah and Caesarius shared any written source, for such a source would have left a deeper similarity both in the anecdotes they re-lated and in the conclusions they derived from them.

It is significant that the actual details of the stories used by both Caesarius and Rabbi Judah bear no special relationship to any reli-gion, either Jewish or Christian. They belong to the realm of popu-lar, supernatural beliefs (or superstitions) that seldom find their way into the theological works of educated scholars—be it in Latin or Hebrew—and, at the same time, were not yet written down in their original language, namely in German.

Caesarius and Rabbi Judah were interested in these popular be-liefs, though for totally different motives. Caesarius introduced Chris-tian dogma into the superstitious stories, finding in them a perfect literary vehicle for his popular ethical teachings. By telling people stories known to them since their childhood, with the addition of discovering Christian morals in them, Caesarius tried to improve the persuasiveness of his sermons. For him, these stories were but tools for the preacher's craft.

As for Rabbi Judah the Pious, his theological method included the idea that God's essence and power were revealed in this world by unusual and unnatural phenomena, not by the natural laws. Con-sequently he was interested in collecting popular tales, whose origin he disregarded. In these stories he found not only morals, but also affirmations of theological ideas. Thus, though their motives were different, these two scholars collected popular German stories, anec-dotes, and beliefs, and incorporated them into their religious works. This is one of the most striking examples of the influence of popu-lar superstition on both Latin and Hebrew theological literature in the Middle Ages.

FOURTEEN

The Desert in Jewish Mysticism: The Kingdom of Samael

In the second part of the *Zohar* we find a unique homily that is intended to explain the reason for the long voyage of the Israelites through the desert after they left Egypt. According to this passage in the *Zohar* (II:183b–184a), the homily was delivered by a strange Old Man, one of a gallery of strange personages who appear in this mystical work. Rabbi Simeon bar Yochai and Rabbi Eleazar, his son, were going on their way with Rabbi Abba and Rabbi Yose, when they met this Old Man, who held a small child by the hand. The Old Man told Rabbi Simeon that he belonged to a group that had retired from the inhabited world into the desert, and, when asked why, he began the homily.

When the Israelites left Egypt, God led them to a terrible desert, the worst in the world. At that time Israel had to complete its numbers to the ideal count of six hundred thousand, and the holy *Shechinah*, the feminine element in the kabbalistic concept of the divine world, had to grow stronger and to rise above all, and it was Israel's duty then to overcome the kingdom of evil. This was the reason that God led Israel to the desert, which was the realm of Samael, the principle of evil in kabbalistic thought. If the desert is Samael's realm, it is because it reflects him. It was the divine purpose that Israel should overcome Samael on his own ground, break his power, and prevent him from ruling anywhere. Had Israel not sinned at that time, God would have delivered the world from Samael entirely; that is why God sent Israel into Samael's fortress.

But Israel did not live up to these expectations, and sinned several times, so all the Israelites, instead of Samael, had to die in the desert. The forty years of wandering in the desert are analogous to the customary punishment of forty beatings. Thus, though Israel did see Samael being led, bound, before them, the divine purpose was not achieved.

The Old Man concludes with a reference to the present and to himself: He and his friends had lived in the desert where they studied the Torah, in order to overcome Samael. They are now returning to the inhabited world, because the time for direct contact with God had come (Rosh Hashanah), and now Samael is dealing directly with God. (See also I. Tishby, *Mishnat ha-Zohar*, vol. II, Jerusalem 1961, p. 584.)

This homily reflects the duality in the concept of the desert in Jewish mysticism, a duality that can be found in the biblical story itself. According to the *Zohar*, the desert is Satan's kingdom, home of the serpent, the most vivid symbol of evil. At the same time, the desert is the place from which redemption must come, for, unless Samael is defeated, redemption is impossible, and it had to take place in the desert—both in the past, in Moses' time, and in the present. However, before redemption can be achieved, the power of evil residing in the desert has to be conciliated and neutralized, in order to prevent its intervention in Israel's religious effort. It is, therefore, not surprising that following the homily in the *Zohar*, the question comes up of Yom Kippur and of the sacrifice of the goat to Azazel. In this biblical context (Leviticus 16:22), the connection between the desert and the power of evil is plainly hinted at, at least as the kabbalists read that passage, and since then speculations about the dwelling of Samael and the way to make contact with him have focused upon the desert. Rabbi Moshe ben Nachman (Nachmanides) hinted at the kabbalistic meaning of this sacrifice to the evil that dwells in the desert in his thirteenth-century commentary on the Bible, and conjectures on this problem abound in kabbalistic literature. This passage in the Zohar (184b) is only one example.

It should be remembered that for most kabbalists the desert was an abstract term, not a sensual reality. The kabbalah originated and developed in Christian Europe, in Provence, northern Spain, Germany, and Italy, at least until the sixteenth century. Very few kabbalists had the opportunity to see a real North African or Near Eastern desert for themselves. Therefore, speculations about the desert tended to be abstract, based upon biblical verses, loaded with homiletical interpretations, while the reality of desert existence was completely obscured. Fixing Samael's residence in the desert was a very good way to get rid of him as a part of reality. Instead, the kabbalists found his traces in the human mind and heart, and thus the fight against the powers of evil came to be associated more with psychology than with geography.

Some of the ideas expressed in the Zohar took centuries to influence Jewish life, practices, and literature, but eventually most of the seeds planted by Rabbi Moshe de Leon, the thirteenth-century author of the Zohar, flourished and bore unexpected results. This is also true of the passage mentioned above. The Old Man and his mysterious group, who went to the desert to continue the task laid upon Israel after the exodus from Egypt, represent a minor episode in the rich fabric of zoharic narrative and homiletics. In the fifteenth century, however, it seems that someone decided to carry on the task of that Old Man.

The year 1490 was believed, by many kabbalists of the day, to be the year of the beginning of the redemption. Yet it passed, and another, too, and, instead of Israel being delivered, the Jews were expelled from Spain. It is natural that a question arose: Why? What went wrong in 1490? We have one of the answers to this question, written in 1519 in Jerusalem by Rabbi Abraham son of Rabbi Eliezer Halevi (studied by G. Scholem in Zion, vol. V [1993], pp. 124–130). Rabbi Abraham explained that the redemption was deferred because of the actions of a certain kabbalist who tried to use magic to bring it about; he almost succeeded, but sinned at the crucial moment, and as a punishment a new, later date was set for the coming of the Messiah.

We know who that kabbalist was: His name was Rabbi Joseph de la Reina, who belonged to a well-known family of kabbalists, the Ibn Gabais. The incident referred to in Rabbi Abraham's story occurred around 1470. Subsequently, the story was told several times, in sixteenth-century Safed, in seventeenth-century Jerusalem, in the circles of the believers in Sabbatai Zevi in the last decade of that century, and many times thereafter.

Much attention centered on the question of how Rabbi Joseph de la Reina intended to bring about the redemption, what magical means he employed, how he overcame Samael and Lilith, and why he committed a grave sin when his mission was almost accomplished. But the crucial problem is, what gave Rabbi Joseph—and others who held the same belief—the ideological basic for his attempt? It seems that the most likely explanation is to be found in the story about the Old Man in the *Zohar*. Like the zoharic figure, Rabbi Joseph also went out, with a small group of disciples, to the desert, to search for Samael and to overcome him. The zoharic passage gave him the assurance that this had been the divine plan from the very beginning, from the moment that God delivered Israel from its exile in Egypt and led it to the desert. Just as the failure of Israel at that time did not convince the zoharic Old Man that the idea itself was unattainable, so it did not discourage Rabbi Joseph de la Reina. If properly prepared and carried out, the task could be accomplished— and it had to be accomplished. God created the desert and gave it as a home to the power of evil; He then began sending holy men, whether a whole nation or chosen individuals, to the realm of Samael so as to overcome him and bring about the redemption of Israel and of the whole world. One failure—or even repeated failures—is not proof that God's plan should not be attempted again, with better preparations and greater care.

The story of Rabbi Joseph de la Reina is just one example, showing how clear was the dual meaning of the desert to kabbalistic circles for many generations, as the divinely ordained battleground between good and evil. For eventually Samael will be overcome in his lair, which is the desert, and the prophecies of the redemption will be fulfilled.

FIFTEEN

Teraphim: From Popular Belief to a Folktale

I

The *teraphim*, mentioned in a verse in Genesis 31:16, which were stolen by Rachel when Jacob and his family fled from Laban, posed a serious exegetical problem to Jewish tradition. The whole episode seems to be problematic, since it could be interpreted to mean that Rachel was so attached to the idols her father worshipped that she had to take them with her, an idea that does not fit the pious, devoted picture of Rachel presented both in the Bible and in Jewish tradition. This problem is closely connected with a second one: What was the nature of these *teraphim*, how were they made, and what could they do?

Many Jewish exegetes followed the idea expressed in *Genesis Rabba*,[1] explaining her strange action as being done with a good end in mind: Rachel did not want her father to continue worshipping these idols, so she stole them. According to this, the *teraphim* were

---

[1] LXXIV, and see Rashi on this verse.

nothing more than the usual wood or stone idols. This interpretation is somewhat unconvincing, however, because there was nothing to hinder Laban from acquiring new ones.

A more popular interpretation is presented in the *Tanhuma*.[2] The *teraphim* were idols that could speak and tell secrets; Rachel was afraid that they would tell Laban the way Jacob and his family and gone, and help in their pursuit. Eventually Laban did pursue and catch Jacob, so that Rachel's act remains partially unexplained nevertheless. This explanation made a distinction between the usual idols and these particular ones, a distinction that was strengthened by the homily in the *Tanhuma* connecting this verse with the verse in Zechariah 10:2: "For the *teraphim* have spoken vanity." Now the question arises: How could the *teraphim* speak, when there are so many descriptions of idols in the Bible stressing that they cannot speak, or hear, or feel, etc.? The answer to this question, offered in the *Tanhuma*, became widely known and serves frequently in Hebrew literature when divination is described. The same description is given in the Aramaic translations of the Bible, and in the narrative homiletical summary of the stories of Genesis in the *Pirkey de-Rabbi Eliezer*.[3] The *teraphim* were made by killing a firstborn man and then preserving him in salty water and different perfumes; he was then put in a special niche with candles lit before him, and he told the future and answered any question put to him. Some authors, who were interested in magic and divination, added more details, many of them gory and disgusting, to describe this practice. Among those details, the most important one is that the *teraphim* actually consisted only of the head and torso of the dead first-born, who was speaking because of the power of a satanic name put under his tongue. The flesh was removed by immersion of the body for a long time in oil or in honey.[4]

---

[2]*Wa-Yeze*, 12.
[3]Ch. XXXVI. In some editions, such as the one with the commentary of Rabbi David Luria, this passage was deleted, probably because of censorship, or because of its repulsive nature.
[4]See the important material on this subject compiled by M. M. Kasher, *Torah Shelemah*, VI, New York 1953, p. 1228.

There are two basic elements in this interpretation. First, anyone using it had to believe in the power of demonic forces to pro-
vide Laban with true information, for otherwise Rachel's action is
pointless. Therefore we find this exegesis accepted by scholars such
as the Ashkenazi Hasidim, who had both belief and interest in
demonological practices, whereas other scholars tried to explain the
matter in a more "scientific" way, by attributing astrological meaning to the *teraphim.* The second element is that an opening had been
created for describing demonological practices, both imagined and
real, according to the beliefs and the environment of any exegete or
scholar dealing with this passage. Thus we may glean important
information about divination practices by following these descriptions as they develop throughout the Middle Ages.[5] Here, however,
we are interested only in the narrative aspect of those beliefs and in
their contribution to Hebrew stories, old and new.

II

An interesting development of this motif is found in Rabbi
Johanan Alemano's *Shaar ha-Heshek,*[6] a kabbalistic, philosophical,
and demonological compilation written in Italy after the expulsion
from Spain. Rabbi Johanan, who was one of the teachers of the great
student of kabbalah and demonology, Pico della Mirandola, was
interested in the writings of the Ashkenazi Hasidim, and used
material attributed to these sages, including sources that have since
been lost. In one part of his book he deals with the problem of love
and desire, and says:

> And so wrote Rabbi Eleazar of Worms, in these words: Most of
> the dead [keep thinking] the same thought that they had in the
> moment when the soul left the body; for many years the soul

---

[5]It is interesting to note that the sixteenth-century author of the *Sefer ha-Yashar,*
in retelling the biblical story, added almost nothing to the version of the *Pirkey
de-Rabbi Eliezer;* see the first edition, Venice 1625, p. 58b.
[6]Ed. Halberstadt, no printing date. Cf. Alemano's *Heshek Shelomo,* on the *Song
of Songs* (Leghorn 1790).

thinks about the same things that it was preoccupied with when
it left the body and remembers them.

There follow expositions of several biblical verses connected by the
author with this phenomenon. Then the author continues in a way
that leaves us wondering whether it is the end of the quotation by
Rabbi Eleazar, or whether Rabbi Johanan himself has resumed writing:

> And I heard something similar from one of the Masters of the
> Art [i.e., magicians], that it was the practice of the early masters, when they gathered great treasures which they wanted to
> protect from other people, they went to someone who was condemned to death and said to him: "Do you want to be saved
> from death?" and the condemned man would answer: "If you will
> save me, I shall be your slave forever." They would answer: "I
> do not want anything from you, except to guard this treasure
> for me with great care, so that nobody can come close to it. If
> you accept this responsibility with all your heart and soul, I shall
> save you from death." The condemned man then accepted with
> great desire and resolution to guard the treasure. Then, even
> while he was feeling this great desire, they cut off his head, and
> his spirit would remain with this same desire to guard the treasure without moving from it, so that no magic used against him
> would be of any avail to make him leave his post; and when
> someone would try to make him go away [by magic] he would
> call other spirits to come and guard the treasure while he is away.
> End of quotation.[7]

This story does not concern itself with Jewish beliefs and exegetical problems, though it is quoted in support of biblical exegesis
by Rabbi Eleazar of Worms, one of the greatest writers of the
Ashkenazi Hasidic movement (d. ca. 1230). It seems that in this case
the Jewish writers were ready to accept non-Jewish magical and
demonological material, because the *teraphim* (which are not mentioned here, although the association probably was present in the

---

[7]Ibid., p. 43a. I am indebted to Prof. I. Tishby for pointing out to me this interesting quotation.

mind of the author) were originally non-Jewish idols; it is natural, therefore, to turn to non-Jewish magicians to collect information about such practices.

Not all popular beliefs developed into popular stories, but many of them did. The following story may serve as an example of how an exegetical motif, supported by popular demonological material, flourished into a full-scale popular tale.

III

The following story was printed in two collections of stories, in *Noreot Anshey Maaseh*[8] and in *Peer Mi-Kedoshim*.[9] There is little difference between the two versions, and it seems to me that the version in *Peer Mi-Kedoshim* is the original one, because it is part of a group of similar stories. It is one of many biographical stories about the Maharal of Prague that circulated in Europe during the end of the nineteenth century:

> When the *Gur Aryeh*[10] was a judge in the great city of Prague, there was a rich man there, who dealt in commissions, and he had a very gifted son, who was regarded by the whole town as a light for Israel. Even though he was very young, only twelve years old, he was one of the best students of the *Gur Aryeh* (may his memory be blessed), and he looked upon him as a son.
>
> Merchants from many countries stayed in the house of the boy's father, two of which [sic] contributed a great deal to his riches by buying large amounts of merchandise through him, and they used to converse with the boy while they were there. From time to time they gave him precious gifts, in order to draw him towards them. The father saw all these gifts but did not pay attention to the matter.

---

[8]Ed. Warsaw, undated, pp. 3–7. From here it was adopted by M. I. Berdyczewski in his *Mi-Meqor Yisrael*, Tel Aviv 1952, pp. 54–57.

[9]Ed. Lvov, undated (probably around 1864); see J. Dan, *The Hasidic Story*, Jerusalem 1975, pp. 212–213.

[10]Maharal is here referred to by the title of his first book, *Gur Aryeh*, an explanation of Rashi's biblical commentary.

When they became close friends with the merchant, the boy's father, and the boy became used to them, one of the two rich men said to the boy's father: "I would like you to pay attention to what we have to say and to the great prospect that we have in mind. We wish to arrange a marriage between your son and the only daughter of a very rich man, a very beautiful girl. So who will inherit all his fortune and his possessions and his treasures but your son? He lives in a certain city, and his name is so and so."

After hearing this offer, the father, when he went to the market on business, inquired about that rich man whose name they mentioned, and everyone told him that that man really had great treasures of gold, and it was true he had only one daughter, and that his greatest wish was to see her married to a man who was dedicated to the study of the Torah. Still, the father was not satisfied, and went to seek God's counsel by asking the great Rabbi, the holy author of *Gur Aryeh*, because he was not only the teacher, Rabbi and *Zaddiq* of the town,[11] but also was like a father to the boy and wished only good to his disciple. The holy Rabbi answered clearly that the idea was good, and that this marriage was right before God and should be arranged.

When he returned home, the merchants who suggested this marriage asked him: "Have you inquired about this matter?" and he told them what he had heard and what he intended to do. Then one of the merchants continued and said: "Then you should know that I myself am this same rich man, whose praise you heard told so widely." The father went again to the Rabbi to ask his advice, and he agreed. The merchants soon went after the boy's father to the Rabbi, the author of the *Gur Aryeh*, and the boy, the bridegroom, was there too, and they shook hands before the Rabbi and agreed about the marriage terms. The Rabbi himself read the marriage contract and blessed the family, and they joined in a happy feast. The bridegroom delivered a learned homily, and the merchants agreed to stay a few more days, to enjoy the feast and be with the bridegroom.

---

[11] The writer uses here a Hasidic term, in a situation preceding the Hasidic movement by two hundred years.

When they decided to go, they asked the boy's father to let the bridegroom come with them to the home of the bride's father, in order that he might meet the bride and her mother. The father was reluctant to send his beloved son into the country, such a long way, before the wedding, but the men implored him to do so until he could not resist, and went to ask the advice of the Rabbi *Gur Aryeh*, and the Rabbi again gave his consent, that the bridegroom should be sent to the house of his father-in-law, to stay there two or three months until he reached his thirteenth birthday.

The men took the boy to that far-away country, and brought him to a large castle, showed him all its rooms, which were all richly furnished, but the boy went here and there and saw neither the bride nor her mother nor any other members of the family. He thought that when he arrived at that place the scholars of the town would come to him and study Torah with him and with the Rabbi of that place, but all his hopes were in vain, for the door was locked, and only the man who claimed to be his father-in-law came to him twice or thrice a day to talk to him. The boy then could not stand it any more and asked him: "What is this? I do not see anybody." The man then took him by his hand and led him from room to room until they reached a small room full of books, by old and new scholars, and said to him: "What do you need that you do not have? Here you have precious books, you can study them as much and as long as you wish."

Let us now cease telling the story of the son and the terrible misfortune that befell him, and speak about his father, whose only son he was, and who was liked by the whole community. Meanwhile, the father was standing by the road waiting for a letter from his beloved son, and sorrow and despair took hold of him when no message came.

He was weeping and praying, but four months passed and neither letter nor message arrived. He wept and complained every day to the Rabbi *Gur Aryeh*, and the Rabbi encouraged him and gave him hope, telling him that nothing had happened to the boy. But the father was going around as if he were out of his mind, and all his relatives and friends asked the Rabbi's advice, for nothing was done without his consent. It is impossible to describe the sorrow and despair of the father and the mother, who were sunk in melancholy; they did not sleep and their tears flowed like fountains. But the Rabbi also did not stop from praying and imploring God, and he himself was very angry that he had made such a great mistake in reading what was destined by the heavenly powers, and his fasting and weeping pierced the windows of heaven. But when he spoke to the father he always encouraged him to hope and be certain that the boy would return home safely and unharmed.

Let us now go back to the story of the boy-bridegroom and the terrible misfortune that befell him; for when he entered that last, small room, before he was over the threshold, the door was closed and locked behind him. Then he heard a voice ringing in his ears, saying: "Oh, you have fallen into the same trap as I; how unfortunate you are; for you shall not leave alive." The boy was silent and listened in wonder, trying to see who was talking to him. Then his eyes saw a head, a very old one, but a head without a body, and that head continued to speak to him: "You thought you had a bride here, or a mother-in-law, or a father-in-law; where are they? Only Lilith is present here, and it is an evil place. Those people whom you saw are priests, hunters for souls, and there is nothing here but *teraphim*."

The boy came nearer, and the head continued its story: "I was also a gifted young scholar, and in my best years they set me this trap and caught me to serve their god, for they possess evil names, which have come from the *teraphim* of Jeroboam ben Nebat, and every eighty years they sever the head of a gifted young scholar who is a firstborn son of a firstborn, on the day that he is thirteen years and one day old, and then they put their evil names under his tongue and he will tell them all that happened in the past and all that is going to happen in the future. Now that my time of service is at an end they chose you to replace me. And look, they give me sacred wine and many candles are lit in front of me."

The boy, who was frightened by what he had heard, asked the head: "If it is so, what should I do? Can you tell me whether there is any way for me to be saved?" The head answered: "The only way is for you to escape through the window here, and if you do not run away tonight, you shall die tomorrow. But I advise you, and may God help you, that when you escape through the window take me on your arms, so that I can show you the way to go. Otherwise you will not succeed, for if someone comes and asks me I shall tell them immediately where you can be found. So if you are ready to listen to me do it wisely, and swear to me that you will do a deed of charity for me by burying my head in a Jewish grave and you will say *Qaddish* for me and do what should be done for my soul."

So the boy collected all his strength and fled through the window with the head, but fear followed him, and the head was telling him: "At this moment the priests are coming to look for you at that place," and kept frightening him every moment.

Before I conclude the story and bring it to its happy ending, dear reader, it is not yet time to rejoice, and we should return and share the sorrow of the people of the town, and the Rabbi *Gur Aryeh* at their head.

The sacred Rabbi was weeping in secret in his soul before heaven and God, and one day before the boy returned safely he declared a day of fasting, and all the people, men, women and children, assembled in the great synagogue. The Rabbi then ordered everybody to recite the first book of Psalms together, and they did so with deep concentration. When they had finished, the Rabbi said: "The boy has not come yet. Therefore I shall preach to you words of moral exhortation." He preached with great fear of God, until everybody had the fear of God in his heart. Then he ordered to recite the second book of Psalms, and when they finished they looked around but the boy still was not there, so the Rabbi delivered another homily, and then he himself recited the third book of Psalms before the praying-stand, and he blew the *Shofar*, and when he finished the boy was brought through the window before the eyes of the whole community, which was very frightened.

The boy then told the whole story to the community, and brought the head to the sacred Rabbi, who said in a loud voice: "All this was intended to happen by the heavenly powers, so that the pure will be saved from evil, and other Jewish souls will be saved, for they were in danger in the future, but now I have taken the evil names from them." So he took the names which were under the tongue of that head and tore them to pieces, and

promised that he would save the head and himself would say
the *Qaddish* for him. It was discovered then, through the boy,
that everything was revealed to the Rabbi from heaven immediately after the boy left town, and he knew everything that was
going to happen. And that night the boy saw with his own eyes
his dead grandfather who came to him and took him through
the window and carried him over villages and towns, a distance
of more than one month's journey, in one night, until he came
safely to his home. All this was achieved by the prayer of the
sacred Rabbi.

IV

While it employs elements that developed within Judaism for
fourteen centuries or more, this story is nevertheless typical of Hebrew narrative literature in the second half of the nineteenth century. The basic plot is almost identical to the description of Rachel's
theft of the *teraphim* as presented in the Midrash. It was necessary
for the boy to steal the *teraphim*—the severed head—in order to prevent his pursuers from finding him by means of its magical powers,
just as Rachel intended to prevent Laban from knowing about their
flight by taking the *teraphim* with her. Other secondary elements are
also identical: The *teraphim* is the head of a firstborn young man;
magical names give it power; candles are lighted and incense burnt
before it, etc. There can be no doubt that the description of the
teraphim in the *Tanhuma*, in *Pirkey de-Rabbi Eliezer*, in the works of
Rabbi Eleazar of Worms, in *Sefer Ha-Yashar* and other sources, ancient and medieval, gave birth to the basic plot of this story.

On the other hand, the way in which this particular story was
built is typical of a much later period. The book in which it is included, *Peer Mi-Kedoshim*, claims to be a collection of Hasidic tales,
and so it is listed in Hebrew bibliographies; but it is not strictly a
Hasidic work. It has some stories about the *Baal Shem Tov* and other
Hasidic sages, but they are a minority in the book. Most of the stories are purely hagiographical, telling wonderful tales about Jewish
sages from many different generations and countries, and the stories that praise Hasidic sages fall into the same category. They pos-

sess no specific Hasidic character, though it may be assumed that the legitimation for Jewish hagiography that was supplied by the Hasidic story—especially by *Shivhey ha-Besht*, published in 1815— helped in the creation of, and the interest shown toward, this literary genre.

We may divide the evolution of this kind of story into two stages, both of them clearly attested by the story translated above. The first is the spreading of hagiographical literature from Hasidic sages to earlier sages, like the Maharal of Prague. The second is the use made by the authors of the second half of the nineteenth century of popular tales and beliefs for creating stories that would fit the mold of hagiographical literature. It is evident that the story about the boy and his adventure with the *teraphim* could have been told—and probably was told—without involving the Maharal or any other sage. It could be a timeless, nameless folktale. But the literary conventions of that age forced the author to adapt the story to the accepted patterns: first, by telling it as a hagiographical story, and second, by including it in a collection with Hasidic legends, thus pretending that it was one of the thousands of stories written between 1850 and 1930 that are loosely described, not always justly, as "Hasidic stories."

SIXTEEN

"No Evil Descends from Heaven": Sixteenth-Century Jewish Concepts of Evil

I

Very few of the main ideas formulated by Jewish thinkers in the sixteenth century in the atmosphere of the Jewish Renaissance had any important impact on seventeenth- and eighteenth-century Jewish thought. Many ideological trends that began in this period either died out or had to wait two centuries or more until the period of the Enlightenment in order to be reborn in new historical and cultural circumstances and then take root. Some of them, like the idea of a Jewish university, had to wait till the twentieth century.

The one school of thought that flourished in sixteenth-century Judaism, as well as in previous and subsequent periods, was the kabbalah. The history of kabbalistic literature marks an uninterrupted creative effort that began late in the twelfth century and continued steadily until the nineteenth century at least. The Renaissance period in Jewish culture is one link in the long chain of kabbalistic literature that, from the beginning of the sixteenth century to the nineteenth, was gaining in impact and cultural influence until it

329

became the dominant popular Jewish ideology and served as a basis for the development of particular trends, sects, and movements.

It is therefore of some scholarly interest to examine sixteenth century kabbalah in comparison with other Renaissance cultural phenomena, and to check whether there is some common element of historical development even though kabbalah continued its steady development while many other sixteenth-century literary and cultural trends, like Jewish historiography or the classically influenced Jewish homily, were discontinued. Did the kabbalists ignore, in the sixteenth century, contemporary events and trends, and thus succeed in being prepared for the changes brought by the reaction of the seventeenth century, or did they participate in the major innovative trends of the Renaissance and still remain ready to adapt to the completely different cultural values of seventeenth-century Eastern European Judaism?

It is our intention here to show, even though limiting ourselves to only one example, that the kabbalah did fully participate in, reflect, and express the major ideological trends of the Jewish Renaissance, but at the same time the kabbalah had the spiritual resources to introduce a drastic change at the end of that century, which enabled it to present the subsequent century with an ideology suited to, and expressing, the new cultural demands.

When speaking about sixteenth-century kabbalah as compared to that of the seventeenth, one really deals with the relationship between two great kabbalists—probably the greatest after the thirteenth century, who lived together in Safed in the second half of the sixteenth century and shared the same disciples, to some extent, namely Rabbi Moses Cordovero and Rabbi Isaac Luria.[1] It is the purpose of this study to present the relationship between their differing mystical systems against the background of the conflicting cultural trends of the sixteenth and seventeenth centuries, and to describe

---

[1]See G. Scholem, *Major Trends in Jewish Mysticism,* New York 1954, pp. 252–258; on the spiritual atmosphere in which these two kabbalists created their systems, see S. Schechter, *Studies in Judaism,* New York 1970, pp. 231–297; R. J. Zwi Werblowsky, *Joseph Karo, Lawyer and Mystic,* Philadelphia 1977, pp. 38–83.

Cordovero as the great spokesman for the sixteenth. We contend that Luria, on the other hand, paved the way for a revolution within the kabbalah, a revolution that made it possible for Jewish mysticism to become the dominant spiritual force in seventeenth-century Judaism.

II

Lurianic kabbalah differed from earlier Jewish mystical systems, first and foremost, in its insistence on describing the beginning of divine history long before the creation.[2] In the Lurianic drama, the creation of the world comes in the third act, while the previous two decide to a very large extent the character and potentialities of all occurrences after the creation. The myths of the *tzimtzum* and the *shevira* are the decisive events,[3] while all the history of the created worlds—including the divine *sefirot*—serves only to enhance the *tikun*, putting to right what wrong in the first two acts. Therefore, there can be no doubt that the main antagonists in the divine drama described by Luria preceded creation and man, who are nothing but latecomers participating in the last act of a mythical struggle. The most extreme and strange theological idea presented by Luria in his mythical symbolism is that the roots of evil are an integral part of the eternal God; they did not emerge within the framework of cosmogony or history, but were present even before the divine *sefirot* were emanated; they are as ancient and eternal as the Godhead (*ein sof*) itself.[4] According to Lurianic theology, the source of evil is com-

---

[2]G. Scholem's descriptions of Lurianic kabbalah are presented in both his *Major Trends*, pp. 258–286, and his *Sabbatai Sevi, The Mystical Messiah*, Princeton, NJ 1973, pp. 22–26.

[3]The myth of the *tzimtzum* is a description of God's withdrawal from a certain part of the universe in which the world was subsequently created; the *shevira* is the myth of God's first attempt to emanate the *sefirot* into the empty space created by the *tzimtzum* and the catastrophic breaking of the vessels that contained the divine light. Evil elements were responsible for both processes.

[4]According to Luria, roots of potential evil that were present in the eternal Godhead remained in the empty space after God's withdrawal in the *tzimtzum*. They were

pletely independent of human action; its future will be decided by the behavior of human beings, but originally evil is one of the basic potentialities of the eternal Godhead.

The concept of evil in the extensive works of Rabbi Moses Cordovero is completely different. It seems to me that it is impossible to harmonize the various references to this problem in Cordovero's works into one systematic, coherent philosophical system;[5] it is better to analyze the conflicting descriptions separately, and then attempt to discover what basic drives, basic intuitions, and major motives are common to these various answers to the problem of the source of evil. Only thus will it be possible to evaluate correctly the relationship between Luria's myth of the source of evil and Cordovero's treatment of the same subject.

In Cordovero's magnum opus of systematic kabbalah, *Pardes Rimonim*,[6] the *Shaar ha-Temurot* (Chapter on Opposites)[7] is dedicated to the nature of evil. Most of this chapter is devoted (like many other parts of that book) to a systematic elucidation of the various traditions in the *Zohar* and other early sources concerning this subject; very little space is allotted to discussion of the basic problem of the source and nature of evil. It is evident that Cordovero was much more comfortable when describing the manifestations of evil in the world than when he was treating the fundamental questions of the origins of evil and its purpose. The first subchapter in this discussion is dedicated, however, to the basic problem.

The key statement concerning our problem is made when Cordovero presents the conclusion of a detailed parable equating the creation with human endeavor. He says: "The truth is that above,

---

called *reshimu*, "impression" or "remnants." These elements became actually evil during the *shevira*. See I. Tishby, *Torat ha-Ra ve-ha-Klipa be-Kabalat ha-Ari*, Jerusalem 1942 (reprinted 1963), pp. 39–61.

[5] J. Ben-Shlomo, *The Mystical Theology of Moses Cordovero* [Hebrew], Jerusalem 1965, pp. 290–291.

[6] The book was completed by the young Cordovero (born in 1522) in 1548, and printed in Cracow in 1592.

[7] This is the twenty-fifth chapter in the book, divided into seven subchapters. Chap. 26 deals with the palaces of the evil powers.

in the world of the divine emanations, no evil thing descends from heaven, for up there everything is absolutely spiritual."[8] While this statement is prepared as an answer, obviously it is nothing but a formulation of a question: Evil cannot be produced by the divine world, because this world is completely spiritual; where, then, is the source of evil?

The parable presented by Cordovero is an attempt to answer this question. Cordovero begins by stating that God created everything in a system of harmony between opposites; therefore every good thing must have its evil counterpart, every holy thing its sinful parallel. But, if so, a similar harmony also should exist at the source, and evil should have a divine manifestation. Cordovero recognizes that the harmony of opposites on Earth does not reflect a similar harmony in the divine realm, and asks:

> If so, where did the evil powers come from, where were the sinful things before they were created? This seems to be a penetrating and difficult question which could confuse the wise, but we have received from our teachers a very good answer to it. This is like the pure wheat, which had been cleaned from every impure element, but still, when a man eats it and the food has been digested in his stomach, a great deal of dirt and excrement will remain there. Now, can we say that when he ate that food he ate dirt and excrement? Of course not, for before it was eaten, the food was clean and pure as it could be, completely separated from dirt and excrement. But after it was eaten, the best part is separated from the food, and the excrement remains, even though it did not exist till then.[9]

In the conclusion of this parable Cordovero presents the statement that no evil descends from heaven, and continues with a neo-Platonic description of the materialization of spiritual things. As they descend downward they are removed from their source, and then

---

[8]*Shaar ha-Temurot*, first subchapter (vol. II, 53c, in the Jerusalem 1962 ed.). Concerning the history of this expression, see M. Halamish, "A Gnomic Collection" [Hebrew], *Sinai* 80 (1977), p. 278.
[9]*Pardes*, 53c.

"there is no way but that the good [food, *ochel*] is separated from good [food] and dirt is created there." Another, similar parable follows:

> Like human semen, which is from the best part of the human body, it is created within the body and originates in the brain, and then comes out from the testicles to the penis. Now, from that very same drop will the embryo be created in the full belly, and other dirty things besides the embryo. Is it conceivable that in the human brain, which is the best part of the body, all that dirt will be created? Of course not, for if it were so, the person would die that instant. But that dirt is created by the descent of that drop from stage to stage, when the best part of it is the origin of the infant and the rest is turned into that dirt. It is the same with the process of divine emanation: In its place of origin, there is no element of evil, but when it is being drawn downwards, the most sacred and pure elements will be separated, and the dirt will remain.[10]

It seems that these parables should not be interpreted too meticulously—for instance, by asking whether the separation of evil from good in the process of emanation and descent does not prove that evil was, at least potentially, part of the divine world. Parables point out the most important element in a thinker's concept, but often obscure secondary points. Cordovero's thesis is quite clear: First, it is imperative for him to state conclusively that no divine evil power exists; second, in answer to the problem of the actual existence of evil, he presents a modification of the neo-Platonic conception of the degradation and materialization of all things as they are being emanated away from their divine source.

Cordovero's attitude is not new in the history of Jewish thought. One of the earliest—and most popular—presentations of this concept is found in the thirteenth-century anonymous ethical work *Sefer ha-Yashar*, which explains the existence of the wicked and wrongdoers in the world as the result of a natural process, like that which

---

[10]Ibid., idem.

causes thorns to be created together with the rose, and dirt together with the fruitful seed of wheat.[11] The author describes the natural force that compels creation to develop in this way as *koah teva ha-beriya*, "the force of the nature of creation." A somewhat similar attitude is found in the early-thirteenth-century *Sefer ha-Hayyim*, which described a power called *reyah ha-avir ha-hay*, "the smell [or spirit] of the living air," which brings into existence dirt, excrement, and unclean beings.[12] Throughout the history of Jewish thought, mystical and nonmystical alike, we find various echoes of these ideas in the works of many scholars. Cordovero, therefore, followed here a clear tendency inherent in the history of Jewish thought.

The fact that this answer to the problem of the origin of evil was often given before does not make it more satisfactory from a theological point of view. Indeed, it is even more difficult within the framework of a mystical system. There is no answer in these parables to the question of the necessity of evil and its purpose. On the contrary, these parables seem to point out that God could not create a good world without an evil element being produced in the process, even if He wanted to. The emergence of evil and dirt in the process of creation seems to be a natural law that binds even God Himself. If that is so, evil need not necessarily fulfill a positive function in the world, for it exists because of basic, independent laws of creation. Of course, every thinker who presented such a system continued to explain how evil benefits the world, for instance by offering the possibility of religious and ethical free choice. Cordovero does so as well. The question of whether God would have created evil in this world were it not necessary according to the natural laws of creation is not answered.

Cordovero did not base his treatment of all theological and exegetical problems connected with the question of the origin of evil on these parables; they are hardly mentioned elsewhere in his voluminous works, and in other contexts he adopts different attitudes. It is important, therefore, to try to discover the underlying, com-

---

[11]Venice 1544, Chap 1.
[12]British Museum Ms. 756, f. 149r. *Sefer ha-Hayyim*, Jerusalem 1977, p. 14.

mon motifs in his different treatments of the various aspects of the problem.

III

Cordovero's attitude toward the problem of the preexistence of evil is best exemplified by his treatment of the medieval Jewish myth of the ancient evil worlds that were destroyed before the creation of this world. This subject in Cordovero's thought was studied in some detail by I. Tishby[13] and J. Ben-Shlomo;[14] it is our intention here to combine it with the general picture of the problem of the origin of evil.

Discussion of the status of the concept of evil in a mystical system should differentiate between explanations of the role of evil in the created world, often (and certainly in Cordovero's thought) a theodicy, and the problem of the source of evil. Theodicy attempts to explain the necessity of an evil element within the created system, and stipulates that its existence is needed in order for the divine creation to produce maximum good. Thus theodicy cleanses the Divinity from any suspicion of containing an evil element. The divine purpose is completely good, even though some of its means necessitate some evil. Evil as such is hated by God and has no place in the divine world or in the ideal state of affairs that will prevail when God's purpose in the creation is ultimately achieved. Evil, therefore, is clearly confined in time and place; it can exist only in the material world, and only as long as the world has not achieved perfection.

Such a theodicy cannot sustain the conception of a preexistent evil power having a place in the divine realm before the creation. Evil is not needed in the preexistent period, and therefore it cannot fulfill any function. If it existed then, it would mean that it was independent, unbound by the confines of time and place needed for it to fulfill its function of helping man make his moral and religious

---

[13]Tishby, *Netivey Emuna u-Minut*, Ramat Gan 1964, pp. 26–27.
[14]Ben-Shlomo, *The Mystical Theology of Cordovero*, pp. 231–238.

choices. Its existence then would denote its divine character, and reflect upon the nature of the Godhead itself. Every mystic whose purpose is to show the complete unity of the divine world and its absolute goodness must, therefore, confine evil to the material world as long as it is imperfect. Any hint at the preexistence of evil would reveal a tendency toward a more mythical, dualistic attitude in the conception of the Godhead.

The key group of symbols used by the kabbalists to denote the preexistence of evil is based on the midrashic cryptic reference to worlds created and destroyed before the present world came into being.[15] This tradition was used by thirteenth-century mystics to create a myth of evil worlds that came into being and then were destroyed because of their complete satanic nature, giving way to the creation of a more harmonious world, in which good and evil were in balance. It seems that the Ashkenazi Hasidim, and especially Rabbi Eleazar of Worms,[16] contributed to the creation of this myth, but it was crystallized in the Tractate on the Left Emanation, written by Rabbi Isaac ha-Cohen in Spain between 1260 and 1270.[17] When I. Tishby presented a brief survey of the development of the mythical element in the kabbalah, he correctly chose this group of symbols as an indicator of the attitudes of every circle of kabbalists and every generation of Jewish mystics toward mythological symbolism when describing the divine worlds.[18] These symbols are central to the zoharic concept of evil,[19] as well as to the Lurianic.[20] For Cordovero, however, they pose a very difficult problem.

---

[15]*Genesis Rabba* 9:2, and compare *Ecclesiastes Rabba* 3:11.
[16]See *Chochmat ha-Nefesh* (Lvov 1876), 12c–d.
[17]The text was published by G. Scholem in *Mada'ey ha-Yahadut* II, Jerusalem 1927, pp. 244–266. A comparison between the Ashkenazi Hasidic treatment of the subject and that of Rabbi Isaac ha-Cohen is included in my paper "Samuel, Lilith and the Concept of Evil," published in vol. V of the *AJS Review*.
[18]I. Tishby, *Netivey Emuna u-Minut*, pp. 25–29.
[19]G. Scholem, "Kabbalot Rabbi Jacob and Rabbi Isaac," *Mada'ey ha-Yahadut* II, Jerusalem 1927, pp. 193–196; I. Tishby, *Mishnat ha-Zohar* I, Jerusalem 1949, pp. 183–184, 296.
[20]See I. Tishby, *Torat ha-Ra ve-ha-Klipa*, pp. 28–34.

When Cordovero attempts to confine the realm of evil to the
created world within the framework of a monistic theodicy, the
zoharic sections dealing with the destroyed evil worlds (whose remnants feed evil in the present world) present enormous difficulties.
Cordovero saw himself as—and to a large extent really was—an interpreter of the *Zohar*. His *Pardes Rimonim* is a Herculean effort to
present zoharic mysticism in a systematic, nonmythical, somewhat
logical form. His major work, *Or Yakar*, is a voluminous, extensive
commentary on the *Zohar*. He could not dismiss zoharic ideas and
symbols as irrelevant or wrong. All his discussions are closely based
on zoharic quotations, even when he clearly departs from ancient
ideas and presents new ones.

In several places in his systematic works[21] (analyzed by J. Ben-
Shlomo[22]), Cordovero interpreted the zoharic story of the destroyed
evil worlds and the kings of Edom (who ruled before the kings of
Israel, according to Genesis 36, and were homiletically identified by
the *Zohar* with the evil worlds). According to Cordovero's interpretation, these worlds were not evil. The story of their destruction is
a veiled symbol for internal divine processes that were going on
within the divine realm before the actual creation. In one of his
several discussions of the subject, Cordovero states: "The matter of
the kings who reigned, this is the secret of the roots of the *sefirot* in
the *chochmah* of *keter*, which vanished. These same roots were emanated stage after stage and existence after existence until the existing things became revealed."[23] Later he explains that their revelation in existence is found also in the realm of *din*, which, according
to the *Zohar*, is the source of earthly evil. In this brief description
Cordovero summed up a lengthy, detailed study of the subject he
presented in the chapters of the first *tamar* of the section *Eyn ha-
Bedolah* in his theological work *Sefer Elima*.[24]

---

[21]*Shiur Komah*, Jerusalem 1966, pp. 130–135; *Elimah Rabbati*, Jerusalem 1966, 57a–
59a; *Pardes Rimonim* I, 25c–d (*Shaar Seder ha-Atzilut*, Chap. 4).
[22]J. Ben-Shlomo dedicated special discussions to Cordovero's interpretation of each
of these sources because of these differences (pp. 232–234, 235–238).
[23]*Elimah Rabbati*, Ein Roi, Tamar VI, Chap. 20 (87d).
[24]*Elimah Rabbati*, Ein ha-Bedolah, Tamar I, Chap. 16–21.

While the details are many, and often discrepancies and even conflicting statements are found in these descriptions (especially when the texts of *Sefer Elima* are compared with the treatment of the subject in his *Shiur Komah*,[25] the dominant elements of the Cordoverian thesis can be clearly stated. The process referred to in previous kabbalistic texts, and especially in the *Zohar*, as the destruction of the evil worlds or the death of the early kings of Edom is not a certain occurrence in a mythical past, but a constant, ongoing process in a most hidden and remote part of the Godhead, in the first *sefirah*, *keter*, which is the divine will. This supreme part of the Godhead is in itself divided into ten aspects, corresponding to the ten *sefirot*. The process of the "death of the kings" occurs between the aspects called *chochmah* and *binah*, the second and third highest aspects within the divine will. In this sublime, hidden part of the Godhead, every thought of existence or creation is still unformed and unclear; it wavers, appears, and vanishes in a constant rhythm. It is as if neither the wish to create nor the plan of creation crystallized in the divine mind. This process of the appearance of the thought and its immediate disappearance is the one referred to by the more mythically inclined *Zohar* as the destruction of the worlds or the death of the Idumean kings.

These roots, or fleeting thoughts, deep in the Godhead and completely remote from even divine existence become, by a slow and gradual process of emanation, the roots of all existence—including earthly evil, but are not specifically concerned with this particular aspect of the creation. Again and again Cordovero stresses that nothing in the divine realm can be called, even symbolically, "a source of evil."

Cordovero's repeated treatments of this subject are in clear contradiction to the descriptions of the *Zohar*, which are relatively clear and emphatic. The term "Edom" itself is indicative of evil, because of its association with Esau and Rome, and therefore with Christianity. Cordovero disregards all these associations, as well as the

---

[25]This book is dedicated mainly to the reinterpretation of the anthropomorphic symbols concerning the body of God, which Cordovero tried to demythologize.

mythical statements of the *Zohar*,[26] thus revealing his insistent aim to cleanse the divine world from any element of evil. The myth of the destroyed worlds is the clearest indication in early kabbalah of the conception of preexistent evil. Cordovero reveals in his treatment of the subject that, for him, evil is an earthly, temporary phenomenon without any possibility of a counterpart or source in the divine realm.

IV

As a systematic thinker, Cordovero could not avoid the problem that naturally arises from his insistence on negating any divine or independent source for evil: How evil, really, *is* evil? If God did not create it, and it did not create itself (as in a dualistic system of thought), what is its nature? Like all kabbalists, Cordovero based his mystical attitude on the premise that everything that occurs on Earth has a counterpart in heaven. What, then, is the divine counterpart to earthly evil?

Cordovero faced these problems and offered his answer in a quite radical manner in his short, popular ethical work, *Tamar Devora* (The Palm Tree of Deborah).[27] This short treatise attempts to lay a kabbalistic foundation for ethical behavior, and is the first of many such kabbalistic works written in the sixteenth century and later. While this book did not gain a very large audience, it was incorporated in other books, like *Reshit Chochmah* by Rabbi Elijah de Vidas,[28] and *Shney Luhot ha-Brit* (*Shelah*) by Isaiah ha-Levi Horowitz,[29] which became one of the most widely read works on Jewish ethics from the seventeenth century onward.

---

[26]Cordovero even wrote a special homiletical exegesis on the names of the kings of Edom in order to show that even their names denoted divine, good processes within the Godhead. See *Elimah Rabbati, Ein ha-Bedolah, Tamar* I, Chap. 17 (57c–58c).

[27]Venice 1589. An English translation by L. Jacobs, *The Palm Tree of Deborah*, was published in London in 1960.

[28]Venice 1579. The author was one of Cordovero's disciples, and used his teachings in many of the book's chapters.

[29]Amsterdam 1653. The whole text of Cordovero's book was included in this work.

The thesis of Cordovero's book is that every human action reflects a divine process, on the one hand, while it influences divine processes in either a positive or a negative way, on the other. There is nothing new to zoharic kabbalists in this idea, but Cordovero's formulation in this brief treatise is a radical and clear one that had, through the works that used it, an enormous impact.

The problem of evil is treated by Cordovero when he deals with the subject of repentance, *teshuva*, in the fourth chapter of the book. It is obvious that during the process of repentance good and evil come into very close contact, and the relationship between them has to be clarified. Cordovero does not choose the easy, conventional way of explaining to the reader that repentance means withdrawing from evil and forsaking it while embracing good ways. He follows the zoharic concept of evil as an emanation from the power of *din* when it leaves the *sefirah binah*, but goes further than the *Zohar* does in his description of the power of repentance.

The process of earthly repentance resembles, according to Cordovero's explanation, the divine process of *sod ha-yovel* (the mystical process of the jubilee): The lower *sefirot*, like all spiritual beings, return to their source as a part of a cosmic cycle of descent and ascent from the Godhead. That source is the third *sefirah*, *binah*, symbolized in the kabbalah by all the relevant terms: Jubilee, the number fifty, and especially *teshuva* (which, of course, means "the returning"). The origin of earthly evil is the point at which the various divine emanations leave the *binah* and assume their particular characteristics; this point of departure is reversed during the process of the Jubliee, and at the place where things had become differentiated they now lose their specific attributes and become part of the divine unity, completely good and completely merciful. The power of *din* participates in this cyclical process, and it, together with all its derivatives, including evil, are reunited within the Godhead, losing all traces of evil. In the next cycle, the same divine elements may return to the revealed world as powers of good.

This mystical cycle, which Cordovero adopted from the *Zohar* to a large extent, makes it possible for him to raise a question not usually discussed in repentance literature: Does *teshuva* affect only the good part of a human being, or does it also affect his evil part? Cordovero's discussion of this problem seems to be somewhat out of character as far as the tone of his argument is concerned; he is more vehement and emphatic than usual in his works.[30] He states clearly: "You should not say that teshuva helps only the holy part in man; rather [it] also [helps] his evil part, which becomes sweetened [i.e., turns into good]." Cordovero then goes on to discuss in some detail a specific example. That example is none other than Cain himself, who, according to kabbalistic myth based on some midrashic homilies, was the son of the snake, that is, of Satan. Cordovero repeats, with his own interpretation, God's words to Cain:[31] "Do not think that because you are from the evil side [that is, the sitra ahra] there is no remedy for you; this is a lie [ze sheker], for if you will attach yourself to the supreme mystery of teshuva and then return from there in the mystery of the good that is rooted there," you will become completely good.

Relying on some zoharic symbols and some radical rabbinic sayings,[32] Cordovero concludes this brief discussion by making it absolutely clear that every evil element in existence, within man and outside, and even the sins themselves, can be turned into good by the process of the Jubilee. The more sins a person had before repenting, the more righteous deeds he is credited with when completing his repentance, for the evil deeds themselves become righteous elements. He even states that if Cain had repented, he would have corrected not only his own sins, but also those of Adam, thus freeing the human race from the curse of the original sin.

The implications of these statements for the history of Jewish mystical thought in the seventeenth and eighteenth centuries are considerable,[33] but they also serve to clarify Cordovero's attitude to-

---

[30]The contemporary problem of the attitude toward the repentant converts to Catholicism in Spain and Portugal may have had some influence on Cordovero's tone here.

[31]This is a part of Cordovero's interpretation of the verse in Genesis 4:7 (see also L. Jacobs's ed., pp. 86–89).

[32]Yoma 86b (sins will become merits after repentance).

[33]M. Piekarz has recently raised the possibility that ideas of the use of sins in order

ward evil in the best way. According to this, evil is not really evil from a divine point of view. The powers of evil are such only temporarily, in their present place in the cycle of the Jubilee. When the time comes—or when repentance is done—they will return to their source in *binah* and will reassume their original good selves. Its appearance as earthly evil is but a stage in the history of a divine particle, which does not affect its inherent, potential goodness. Spiritual power cannot be lost, even the spiritual power used to commit the worst crimes, like murder; it waits until it can return to the root of everything in *binah* and then will be transformed into goodness equivalent in its degree to its former degree in the realm of evil.[34]

In a mystical way Cordovero revives here the philosophical attitude that denied the very existence of evil and explained it away as a lack of goodness or as "in the eye of the beholder," that is, man alone. But Cordovero is even more radical: He does not deny the actual existence, or even the ferocity, of earthly evil; he just denies that it is really and constantly bad. Evil is ephemeral, while good is eternal. Therefore good is dominant even among the characteristics of the most starkly evil elements; when the Jubilee cycle is completed, it will be evident that evil was just a temporary mask on the face of divine goodness.

The three examples discussed here, even though different in their detailed theological implications, do form a whole as far as Cordovero's intuitive attitude toward evil is concerned: God had no intention of creating evil; some dirt and excrement naturally are to be expected when some good process is going on. Traditional myths concerning preexistent evil should be reinterpreted to prove that they denote perfectly good processes within the highest realms of the Godhead; and even human evil and sins are but a transitory phase

---

to enhance the redemption could develop in rabbinic, non-Sabbatian ethical literature. See his *The Beginning of Hasidism* [Hebrew], Jerusalem 1978, pp. 175–268.
[34]Cain, for instance, was regarded as the source of the soul of the Messiah, even by Rabbi Hayyim Vital, the great disciple of Luria, who regarded himself as possessing a part of the Messiah's soul. See his *Sefer ha-Hezyonot*, ed. A. Z. Eshkoli, Jerusalem 1954, pp. 204–205 et passim.

in the cosmic divine cycle, and they reveal their truly good selves when they return to their divine source. All three theses are united by the basic axiom: No evil descends from heaven.

V

Cordovero is a unique figure in the history of Jewish thought in many respects, but not in his attitude toward evil. While many of his formulations and theological theses are his own, in his basic attitude he represents cultural and ideological processes both within the kabbalah and in the general Jewish culture. Tishby has already pointed out that Cordovero represents the culmination of a process, begun in the fourteenth century, of withdrawing from the mythological symbolism of the *Zohar* and adopting a more philosophical symbolism.[35] As far as the history of the conception of evil in kabbalah is concerned, even the *Zohar* itself is less radical than its source, the writings of Rabbi Isaac ha-Cohen. It is clear, however, that in denying the preexistence and divinity of evil Cordovero gives expression to the prevailing attitude among the kabbalists of his age and in previous generations. Many kabbalists avoided the problem completely, dealt with it in neo-Platonic terms like Rabbi Johanan Alemanno,[36] or obscured it, like Rabbi Meir ibn Gabai in his popular summary of the kabbalah, *Avodat ha-Kodesh*.[37]

This process within the kabbalah coincided with a similar one in nonkabbalistic circles. It is impossible to review all the many facets of Jewish sixteenth-century thought, but it is clear that the dominant atmosphere concerning the origin and nature of evil is exactly the one reflected in Cordovero's discussions, though the symbolism and terminology are completely different. Rabbi Judah Moscato, one of the most typical of Jewish thinkers of the period and one whose writings reflect the impact of the Italian Renaissance upon

---

[35]I. Tishby, *Netivey Emuna u-Minut*, pp. 23–26.
[36]Thanks are due to Dr. M. Idel, who studied Alemanno's works and discussed his results with me.
[37]Mantua 1545.

Judaism more clearly than many others, can serve as an example.[38] Moscato dedicated a special sermon to the problem, one that was included in his book *Nefutzot Yehuda*.[39] This sermon is titled appropriately: "No evil descends from heaven." Using rabbinic and philosophical sources, Moscato explains that all evil originates in man, and that the abolition of evil is dependent upon human ethical and religious behavior. Moscato was not a kabbalist,[40] even though he quoted kabbalistic sources occasionally. In this sermon he did not quote the *Zohar*, but relied on other sources to make his point. The homily does not reveal any polemical motives, as do some other parts of this book, so that it seems that Moscato did not expect anyone to hold different views than the ones expressed by him. Moscato's example may indicate that Cordovero's basic views were the common ones found in Jewish intellectual circles in the sixteenth century.

Another example that should be briefly mentioned is the sixteenth-century attitude toward witchcraft and demonology. Jewish thinkers, like non-Jewish ones, were almost unanimous in this period in their complete belief in the veracity of demonic phenomena, and one cannot find any significant difference between kabbalists and nonkabbalists in their acceptance of witchcraft and demonology as integral parts of natural and human laws. The *Zohar*, three centuries earlier, emphasized the link between Satan and demonic forces (an idea almost completely absent from pre-thirteenth-century Jewish thought), and some later kabbalists developed this theme.[41] In the sixteenth century, however, we find kabbalists discussing demonic forces in great detail, without ever linking them with any

---

[38]See J. Dan, *Hebrew Ethical and Homiletical Literature* [Hebrew], Jerusalem 1975, pp. 188-197; I. Bettan, *Studies in Jewish Preaching*, Cincinnati 1939, pp. 192-226.
[39]*Nefutzot Yehuda* was first printed in Venice in 1589. This homily is the fourty-eighth chapter in the book (Warsaw 1871 ed., pp. 124-128).
[40]Moscato's attitude toward the kabbalah and the structure of one of his homilies are discussed in my paper in *Sinai* 76 (1975), pp. 209-232.
[41]A clear example is Rabbi Menahem Tziyoni's treatise on evil, *Tzfunei Tziyoni*, ms. Oxford 1651. See J. Dan, *The Esoteric Theology of the Ashkenazi Hasidim*, Jerusalem 1968, pp. 259-260.

supreme principle,[42] and certainly without identifying witches as the servants of Satan (at the time that the witch-hunts in Europe were in full force). This fact seems to indicate that Jewish thinkers did not find any evidence in this realm for the power, or even the existence, of a principle of evil that had emissaries throughout creation. Their basic disbelief in the divinity of the source of evil prevented them from seeking such evidence. Thus we find both sixteenth-century and seventeenth-century thinkers, most notably Rabbi Manasseh ben Israel in his *Nishmat Hayyim*,[43] who could use evidence derived from the realms of witchcraft and demonology to prove, for instance, the eternity of the soul, without for a moment doubting that these phenomena might have a source different from the Creator of all natural existence. In this they were returning, in a completely different way, to views held by the theologians of the Ashkenazi Hasidic movement in the twelfth and early thirteenth centuries,[44] in prezoharic times. If no evil can descend from heaven, all worldly phenomena should be explained as the workings of the one and good God.

The clearest example of this prevailing attitude among sixteenth-century thinkers is found in their treatment of historical occurrences in their own times. One might expect people who have witnessed, or even suffered, the tortures of the period of the expulsion from Spain and Portugal and the undisturbed rule of the Inquisition to express some doubt as to whether all these misfortunes were caused by God Himself, or whether an evil power had anything to do with them. I have been unable to find such themes in that period. It seems that the belief that God Himself instigated all these tortures, for one reason or another, is almost universal. The postexpulsion thinkers,

---

[42]Johanan Alemanno is a perfect example. Demonology and witchcraft play a major role in his works, yet they are not connected with any divine power antagonistic to God.

[43]Amsterdam 1652. This seems to be the book that includes the most detailed discussions concerning witchcraft and demonology in that period, yet the only theological implications from the vast material are those relating to the eternity of the soul

[44]See *The Esoteric Theology of the Ashkenazi Hasidim*, pp. 184–202.

beginning with Rabbi Joseph Yavetz and Rabbi Isaac Abravanel, were building their theodical systems, counting human sins that had caused the destruction of Spanish Jewry and revealing in the suffering a divine promise for an imminent messianic redemption.[45] The minority who did not adopt a clearly theodical attitude tried to formulate socioeconomic explanations for the misfortunes of exilic Judaism, like the views expressed in Solomon ibn Verga's *Shevet Yehuda*.[46] Again, no worldly evidence could shake Jewish thinkers in the sixteenth century from their deep conviction that no evil descends from heaven.

This background may help us understand the force of the Lurianic revolution in Jewish thought. When explaining the rapid spread of Lurianic concepts in the late sixteenth and early seventeenth centuries, G. Scholem pointed out that Luria put the desired emphasis upon the exilic state of the Jewish people by making the exile of the Godhead the cornerstone of his mythological system.[47] It seems that our analysis may add another element to that picture. One may wonder whether Jews could really be happy with an ideology that was going farther and farther away from the concept of an independent, preexistent evil power, when history developing all around them was proving time after time the rule of evil in this world. It seemed as though Satan was constantly advancing in his role in history, while receding from the ideological systems presented by Jewish thinkers.

When Lurianic mysticism began to spread, putting forward the concepts that evil is the ruler of this world, and that evil was in a constant—and often winning—struggle against God, reality seemed to prove the veracity of this most mythological of all Jewish theologies. When Luria explained the power of the Gentiles as derived from the power of Satan, his ideas were much more easily accepted than

---

[45]H. H. Ben-Sasson, "Dor Goley Sefarad al Atzmo," *Zion* 26 (1961), pp. 23–64.
[46]I. Baer, "Yediot Hadashot al Sefer Shevet Yehuda," *Tarbiz* 6 (1935), pp. 152–179; J. Dan, *Ethical and Homiletical Literature*, pp. 184–188.
[47]G. Scholem, *Major Trends*, pp. 248–251.

theories explaining that the tortures inflicted by the Gentiles on the Jews sprang from God's eternal love for the people of Israel.

One many surmise that the fierce revolutionary process by which the Jewish Renaissance-influenced theology of the sixteenth century was replaced by Lurianism in the first half of the seventeenth century was enhanced by the enormous gap created by thinkers like Cordovero and Moscato between theology and national and private experience. Lurianic myth became the dominant Jewish ideology because it succeeded in creating a harmony between its symbols and Jewish reality, while destroying the harmony in the divine worlds and postulating that evil did indeed descend from heaven.

SEVENTEEN

Manasseh ben Israel's Nishmat Hayyim and the Concept of Evil in Seventeenth-Century Jewish Thought

I

Rabbi Manasseh ben Israel's *Nishmat Hayyim*, an extensive theological work, was written in the last decade of the seventeenth century before the onset of the Sabbatian crisis[1] that changed Jewish culture for generations to come. A study of Rabbi Manasseh's position on basic theological and cultural problems can shed light on the relationship of seventeenth-century Jewish scholars to their past traditions and on the main tendencies beginning to emerge at that time that shaped the cultural trends of the following decades. Rabbi Manasseh's work is not one of great originality. Its importance lies in its extensive coverage of many key issues; the author's positions reveal the attitude of a significant group of Jewish intellectuals of that time toward these issues. This analysis is based on the assumption that a thinker's views on the problem of evil is one of

---

[1]Rabbi Manasseh finished writing the book in 1652, and it was published later that year in Amsterdam. Quotations in this paper are according to the Samiel Zackheim ed. (Lemberg 1858).

the most important, though often intuitive, indications of his general religious, philosophical, and cultural views. In addition, *Nishmat Hayyim* is one of the most detailed—if not the most detailed—analysis in Hebrew of the demonic world and all its aspects in a systematic manner. It is therefore crucial to an understanding of the concept of evil in seventeenth-century Jewish culture and theology.

In the beginning of the seventeenth century, two alternative conceptions of evil existed in Jewish thought. The first was a direct continuation of the concept developed in the works of most sixteenth-century Jewish thinkers, kabbalists and non-kabbalists alike, according to which "no evil descends from Heaven."[2] This view, most clearly expressed by Rabbi Moses Cordovero, the great pre-Lurianic kabbalist in sixteenth-century Safed, described all the phenomena of evil found within the created world resulting from human misbehavior—an inevitable development of natural forces within the framework of creation but having no connection to God's original design of the universe and having no bearing on the structure of the divine world. This attitude was not originally developed by Cordovero, but has its roots in thirteenth-century Jewish thought, which was temporarily submerged when the fierce dualistic mythologies of Rabbi Isaac ha-Cohen and the *Zohar* were introduced in the second half of that century.[3] In the fourteenth century and later, many kabbalists deemphasized the dualistic, mythological symbolism of the *Zohar*, and by the sixteenth century most of them—as well as the nonkabbalistic thinkers—held the view that "no evil descends from heaven" and that the roots of evil phenomena are found within creation, in man and in nature, and are not the result of a conflict within the divine world.

While this conception was the dominant one, the great cataclysm of the expulsion from Spain, the mass conversion of Spanish and Portuguese Jews, the hardships suffered by the wandering mul-

---

[2] " 'No Evil Descends from Heaven'—Sixteenth-Century Jewish Concepts of Evil," in *Jewish Thought in the Sixteenth Century*, ed. B. D. Cooperman, Cambridge, MA and London 1983, pp. 89–105.
[3] See my paper "Samael, Lilith and the Concept of Evil in Early Kabbalah," *AJS Review* 5 (1980) pp. 17–40.

titudes who could not find a new place to settle, and the Inquisition's horrors in persecuting Marranos all led to the emergence of a completely different concept of evil that, in many ways, was a return to the symbolism of Rabbi Isaac ha-Cohen and the *Zohar*. Kabbalists who were intensely aware of the horrors of the exile wrote extensive and detailed messianic works,[4] some of them in Spain before the final expulsion (including, probably, the historical Rabbi Joseph de la Reina),[5] and many of them immediately after the expulsion, when they moved through the Ottoman Empire toward *Eretz Yisrael* and settled mainly in Jerusalem and Safed. The most important figure in this school was Rabbi Abraham be-Rabi Eliezer ha-Levi, who wrote several intensely messianic, mythological, and dualistic treatises in Jerusalem in the first decades of the sixteenth century.[6] To this school must be attributed a major kabbalistic work—*Galyah Razah*. Though it has been hitherto unstudied and its theology unclarified, important discoveries have recently been made concerning its theological characteristics.[7]

Though extremely important from a historical-cultural point of view, this school had minimal impact in the first half of the sixteenth century. The main Jewish scholars who dedicated their works to the theological consequences of the expulsion from Spain, like Rabbi Joseph Yavets, Rabbi Yehudah Abravanel, Rabbi Solomon ibn Verga, and others, do not reveal any similar attitudes. The many kabbalists and somewhat kabbalistic authors in sixteenth-century Italy disregarded this alternative theology completely. Most of the great writers in Safed—kabbalists and writers of ethical, homiletical, and kabbalistic works—followed the concepts found in Moses Cordovero's theology. The almost single exception, but the one that

---

[4]G. Scholem, *Major Trends in Jewish Mysticism*, New York 1954, pp. 244–251.
[5]G. Scholem, "Rabbi Joseph De la Reina, the Case History," *Studies in Jewish Religious and Intellectual History Presented to Alexander Altmann*, eds. S. Stein and R. Loewe, University of Alabama 1979, pp. 101–108 of the Hebrew section.
[6]G. Scholem, "The Kabbalist Rabbi Avraham berabi Eliezer ha-Levi" (Hebrew), *Kiryat Sefer* II (1925/1926), pp. 101–141, 269–273; VII (1930/1931), pp. 149–165, 440–455; idem, *Ma'amar Meshreh Kitrin*, Jerusalem 1978, pp. 7–42.
[7]R. Elior, *Galyah Razah*, Jerusalem 1981.

counted most from a historical point of view, was Rabbi Isaac Luria, the founder of Lurianic kabbalah, which had a major impact on seventeenth-century Jewish thought. In Luria's kabbalah we find the maximum development of the ideas of Isaac ha-Cohen, the *Zohar*, and Rabbi Abraham ha-Levi, in which a theology was presented that placed the dualistic conflict between good and evil at the heart of the divine world, before the process of creation began and even as a cause for this process. A detailed mythology was developed by Luria[8] in which the eternal conflict between good and evil is symbolized, to be resolved only when the messianic process ends in victory and evil is abolished, first from the divine world and then from the earthly one. Dualistic symbolism and messianic mythology were merged in Lurianic kabbalah into a systematic whole, giving a new meaning to religious commands, for every human deed, be it good or evil, contributes to one or the other of the divine powers in conflict. Dualistic symbolism thus became an integral part of actual, everyday Jewish religious practice.

These two conflicting conceptions—Cordovero's and Luria's—were fully developed when the seventeenth century began, and at that time Cordovero's theory was dominant within Jewish culture. At first, Luria's kabbalah was disseminated out of Safed very slowly by Rabbi Israel Saruk[9] in a different variation that did not emphasize messianic and dualistic symbolism in the same way. Only in the second and third decades of the seventeenth century did it begin to have some impact, a process that increased in speed and depth in the decades before the Sabbatian upheaval. Rabbi Manasseh ben Israel began to work on his *Nishmat Hayyim* when these two alternative concepts of evil existed in Jewish culture side by side, each supported by contemporary thinkers and by great kabbalistic works from Safed, waiting for history to decide which one would become supreme and dominant in the second half of the seventeenth century.

---

[8]G. Scholem, *On the Kabbalah and Its Symbolism*, New York 1965, pp. 110–117.
[9]G. Scholem, "Rabbi Israel Saruk—A Disciple of Luria?" (Hebrew), *Zion* V (1940), pp. 214–243.

II

Rabbi Manasseh ben Israel did not write *Nishmat Hayyim* in order to present his views concerning the existence of evil in the world or its divine sources. This book was a part of his general scholarly work in commenting on the analysis of biblical theology.[10] The most important idea expressed in this work is that the Bible *does* include references to the eternity of the soul, a celebrated exegetical problem from midrashic literature and throughout the Middle Ages. Like many other works by the same author, *Nishmat Hayyim* presents an exegesis of relevant biblical passages to prove that the Bible regards the soul as eternal, to receive its due after the body's death and to be resurrected in the messianic future.

However, the author dedicated only part of the first section (out of four) in his work to this central problem.[11] Most of the book is dedicated to a detailed analysis of the nature of the soul and its relationship to the body. In the course of this analysis, Ben Israel presents a most impressive anthology of views concerning the soul; it is an anthology of encyclopedic dimensions—seldom, if ever, surpassed in erudition in the history of Jewish culture. Hundreds of sources are cited verbatim, most of them non-Jewish. The author quotes extensively from ancient Greek and Roman philosophers, not only from Plato and Aristotle, but also from dozens of lesser figures in classical Greek and Roman philosophy and literature; this is probably the first appearance for some of them in a Hebrew work. These are followed by the Church fathers and many medieval Christian and Muslim philosophers, historians, and writers. Renaissance and contemporary seventeenth-century figures abound as well, without any discrimination. It is certain that the author did not study all of these sources in the original, but made extensive use of non-Jewish summaries of views on psychology written in the Renaissance and

---

[10]A general description of the works of Rabbi Manasseh is found in C. Roth, *Life of Manasseh ben Israel* (1934).
[11]Part I, Chs. 3–10. The remaining chapters of the first part of the book deal with the talmudic and kabbalistic views on the subject.

after that period. Even taking this into account, his erudition is astounding.

Ben Israel has no hesitation in presenting non-Jewish sources on the same basis as Jewish ones,[12] and he does not always prefer a Jewish source over a classical or Christian one. His attitude toward medieval Jewish philosophers is decided by a comparison of their views with his own. He often brings forth quotations and arguments from Christian sources in order to refute the views of a celebrated Jewish thinker.[13] A criticism of *Nishmat Hayyim* has been that this is not a book but an indiscriminate collection of quotations, collected and presented unsystematically. My impression is exactly the opposite. It is rare to find an author presenting such a wide selection of views and sources without for a moment losing his main purpose, putting every quotation in exactly the right perspective in order to support the main thesis of the book as a whole. This is a work written by a most confident, determined thinker, whose attitudes contain no elements of ambiguity; right and wrong in this variegated presentation of different ideas are never obscured.

The main thesis of this work is the rejection of the Aristotelian conception of the soul and the upholding of the Platonic one (according to the author's understanding of Platonism, briefly discussed below). Ben Israel insists on the separate existence of the soul, completely independent of the body, preexisting in the divine realm and returning there after the completion of its task within the body. All Aristotelian references to the relationship between the soul and physical functions are rejected vehemently and decisively, and, if there is a classic demonic picture in this book, it is that of Aristotelian

---

[12]In the last paragraph of the introduction to the book, the author apologizes for his extensive use of non-Jewish sources, explaining that one should accept truth from whomever states it, and a scholar should be able to distinguish between what should be learned and what should not. Concerning his attitude toward these non-Jewish scholars, see below and section V of this paper.
[13]Thus, the second part of the book, which is concerned mainly with the problem of the nature of the soul, begins with a detailed refutation of the views of Rabbi Isaac Arama, the fifteenth-century author of *Akedat Yitzhak*, a refutation that is supported by quotations from many non-Jewish neo-Platonic writers.

philosophy. All the hundreds of quotations brought forth in this work are systematically divided between those belonging to the Aristotelian school—even if remotely—and those brought down by the author in order to refute these views. Human thought, be it Jewish, Christian, or Muslim, is neatly divided into these two conflicting schools, with all that is wrong found in one and all that is right found in the other. *Nishmat Hayyim*, therefore, is extremely critical of the Jewish rationalistic philosophy of the Middle Ages, especially the Maimonidean school, though Ben Israel does not often confront Maimonides directly, preferring to attack the works of his followers or to reinterpret some of his ideas.

Because of this anti-Aristotelian attitude at its ideological core, *Nishmat Hayyim* is one of the most significant post-Renaissance Hebrew works reflecting the cultural attitudes of the Renaissance period in which, both in general and in Jewish culture, are found a strong opposition to Aristotelianism and a new embracing of Platonic and neo-Platonic philosophy. Classical and medieval neo-Platonic philosophers were the focus of a new intellectual group that read their works and used them in order to create new ideologies. Jews and non-Jews alike spoke about "the divine Plato." When Ben Israel adopted this attitude, he was not opposing the main cultural trends of his generation (or previous generations), but rather following, with unusual erudition, the main spiritual currents of his time.

The author's attitude toward the kabbalah is to be understood within the same framework. Rabbi Manasseh repeatedly states in this book that Rabbi Simeon's conceptions should be accepted in their entirety, completely embraced and followed, referring, of course, to the teachings of the *Zohar*.[14] There are many dozens of zoharic quo-

---

[14]In the concluding paragraph of the book, the author declares (Part IV, Ch. 23, p. 74d):

> I know that there are some statements in this book which are not going to be well received by those philosophers who always seek logical proof, but I have already stated that I have sworn to uphold the teachings or Rabbi Shimon bar Yohai, and I shall not stray from my belief in him. After all, whether I turn right to the Torah of Moses and the teachings of our rabbis, or if I turn left towards the works of the philosophers, it is always necessary to believe in

tations in this work, all of them supported completely by the author and brought down in order to refute this or that Aristotelian postulation (he often uses zoharic quotations in order to argue against Jewish thinkers). There is no doubt that Ben Israel regarded the *Zohar* as a part of ancient Jewish tradition, equal to talmudic and midrashic traditions in antiquity and authority; but, while some midrashic sayings pose a problem to his attitude and have to be reinterpreted in order to be integrated into his theology of the soul, the zoharic quotations are brought as final proof, not needing any emendations in order to be accepted completely. Rabbi Manasseh regarded the *Zohar* as one of the most—or even the most—perfect Jewish presentation of the Platonic view of the essence of the soul and its fate both before and after its existence within the body, and he quotes from the *Zohar* with wholehearted support.

His complete agreement with the *Zohar* is reflected in his attitude toward other kabbalists. He made no distinctions between "correct" kabbalists and "incorrect" ones, as he did concerning Jewish philosophers. Kabbalah, for him, meant the teachings of the *Zohar*, followed by all other kabbalists,[15] and the whole kabbalah was an expression of the true philosophy, namely Platonism. It is interesting to note that Ben Israel does include Luria within this framework, and, although he was more familiar with the narrative traditions from the disciples of Luria and the stories of Safed than with Lurianic theology and symbolism, he does state that Luria and his disciples belong to the camp of those who know and understand the true character of the soul, and their teachings should be accepted and followed.

---

       everything that Rabbi Shimon bar Yohai believed in. He was the last of the scholars of the Mishnah and the first in his importance, and he was almost unparalleled among all the wise men of Israel. He ascended to Heaven and returned and was a father to all the sons of Israel.

Similar expressions concerning the *Zohar* and its author are found throughout the book.

[15]Among the kabbalistic works quoted often in the book we find Rabbi Shem Tov ben Shem Tov's *Sefer ha-Emunot*, the commentary on the Torah by Recanati, *Sefer ha-Kanah*, the *Bahir*, and many others, but there is no doubt that the major source is the *Zohar*.

Can we, therefore, regard Ben Israel in *Nishmat Hayyim* as a kabbalist? Can we view the theory of the soul presented in this work as a kabbalistic one? Certainly there is no conflict between the quotations that the author uses in this work and the teachings of the kabbalah, nor is there any deliberate distortion of usual kabbalistic views of this subject. It is doubtful, however, whether this work can rightfully be described as kabbalistic, and this doubt is closely connected with Rabbi Manasseh's concept of evil.

III

The third and fourth parts of *Nishmat Hayyim* are dedicated to the description and analysis of various phenomena that are usually described as demonic. This is probably the most detailed presentation of such phenomena in a systematic way in Hebrew, and there can be little doubt that the author did not dedicate so much effort and space to this subject just because his argument required it; Rabbi Manasseh reveals intense curiosity about every bit of information relating to this field, and there is a basis for the assumption that the whole field of the supernatural appealed to him. Yet, the presentation of these chapters is closely and systematically related to the previous parts of the book, and, like Rabbi Judah the Pious in the twelfth and thirteenth centuries, Rabbi Manasseh discussed demonology in detail out of both theological necessity and personal curiosity.[16]

Theologically, Ben Israel uses the whole range of supernatural and demonic phenomena to enforce his main thesis throughout the book: that the soul is an independent power within the body, it can be separated from it, it was separated from it before its entrance into it, and it continues to exist after death. Therefore, there can be no doubt that souls of the dead do wander and can appear soon after, or many years after, death.[17] The best example of such independence is the phenomenon of transmigration of souls from body to body

---

[16]Concerning Rabbi Judah the Pious, see my notes in "Samael, Lilith," pp. 26–32.

[17]See Part III, Ch. 11, pp. 48c–49c; and compare Ch. 10, pp. 47a–c.

(*gilgul, ivur*, later known from the Yiddish as a *dybbuk*). The fact
that souls can wander from body to body is the clinching proof of
their independence of any specific body and their ability to have a
separate existence.[18] This is, for Ben Israel, the final refutation of the
Aristotelian attitude that sees the soul as an appellation to some of the
physical functions of the body. To support his view, Ben Israel collected in the fourth part of *Nishmat Hayyim* a very important anthology of such phenomena, including examples from Luria's Safed[19]
(it should be taken into account that *Nishmat Hayyim* was written
hardly a hundred years after the first appearances of narrative descriptions of a *dybbuk* in Hebrew literature).

While the close connection between appearances of the souls
of the dead and the transmigration of souls to the main thesis of his
work concerning the nature of the human soul is self-evident, Rabbi
Manasseh does not limit his discussion to these obvious examples.
The whole realm of the supernatural and the demonic is relevant to
this problem, according to him. The power of holy names,[20] the
prophecy of dreams,[21] human spiritual ailments like epilepsy[22] and
impotence (on the day of the wedding),[23] the ability of birds to reveal the future,[24] the various powers of witches and sorcerers, and

---

[18]See mainly Part IV, Chs. 10–12, pp. 67c–68d.

[19]Part III, Ch. 10, pp. 47c–48d; Part IV, Ch. 20, pp. 72c–73b.

[20]In Part III, Ch. 4 (pp. 46a–c), the author connects the use of holy names with
necromancy, thus proving that these names evoke souls that can reveal hidden
truths; a detailed discussion of the powers of such names is found in Part III,
Ch. 26 (pp. 61c–62d), which is followed by an explanation of how evil and demonic names can reveal true information (pp. 62c–63b).

[21]This is one of the main points raised by the author, to which he frequently
returns, because of the belief that dreams represent information gathered by the
soul when it departs from the body during sleep. The main exposition is in Part
III, Ch. 5, pp. 44a–45d.

[22]Part III, Ch. 9, pp. 46c–47b.

[23]Part III, Ch. 18, pp. 54a b. Other ailments and remedies, including amulets,
serve to prove the same point; see Part III, Ch. 25, pp. 59a–d.

[24]Part III, Ch. 22, pp. 56c–57d. Many other subjects connected with prophecy
are discussed in the same way, like the "dream question" (Part III, Ch. 6, pp.
45c–46b) and speech, especially prophetic speech, found in just-born infants like
Nachman Ketofa, the hero of the famous "prophecy of the child" and similar
Jewish and non-Jewish stories (Part III, Ch. 15, pp. 52c–d).

many other topics are cited, described, and discussed.[25] Large sections are dedicated to the demonstration that demons do exist[26] and that they can have sexual relationships with human beings of the opposite sex (*succubi* and *incubi*),[27] and so forth. The healing powers of amulets and other forms of popular medicine are included in the discussion.[28] Even astrology is cited, and Maimonides' opposition to it is explained away by the author.[29] It seems that Rabbi Manasseh regarded any doubt concerning the veracity of even one supernatural or psychic phenomenon as a threat to the theological integrity of his thesis concerning the eternity of the soul. His encyclopedic erudition and keen interest concerning these phenomena make this part of the book a masterpiece among Hebrew works in this field.

In the opening chapter of the discussion of the demonic and the supernatural, Ben Israel explains his methodical approach. Everything can and should be proved in three ways: by tradition (kabbalah), by logic (*mofet*), and by the senses (*be-hush*).[30] While the first two are traditional methods, according to medieval Jewish philosophy since Saadia Gaon, Ben Israel's insistence on the third reveals something close to scientific inquiry. He analyzes the testimony of various authors who witnessed such phenomena and recorded

---

[25]A detailed description from the *Zohar* of the powers of demons is a basis for many of his remarks concerning witchcraft (Part III, Ch. 27, pp. 60a–c). Witchcraft in general is described in Part III, Ch. 20, pp. 55a–d, and many examples of the deeds of witches and sorcerers are brought out in Part III, Chs. 23 and 24, pp. 58a–59b.

[26]See especially Part III, Ch. 14, pp. 51c–52b. A comparison between demons and human beings, and the meaning of death in each case, is found in Part III, Ch. 13, pp. 51a–b. The systematic explanation of the veracity of the existence of demons is found in Part III, Ch. 12, pp. 49c–50d. A comparison between wonders made by God and those brought about by sorcerers and demons is found in Part III, Ch. 30, pp. 63a–d.

[27]Part III, Ch. 16, pp. 52c–53b.

[28]Part III, Ch. 25, pp. 59a–d. The belief in the evil eye is brought forth in the same manner (Part III, Ch. 27, pp. 61a–b), as well as beliefs such as the victim's blood pointing at the murderer (Part III, Ch. 3, pp. 43c–44b), or the intuitive fear when a criminal approaches (Part III, Ch. 4, pp. 44a–b), and many others.

[29]Part III, Ch. 21, pp. 55c–56d.

[30]Part III, Ch. 1, pp. 42a–b.

them in their works and accepts them as scientific facts; sometimes, though not as a central theme, he also tells of some personal experiences. The factual, scientific, and experimental elements in his discussion do not cause him to neglect logical analysis and traditional support, which is often based on the demonology of the *Zohar* and other rabbinic and kabbalistic sources. Still, *Nishmat Hayyim* should not be regarded as a deliberate step toward experimental science in the history of Jewish thought; it seems that the main reason for the presentation of so much material of this sort is an instinctive awareness of the rhetoric powers of such a presentation. With all respect to logic and tradition, in cases involving the supernatural a trusted witness is the most important proof.

This attitude makes the *Zohar* a central source for the second half of *Nishmat Hayyim*, and its demonology serves to prove the traditional acceptance of such phenomena in Judaism.[31] It is all the more remarkable, therefore, to find that Rabbi Manasseh succeeded in representing such a detailed picture of the demonic world without directly dealing with the problem of the roots and nature of evil in this world. A description of Ben Israel's concept of evil should, therefore, rely more on what he does not say than on what he does.

The unique position of the *Zohar* in the history of Jewish thought (following the teachings of Rabbi Isaac ha-Cohen) is that demonic phenomena are related to and reveal the powers of the *sitra ahra*—the other side or left side, namely the evil element within the divine world. The *Zohar* and all the kabbalists who followed it, including, in this field, Lurianic kabbalah, regarded demons, witches, and their deeds as parts of the cosmic conflict between good and evil that is the worldly reflection of the mythological struggle between God and Satan. Zoharic dualism clearly comes to the foreground when these subjects are described.

In *Nishmat Hayyim* Rabbi Manasseh achieved a remarkable literary and theological aim when he successfully discussed zoharic de-

---

[31]The author often accompanies the quotations from the *Zohar* with a line of praise; see, for instance, Part II, Ch. 29, pp. 40d–41a; Part III, Ch. 27, p. 60c.

monology for dozens of pages without any reference to zoharic dualism. The term *sitra ahra* is hardly mentioned, and, when it does appear, it is made into a harmless synonym for a demon or the evil inclination of man. Using a dualistic main source, Ben Israel presents a nondualistic picture. For him, supernatural and demonic phenomena are part of nature, and when the reason for their existence has to be mentioned—which happens very seldom—it is said that they reflect God's greatness by demonstrating the independence of the soul, thus confirming the author's main thesis. Evil in this world is explained as resulting from the human *yetzer hara*, the inclination toward evil, which is necessary in order to enable man to choose between good and evil and achieve, if he chooses correctly, his religious aims after death. There is no place in this system for any dualistic element, either in this world or in the divine realm. This is an extensive picture of a demonic world—without a devil.[32] There is no conception of a uniting force that governs all these phenomena, so that there is no possibility of a larger theological significance of the demonic beyond proving the nature of the soul or some other very limited benevolent theological aim.

Rabbi Manasseh ben Israel, when presenting a detailed description of the powers of evil, is completely satisfied within the framework of the Cordoverian system according to which "no evil descends from heaven." He goes even further by questioning the evil nature of many of these phenomena. In this sense, *Nishmat Hayyim* is probably the most impressive demonstration of the negation of the zoharic doctrine of evil, and, like Cordovero, it relies directly upon the *Zohar* itself. The *Zohar* is a Platonic, anti-Aristotelian source, which proves, both as an expression of ancient, sacred tradition and as a body of factual observations, that Judaism has always been Platonic in its conception of the soul.

---

[32]When the author uses the term "Satan" (usually when following his sources), the reference is to nothing more than a demon or the manifestation of the evil *yetzer* or a prosecuting angel. See, for instance, Part III, Ch. 27, pp. 60c–61b.

IV

The absence of the zoharic concept of evil from Ben Israel's *Nishmat Hayyim* is not the only element missing in his book from the most basic zoharic symbolism. There is almost no trace in this work of the dualism of male and female that holds a central position in the intensely sexual system of symbols developed in the *Zohar*; nor do we find any trace of zoharic messianism. These two elements are present in the zoharic treatment of the soul, for the structure of the soul reflects the structure of the divine world according to the *Zohar*, which makes sexual symbolism relevant; and zoharic eschatology contains intense messianic elements. When Rabbi Manasseh chose his quotations from the *Zohar*, he deliberately neglected any use of these symbols. We can even go further and state that the zoharic system of the *sefirot* and the multiple mythological powers within the Godhead are completely absent from Ben Israel's presentation.

Nishmat Hayyim is in no way a kabbalistic work, for the key symbols that the kabbalists employ in their descriptions of the created world, as well as of the Creator, are deliberately and consistently neglected. Ben Israel presents in this work a curious attitude of nonkabbalistic kabbalism—accepting the kabbalah as a revelation of ancient divine truth, while completely disregarding the contents of this truth, save for the few elements of demonology and psychology needed directly for this thesis. This is no accident, for Ben Israel conclusively proves in his careful and systematic use of a variety of sources that he is capable of understanding and analyzing ancient works in an exemplary manner. He takes from the *Zohar* only what he wants and needs and disregards the rest, which is the essence of the *Zohar*. If he were critical of the zoharic mystical and mythological worldview, he could have omitted the many expressions of reverence and dependence on the *Zohar* found in *Nishmat Hayyim*. It seems that the *Zohar*, like the Bible, became, in the culture to which Rabbi Manasseh belonged, the kind of book from which one chooses only those quotations that serve one's purpose; but, unlike the Bible, one does not have to explain the contradictions, real or apparent, between one's presentation and other verses.

With the *Zohar* this is not necessary; it is legitimate to utilize whatever seems to be suitable without commenting on the omissions. The *Zohar* was regarded as a source for positive reliance when possible, but disregarded when a possibility of a conflict existed.

Nishmat Hayyim was written when the impact of Lurianic kabbalah was reaching its zenith and when the Sabbatian crisis was approaching. There is no reference in *Nishmat Hayyim* to Lurianic theology,[33] thus we cannot know whether Rabbi Manasseh was even aware of the existence of this new mythological system, which also included a very detailed concept of psychology. It is possible to surmise that even if Rabbi Manasseh knew something of Lurianic theology, he would have disregarded it completely, as he did the main ideas of zoharic mystical symbolism.

Rabbi Manasseh ben Israel's concept of evil can be seen as the direct continuation of the mainstream attitude of the kabbalists and nonkabbalists of the sixteenth century, excluding the emerging messianic mythology that was closely connected with the theological dualism of Rabbi Abraham ha-Levi and others. He goes one step further and, together with the neglect of the zoharic dualistic symbolism, also disregards zoharic sexual and messianic symbolism, an attitude in which he is not alone. But the result of this process seems to be the abolishment of the kabbalistic *sefirot* symbolism as a whole, thus severing any connection to the kabbalah as such and converting the *Zohar* into a treasury of ancient quotations to be used in an arbitrary fashion.

Each of these steps carried Ben Israel, and others like him, farther away from the dominant cultural trends in Jewish thought in the seventeenth century. If Rabbi Manasseh's attitude had been prevalent, Sabbatianism would not have been possible. Nathan of

---

[33]Several times the author quotes stories from Luria's Safed, as they were presented in the letters of Shlomoh Shlumil of Dreznitz. See, for instance, Part III, Ch. 7, pp. 46a–c, where the source is clearly identified. There are some references in the book to the kabbalistic works of Luria's disciples (for instance, *Sefer ha-Kavanot*, Part IV, Ch. 13, p. 69b), but no reference to the basic idea and terminology of the Lurianic kabbalah is found.

Gaza's message to the Jewish world, which transformed the history of Jewish thought in 1665 and 1666, was based completely on the intensified symbolism concerning the powers of evil, the sexual divergence in the divine world, and the messianic mythology that Luria developed on a zoharic basis. Sabbatian theology can be viewed as a further intensification of elements from these fields found in the *Zohar* and developed in Lurianic kabbalah, to which the Sabbatian thinkers added another extreme dimension. While the process leading from the *Zohar*, through Luria, to Nathan of Gaza and Michael Cardozo is one in which there is more dualistic symbolism, more sexual symbolism, and more messianic mythology, Rabbi Manasseh ben Israel and others like him were leading in the opposite direction, even reaching a breakaway point from the most basic kabbalistic symbols.

The history of the second half of the seventeenth century proved that Jewish thought and culture were not following the direction prescribed in *Nishmat Hayyim*, but rather the opposite. The slow process of the demythologizing of the *Zohar*'s symbolism, which began in the fourteenth century, was reversed by Luria, and the appearance of the Sabbatian movement was the result of the victory of Luria's dualistic mythology, which served as a basis for Sabbatian theology.

V

A final note is necessary concerning the relationship between *Nishmat Hayyim* and eighteenth-century Jewish Enlightenment. Many characteristics of this work seem to be indicative of the approaching Enlightenment: the equal use of Jewish and non-Jewish sources, the tolerant attitude toward the works of Christians and Muslims, the intensive study of classical and other non-Hebrew works, the scientific attitude and search for factual confirmation of a thesis, and several other such elements. Of course, the very use of the *Zohar* is unimaginable in a work written during the eighteenth-century Enlightenment, but, as we have shown, the process of minimizing the impact of kabbalistic symbolism, if not of the kabbalistic text, turned *Nishmat Hayyim* into a non-kabbalistic work.

However, *Nishmat Hayyim* cannot be regarded as an "Englightenment" work, or even as one leading toward the same cultural atmosphere that prevailed among the teachers of the Enlightenment. One basic and important difference sets it apart and makes *Nishmat Hayyim* a typical seventeenth-century or earlier Jewish work, and that is its attitude toward non-Jewish sources.

Rabbi Manasseh ben Israel declares several times in this work, both generally and concerning specific details and specific works, that the non-Jewish sources are important because they retain lost Jewish sources. The old medieval belief—found in the writings of some of the philosophers and developed further by Jewish scholars of the Renaissance, especially in Italy—that the Greek philosophers were students of the Jewish kings and prophets is the dominant motive behind Ben Israel's extensive use of non-Jewish sources.[34] He had no doubt that Plato had the true explanation of the essence of the soul, but he had no doubt either that Plato received it from King Solomon. According to Ben Israel, everything that is true in the works of non-Jewish scholars, including that of the Church fathers, comes from Jewish traditions that were not preserved in their original Hebrew version. This attitude enables Rabbi Manasseh to treat the works of Plato and the pagan, Christian, and Muslim neo-Platonists as members of the same school, one that includes the Bible itself, the *Zohar*, the talmudic and midrashic traditions, and the works of Jewish neo-Platonists.

---

[34]In the conclusion of the introduction to his book, after explaining his use of non-Jewish sources (see note 12), the author states:

> You will see throughout this work that in every place where I shall mention their [i.e., the non-Jewish scholars] names or their language [i.e., quotations], it is my intention to show how they had received most of their knowledge concerning divine things from our ancients, and that was their basis and proof. Sometimes I use their words because they have accidentally spoken in the correct way intended by Scriptures. Thank God, I have not studied non-Jewish scholarship consistently for its own sake, but have studied the works of the Kabbalists, who knew everything that is precious.

Similar declarations, supported by specific examples, abound throughout the book.

This belief is essentially different from that of the scholars of the Jewish Enlightenment, who regarded non-Jewish methods, scholarship, and sources as different from the Jewish ones and as realms of culture to which the Jews must adapt while changing their own culture. Ben Israel is as far from such a position as the *Zohar* or Luria were, believing vehemently in the universal superiority of Jewish culture. Thus, while adapting some of the external elements of non-Jewish culture, Rabbi Manasseh ben Israel is no closer to the spiritual world of the Enlightenment than any other medieval Jewish thinker.

EIGHTEEN

Samael and the Problem
of Jewish Gnosticism

I

It was Alexander Altmann, in several of his studies, who introduced into Jewish scholarship the problem of the relationship between Jewish and gnostic ideas and texts in a modern, unbiased way.[1] Before him, for nearly a century, in discussions of this sub-

---

[1] See especially his articles: "The Gnostic Background of the Rabbinic Adam Legends," in his *Essays in Jewish Intellectual History*, Hanover, NH: University Press of New England 1981, pp. 1–16; "A Note on the Rabbinic Doctrine of Creation," in his *Studies in Religious Philosophy and Mysticism*, London: Routledge & Kegan Paul 1969, pp. 128–139. Altmann's studies belong to a scholarly tradition that is expressed, for instance, in M. Friedläander, *Der Vorchristliche jüdische Gnosticismus*, Göttingen: Dandenhoef & Ruprecht 1898, and was followed to some extent by Saul Lieberman, in his interpretation of the Ben Azzai narratives in the Tosefta; see his *Tosefta ki-Feshuta, Hagiga*, New York: The Jewish Theological Seminary 1962, pp. 1292–1295. For a more recent examination of rabbinic sources in this fashion, see B. A. Pearson, *Gnosticism, Judaism and Egyptian Christianity*, Minneapolis: Fortress Press 1990.

ject, following Heinrich Graetz's *Gnosticismus und Judentum*,[2] the analysis of this relationship was dominated by prejudice and preconceptions concerning the destructive and heretical nature of gnosticism. Altmann expressed a much more balanced view, influenced, to some extent, by Scholem's contributions to this subject.

The place of Samael in Jewish traditional, esoteric, and mystical literature is relevant to the more general problem, because, unlike other parallels between Judaism and gnosticism, in this case we have several historical facts that can serve as a good starting point for any analysis. The highly speculative nature of the discussion of some common motifs in Jewish and gnostic concepts can be avoided, and historical analysis can proceed on relatively firm ground.[3]

The subject of Samael is indicative and meaningful because there is no doubt that in postzoharic Hebrew literature and thought this became the most prominent and significant name of the devil. It did not remain confined within the esoteric literature of the kabbalah, but became dominant in folklore and folktales, and was integrated into everyday language. Indeed, Samael joined the tetragrammaton itself in becoming a name the pronunciation of which is forbidden; its first two letters, *samech-mem*, became the colloquial reference to the devil, so that the utterance of the full name would not invoke him and put the speaker in danger. On the other hand, its place in gnostic literature is clear and his presence unambiguous. Therefore, this is one of the uncontroversial connections between the Jewish esoteric tradition and gnosticism. An examination of the context in which Samael was integrated into medieval Jewish texts can, therefore, reveal at least one aspect of the relationship between Jewish thought and gnosticism.

The development of the concept of Samael in Jewish tradition can be divided into several stages, the earliest of which was its use in the pseudepigrapha of the Second Temple period. This is followed

---

[2]Krotoschin, 1846. A photocopied edition was published in 1971: Richmond, England: Gregg.
[3]For a survey of the attitudes toward the gnostic element in Jewish mysticism, see J. Dan, "Jewish Gnosticism?" *Jewish Studies Quarterly* 2 (1995), pp. 309–328.

by its integration in midrashic literature and in the texts of Hechalot and Merkavah mysticism. These sources served as a basis for its various meanings in early medieval midrashic literature (especially the Pirkey de-Rabbi Eliezer), and in early kabbalistic works of the late twelfth century and the thirteenth.

Samael first appears in Jewish apocryphal literature during the Second Temple period and immediately after its destruction.[4] The first reference to him may be found in the Book of Enoch,[5] and if it was indeed part of the Enoch tradition,[6] it spread from there to other treatises of ancient Jewish pseudepigrapha, especially the Greek Baruch and the Ascension of Isaiah. While many details are still obscure, it can be stated with confidence that before the emergence of gnostic literature in the second century on the one hand, and rabbinic literature on the other, Samael was known to be the dominant evil figure in the story of the Garden of Eden, connected with the temptation of the snake, and associated with the narrative of the angelic rebellion against God that developed from the story of giants in Genesis 6. The Greek book of Baruch, which is often regarded as including influences from Egyptian magical texts and even

---

[4] A brief survey of the history of Samael is found in G. Scholem's article in the Encyclopedia Judaica, vol. 14, pp. 719–720; reprinted in his Kabbalah, Jerusalem: Keter 1974, pp. 385–389, and bibliography there. I have been assisted in this study by two M.A. dissertations on the subject, one by Idit Pintel (Jerusalem 1981), and one by Claudia Rohrbacher-Sticker (Berlin 1991).

[5] F. Martin, Le Livre d'Henoch, Paris: Letouzey et Ane 1906, p. 12; Charles, Apocrypha and Pseudepigrapha of the Old Testament vol. II, Oxford: Clarendon 1913, pp. 164, 167, 191; A. Kahana, Ha-Sefarim ha-Hizonim I, Tel Aviv 1937, pp. 21, 26, 31, 38, 63; A. Lods, Le Livre d'Enoch, Paris: E. Leroux 1892, pp. XXXI, XLVI; S. Hartum, Ha-Sefarim ha-Hizonim, vol. I, Tel Aviv: Yavneh 1967, pp. 16–17, 34–35. See also I. Levi (in a book review) REJ 1897, pp. 156–157; and see note 6.

[6] This cannot be taken for granted because of the many variants in the versions of the work that have reached us. The name usually identified as Samael appears in forms like Semiel, Sammane, Samiel, Samsapeel, Satariel, etc. Recent discoveries and research have not made the presence of Samael in Enoch I or II more probable. The Aramaic sections published by J. T. Milik, The Book of Enoch: Aramaic Fragments of Qumran Cave 4, Oxford: Clarendon Press 1976, do not include his name. See also J. H. Charlesworth, The Old Testament Pseudepigrapha, vol. I, London: Darton, Longman & Todd 1983, p. 15.

gnostic ones,[7] describes Samael as planting the Tree of Knowledge (which is identified as a grapevine); this caused divine anger, which resulted in his banishment. Because of his envy, he seduced Adam into sin. This text includes also the depiction of Samael as assuming the form of the snake, and also the traditional rabbinic legend of the diminution of the moon because of its opposition to its place in creation.[8] This text is undoubtedly a central source for some of the motifs that were introduced into Hebrew texts centuries later in the *Pirkey de-Rabbi Eliezer*.

Samael is also mentioned in the Ascension of Isaiah,[9] in the description of the first firmament, parallel to the terms Satan and Beliar. It is usual to divide the work between a Christian work and an earlier Jewish work, and this name seems to be included in the Jewish one. These texts clearly indicate that the image of Samael as an evil power is present in the literature that served Jewish thinkers in Late Antiquity and early Christian works in the development of their worldview, as well as their biblical exegesis.

The second stage in the development of the image of Samael is found in the early gnostic sources. Gnostic literature, especially Ofitic gnosticism, used the name Samael as a Semitic name, and usually it was interpreted as being derived from *summa*, a blind power.[10] He is

---

[7]See H. E. Gaylord, "Greek Apocalypse of Baruch," in Charlesworth, *Pseudepigrapha* (see note 6), pp. 653–680 (bibliography on p. 661), Chs. 4, 8–9 (pp. 666–667.) The Slavonic text of this apocalypse has "Sataniel" instead of Samael.

[8]Compare Bavli *Chulin* 60a and *Midrash Konen*, in A. Jellinek, *Beit ha-Midrash* part II, 3rd ed., Tel Aviv: Wahrman 1967, p. 26.

[9]G. H. Box, *The Apocalypse of Abraham and the Ascension of Isaiah*, New York: Macmillan 1919, p. XLIII; E. Tisserand, *Ascension d'Isaie*, Paris: Letouzey et Ane 1909, pp. 42–56; R. H. Charles, *The Ascension of Isaiah*, London: Adam and Black 1900, pp. 13, 15–16, 41–43; M. A. Knibb, "Martyrdom and Ascension of Isaiah, in Charlesworth, *Pseudepigrapha*, vol. II (1985), pp. 151, 156–157, 164.

[10]The description of Samael as blind is current in Hebrew medieval sources, especially in the Treatise on the Emanations on the Left by Rabbi Isaac ha-Cohen (see below). It is surprising, however, that Gershom Scholem deduced from this that the medieval kabbalists had access to ancient gnostic sources that utilized this motif. See his *Origins of the Kabbalah*, trans. A. Arkush, ed. R. I. Zwi Werblowsky, Princeton, NJ: Princeton University Press 1986, p. 295, note 190. It

a part of the list of Hebrew names, most of them biblical divine names, that are associated with the evil creator, Yaldabaoth.[11] Among the gnostic references to evil and to Samael, one of the more relevant is the description of the figure of Gamaliel in the Gospel to the Egyptians, a treatise found in the Nag Hammadi library.[12] The use of such a term for a power of evil can be explained as the result of the Jewish tradition that the snake, before it was cursed following the temptation of Adam and Eve, had the form of a camel (gamal).[13] As a punishment for his part in this narrative, his legs were cut by God. This is stated also in the PDRA version of the narrative (see below), in which Samael is described as riding this camel-snake and inspiring him in the process of leading Adam to sin. The Coptic text is usually identified with Sethian gnosis, which is one of the most intensely mythical and dualistic among the gnostic sects. This text also includes a reference to "the Great Demon," reminiscent of a sentence concerning Lilith in the Pseudo-Ben Sira narrative.[14] Another relevant reference is found in Epiphanius's *Panarion*,[15] in which the development of the hierarchies in the divine realms is portrayed as the emergence of four Aeons from the womb, which in

---

is hardly surprising that a Hebrew writer intensely interested in this demonic figure would use this interpretation. The only conclusion to be derived from the many references to blindness in sources in a dozen languages, ancient and medieval, is that his name was understood as having a Hebrew (or Aramaic) origin, and its meaning is to be sought in that language.

[11]Concerning Yaldabaoth, the origin of the name, and its significance concerning the relationship between Judaism and gnosticism, see J. Dan, "Yaldabaoth Once More," *Proceedings of the Tenth World Congress of Jewish Studies*, sec. III, vol. I, Jerusalem 1990, pp. 253-259; idem, "Yaldabaoth and the Language of the Gnostics," M. Hengel Festschrift (in press).

[12]Corpus III, treatise 2; translated in J. M. Robinson, *The Nag Hammadi Library in English*, New York: Harper & Row 1977, pp. 199-201.

[13]See below, in the beginning of *Pirkey de-Rabbi Eliezer*, Ch. 3.

[14]The ninth-century Hebrew narrative work, *Alpha-Beta of Ben Sira*, includes a story concerning the relationship between Lilith, Adam's first wife, and an unidentified "great demon." This could have served the later concept of Lilith as Samael's wife. See J. Dan, "Samael, Lilith and the Concept of Evil in Early Kabbalah," *AJS Review* 5 (1980), pp. 15-40.

[15]*Panarion* XXV, 5.1; see the translation in W. Foerster, *Gnosis*, vol. I, p. 317.

their turn produced another fourteen, and created the "right side and the left side," the realms of light and darkness. The concept of the "Emanations on the Left" is one that has clear gnostic anteced-ents (though, obviously, these systems could have evolved indepen-dently).[16] Numerous other references to this figure in gnostic litera-ture clearly demonstrate that the tradition that began in the Jewish texts of the Apocrypha and pseudepigrapha flourished within gnos-ticism and had an impact on its interpretations of biblical narratives.

The third stage in the development of the concept of Samael is found in the early strata of talmudic-midrashic literature, which include very few references to this name, and its place in the Jewish concept of the realm of evil is marginal at best. On the other hand, in later midrashic literature, the frequency of the use of this name increases meaningfully, and by the fifth or sixth century it became one of the most prominent names in the demonic pantheon.

Among the meaningful references to Samael in the classical layer of midrashic literature, his role in the story of the sacrifice of Isaac by Abraham should be emphasized. According to the *Bereshit Rabba* text,[17] it was Samael who tried to influence Abraham not to sacri-fice Isaac, and thus to transgress God's command. This extensive midrash on Genesis does not mention Samael in the context of the Garden of Eden narrative; one may wonder whether his role as tempter in the case of Abraham reflects a possibility that he was involved in the earlier, more successful, situation. This text, how-ever, does not clarify the relationship between Samael and God. It is unclear whether the temptation by Samael was a part of the trial

---

[16]It should be noted that, within the context of the struggle of the Church fa-thers against gnostic dualism, the figure of Satan is sometimes presented as evil only in a temporary context, that is, his rebellious nature is transitory and will be mitigated. Thus, for instance, Origen explains (in an antignostic polemical context) that in the future Satan will lose his evil and will be reintegrated in the spiritual celestial realms after the destruction of material existence. See *De Princ.* III, 6:5; Koetschav, ad. cit, pp. 286–287; J. Meyendorf, *Christ in Eastern Christian Thought*, 1975, p. 54.

[17]Ch. 56, sec. 4; see Theodor-Albeck edition, vol. II, pp. 598–599 and the notes there.

of Abraham by God, or whether he was acting on his own, fulfilling his designated role in creation. There is no reason no believe that Samael has an independent theological status in this midrash.

Much more material concerning Samael is found in later midrashic collections, most of which were composed in the early Middle Ages. In *Exodus Rabba*[18] Rabbi Yossi states: "What are Michael and Samael like? Like a defender and a prosecutor who stand and argue, one speaks and then the other speaks, until they each finish what they have to say . . . thus Michael and Samael stand in front of the *Shechinah*, the Satan speaks against (*mekatreg*) and Michael points out the merits of the people of Israel. . . . " Here Satan and Samael are obviously synonyms, thus making Samael present or implied wherever Satan's role as prosecutor is discussed. Coupling him with Michael, however, makes it impossible to view Samael as anything but a servant of God, holding an unpleasant but necessary position in the celestial court.

The same midrash[19] places Samael in this role as a participant in the drama of the parting of the sea before the people of Israel when they were fleeing from the hosts of the Egyptians. Samael is quoted as saying before God: "These people have been worshipping idols until now, and for them you part the sea?" The text uses the verb *lekatreg* to characterize his action. Samael is just a proper name for the more general "Satan" in such contexts.

The late midrash *Deuteronomy Rabba* has a slightly more accurate description of the relationship between Samael and Satan: Samael was waiting to take the soul of Moses, fulfilling the role of the Angel of Death, and is called "the head of all the satans."[20] This is clearly an attempt to give Samael a specific standing among the powers of evil. It should be remembered, however, that this midrashic collection may have been edited after the *Pirkey de-Rabbi Eliezer*; Samael's designation as "the head of all the satans" may have been influenced by his role as the chief rebellious angel in that midrash.

---

[18]Ch. 18, sec. 5.
[19]Ch. 27, sec. 7.
[20]Ch. 11, sec. 9.

Still, such a description in an influential text at the beginning of
Jewish medieval culture may have helped in singling out Samael as
an important name, superior to other designations of the powers of
evil. There is no doubt that a process can be discerned here in which
the name Samael is in ascendance compared to other terms, while
no meaningful change of function or position can be identified.

Other texts supply more direct information concerning Samael.
In *Midrash Konen*, a late cosmogonical and cosmological work, the
structure of hell, *gehinom*, is described; each section of hell has a ruler
(*sar*). The ruler of the first section is called Kippod (porcupine), the
second is called Nagadsaniel (the name may include the verb *nagad*,
"opposing"), and the third is Samael.[21] Another, somewhat similar,
text describes Samael physically: His height is (a walk of) five hundred years, he is full of eyes of fire, and his functions include those
of the Angel of Death.[22]

Several sources identify Samael as the Prince of Evil Rome. One
of the most powerful descriptions of this role is found in a late
midrash, quoted in the *Yalkut Shimoni*.[23] According to this narrative, the verse in Genesis 25:22 describing the turmoil in Rebecca's
womb before giving birth was the result of Samael's attempt to kill
Jacob in his mother's womb; Jacob was saved by Michael, who
wanted to burn Samael in fire. God's solution for this conflict was
to "put a court between them," that is, to give them specific roles in
His court, so that their conflict would be expressed in the formal-
ized structure of a legal debate. This legend denotes the conflict
between Jacob and Esau, between Israel and Rome, as one between
Samael and Michael, as if the two angelic principals of the two nations tried to kill each other in their mother's womb. There is no
doubt that this legend uses the identification between Samael and
Rome and between Esau and Rome, and at the same time "explains"
the establishment of the divine court in which Samael and Michael

---

[21]*Midrash Konen* (see note 8), p. 30.
[22]*Midrash Alpha Betot*, in *Batey Midrashot*, ed. S. A. Wertheimer, vol. II, Jerusalem: Rav Kook Institute 1995, pp. 431–434.
[23]*Bereshit*, par. *Toledot*, 110. The source was probably *Midrash Avkir*.

have opposing, but necessary, functions. This legend did not hesitate to designate Rebecca as the mother of Rome, and Esau as the
physical presence of Samael in her womb.

An apocalyptic dimension is associated with some expressions
of the identification between Samael and Rome. The Talmud[24] takes
the verse Isaiah 63:1, "who is coming from Edom, red-clothed from
Bosra," which is usually interpreted as a description of the avenging
God, as the Prince of Rome, who is going to "make three mistakes";
this is developed in a medieval midrash, Bereshit Rabbati of Rabbi
Moshe ha-Darshan, into an apocalyptic description in which Samael
plays the major role. It is evident that in this description the concept of Samael is nearly identical to that found in Hechalot Rabbati.

Corresponding to the use of the name in talmudic literature,
Samael became prominent in Hechalot and Merkavah literature. In
Hechalot Rabbati, one of the most intense mystical works in this literature, Samael is portrayed as the Prince of Rome, the enemy and
prosecutor of the Merkavah mystics. Yet his role is clearly that of a
member of the celestial court, obeying divine commands after trying to shape them. He derives his authority from God's decrees,
though as the embodiment of the evil empire he is full of spite and
enmity toward Judaism. No trace can be found in this literature of
Samael's role in the temptation of Adam and Eve, or to his rebellion against God. One of the key scenes in Hechalot Rabbati, which
serves also as a basis for the narrative and poetic versions of the
martyriological legend of the ten martyrs, describes Samael as insisting on the execution of ten sages to absolve the crime of the ten
brothers of Joseph who sold him into slavery. God, according to these
sources, agrees, but puts forward a condition: Samael must agree to
the complete destruction of Rome. In his hatred for Israel, Samael
accepts and sacrifices his domain.[25] A detailed analysis of the role of

---

[24]Bavli Makot 12a.
[25]A detailed edition of all the texts relevant to this narrative has been published
by Gottfried Reeg, Die Geschichte von den Zehn Märtyrern, Tübingen: J.C.B. Mohr
(Siebeck) 1985, and detailed bibliography there. See also J. Dan, "The Origins
and Meaning of the Narrative of the Ten Martyrs," Studies in Literature Presented
to Simon Halkin, Jerusalem: Magnes Press 1973, pp. 15–22.

Samael in this literature cannot be presented here;[26] it is clear, however, that in this literature Samael is the dominant evil power, representing the evil empire of Rome, and a servant of God whose main
purpose is to harm the people of Israel.

The conclusions that can be drawn from this brief survey concerning the early history of Samael in Jewish literature are as follows.

1. The name Samael is a marginal one in the terminology concerning evil in the classical period of the Talmud and Midrash
   in Late Antiquity, the period corresponding to that of the
   texts of *Hechalot* mysticism, especially *Hechalot Rabbati*. It is
   probable, therefore, that the intensification of the identification of Samael with the Prince of Rome, thus increasing his
   evil and centrality in the concept of evil, was the result of
   original usage among these mystics and does not reflect the
   common terminolgy of rabbinic Judaism at that time.

2. During the later period, in which midrashic collections like
   Exodus Rabba, *Deuteronomy Rabba*, *Avkir*, *Konen*, and *Bereshit
   Rabbati* were edited, a process can be discerned in which
   Samael increasingly assumes the functions of other demonic
   powers, like Satan and the Angel of Death. The name Samael
   becomes more common among such terms, and it slowly assumes the position of "the head of all the satans." This process occurred at the same time that the *Pirkey de-Rabbi Eliezer*
   was edited.

3. The roles of Samael in these *midrashim* are: the tempting of
   individual figures (Abraham) or collective ones (Israel) to
   transgress God's commands; serving as the Prince of Rome,
   and thus the archenemy of Israel and a central player in the
   apocalyptic drama; serving as the Angel of Death and looking like this evil entity; identifying with Edom and Esau;
   sometimes trying to harm Israel in a direct, violent way, in
   the womb of Rebecca and when crossing the sea; acting as

---

[26]Such an analysis is included in Claudia Rohrbacher's work (see note 4).

the *kategor* of Israel in the divine court; assuming charge of a portion of hell.

4. The essential characteristic of Samael, the one for which no other name or title but Samael is appropriate, is the association with Rome. In this sense, the field of meanings of Samael in the midrash exceeds, only in a minimal way, that found in *Hechalot Rabbati*.

5. Despite the fact that most—and probably all—of these texts originated in a period in which Samael's presence in gnostic texts has been established, and that there is a process of increase of this figure's centrality in Hebrew texts, no definite gnostic motif can be discerned. The process of Samael's ascendancy in Hebrew texts in no way reflects the influence of particular gnostic myths and ideas.

6. By the beginning of Jewish culture in Christian Europe, Samael had been established as "the head of all the satans" and as the representative of Rome, and therefore also of Christianity. The background of his becoming the most important Hebrew term for a celestial power of evil had been prepared by centuries of development, most probably in an autonomous way, in midrashic literature.

II

The most important text that shaped the figure of Samael in medieval Hebrew culture is the *Pirkey de-Rabbi Eliezer*, Chapter 13. The text reads:

Envy, desire and [the drive for] honor make a person lose his world. The ministering angels said before God: Master of all the universes, "What is man that thou doth regard him . . . man is like a breath" (Psalms 144: 3–4), "Upon Earth there is not his like" Job 41:33). He said to them: In the same way that you praise Me in the celestial realms, he declares My unity in the lower ones. Not only this, but can you stand and call names to all the creatures? They stood and could not. Immediately Adam stood and called names to all the creatures, as it is said

(Genesis 2:20), "and the man gave names to all cattle," etc. When the ministering angels saw that, they said: If we do not conspire to [cause] Adam to commit a sin before his creator, we shall never be able to confront him. And Samael was the great prince in heaven; the holy beasts and the *seraphim* had six wings, Samael had twelve wings. He took his cohort and descended. He observed all the creatures created by God and did not find among them a wise one for making evil like the snake, as it is said: "Now the serpent was more subtle than any other wild creature" (Genesis 3:1). And his image was like that of a camel. He ascended and rode him. The Torah was crying and saying: Samael, it is just now that the world was created, is it time to rebel against the Creator? "Now in the upper realms will ascend the Master of the Universes," "You shall laugh at a horse and his rider." [27] This is like a man who has an evil spirit; all the deeds that he does, does he do it by his own thought? And all the words that he says, does he speak his own mind? All he does and speaks is from the thought of the evil spirit that is over him. In the same way, the snake, all the acts he committed and all the words that he spoke he did not do or speak but from the mind of Samael, and about him the verse says, "in his mind he will drive the wicked" (Proverbs 14:32).

This is like a king who married a woman and made her the sovereign of everything he had, precious stones and jewels. He told her: All I own will be in your hand except this barrel, which is full of scorpions. An old man came to her and asked for vinegar. He said to her: What does the king give you [or: How does the king treat you]? She answered: All he had he gave me except this barrel, which is full of scorpions. He said: But all the jewels[28] of the king are in this barrel, and he did not tell you this only because he wants to marry another woman and give it to her. The king is Adam; the woman is Eve; the old man asking for vinegar is the snake; and about them the verse says: "There the doers of evil have fallen" (Psalms 36:13).

---

[27] Compare Exodus 15:1.
[28] The author uses a Greek term, *kuzmin*, which is used several times in talmudic and midrashic literature for "jewelry."

The snake was debating with himself: If I speak to Adam, I know that he will not listen to me, for it is always difficult to sway man from his opinion. I shall speak to the woman, because her mind is easy, I know that she will listen to me, for women accept [obey] all people, as it is said: silly without knowing anything (Proverbs 9:13). The snake went and asked the woman: Is it true that you are ordered concerning the fruit of this tree? Eve told him: Yes, as it said, "from the fruit of the tree in the garden" (Genesis 3:3). In these words of hers he found an opening to enter and said: This command is nothing but an evil eye [or: stinginess]. For when you eat from it you shall be like God; in the same way that He creates worlds and destroys worlds, so you shall be able to create worlds and destroy worlds. In the same way that He causes death and life, so you shall be able to cause death and life, as it is said: For God knows that the day you eat from it your eyes will be opened. The snake went and touched the tree. It cried and said: Wicked one, do not touch me, as it is said: "The foot of pride will not come to me . . . there fell the workers of wickedness" (Psalms 36:12). The snake then went and told the woman: Here, I have touched the tree and did not die, you should also touch it and shall not die. The woman went and touched the tree. She saw the Angel of Death coming in front of her, and said: Now probably I shall die, and God makes him another woman and gives her to Adam; but I shall make him eat with me; if we die, we shall both die, and if we live, we shall both live. So she took from the fruit of the tree and gave from its fruit to her husband to eat with her, as it is said: "She took from its fruit and ate and gave also to her husband" (Genesis 3:6). When Adam ate from the fruit of the tree he saw himself naked, his eyes were opened and his teeth were dulled. . . .

In the continuation of the story, Samael appears only in the conclusion (Ch. 14), when God punishes the participants in the transgression: He throws Samael and his cohorts from their holy place in heaven, and he cuts the feet of the snake and curses him.

Samael, therefore, is mentioned by name only twice, at the beginning of the story and at its end. He may be present throughout the story as the one who speaks in the voice of the snake, but this is stated only in the beginning and is not repeated in the story it-self, which can be told independently of this element. The one im-portant statement of this narrative concerning Samael is his desig-nation as the head of a celestial rebellion, punished by exile to Earth, an element not found anywhere else in previous talmudic, midrashic, or *Hechalot* and *Merkavah* texts. This rebellion is described as the result of the angels' envy concerning the wisdom of Adam and God's love for him. The Garden of Eden narrative is therefore portrayed as a conspiracy to incite Adam to sin and deprive him of his fa-vored position in the eyes of God. The snake is described as the instrument of Samael and not as an independent actor in this drama.

There can be no doubt that a new dimension has been intro-duced here into the concept of evil in rabbinic tradition. There is, on Earth, an independent power of evil that received its present po-sition as a result of its enmity toward man. The long tradition that describes angelic powers as opponents of the creation of man and of giving the Torah to Israel has been crystallized here in the figure of one power, Samael. There can be no doubt that this text represents, from a Jewish medieval point of view, the most explicit source for any dualistic concept of the universe, creating an image of a celes-tial opponent to God who acts independently against man. Com-bined with the process we have identified in the midrashic material, it is no wonder that in the Middle Ages Samael was regarded as the central, most important name of Satan.

The problem facing us is: Do the innovative elements in the *Pirkey de-Rabbi Eliezer* narrative represent an intrusion of gnostic at-titudes into Jewish tradition? A negative answer is rather obvious. The devil as a fallen celestial power is a concept deeply embedded in Christian tradition, without any need for gnostic myths to ex-plain it. Its roots are easily found in the Apocrypha, and thus it can be described as a Jewish narrative returning to its cultural source. Gnostic writers undoubtedly utilized the same sources, and the de-velopment of Samael in their writings can be regarded as a parallel development to the process found in the Hebrew works. There is no element here that necessitates the assumption that the gnostic branch of this narrative and the Jewish one met again in Late Antiquity or the early Middle Ages to shape the narrative that influenced medieval Jewish concepts of evil.

The common denominator of these stages in the development of the figure of Samael in Hebrew texts (except in non-Hebrew gnostic literature) is that they all appeared in literary sources that do not represent a definite ideology. Samael, in all these cases, is an actor in mythical dramas in the celestial and earthly realms, but his figure is not integrated into a wider, more comprehensive system of cosmology or theology. In the *Pirkey de-Rabbi Eliezer*, his role undoubtedly marks a new departure concerning the concept of evil in Judaism, and he is granted a measure of independence not found in earlier references. Yet this late midrash cannot be characterized as presenting an innovative system of thought in which a new concept of evil serves as an important component. Near the end of this work (Chapter 47), the Yom Kippur service is described, and Samael is presented there in his traditional role of the *kategor*, the one who presents the sins of the people of Israel before the divine court and attempts to incite God to punish them—a role similar to that described in *Hechalot Rabbati* (incidentally, in this text Samael seems to be identified with the biblical Azazel, an identification that had meaningful consequences in the High Middle Ages). The first text in which Samael is integrated into a universal, systematic myth is the Treatise on the Emanations on the Left by Rabbi Isaac ha-Cohen, written in Castile in the second half of the thirteenth century.

In this treatise, which Gershom Scholem sometimes characterized as "gnostic," the basic concepts of kabbalistic dualism were formulated. Rabbi Isaac divided the celestial realms into two symmetrical hierarchies, the right side representing the powers of good and the left side the powers of evil. Both have a common source within the upper divine emanations, but they operate in the universe in two parallel systems of seven emanations. Rabbi Isaac was the first, as far as we know today, to unite all evil phenomena into one hierarchy, including earthly maladies like leprosy and rabies. The various groups of demons originate from different points in this hierarchy. He presented Asmodeus as a lower satanic figure within this system (no previous text presents this figure in connection with

Samael, and some of them describe him as having good characteristics as well as evil ones). His most dramatic new myth, which became dominant in Judaism for many centuries, is that of the couple
ruling the "left side"—Samael and Lilith, who are presented as the
parallel of God and the *Shechinah* on the right side. Thus, an erotic
drama has been introduced in the realm of evil; Rabbi Isaac describes
an "elder Lilith," who is Samael's spouse, and a "young Lilith," who
is the spouse of Asmodeus but is coveted by Samael, causing turmoil in the realms of evil. Lilith is a well-known figure in Hebrew
demonology; talmudic literature portrays her as the first, demonic
spouse of Adam and a rival of Eve, and she is sometimes described
as the mother of demons. For at least a millennium, and probably
much longer, Samael and Lilith played their parts in Jewish beliefs
without ever meeting each other. It was Rabbi Isaac ha-Cohen who
brought them together and made them the main characters in his
dualistic drama.[29]

Rabbi Isaac's myth seems to have had very little influence, even
in his own circle of mystics. It is not found in the writings of his
brother, Rabbi Jacob, and only one follower—Rabbi Moses of Burgos,
who wrote commentaries on most of Rabbi Isaac's works—devoted
a treatise to the subject.[30] It had real influence in the one place that

---

[29]From a purely theological point of view, it is unclear how deep-rooted is the
dualism described by Rabbi Isaac. Some references seem to indicate that the system of the powers of evil on the left side is an equal parallel to the divine *sefirot*,
thus making these powers divine emanations in the full sense of the term, parts
of an evil pleroma. Other references lend themselves to the interpretation that
they belong to the angelic realms, within the created celestial worlds far below
the divine spheres. Dr. A. Farber-Ginat made a strong case for the concept that
this system is indeed a low one, mainly angelic in character. It seems to me that
further study is needed to clarify this problem. The further development of this
myth in the *Zohar*, however, clearly finds evil parallels to the divine *sefirot* themselves. See Farber-Ginat's M.A. thesis, *The Commentary of Rabbi Jacob ha-Cohen
on the Chariot*, Jerusalem 1978.

[30]*Ha-'Amud ha-Semali*, "the Left Pillar," published by Scholem in *Tarbiz*, vol 4
(1933), pp. 207–225. It should be noted that the sources and references that he
uses differ considerably from those of Rabbi Isaac, his teacher. This strongly
suggests that many of these references are pseudepigraphic. Scholem, in one
discussion of this work (*Origins of the Kabbalah*, pp. 293–297), tended to give

really counted—the *Zohar* itself, which was written about a generation after Rabbi Isaac's treatise. Rabbi Moses de Leon, the author of the *Zohar*, used this myth to create the world of the *sitra ahra*— "the other side" (meaning the left side), which became one of the characteristics of kabbalistic writings for several centuries, and made the dualistic attitude a central feature of Jewish mystical thought.

The problem facing us is whether there was an intrusion of gnostic sources between the *Pirkey de-Rabbi Eliezer* and the Treatise on the Emanations on the Left—that is, between the eighth and the thirteenth centuries—that shaped the dualistic tendencies in the kabbalah and made it possible to characterize kabbalistic thought as "gnostic" not only in a typological sense (which is, after all, an arbitrary use by scholars who may or may not like such a usage), but also in a historical sense—that is, the reappearance of ancient sources and ideas, from either a Jewish or a non-Jewish origin, that gave their character to the kabbalistic concept of evil. We have not found, in the ancient references to Samael in Hebrew, any element that necessitates the assumption that gnostic sources, Jewish or Christian, were used. The *Pirkey de-Rabbi Eliezer* reintroduced some of the elements found in the Apocrypha, not in gnostic literature. Did something happen in these five centuries that can explain the introduction of a dualistic myth woven around Samael as the result of a new meeting between medieval Judaism and gnosticism?

It is well known, though often forgotten, that a negative can never be conclusively proved. It is the thesis of this presentation that the development of the figure of Samael in Jewish medieval mystical literature is the result of the development of ancient, known, and non-gnostic sources and the individual creativity of the medieval scholars. The best one can do in presenting a historical analysis is to take into account, and try to exhaust, the information inherent in the sources known to us, and use them to present a picture that reflects the present stage of our knowledge. No one can know if there

---

credence to Rabbi Isaac's claim that he had in his possession ancient texts and traditions. This claim is not supported by any other writer, not even Rabbi Isaac's brother or his disciple, Rabbi Moses of Burgos.

were sources that have not reached us, and certainly no historian can claim knowledge of what is written in nonexistent documents (a mystic, of course, can and does). Historical study never reaches ultimate truth; it can and must present an exhaustive picture of present knowledge, and humbly wait for future discoveries. Adopting this methodological principle, it is possible to show that the development of the figure of Samael can be explained on the basis of internal development and the influence of non-gnostic sources; if there is any similarity to gnostic ideas in the medieval kabbalah concerning Samael, it should be described as typological rather than historical.[31]

Samael was introduced into kabbalistic literature by the author of the first kabbalistic treatise that reached us—the Bahir, written probably in the next-to-last decade of the twelfth century (ca. 1185). The last section of this work, paragraph 200 in Margalioth's edition, is the only extensive quotation found in whole book. The author used many sources, and quoted throughout the work sentences and paragraphs from them; in most cases he adapted and changed them. Paragraph 200 is an exception: It consists of a long quotation, with only few changes, from Chapter 13 of the Pirkey de-Rabbi Eliezer, describing Samael's rebellion and his role in bringing Adam and Eve to sin.

Sefer ha-Bahir was keenly interested in the problem of evil, and several sections are dedicated to the subject.[32] In the beginning of the book is a discussion concerning the relationship between good and evil in the process of the creation and divine providence for the universe, and it seems that a link is formed, in a neo-Platonic fashion, between matter and spirit on the one hand and good and evil on the other. In other sections, the figure of Satan represents temptation and threat posed to Moses and the people of Israel. In several sections new terminology is introduced to describe evil; it constitutes

---

[31]I use the term "typological" where some would use "phenomenological"; this is because "phenomenological" has been so much used and abused in recent writing that it has lost its power to clarify.

[32]They have been analyzed by Scholem, Origins of the Kabbalah, pp. 147–151 et passim; and compare his discussion of the concept of evil in the kabbalah, in On the Mystical Shape of the Godhead, New York: Schocken 1991, pp. 56–86.

the left hand of God, and its fingers are the evil emissaries that spread evil among men. Evil is identified with the left and with the north (the picture presented in *Pirkey de-Rabbi Eliezer* concerning the unfinished northern corner of the universe from which demons and troubles enter the world may have had some influence). Section 199 can be seen as presenting a proximity, not an identity, between femininity and evil. The only name used for the devil in the body of the book is Satan; Samael is found only in the last section, in the quotation from the Midrash.

On a minimal level, no meaningful development of the figure of Samael is found in the *Bahir*; it follows the Midrash without any addition. Yet the very fact that this description of the origin of evil in the Garden of Eden was included in the *Bahir* gave that myth legitimation and a meaningful presence in the emerging schools of kabbalists in Europe. While the author does not identify Samael as the evil element in other sections of the book, his readers may be justified in doing so. From that time onward, users of the *Bahir* could relate the variegated discussion of evil in the *Bahir* to the figure of Samael. One particular contribution in this direction is found in the *Bahir*'s next-to-last section, no. 199, which immediately precedes the quotation from the PDRA. Here the author identifies femininity with openness to evil suggestions and seduction; this is his direct contribution to the elucidation of the Garden of Eden narrative. Though no definite erotic element is introduced here, a suggestion that there could be such a dimension in the relationship between humanity and evil is implied, and could be used by later interpreters of these passages.

The kabbalistic treatments of the subject of evil immediately following the *Bahir*, in the schools of Provence and Gerona, are remarkable in their neglect of the theological problem of the autonomy and independence of evil on the theological level, and the absence of speculations concerning Samael on the mythical level. Rabbi Isaac the Blind did not discuss this problem in his Commentary on the *Sefer Yezira*, despite the existence of some phrases in this work that may suggest a good-evil dualism. He did refer to it in the context of the historical evil of Amalek, to which he attributed celestial origins.[33] The one detailed discussion of the subject is found in a brief text, The Secret of the Tree of Knowledge, which Scholem identified and published as a work by Rabbi Ezra ben Shlomo of Gerona.[34] This work seems to be a refutation of the mythical suggestions of the *Bahir* concerning the position of evil within God, and an insistence that evil is the result of Adam's deeds, rather than any intrinsic duality within God or the universe. The figure of Samael is not developed in this treatment of the ancient narrative. This treatise seems to represent a denial of the dualistic tendencies inherent in the *Bahir*, and an adherence to the rationalistic concept that evil is an absence rather than a mythical figure.

The major change in this situation and the direct link between the *Bahir* and the intense myth of Rabbi Isaac can be identified in the works of Rabbi Moses ben Nachman (Nachmanides). In his Commentary on the Torah and other works, an intensification of the significance of the powers of evil can be discerned on several levels. His profound interest in demons and other supernatural phenomena can be understood in the context of the controversy against rationalism, especially concerning the creation of the world and the nature of miracles. Nachmanides viewed Aristotelian rationalism as one that adopted a scientific view of the universe, denying the existence of nontangible spiritual phenomena that defy the laws of nature. His defense of the biblical concept of creation as a supreme miracle, and of miracles as divine interventions in the universe, led him to use the realms of demons, magic, and witchcraft as examples of the universe's expression of its independence from the tyranny of the laws of nature.[35]

---

[33]See the analysis of that paragraph in H. Padaya, "Pegam ve-Tikkun shel ha-Elohut be-Kabbalat Rabbi Yizhak Sagi Nahor," *Proceedings of the Second International Conference on the History of Jewish Mysticism: The Beginnings of Jewish Mysticism in Europe*, ed. J. Dan, Jerusalem 1987, pp. 157–286.

[34]In his essay on "Good and Evil in the Kabbalah," in *On the Mystical Shape of the Godhead*, pp. 65–68.

[35]A similar phenomenon can be found in Ashkenazi Hasidic literature, which used demonic phenomena to illustrate the miraculous nature of divine revelation. In this context they described and analyzed in depth a particular magical practice, that of the demons of oil. See in detail J. Dan, "Sarey Kos ve-Sarey Bohen,"

Nachmanides' contribution to the theological problem of the position of the powers of evil and, at the same time, the meaning of Samael can be found in his discussion of the biblical commandment concerning the sending of a goat (*seir*) to the desert to Azazel on Yom Kippur.[36] This biblical text (Leviticus 16) is extremely suggestive concerning the independence of the powers of evil, and has been recognized as such in midrashic literature, because the verse demands that one goat be sacrificed to God and one sent to Azazel. Nachmanides does not completely deny these dualistic implications, and his main contribution to our subject is the identification of Azazel with Samael. He quotes a long paragraph from the *Pirkey de-Rabbi Eliezer* (Chapter 46), the description of Samael receiving the goat as a bribe on the Day of Atonement; then he responds to the possible interpretation of that passage as indicating idolatrous sacrifice, and says:

The Torah has completely forbidden the acceptance (of idols) as deities and all worship of them, but the Holy One blessed be He commanded that on the Day of Atonement we send a goat to the desert—to the prince in charge in the places of desolation. It (the *seir*) is appropriate, because he is its master, and from the emanation of his power emerge drought and desolation, for he is the source of the stars of the sword and bloodshed and wars and conflicts and injuries and inflictions and separation and destruction. In general he is the soul of the sphere of Mars, and his share among the nations is Esau, who is a people that inherited the sword and wars; and from among the animals his lot is the goats and the *seirim*, and in his lot are also the demons who are called *mazikim* in the language of our sages, and in the language of scriptures *seirim*, for he and his people are called *Seir*. And the meaning of the sending of the

Tarbiz 32 (1963), pp. 359–369. This analogy had a meaningful influence on Rabbi Isaac ha-Cohen, who ignored the analogical nature of the Hasidim's discussions and actually connected the "realm of demons" and the "realm of prophecy."
[36]For a detailed analysis of this passage in Nachmanides' Commentary, see my study "Nachmanides and the Concept of Evil in the Kabbalah," *Proceedings of the Girona Conference on Nachmanides* (1994) pp. 161–179.

goat is not that it is a sacrifice that we offer to him, but that
our only intention is to obey the will of our Creator who commanded us.[37] (With modifications.)

The whole paragraph is an explanation of Samael's name and
function, as the author declares in the beginning of this discussion
where he summarized the quotation from the *Pirkey de-Rabbi Eliezer*.
The traditional elements in this description are the identification of
Samael with Esau and with the territory in which the sons of Esau
settled, Seir. This name serves to connect the goat that is sent to
the desert—called *seir*—with the Prince of Esau, Samael. As Esau also
represents Rome, the domain of Samael includes all the military
characteristics of Esau-Edom-Rome. Thus Samael is conceived as the
celestial principle that is in charge of everything connected with war,
bloodshed, and destruction. Its position in the universe is defined
in astrological terms, as the moving force ("soul") of the sphere of
Mars, the red (*adom*, Edom) star. He is the source of the suffering
that emanates from that sphere and the cause of desolation and the
inflictions on the inhabitants of Earth. He is also the Prince who
rules all the demons, and this is proved by the linguistic identification of *seirim*, the biblical term, with *mazikim*, the rabbinic term,
both indicating *sheydim*, demons.

This is a description of Samael and the realm of evil that is
radically different from the ones found in the *Bahir* and in the works
of other Gerona kabbalists. His domains include a celestial region,
from which his power emanates down to Earth. The demons are his
subjects and all evil that people do on Earth is the result of his influence. It cannot be doubted that this formulation assisted Rabbi
Isaac ha-Cohen in his much more detailed description of the "emanation on the left." It should be noted that Samael is portrayed by
Nachmanides as a source of emanation (*me-azilut koho*), something
that is absent from any previous description of this power. "Emana-

---

[37]C. B. Chevel, Ramban's *Commentary on the Torah*, vol. III, New York: Shilo
1974, pp. 217–222 (in the original Hebrew ed., Jerusalem: Rav Kook Institute 1964,
vol. II, p. 89).

tion" should not be understood in this context as indicating divine emanation in the kabbalistic sense; it can be read as a reference to the influence of the planets, in the astrological meaning of the term. Samael, however, is clearly depicted as a spiritual entity; it is not identified with the planet Mars, but with the "soul" of the sphere, the spiritual driving-force inherent in it.

The stages of the development of the concept of Samael between the beginning of the Middle Ages and the High Middle Ages can be presented as follows.

1. Samael is described as the chief rebel against God and the power responsible for the sins of Adam and Eve in the Garden of Eden, speaking from the mouth of the snake, in the *Pirkey de-Rabbi Eliezer*. Samael was conceived as an independent evil power once this midrash became known.

2. The *Bahir* uses this midrash and other sources, giving legitimacy to the inclusion of this material in the speculation of the kabbalists. The author, however, does not use Samael's name when describing the powers of evil in his original formulations.

3. The early Gerona kabbalists modify the *Bahir*'s views and present no further development of Samael's powers.

4. Nachmanides presents Samael as the lord of all demons, the power responsible for bloodshed and destruction, and connects him with the celestial realm as "the soul of the sphere of Mars," from which evil emanates to Earth.

5. Rabbi Isaac ha-Cohen in Castile utilizes Nachmanides' statements when he creates the elaborate myth of Samael and Lilith as the governing powers of the "emanation on the left."

6. The author of the *Zohar* utilizes the myth presented in Rabbi Isaac's works to create the elaborate kabbalistic myth of evil.

The common denominator of all these stages is that we do not have to postulate the intrusion of gnostic elements in any of them. It is most clear in Nachmanides' presentation that his main addition to previous characteristics of Samael is taken from an astrological context rather than a gnostic one. Despite a radical development

in the concept of Samael in Hebrew writings, during the five hundred years that separate the late midrash from Nachmanides, there
is no indication of any gnostic element being utilized in this process. There is no reason to suppose that decades later Rabbi Isaac
ha-Cohen suddenly discovered a whole library of gnostic sources that
no one, either in his own time or before or after, was aware of or
used in his speculations. The history of Samael in Jewish literature
and mystical speculations is a meaningful example of the possibility
of parallel development of an ancient Jewish concept independently
in ancient gnosticism and in medieval Judaism, without any further
interaction beyond their common source in the Apocrypha.

NINETEEN

Nachmanides and the Development of the Concept of Evil in the Kabbalah

I

The golden age of the kabbalah in Spain, in the second half of the thirteenth century and the beginning of the fourteenth, mainly in Castile, is the period in which the kabbalistic concept of evil took shape and was expressed in the most forceful manner. The *Zohar* presented a dualistic concept of existence,[1] in which a continuous struggle between the divine powers of goodness and those of the evil powers, the *sitra ahra*, "the Other Side" (that is, the left side), characterizes and decides the fate not only of man, but also that of the divine realm. The lowest part of the divine world, the feminine divine power, the *Shechinah*, is described as the main battleground

---

[1]See G. Scholem, "Good and Evil in the Kabbalah," in his *On The Mystical Shape of the Godhead*, New York: Schocken 1991, pp. 56–86; I. Tishby, *The Wisdom of the Zohar*, vol. I, Oxford: Oxford University Press 1989; idem, "Mythological versus Systematic Trends in Kabbalah," in J. Dan, ed., *Binah*, vol. II, *Studies in Jewish Thought*, New York; Praeger 1989, pp. 121-130.

between good and evil. The intense zoharic myth on this subject, developed in rich, suggestive images, had great impact on subsequent Jewish mysticism throughout the ages.[2] A further intensification of this dualistic myth marks the modern stage in the history of Jewish mysticism, in the teachings of Rabbi Isaac Luria in Safed in the sixteenth century.[3] For nearly seven hundred years, the dualistic concept of evil has characterized Jewish mysticism in various degrees of intensity. The problem of the origins of this concept and the ways in which it developed is, therefore, a most meaningful one in any attempt to understand the development of Jewish mysticism and Jewish thought. This study is dedicated to an attempt to identify the role of Moses ben Nachman in Gerona in this enormous process in the first half of the thirteenth century.

There can be very little doubt concerning the direct sources from which the author of the *Zohar* derived many of the elements that combined to develop his myth of the *sitra ahra*: These were the writings of Rabbi Isaac ben Jacob ha-Cohen, who flourished in Castile in the second half of the thirteenth century, and who was the author of the paramount work of kabbalistic dualism: the Treatise on the Emanations on the Left, published by Gershom Scholem nearly seventy years ago.[4] In this work, Rabbi Isaac presented a

---

[2]For a review of later developments, see J. Dan, "Gnostic and Kabbalistic Dualism," in *Binah*, vol. III, *Studies in Jewish Intellectual History in the Middle Ages*, New York: Praeger 1994, pp. 19–34; and compare idem, "The Concept of Evil in 16th Century Jewish Thought," in I. Twersky, B. Septimus, eds., *Jewish Thought in the Sixteenth Century*, Cambridge, MA: Harvard University Press 1987, pp. 63–76.

[3]A detailed description of this chapter in the history of Jewish concepts of evil is found in I. Tishby, *Torat ha-Ra veha-Kelipah be-Kabbalat ha-Ari*, Jerusalem: Schocken 1942.

[4]*Maamar al ha-Azilut ha-Semalit*, published in a collection of works by Rabbi Isaac and his brother, Rabbi Jacob ha-Cohen, in *Madaey ha-Yahadut*, vol. II (1927), pp. 244–264. An English translation of this treatise is found in J. Dan and R. Kiener, *The Early Kabbalah*, New York: Paulist Press 1986, pp. 165–182. It should be noted that in Scholem's study the relationship between Rabbi Isaac ha-Cohen and the *Zohar* was not stated clearly, because at that time Scholem had not yet arrived at a definite conclusion concerning the time in which the *Zohar* was composed, so that the possibility that Rabbi Isaac was influenced by the *Zohar*, not vice

scheme of a hierarchy of evil powers that corresponds to the holy system of the divine powers, the *sefirot*, on the right side. The leader of the powers of evil is Samael,[5] and he is supported by his feminine counterpart, Lilith.[6]

Rabbi Isaac ha-Cohen was not supported by the group of the kabbalists to which he belonged when he developed his unique concept of evil. The writings of his father, Rabbi Jacob, do not include it, and neither do those of his brother, also named Rabbi Jacob.[7] The only kabbalist from this circle who deals with this subject was Rabbi Isaac's disciple, Rabbi Moses of Burgos, who wrote commentaries on his teacher's works. His treatise, *Ha-Amud ha-Semali* (The Pillar of the Left), is based on Rabbi Isaac's treatise, though in many respects it is different from the earlier work.[8]

Rabbi Isaac's work is a model of kabbalistic pseudepigraphy. He cites dozens of sources and traditions, most of which are completely

---

versa, was regarded as probable. Only later did Scholem prove conclusively that the *Zohar* was written in the end of the thirteenth century, and that the works of the Cohen brothers from Castile were among its major sources. See J. Dan, *Gershom Scholem and the Mystical Dimension in Jewish History*, New York: New York University Press 1987, pp. 203–204 et passim.

[5]Concerning the history of Samael in the Apocrypha and pseudepigrapha, in talmudic and midrashic literature, and in the kabbalah, see G. Scholem, *Kabbalah*, Jerusalem: Keter 1974, pp. 385–389, and bibliography there. See also J. Dan, "Samael and the Problem of Jewish Gnosticism."

[6]This is the first time that the pair of Samael and Lilith is presented as a couple; both of them existed for many centuries—even millennia—in Jewish culture, yet Rabbi Isaac was the first to describe them as connected to each other. See J. Dan, "Samael, Lilith and the Concept of Evil in Early Kabbalah," *AJS Review* V (1980), pp. 17–40. There is another text in which this connection is found, but it is undated, and probably is the result of the influence of the Treatise on the Emanations on the Left. See G. Scholem, "Sidrey Shimusha Raba," *Tarbiz* 16 (1945), pp. 196–209.

[7]Compare D. Abrams, *The Book of Illumination of Rabbi Jacob ben Jacob ha-Kohen*, Ph.D. thesis, New York University 1993 (UMI, Ann Arbor 1994).

[8]This work was published by G. Scholem in *Tarbiz* 4 (1933), pp. 207–225. It should be noted that one of the differences between the two treatises is found in a different list of sources, most of which are completely fictional. Rabbi Isaac does not mention any Geronese source for his tradition, true or fictional, while Rabbi Moses attributes some of his statements to Nachmanides.

or partially fictional.[9] It is probable, according to present knowledge, that the intense dualism was the original contribution of Rabbi Isaac to this subject, as was his description of a messianic myth, not found in earlier kabbalistic sources.[10] Yet the question should be asked: Did Rabbi Isaac follow an earlier kabbalistic tendency that assisted him in formulating his concept of the hierarchy of evil powers? If there is such a trend in earlier kabbalah, it should be sought in Gerona, the great center of kabbalistic creativity in the first half of the thirteenth century. Many aspects of the teachings of Rabbi Isaac and his brother, Rabbi Jacob, are based on the speculations of the kabbalists of Gerona. Could this subject be one among those in which the Castile kabbalists developed the teachings of their Geronese predecessors?

When Gershom Scholem wrote an essay on the concepts of good and evil in the kabbalah,[11] he dedicated a section to the concept of evil among the kabbalists in Gerona. The example he chose to present was a treatise called the Secret of the Tree of Knowledge, an anonymous brief work, which he tended to identify as a work by the earliest Gerona kabbalist, Rabbi Ezra ben Shlomo. It is not certain that Rabbi Ezra is indeed the author, but it is very probable that it does express the views concerning evil among the early kabbalists in the Gerona circle.

Rabbi Ezra, like his colleague Rabbi Azriel, is among the first authors who quote and use extensively the *Bahir*, which was writ-

---

[9]His reliance on *Hechalot Zutarti* is pure fiction, while the tradition he claims to have received from Rabbi Eleazar ben Yehudah of Worms, the great writer of Ashkenazi Hasidic esoteric works, is only partially so. It can be shown that Rabbi Isaac utilized a commentary by Rabbi Eleazar concerning the nature of the worlds that were destroyed before this world was created (a legend found in *Bereshit Rabba*), and introduced into it dualistic elements that were not in the original exposition, which is found in Rabbi Eleazar's *Chochmat ha-Nafesh*. See Dan, "Samael, Lilith," (see note 5).

[10]See J. Dan, "The Emergence of the Messianic Mythology in Thirteenth-Century Kabbalah in Spain," in *Occident and Orient: A Tribute to the Memory of A. Scheiber*, Budapest and Leiden: Brill 1988, pp. 57–68.

[11]See note 1.

ten, most probably, in the end of the twelfth century.[12] The concept of evil in the works of these early kabbalists in Gerona should,
therefore, be compared to that of the *Bahir*. If Rabbi Ezra is the
author of the Secret of the Tree of Knowledge, then his attitude
toward that realm should be regarded as completely opposed to that
of the *Bahir*. These two treatises express the two main directions in
the kabbalistic understanding of the problem of evil.

The teachings of the *Bahir* concerning evil include several elements that are very difficult to harmonize. There is no doubt that
his interest in the subject is unusual, compared to other Jewish works
of the twelfth century: The rationalists of that period hardly recognized it as a major theological problem, and treated it as a marginal
one. Rabbi Abraham bar Hijja and Rabbi Judah be Barzilai neglected
it almost completely, as did Maimonides. The fact that several significant sections in the *Bahir* are dedicated to it already makes it an
exception in its period. The author seems to identify the duality of
matter and form, which he presents in terms derived from Bar Hijja,
with that of good and evil. This duality characterizes, according to
him, divine power, and is an integral element in the nature of God
and that of creation as a whole.[13] In other sections, the powers of
evil are identified as the fingers of the divine hand (probably the
left hand), which tempt man and bring harm and sin to the world,
even though they are a part of the anthropomorphic image of God.[14]

---

[12]G. Scholem, *Origins of the Kabbalah*, trans. A. Arkush, ed. R. J. Zwi Werblowsky,
Princeton, NJ: Princeton University Press 1986, pp. 35–197. The date of the *Bahir*'s
appearance can be decided by its use of the works of Rabbi Abraham bar Hijja,
Rabbi Abraham ibn Ezra, and, probably, some terms taken from the early translations of Judah ibn Tibbon; these sources extend to the seventh decade of the
twelfth century. It is reasonable, therefore, to assume that the book was written
in the eighth or ninth decade of that century. It is an unanswered question
whether the early kabbalists in Provence—especially Rabbi Isaac the Blind, who
wrote in the very end of the twelfth century and the beginning of the thirteenth—
were familiar with it. Rabbi Ezra's extensive use of the *Bahir* can be regarded as
the earliest combination of Provencal traditions with those of the *Bahir*.
[13]Margalioth's ed., secs. 10–13.
[14]Ibid., sec. 165.

The last section of the work is dedicated to an adaptation of the *Pirkey de-Rabbi Eliezer* narrative concerning Samael, Adam, Eve, the snake, and original sin.[15] In these and other *Bahir* discussions, except for the last, evil is presented as an integral part of the divine world and an element in the divine direction of worldly affairs; yet it acquires in these descriptions a mythological dimension completely absent from previous Jewish traditions concerning this subject. The last section, however, does not clearly identify Samael as a part of the divine system; rather, following the late midrash, he is a rebel against God, and Adam's sin is the result of his scheming against the divine order of the world. This is presented not as a theological statement, but only as a part of the midrashic narrative.

While some aspects of the *Bahir*'s concept (or concepts) of evil are not completely clear, it is evident that the direction pointed to by them is one of increased mythologization and a tendency to regard evil at least as a partially independent enemy of man, if not of God. The zoharic dualism is not found in the *Bahir*, yet this early treatise does point in that direction. Comparing the *Bahir* to other works of its period, it can be viewed as a radical statement concerning the centrality of the power of evil in creation.

The treatise the Secret of the Tree of Knowledge points in exactly the opposite direction. Not every sentence in this brief work is clearly understood, but it is obvious that its main thesis is that the sins of Adam and Eve were committed because of their own disobedience to God, deriving from their human nature. Evil is not a part of the divine figure or the divine system of creation; it was introduced into the world by the sins of man. It is probable that this treatise is a deliberate response to the *Bahir*'s attitude, a deliberate opposition to the mythical tendencies in the early treatise that attribute the origin of evil to elements outside of man himself.

---

[15]*Bahir*, sec. 200, PDRA Ch. 13. It should be noted that section 199 of the *Bahir* includes a brief statement that "the soul of the masculine is derived from the masculine and that of the feminine from the feminine, and the feminine element is always open to the impact of evil."

Rabbi Ezra's concept of evil can be regarded as a formulation, in a kabbalistic context (though one that does not use intensely kabbalistic terminology and symbolism), of the basic tendencies of Jewish rationalists, especially those among them who absorbed neo-Platonic doctrines, to regard evil as an absence rather than as an entity of ontological meaning. This is also attested by the attitude found in the other works of Rabbi Ezra and Rabbi Azriel, who did not follow the *Bahir*'s direction. The *Bahir*, on the other hand, seems to be developing attitudes found in *Hechalot Rabbati*, describing Samael as the Prince of Rome and the celestial opponent of the people of Israel, and the *Pirkey de-Rabbi Eliezer* tradition, derived from ancient sources, concerning Samael as a rebel against God. These two conflicting concepts seem to have coexisted in the beginning of the thirteenth century, presenting the kabbalists of Gerona with a choice between the denial of evil's divine dimension and its mytho-logical intensification. By the end of that century the second direc-tion achieved complete victory in the writings of Rabbi Isaac ha-Cohen and the *Zohar*. What is Nachmanides' place in this process?

II

It is impossible to survey in this paper all aspects of Nachmanides' attitude toward evil. The problem includes several theological discussions found in his works, the question of the place of evil in his eschatology and in the process of creation, and especially his unusual attention to demons and supernatural phenomena, in which Nachmanides showed great interest and original formulations. We shall concentrate this discussion on the concept of Samael, which represents the basic choice between mythologization or negation of the ontological nature of evil. The key section in which Nachmanides discussed this problem is found in his Commentary on the Torah, Exodus 14, concerning the sacrifice to Azazel.

It is no accident that Nachmanides dedicates his commentary on verse 14:8 to a discussion of the principle of evil. The verse is one of the most perplexing ones in the Pentateuch concerning the unity of God and the position of demonic and evil powers. The legal demand posed by this verse, that during the Yom Kippur ritual one goat will be sacrificed to God and another should be given to Azazel, can easily be interpreted as indicating some kind of dualism and the worship of Satan and demons. It is no wonder that several Jewish medieval commentators dedicated much effort to elucidate this verse in a way that would deny such a possibility, and that they utilized old midrashic discussions of the subject to enhance their own conceptions. Nachmanides begins his commentary on this verse by presenting an anthology of previous discussions, to which he adds his own critical assessment.

He first quotes Rashi on this verse, who interprets Azazel as a geographic term. Azazel, according to Rashi, is "a tall, hard rock, a high mountain." [16] Nachmanides continues by presenting the midrashic source for Rashi's statement, and indeed the ancient source includes both Rashi's conclusion and his proof-text, as well as an insistence, based upon another term in this context, "to the desert." [17] According to this interpretation, the verse under discussion is not theological in any way; it demands that one goat should be sent free to the desert, to a high and hard mountain-rock, without connecting it with any ritualistic significance. Nachmanides himself continues to present a linguistic interpretation of the term *azazel* that fits this concept. He says that, if so, the word includes a doubling of the letter *z* in order to denote hardness, something common in Hebrew, and it should be connected with the term *izuz* in Psalms 24:5, which is derived from the same root, *oz* (power, courage; here interpreted as "tough"), and the *z* is doubled for emphasis.

If all that Nachmanides wanted to achieve was to present an interpretation that will seemingly overcome the danger of a dualistic concept, he could have stopped here, like Rashi. It may be surmised that he was well aware of the inadequacy of this exegesis. It

---

[16]Rashi bases his interpretation on the term presented in a verse later in this chapter, verse 22, in which Azazel is equivalent to *eretz gezera*, a forbidden territory. The important point in this commentary is that Azazel is identified with a territorial term, and therefore cannot be a divine entity.

[17]The author calls this text *torat Kohanim*.

does not solve the problem of the reason for the presence of the second goat in this ritual, nor does it explain why should it be sent to the desert. Even more, it does not do justice to the full power of the term *azazel* in Hebrew, which cannot be denied by the simple identification with tough, forbidding terrain. Nachmanides goes on, presenting and analyzing the commentary of Abraham ibn Ezra on this verse.

Nachmanides begins by presenting a quotation from the talmudic discussion of the subject that Ibn Ezra included in his commentary in a critical manner. In the Talmud, Rav Shemuel addressed the difficulty in the verse that states that the goat, the *seir*, which is sacrificed, is sacrificed to God. From this it may be surmised that the second *seir* is not to God, but to some other divine or demonic power. Shemuel therefore stated that even though it is said in the verse that the first goat is to be sacrificed to God, the second one, the one sent to the desert, is also to God. To this Ibn Ezra retorted that Shemuel's statement is superfluous because the second goat is not sacrificed, therefore the verse did not have to designate it to God; only that which is actually sacrificed has a ritualistic meaning.[18]

This opening of the exegesis of the verse consisted actually of the presentation of two interpretations, both of them midrashic— one as brought by Rashi, the other as used by Ibn Ezra. Both share the complete denial of any reference to the powers of evil and their role in the Yom Kippur ritual. Nachmanides continues his presentation, however, as if these two statements have not been made at all, or at least they do not carry any weight concerning the true meaning of the verse. He turns now to use enigmatic language, demonstrating by this that there is a great secret hidden in this verse:

> If you could understand the secret that is after the word *azazel* then you shall understand his (Azazel's) secret and the secret of his name, because there are other such references in the Bible. And I shall give you a hint that will reveal a portion of the

---

[18]This discussion compares the other elements in it that neither Nachmanides nor Ibn Ezra chose to quote.

secret: When you shall be thirty-three years old you shall know it.[19]

These words are not those of Nachmanides; they are quoted from Ibn Ezra. The secret denoted here is a reference to a verse that is found thirty-three verses after the one under discussion, and this is the meaning of the number included here as an age to be attained. That verse includes a reference to the forbidden sacrifices to the *seirim*, the demonic powers (17:7). This awkward hide-and-seek by Ibn Ezra is needed in order not to give a clear hint concerning the possibility that behind the biblical text there is indeed a recognition of the sacrifice to the demonic powers, while the author definitely seems to think that is the case.[20]

After quoting Ibn Ezra, Nachmanides proceeds to discuss his exegesis and says: "Rabbi Abraham is really faithful in his spirit, and I shall not be the gossip who will reveal his secret, even though our sages, of blessed memory, have already done so in several places. They said in Genesis Rabba on the verse 'The *seir* will carry upon it' (verse 22 in this chapter), that this is Esau, who was described as a hairy person (Genesis 27:11) by his brother Jacob.[21] The continu-

---

[19]See Shevell's note, p. 88.

[20]Ibn Ezra's position can be compared to that of Maimonides, who wrote about it several decades later. According to Maimonides, several biblical injunctions and commandments have to be understood as accommodating the Israelites' devotion to the worship of idols, and divine inability to completely forbid them to follow such customs. Thus, even the practice of sacrifices in the tabernacle and Temple is explained as God's inability to forbid such pagan customs completely, and His preference that if they do sacrifice animals because they are as yet unprepared for spiritual faith, they should at least dedicate them to God Himself. There is a talmudic basis to this exegesis. See, concerning this, Stephen Benin, "The Footprints of God," *Divine Accommodation in Jewish and Christian Thought*, Albany, NY: SUNY Press 1993. It seems that Abraham ibn Ezra viewed this concept as the esoteric meaning of this verse, namely, that God commanded the sending of the *seir* to the desert as an accommodation, to prevent the people from doing worse rituals of idolatry. It should be noted, however, that no clear reference to the meaning of the name *azazel* is included in this esoteric hint, despite the author's promise.

[21]In Hebrew, of course, *sair* (hairy) and *seir* are spelled the same way. So, also, is the Edomean mountain, Har Seir, which has been described as the abode of the Edomites (sons of Esau).

ation of the verse, '(will carry) all their sins,' should be read as 'the sins of the sons of Jacob.' " [22]

From here Nachmanides proceeds to the heart of his exegesis, the main point of which is the identification of Azazel with Samael. This identification is neither mentioned nor hinted at in any previous commentary to this verse, ancient or medieval (except the author's direct source), yet it seems to be taken completely for granted by Nachmanides, as if there were no doubt about it. By doing this, the author forsakes all attempts to describe Azazel as a place rather than a demonic entity, and the theological significance of the verse interpreted here is clearly revealed. His means of creating this connection is a passage from the midrash *Pirkey de-Rabbi Eliezer*, a text whose importance concerning the history of Samael has already been pointed out.

Nachmanides quotes:

It is explained, concerning this matter, in the Chapters of Rabbi Eliezer the Great: This is why they used to give to Samael a bribe on Yom Kippur, so that he will not annul their sacrifice. As it is said [in this verse], one lot to God and one lot to Azazel; the lot of the Holy One blessed be He to an *olah* sacrifice, and the lot of Azazel the goat (*seir*) of sin, and all the sins of Israel are on it, as it is said, "and the *seir* will carry upon it." Samael observes that no sin can be found in them on Yom Kippur, and says in front of the Holy One blessed be He: Master of all the universes, You have on Earth one people that are like the ministering angels in heaven. In the same way that the ministering angels are barefoot, so is Israel barefoot on Yom Kippur. In the same way that the ministering angels do not eat and drink, so are the people of Israel without eating and drinking on Yom Kippur. In the same way that the ministering angels do not have joints,[23] so Israel is standing on its feet on Yom Kippur. In the

---

[22] "Their sins" is *avonotam*, which should be read, according to this exegesis, *avonot tam*, when *tam* is the appellation of the patriarch Jacob (following Genesis 25:27)
[23] That is, their legs are "straight," without joints, as the prophetic vision attests (Ezekiel 1:7), and therefore they cannot sit; this belief had meaningful consequences in talmudic and *Hechalot* literature. Elisha ben Avuyah, the colleague

same way that peace is present in the midst of the ministering angels, so is peace present among the people of Israel on Yom Kippur. In the same way that the ministering angels are pure of any sin, so are the people of Israel pure of any sin on Yom Kippur. And the Holy One blessed be He hears the testimony concerning Israel from their prosecutor,[24] and extends His forgiveness over the temple and the priests and all the congregated people, as it is said: "He will absolve the holy temple."[25] This is the end of this tradition.

This idealized picture of the Yom Kippur ritual, quoted by Nachmanides from the *Pirkey de-Rabbi Eliezer*,[26] is significant in that it leaves no doubt that the *kategor* is a servant of the divine court, not an independent evil power. When the people of Israel follow the rituals correctly, the prosecutor turns into a witness to the people's perfection and enhances divine absolution for them. This is a very different power from the rebellious Samael of Ch. 13 of that midrash. The main point, however, for Nachmanides' presentation is the opening sentence, in which all this idealized description is connected— and made dependent on the bribing of Samael by sending to him the second goat.

---

of Rabbi Akiva in the "entering to the *pardes*" and the ascension to the chariot, saw Metatron sitting on a throne in the entrance to the seventh *hechal*, and concluded that "there may be two powers in heaven," a mistake for which both Aher and Metatron were severely punished (see Bavli *Hagiga* 15b and Third Enoch, Ch. 15). The mistake was caused by Metatron's sitting, which proved that he was not an angel, for they do not have joints and cannot sit. The solution in Third Enoch is the identification of Metatron with the human being Enoch son of Jared; as an ex-human, Enoch-Metatron could sit. See J. Dan, *Ancient Jewish Mysticism*, Tel Aviv: MOD 1993, pp. 108–124.

[24]The term used here, *kategor*, is the traditional talmudic-midrashic term describing the celestial power in the divine court whose duty is to bring forward before God all the sins of Israel and demand punishment for them. In *Hechalot Rabbati* this duty is assigned to Samael, who also serves as the celestial prince of Rome and its protector.

[25]Leviticus 16:33.

[26]Chapter 57, with several versions that differ from the texts we have; see Shevell's notes there, pp. 88–89.

Nachmanides seizes this element and separates it from the rest of the tradition in an unambiguous manner: "We have thus been informed of his name and his functions," namely, Samael has been identified as the power to whom the goat is given, and his position has been described. The long quotation was copied mainly to bring Samael into the foreground of the discussion of the goat to Azazel. From here Nachmanides proceeds to describe Samael using his own terms:

> And this is the secret of the matter, that they were worshipping foreign gods, which are angels, and giving them sacrifices. . . .[27] And you should observe what is stated in the scriptures and in the tradition, for the Torah has completely forbidden the acceptance of their divinity and any act of worship for them, but the Holy One blessed be He ordered that a *seir* will be sent to the desert on Yom Kippur, to the prince who governs the places of desolation. And this is appropriate for him, because he is its master, and from the emanation of his power desolation and desert is derived. This is because he is the cause of the stars of the sword and of bloodshed, of wars and struggles and wounds and blows and conflict and destruction. The principle is that [he is] the soul of the sphere of Mars. And his lot among the nations is Esau, which is a people who inherited the sword and wars. And among the animals [his lot is] the *seirs* and the goats. And his lot also includes the demons who are called maleficia,[28] by our rabbis. And the biblical verse calls them *seirim*, for he and his people are called Seir.

I believe that this passage can be characterized as the earliest Hebrew comprehensive description of a devil's domain in so many aspects. Nachmanides draws the borders of Samael's realm on several levels. He is the ruler of the goats and the *seirim* among ani-

---

[27]The author quotes here the verse from Ezekiel 16:18–19, and interprets it as a description of sacrifices to angelic powers.

[28]The Hebrew term *mazikim*, literally, "those who cause harm," can be translated, I believe, in this context by the term denoting the evil activities of demons in their capacity of being the devil's servants.

mals, of Rome and the Gentiles descended from Esau among human beings; he is the master of desolate and destroyed territories. Of human activities, he is the master of war, bloodshed, weapons, and wounds. He is the master of demons and other evildoers, a concept that is innovative and meaningful in the long process of the assemblage of all beings who are dangerous to human life under the auspices of the theological entity assigned to be the master of all evil.[29] This is an innovative, even revolutionary, picture, presented here in Nachmanides' own words and terminology. Many of the main aspects of this description are repeated, in various forms, elsewhere in Nachmanides' works.[30]

The author presents the boundaries of Samael's domains, and he also devotes one brief sentence, yet a most important one, to designate the source of the devil's powers. He uses strictly astrological terminology in defining Samael's powers. He is the "cause," meaning the spiritual, essential source of potency, of the stars that are characterized as those responsible for war and bloodshed, and, in principle, he is the "soul," that is, the intrinsic spiritual drive, within the sphere of the fifth planet, Mars. This makes him independent of human affairs, because the sphere and its intrinsic driver are an integral part of the cosmic constellation. Nachmanides also uses the term azilut, a Hebrew word adopted in the previous century by various Hebrew writers to designate a process of emanation. Here the emphasis in the use of the term may be more on the astrological concept of influence than on the purely theological neo-Platonic concept of emanation.[31]

---

[29]Classical Hebrew sources, and many early medieval ones, did not regard the realm of demons, witches, and spirits as being part of an evil realm governed by the devil. This process occurred in the period under discussion here, and Nachmanides' statement is a major step in this direction.

[30]See especially his sermon Torat ha-Shem Temimah, Shevell's ed., pp. 146–149, 171.

[31]There is no textual reason to associate the use of this term here with the kabbalistic concept of the emanated sefirot. The context seems to be essentially cosmological.

From a theological point of view, this paragraph should not be regarded as a depiction of a divine power of evil. Its innovative character lies in the concept of concentration, uniting all elements of earthly and cosmic evil under the power of Samael. The theological consequences are discussed by Nachmanides in the continuation of his commentary. But before turning to the analysis of that part, another aspect should be presented: the influence of language on the picture drawn by Nachmanides concerning the nature and meaning of Samael.

It is very difficult, when dealing with an exegetical text, to distinguish between theological and exegetical-linguistic drives that shape the author's presentation. It may be argued that such a separation did not exist in the mind of the author, and even the positioning of the question reflects modern bias, which tends to diminish the pure textual impact of scriptures. Be that as it may, in this case, Nachmanides demonstrates the fullness of the powers inherent in textual-traditional terminology; so much so that one may assign to the intrinsic force of this process a major part of the responsibility for the innovative character of his formulations.

The starting point of this essay on the power of evil is the biblical term central in this verse and this chapter: *seir*. In the immediate context, *seir* is a goat, a sacrificial animal. Yet not for a moment can it be forgotten that this very term has two other biblical meanings: It is a geographic term referring to the Edomean mountain range in the southern Trans-Jordan; and it is the central element in the description of Esau, Jacob's evil twin brother. Esau's hairiness distinguished him from his twin, Jacob, from the beginning, and when Rebecca wanted to present Jacob to the blind Isaac in the guise of his brother, she made him wear a goat's fur.[32] The separation between Jacob and Esau, which was later conceived as that between Jews and Gentiles, is one between the "hairy one"—*sair*, and the one who is not.

These three biblical meanings were developed in talmudic-midrashic literature. The mountain of Seir, the residence of the

---

[32]See Genesis 27:11–17.

Edomites, was identified with the residence of the sons of Esau, following the biblical tradition.[33] To these three, a fourth one should be added that is emphasized in this context by both Ibn Ezra and Nachmanides—*seirim* (plural form) as a reference to both pagan deities and demonic entities that may be the subjects of erroneous, sinful human worship. Yet a completely new dimension of meaning was given to these terms when the Roman Empire was identified in talmudic literature with the term Edom. This word became one of the most hated ones, representing the rule of evil on Earth. This gave rise to the identification of Rome—and Gentiles in general—with Esau, disregarding completely the obvious fact that Esau was the son of Isaac, the grandson of Abraham, and the twin brother of Jacob.[34] The identification of Seir-Edom-Esau-Rome is a prominent, unambiguous linguistic phenomenon of talmudic Hebrew. In this identification, hatred and rejection are the most powerful elements, increasing every decade with the tragic and destructive struggles between the Jews and the Romans.

Nachmanides utilized, as has been shown, all these elements. He added to them another one, which is not completely original, but was inherent in this combination from the beginning: the word *adom*—red—associated with the people of Edom in biblical metaphors, meaning blood (and also, in biblical terminology, sin[35]), and the name of the red planet, long believed to be responsible for warfare and bloodshed (hence its name Mars, the god of war), whose reddish image was understood to be connected with blood. Nachmanides could thus confidently present the linguistic unity of *seir*, Edom, Esau,

---

[33]The settlement of the descendants of Esau on the mountain of Seir is explicitly stated in Genesis 36:8.

[34]This identification became so deep-rooted that medieval legend attempted to identify the descendants of Esau as the founders of the city of Rome. This is found in embryonic form in the tenth-century book of Jossipon and in a developed, extended form in the sixteenth-century novel concerning the employs of Zefo ben Elifaz, the grandson of Esau, which constitutes a Hebrew version of the epic of Rome's founding, in the *Sefer ha-Yashar*.

[35]See, for instance, Isaiah 1:18.

Rome, red, blood, sin, and the planet Mars. The unity of diverse elements presented in this paragraph by Nachmanides is brought together by the history of the linguistic elements that constitute it. It is a Hebrew construct founded upon the development of the Hebrew language in the preceding two millennia. Demons and evil planets, evil empires and evil people, sinister celestial forces and disastrous historical memories are brought together and bound into one comprehensive picture of an earthly and cosmic evil realm.

In this intricate linguistic equation the most important element is missing: Samael himself. His name does not include any of the connotations listed above. The traditional derivations of his name—left, north, and blindness—are not inherently connected to any of the terms in these sequences. Yet it is clear that Nachmanides deliberately introduced the long quotation from the *Pirkey de-Rabbi Eliezer* in order to make this name the central appellation of evil, the word binding together all the variegated realms he described. Here, it seems, the reasons should be regarded not as linguistic, but as being derived from a textual situation. The unavoidable fact is that in three key texts that Nachmanides utilized in formulating his concepts, Samael is the dominant appellation of the devil. These three are *Hechalot Rabbati*, *Pirkey de-Rabbi Eliezer*, and the *Bahir*. The first is the most forceful presentation of Samael as the celestial power in charge of Rome and the instigator of evil designs against the people of Israel. The second continued in this characterization, but added to it the rebellion of Samael and his identification with Satan and the snake in the story of the Garden of Eden, and thus with human sin and death. The third introduced the *PDRE* concepts into a kabbalistic context by adapting its narrative, and, by inference, thus gave the name Samael to other, unnamed, functions of evil described in the *Bahir*.

The original contribution of Nachmanides can therefore be defined as the bringing together of the linguistic sequence with the textual one, to which he added an element absent in all of them—astrological terminology. These new characterizations, which connected Samael with the terms "emanation," "sphere," and "cause," give the contemporary medieval scientific-cosmological placing of

Samael. It turned Samael into a contemporary relevant power, not only the subject of ancient legends.

The absence of a crucial aspect has to be emphasized. Samael had very old roots in gnostic literature, based, undoubtedly, on his presence in apocryphal and pseudepigraphical Jewish literature of the postbiblical period. The early kabbalah, especially the *Bahir*, has been described as the expression of the reappearance of gnostic elements in medieval Judaism.[36] Yet Nachmanides does not use, and leaves no place for, the inclusion of gnostic elements in the newly emerging figure of Samael. We find no reference in this description to any of the common motifs concerning this power that characterize its position in gnostic literature,[37] and the new components presented here are derived, as shown above, from astrological and cosmological contexts. The development of the figure of Samael in the writings of Nachmanides does not support the thesis that the kabbalah of that period can be characterized by the absorption of gnostic elements and making them central in the development of Jewish mystical thought.

III

Nachmanides was keenly aware of the theological tension surrounding his discussion of Samael and Azazel, and that the main problem presented by the verse interpreted here is that of the independence of the power of evil. The next section of this exegesis is

---

[36]A great deal has been written concerning the problem of the place of gnosticism in the early kabbalah and the *Bahir*. Some of the nineteenth-century scholars took it for granted, and Scholem analyzed it in detail in his studies of that period. See especially *The Origins of the Kabbalah*, pp. 67–97. Compare J. Dan, "Jewish Gnosticism," *Jewish Studies Quarterly* 2 (1995) pp. 309–328.

[37]There is no connection between Samael and the process of the creation, or its relationship with other divine or evil powers. Even the most elementary one—the explanation of his name as derived from "blindness"—is not presented or hinted at, even though a short while after Nachmanides we do find it in the *Meirat Einayim* of Rabbi Isaac of Acre, and, indirectly, in the Treatise on the Emanations on the Left by Rabbi Isaac ben Jacob ha-Cohen.

dedicated to an attempt to clarify the relationship between Samael's evil deeds and the omnipotence of God. He tries to explain this by a detailed parable:

> The intention of the sending of the *seir* is not that we present a sacrifice to him (i.e., to Samael)—heaven forbid. The intention is that we obey the will of our Creator, Who ordered us to do that. This can be expressed by a parable. It is like someone preparing a feast for his master, and the master ordered the person who is preparing the feast: Give one portion to this certain servant of mine. The person preparing the feast does not give anything (of his own) to that servant, and does not do anything in his honor. He gives everything to the master, and the master gives a prize to his servant. And he (the person preparing the feast) has obeyed his master's command and did everything in honor of the master. The master, because of his love for the one preparing the feast, wanted all his servants to enjoy it, so that he (the particular servant) will praise him and will not speak against him.
>
> This is the meaning of the (priest) giving the lots. If the priest were to dedicate them explicitly to God and to Azazel, he would have seemed to be worshipping him and swearing in his name. But since he put both of them at the gate of the tabernacle, for both of them are a gift to God, and He gave from them to his servant the proper portion which he deserves from God, and He made the lots and his hand gave them the portion.

In the parable and in its interpretation, Nachmanides has one paramount purpose: to deny any possibility of understanding this ritual as if man is worshipping Azazel by the gift of the *seir*. Man only obeys God; it is purely God's decision to give a portion to one of his servants. Man obeys this divine decision in the same way that he follows all the other divine commandments. Therefore, there cannot be any trace of idolatry or devil-worship in this ceremony.

While absolving man from any trace of intention to worship Samael, Nachmanides problematizes the relationship between God and Samael. If we accept Nachmanides' exegesis, it means that man has nothing to do but follow divine commands, even those that seem strange to him. But why did God give such an order? The answer to this is found in a hint within the parable, which is not repeated in the explication. God wants all His servants to enjoy the feast, so that even the particular servant who presumably is not inclined to do so will praise the person who prepares it. This He can achieve by ordering man to give that portion to Azazel. No direct relationship is thus created between Azazel and man, but one wonders why God has to give a specific "bribe" to that servant. In a subtle way, divine omnipotence seems to have some limitation in the case of Azazel. Man is not obligated to give an offering to the devil, but God is.

On the other hand, the structure Nachmanides presents is one in which there cannot be any doubt that Azazel and Samael are servants of God and that they belong to the celestial court. Samael, in this structure, cannot be regarded, on the one hand, as a rebellious angel positioning himself in opposition to God; neither can he be regarded as a part of an "emanation on the left," an independent system of evil powers opposing the good ones. Samael here essentially fulfills his ancient role as presented in *Hechalot Rabbati*: He is the representative of earthly evil powers, but he does not have independent authority. He has to acquire divine permission to carry out any act against Israel, and he therefore observes their sins in order to use them as arguments. Yet one wonders why, in such a structure, he has to be bribed by being honored as if he were receiving a sacrifice that is equal to God's. The need to bribe him does express some belief in his authority to make independent decisions, a process that the bribe attempts to influence.

In this section, as in many others in Nachmanides' commentary, one should not expect to find a comprehensive theological discussion. Nachmanides states here, as he does so often in the kabbalistic discussions in this work, that "we cannot explain" this in full. This is the reason that several kabbalists in the next two generations wrote extensive commentaries on Nachmanides' "secrets." While complete analysis of all the elements that converge in this section is impossible, one more point should be discussed, because the author himself makes the point in strong terms in the end of this exegesis: the meaning of this verse as a refutation of Aristotle's philosophy.

IV

It is my suggestion that the strengthening of the image of the powers of evil, the convergence of many old and new motifs in the creation of a new, empowered figure of Samael, in Nachmanides' Commentary, has been motivated by the fierce anti-Aristotelian sentiments of the author. The centrality of the great controversy concerning the study of rationalistic philosophy among the kabbalists in Gerona has been demonstrated by several studies.[38] One should not be surprised, therefore, to find that this exposition of the role of evil is concluded by a fierce statement against "those who follow[39] the Greek one, who deny everything that they cannot sense, and he and his evil disciples are so crude as to suspect[40] that anything that he cannot reach by his discourse is not true." What is the relationship between Aristotelianism and the powers of Samael?

The particular example that the author gives is necromancy, and by inference the subject is the existence of the spirits of the dead, the powers of sorcerers and witches who invoke them, and the de-

---

[38]See Scholem, *Origins of the Kabbalah*, pp. 393–430, and J. Dan, *Jewish Mysticism and Jewish Ethics*, Seattle and London: Washington University Press 1987 et passim, and especially my study "The Cultural and Social Background of the Emergence of Traditional Ethical Literature," in *Shlomo Pines Jubilee Volume*, Part I, ed. M. Idel, E. Schweid, and Z. Harvey, Jerusalem 1988, pp. 239–264. The main thesis is that Rabbi Isaac the Blind's prohibition concerning the writing of kabbalistic works turned the Gerona authors toward publication of traditional works of ethics, directed mainly against rationalistic ethics, in the framework of the great controversy.

[39]I do not believe there can be any doubt that by "those who follow" here and "evil disciples" in the continuation of the sentence the author refers to Maimonides and his followers. Politics prevented Nachmanides (and many others) to confront Maimonides directly, but the attack against Aristotle is not directed against Arab or Christian thinkers; it is the Jewish rationalists who are under attack.

[40]The author uses the term *lahashod*, "to suspect," instead of *lahashov*, "to think," because their reasoning should not be adorned by a verb connected with "thought."

mons that often participate in such practices. These three elements, to which Nachmanides often alludes in many of his works, represent theological beliefs rather than superstition. Their existence expresses faith in the afterlife and in the separate existence of the soul, while witchcraft and demonology represent the supernatural, which should be called, in this context, "the miraculous." Several sections of Nachmanides' sermons are dedicated to argumentation against the rationalists and particularly Aristotle, concerning the truth of miracles, a subject closely connected with that of the creation. It seems that Nachmanides believed that the denial of creation is equivalent to the denial of miracles and of supernatural phenomena, because all of them represent the belief in a God Who is active in the world. An eternal, uncreated universe means the absence of divine intervention in worldly affairs. In such a world, the laws of nature are eternal and unchanging, allowing no exceptions. Miracles and miraculous phenomena are impossible in such a world, because they denote an intervention from the outside or the existence of a different set of laws, which the concept of the eternal universe does not allow. For Nachmanides, the creation, the miracles, and the supernatural became united in the defense of the concept of an active God Who governs the universe exercising His will in the forms of cosmogony, in breaking His own laws by incurring miracles, and hinting at the existence of realms beyond the physical world by the existence of supernatural powers.

Nachmanides was not the only one in that hectic period to realize this. This best-known example of such awareness was the accusation that Maimonides denied the existence of demons. This argument, it was quickly proved, was the result of a mistake in the Alharizi translation of the Guide to the Perplexed.[41] But even though Maimonides did not state such a belief explicitly, the suspicion that his picture of the world did not allow such supernatural creatures

---

[41]Concerning this accusation and the mistranslation that caused it, see Daniel J. Silver, Maimonidean Criticism and the Maimonidean Controversy, Leiden: Brill 1965, p. 158.

to exist persisted.[42] It is evident, however, from the text under discussion and other expressions in Nachmanides' works that, for him,
the belief in the existence of demons, spirits, and witchcraft divided
Aristotelian scientists and rationalists from the believers in Jewish
tradition.

It is evident, therefore, that Nachmanides' discussion of Samael
and his powers is far removed from any dualistic drive. There is no
similarity whatsoever between his basic attitude and that demonstrated by Rabbi Isaac ha-Cohen a generation later. The question
of the existence of evil on Earth and its sources was not paramount
in his mind. The main subject was divine providence and active
direction of existence, and its religious implications, including some
halachic principles.[43] The exegetical discourse is directed toward removing any possibility of understanding the verse as demanding
sacrifice to Satan, and the contemporary ideological discourse is
directed to demonstrating the miraculous nature of divine providence
by the creator. Both motives are categorically opposed to the emergence of dualistic tendencies.

---

[42]This may be another reason why Nachmanides did not attack Maimonides directly: He did not have a clear textual basis for such a confrontation.
Nachmanides was in similar situation concerning the subject of the creation. On
the face of it, Maimonides seemed to support the concept of the creation and
claimed that Aristotle did not succeed in proving logically that the universe was
eternal. Many medieval and modern thinkers believed that Maimonides chose
not to state exoterically his true opinion on this matter, and I believe that
Nachmanides was one of them.

[43]One of the most important hidden elements in this controversy was the problem of sacred time. If the universe is eternal, the concept of a "holy day" loses its
meaning. Sabbath cannot be the seventh day after the creation, and Rosh
Hashanah cannot be the day creation began. The division of the year into weeks
and months becomes arbitrary, as there is no meaningful starting point. As so
much of the halachah is based on specific sacred times, the adoption of the concept of a noncreated world is intrinsically anarchic and antinomianistic. This
argument was not used in the open debate, probably because of the existence of
the Mishneh Torah, which includes the great codes concerning the observance
of sacred time. Yet it gave power and persistence to the controversy concerning
the creation.

This is as far as we can go in understanding Nachmanides' considerations and motives. From this point of view, Nachmanides can be regarded as a faithful follower of Rabbi Ezra, his teacher, if he indeed was the author of the "Secret" published by Scholem. His concept of evil can be regarded as one opposing any possibility of recognition of an independent opponent of God. Yet texts have lives of their own, and often they may become part of a process that the author never intended to support. Within the thirteenth-century process of the development of the concept of the "left emanations," the description of Samael by Nachmanides has a position rather different from the author's intentions.

Compared to Rabbi Ezra's treatise, it is evident that Nachmanides did not attribute the emergence of evil to the Garden of Eden narrative. Samael is a cosmic power, and, as "the soul of the sphere of Mars" his impact is not dependent on Adam, Eve, and the snake. His domination of the realm of evil is cosmic in nature, and is closely associated with the structure of other universal powers. It is not of human origin, nor is it directly connected to the divine realm. It is doubtful whether Nachmanides intended his analysis of the position and powers of Samael to increase the dualistic element in the kabbalah, yet it is probable that his followers, especially Rabbi Isaac ha-Cohen, were influenced by the elevation of Samael to a cosmic position and were assisted by these ideas in the formulation of the realm of emanations of the left.

The kabbalists of Gerona in the first half of the thirteenth century did not develop the myth of the powers of evil as presented in the Bahir, nor did they introduce any gnostic elements into the concept of evil in the kabbalah. The writings of Nachmanides express an increase in the interest in this subject and its integration in the new worldview that this school formulated. These elements were later used by Rabbi Isaac ha-Cohen and Rabbi Moses de Leon in developing the dualistic myth of Samael in the second half of that century.

TWENTY

Kabbalistic and Gnostic Dualism

Jewish mysticism has often been described by scholars of the nineteenth and twentieth centuries as being "gnostic." Sometimes this designation has been meant as a compliment, but more often it has not. The term has referred, in most cases, to the kabbalists' concept of evil as an independent divine power, resembling the evil creator found in the works of several gnostic sects. This study is an attempt to analyze the analogy and the nature of the resemblance between these two major mystical schools.

A close link exists between the concept of evil in Jewish mysticism and the problem of the gnostic element in kabbalah and other mystic currents within Judaism. This perception occasionally leads to the indiscriminate equation of gnostic principles in kabbalah with the dualistic conception of reality as a struggle between the divine powers of good and evil—as if this dualism were the sole character-

This article was first published in *Da'at, Journal of Jewish Philosophy and Kabbalah* 19 (1987), pp. 5–16. The translation/adaptation is by Dena Ordan.

istic of gnosticism. Thus, Gershom Scholem's designation of Hechalot and Merkavah mysticism as "Jewish gnosticism" was critically received,[1] primarily on the basis that early Jewish mysticism lacks a dualistic concept of good versus evil. It should be noted, however, that gnosticism has many other distinguishing characteristics that are equal in importance to the dualistic principle. This study concentrates primarily on a comparison of gnostic dualism with the dualism found in various strata of Jewish mysticism.

Confusion results in part from the complexity and manifold interpretations of the term "gnosticism" as used by scholars without specifying its meaning in a particular context. This study will distinguish between the historical and the phenomenological significance of the term.

Historically, "gnosis" or "gnostic" refers to a concept or trend associated with any of dozens of sects, flourishing in the Orient and subsequently in Europe, from the second to the twelfth centuries. In this context, the contention that early kabbalah is gnostic means, for example, that the early Provençal kabbalists were influenced by the Catharist and Albigensian heresies, or that some of their ideas (not necessarily in the realm of good versus evil, but the transmigration of souls, for example) were borrowed from their gnostic neighbors. Hechalot literature is gnostic if we assume that the depiction of divine powers in Hechalot and Merkavah treatises was influenced

---

[1]Scholem's use of the title "Merkabah Mysticism and Jewish Gnosticism" for a chapter in his book Major Trends in Jewish Mysticism aroused little comment upon the book's publication (New York: Schocken 1941), or upon its 2nd ed. (1954). However, considerable discussion followed publication of Jewish Gnosticism, Merkabah Mysticism and Talmudic Tradition, New York: Jewish Theological Seminary 1960. See D. Flusser, "Scholem's Recent Book on Merkabah Literature," Journal of Jewish Studies 11 (1960), pp. 59–68; I. Gruenwald, "Knowledge and Vision," Israel Oriental Studies 2 (1973), pp. 64, 88–107. Hechalot literature describes the ascent of the mystic through the celestial palaces, while Merkavah mysticism centers on the mysteries of the divine throne-chariot. Those who achieve the ascent are referred to as yordey merkavah, "descenders to the chariot." See Encyclopaedia Judaica (hereafter, EJ), vol. 10, pp. 479ff; G. Scholem, Major Trends in Jewish Mysticism, pp. 46–47.

by the gnostic doctrine of the pleroma and the *aeons*.[2] This sense of the term gnostic ignores specific content to a certain extent, focusing instead on historical ties to phenomena commonly identified as gnostic in the history of heretical Christian sects.

In contrast, gnostic in the phenomenological sense focuses on content rather than history. It assumes the existence of an abstract gnostic type of mysticism, identifiable by such characteristic ideas as the bisexual aspect of God, a dynamic stratified pleroma of divine powers, a myth relating the detachment of part of the divine world and its displacement from its proper place, the saving power of esoteric knowledge (the gnosis), and, of course, the dualism of good versus evil. This is not a historical assessment, but rather a typological evaluation of religious thought. Kabbalah can be said to be gnostic if we find phenomenological similarity between kabbalistic mysticism and a particular gnostic doctrine as understood by the speaker; this does not imply a direct historical influence of gnosticism on kabbalah. (In this context, no attempt is made to determine whether the kabbalists were subject to external influences, or whether their ideas were the result of internal developments in Judaism in general and Jewish mystical sects in particular.)

These two senses will be dealt with separately in the following discussion, and a distinction will be made between the assumption of historical ties between gnosticism and Jewish mysticism, and of phenomenological-typological parallels between kabbalistic and gnostic thought processes. In each case, the evidence must be relevant; historical claims must be based on pertinent historical parallels, while phenomenological arguments must show similarity in the central concerns of gnosticism on the one hand and Jewish mysticism on the other.

---

[2]The gnostic doctrine of the aeons, especially as taught by the Valentinians, refers to the group of divine eternal beings that emanated from the Deity and serve as intermediaries between him and the world. On the *aeon* in kabbalah, see *EJ*, vol. 10, p. 506. The pleroma is the fullness of being of the divine life, held in gnosticism to comprise the aeons as well as the uncreated monad or dyad from which they have emerged.

The same distinction applies to the concept of dualism. Dualism in Jewish mysticism is open to historical analysis aimed at uncovering actual contact between Jewish mystics and gnostics, or to phenomenological treatment, based on similarities between gnostic dualism and Jewish sources (without attempting to establish the existence of historical influence). This methodological distinction will be the guiding principle in the attempt to uncover the relationship between gnosticism and Jewish mysticism.

GNOSTICISM AND *MERKAVAH* MYSTICISM

Historians have not reached a definite consensus with regard to two basic questions concerning gnosticism: (1) the position of the dualism of good versus evil in gnostic thought in general, and (2) the origins of this dualism. The earlier widely-held opinion that dualism, as derived from Persian Zoroastrianism, was the defining characteristic of historical gnosticism is no longer accepted. Many extant gnostic texts lack clear-cut dualistic views, and some important gnostic schools, like the Valentinian, did not assign a central role to the mythological struggle between divine forces of good versus evil. Moreover, the characteristics of Persian religion during the period under discussion are obscure, and it is debatable whether it embraced the extreme dualism found in later Persian sources.[3]

Nevertheless, recent discoveries and extensive study of the Nag Hammadi texts demonstrate that, between the second and fourth centuries, certain streams of gnostic thought did develop a starkly dualistic myth. (However, this myth was not accepted by all gnostic sects.) At the core of this myth stands a creator—the demiurge—a rebel against the divine, a satanic force opposed to the Good Deity of the upper realms and to His faithful terrestrial servants, the gnostics. This myth also often has anti-Semitic overtones, identify-

---

[3]See R. C. Zaehner, *The Dawn and Twilight of Zoroastrianism*, London: Weidenfeld & Nicolson 1961.

ing the biblical creator and God of Israel with the demiurge, and the people of Israel, His chosen people, as satanic. The lack of parallels of this extreme dualism among the Oriental religions and the absence of clear sources for this myth imply that it is the product of internal processes within the gnostic sects themselves, nurtured in part by the Christian nature of these sects and partly by the Jewish origin of some of the extreme views described above. The contention that the anti-Semitic nature of gnostic dualism negates the possibility of Jewish origins unfortunately does not hold water. Although not sufficiently verified, the hypotheses linking the emergence of gnostic dualism with the crisis of the destruction of the Second Temple and the appearance of apocalyptic concepts,[4] and/or with the spiritual phenomena found in the Dead Sea scrolls,[5] remain under consideration.

Examination of the Nag Hammadi and other gnostic texts has uncovered interesting parallels with *Hechalot* and *Merkavah* literature. Although of secondary importance, the motifs are sufficient to prove the existence of a modest interchange of ideas between early gnostics and Jewish mystics in the talmudic era.[6] In light of this mutual influence, it is significant that Jewish mystics did not adopt the dualistic aspect of gnosticism even as the mystical school of thought incorporated other characteristic ideas such as a divine pleroma,[7] and

---

[4]For the hypothesis linking gnosticism and the destruction of the Second Temple, see R. M. Grant, *Gnosticism and Early Christianity*, New York: Columbia University Press 1959, pp. 313ff.

[5]For a detailed bibliography and discussion of the relationship between gnosticism and the Dead Sea scrolls, see E. Yamauchi, *Pre-Christian Gnosticism*, London: Tyndale Press 1973, pp. 151–156.

[6]See, for example, I. Gruenwald, "Jewish Sources for the Gnostic Texts from Nag-Hammadi," *The Proceedings of the Sixth World Congress of Jewish Studies* 3 (1977), pp. 45–56.

[7]In my opinion, the specific terminology applied to the divine powers in *Hechalot* literature—"God of Israel," "Yah, the Lord of Hosts"—and that accompanies the use of "angelic names"—Akhatriel, Zaharriel, etc.—demonstrates the significance of these powers as partners in the divine realm. The later concept that distinguishes between a divine power and a created angel has no relevance in *Hechalot* literature.

perhaps the distinction between the Supreme Deity and the demiurge—the God of Genesis (*yotzer bereshit*).[8]

Hechalot and *Merkavah* literature contain no descriptions of autonomous satanic forces opposing the divine; rather, such forces emerge on a contextual basis as in the legend of the ten martyrs, where Samael appears as the Prince of Rome, one of the many princes of the nations who implement divine will. By no means is he ascribed autonomous status.[9] Similarly, the mystical literature dealing with the story of the Flood, where the appearance of rebellious angelic powers would be natural, lacks independent forces of evil.[10] Moreover, although the conception of "two divine powers" ascribed to Elishu ben Abuya (Aher) is clearly dualistic, it relates to two complementary forces, not implacably opposed enemies. Aher's assumption, when he saw Metatron sitting on a throne in the seventh palace, resembling God in every way, that "Indeed, there are two divine powers in heaven!" is based on Metatron's similarity to God, not his disparity.[11] Furthermore, although early Jewish esoteric literature emerged in a historical environment containing strong dualistic elements, and dealt with ideational contexts in which such dualism would be apposite, our extant texts show not the slightest evidence of dualism. Thus, even if we postulate the existence of unpreserved texts or a suppressed stratum of radical Jewish mysticism—inferred from the polemical nature of certain aspects of extant *Hechalot* literature—our sources indicate that the dualism that opposed the God of Genesis to the Supreme Deity contained no ascription to the realm of good or evil.

------

[8]*Yotzer bereshit*—Creator of the world. For a brief discussion of the *yotzer bereshit* in *Merkavah* mysticism, see Scholem, *Major Trends*, p. 65.

[9]For a discussion of the legend of the ten martyrs, see J. Dan, "The Concept of History in Heikhalot and Merkabah Literature," *Binah*, vol. 1, New York: Praeger 1989, pp. 47-58.

[10]For example, Uzza and Azzael, the angels mentioned in this context in Third Enoch and in other *Hechalot* tracts in connection with the fallen angels, lack independence and bow to the will of God. See H. Odeberg, *3rd Enoch, or The Hebrew Book of Enoch*, New York: Ktav 1973, pp. 10-13.

[11]Odeberg, *3rd Enoch*, p. 44.

No polemic against the dualism of good versus evil appears in *Hechalot* or *Merkavah* literature; evidently, this train of speculation was foreign to its worldview. Thus, if Scholem's designation of this literature as gnostic is apt, it must have another basis. Scholem grounded his view mainly on phenomenological similarities (while suggesting interesting historical parallels as well), but gnostic dualism was not one of them. It is historically clear that even if Jewish mystics were familiar with gnostic dualism, their unequivocal rejection of this idea completely obviated the need to deal with it. (It may be suggested that, conversely, gnostic dualism can be seen as an offshoot of the Jewish concept of "two divine powers"; this possibility does not, however, change the historical evidence regarding the attitude of Jewish mysticism to gnostic dualism.

SEFER HA-BAHIR

Medieval Jewish mysticism developed from earlier forms of Jewish mysticism, the *maaseh Merkavah* and *maaseh bereshit*.[12] The combination of ideas from both *Hechalot* and *Shiur Komah* mysticism and *Sefer Yezira*[13] led to the creation of the kabbalistic doctrine of *sefirot*,[14] whose elucidation was the focus of the esoteric lore of the Ashkenazi Hasidim of the twelfth and thirteenth centuries.[15] The appearance of dualistic doctrines in medieval Jewish mysticism was a contemporaneous development, because the doctrines bequeathed by early Jewish mysticism contained no hint of dualism.

---

[12]*Maaseh bereshit* refers to the esoteric traditions focusing on Genesis 1.

[13]*Shiur Komah* mysticism, literally the "measure of the body" of God, is the esoteric doctrine concerning the appearance of God in a quasi-bodily form (*EJ*, vol. 14, p. 1417). *Sefer Yezira*, the Book of Creation, is the earliest extant Hebrew text of systematic speculative thought, a mystical discourse on cosmology and cosmogony (*EJ*, vol. 16, p. 782).

[14]*Sefirot* is a fundamental term in kabbalah. It was coined by the author of *Sefer Yezira*, to designate the ten primordial or ideal "numbers" (*sefirot*). The term's meaning expanded to denote the ten stages of emanation that form the realm of God's manifestations in His various attributes (*EJ*, vol. 14, p. 1104).

[15]*Ashkenazi Hasidim*: a pietist movement in Germany that produced original ethical and mystical thought (*EJ*, vol. 7, pp. 1377–1383)

There is, of course, a possibility that unknown traditional conduits conveyed dualistic ideas to the medieval sages. Even though early Jewish mysticism lacks such concepts, the influence of gnostic sources unknown to us, whether Jewish or Gentile, on the early kabbalists is not entirely out of the question. Nonetheless, it should be stressed that even where our sources imply the existence of suppressed traditions, as in Rabbi Eleazar ben Judah of Worms's mystical description of the "crown called Akhatriel," or the doctrine of *sefirot* in *Sefer ha-Bahir*,[16] no traces of specifically gnostic dualism are evident. Moreover, the philosophical systems of sources associated with figures like Rabbi Aaron of Baghdad or Joseph ben Uzziel contain no references to a mythological treatment of opposing forces of good and evil. In conclusion, at present we have no evidence that medieval Jewish mystics inherited a gnostic-dualistic myth from ancient sources, Jewish or Gentile.

It is a moot point whether the concept of the Deity in *Sefer ha-Bahir* incorporates dualistic elements. The pertinent section of the book (probably based on Rabbi Abraham bar Hijja), a commentary on the primal chaos (Genesis 1:2), appears to be a speculative cosmology. However, the equation of chaos, matter, and evil by the author of *Sefer ha-Bahir* is probably based entirely on known sources, beginning with the midrashic statement linking chaos with evil (*Midrash Rabbah* Genesis 1:9) and extending to Rabbi Abraham bar Hijja's interpretation in *Hegyon ha-Nefesh*.[17] Other passages in *Sefer ha-Bahir* equate evil with the anthropomorphic figure of the Deity, especially his left hand and fingers. Even if *Sefer ha-Bahir* contains overtones of the potency and independent existence of evil, no hint

---

[16]On "the crown called Akhatriel," see J. Dan, "The Emergence of Mystical Prayer," *Studies in Jewish Mysticism*, ed. J. Dan and F. Talmage, Cambridge, MA: Association for Jewish Studies 1982, pp. 85–120. *Sefer ha-Bahir* is the earliest work of kabbalistic literature and the earliest source that deals with the realm of the *sefirot*; see *EJ*, vol. 4, p. 96ff.

[17]*Midrash Rabba*, trans. H. Freedman, London: Soncino Press 1951. For an English translation of *Hegyon ha-Nefesh*, see *The Meditation of the Sad Soul by Abraham bar Hayya*, translated with an introduction by Geoffrey Wigoder, New York: Schocken 1969.

of the existence of a second anthropomorphic divine figure, antithetical to the Deity, is found; the work's anthropomorphism depicts evil as belonging to and purposefully emanating from the Deity, not as an autonomous rebellious force.

Another major passage in the *Bahir* links evil with the tradition describing Samael, riding on the serpent, as the prime mover in the "fall from Paradise." (This tradition first appears in Enoch, but its most important Hebrew version is found in Chapter 13 of *Pirkey de-Rabbi Eliezer*.)[18] These bold mythological elements are apparently based on the internal development of known apocalyptic and midrashic motifs. The outstanding exception, *Sefer ha-Bahir* (passage 199), testifies to the existence of the principles of good versus evil, identifying them with the male and female principles in the material world. I believe that both this passage and the passage concerning the "princess who came from afar" (*Bahir* 132) incorporate early gnostic doctrines of good and evil, thereby laying the foundation for the development of a dualistic theory of good and evil in later kabbalah. Nonetheless, the significance of these elements in the doctrines of *Sefer ha-Bahir* should not be overrated, nor does evidence exist that later kabbalists adapted these specific passages in the development of a comprehensive doctrine of evil.

The doctrine of evil in early kabbalah is rooted primarily in the works of three kabbalists: Rabbi Isaac the Blind's statements on evil, particularly his commentary on Amalek (Exodus 17:16), Rabbi Ezra ben Shlomo of Gerona's well-known treatise *Etz ha-Daat* (the Tree of Knowledge), and Nachmanides' commentary on the scapegoat (Leviticus 16:8). Rabbi Isaac the Blind's commentary exhibits primitive dualistic leanings, but no evidence of external influence. Rabbi Ezra's text, of greater significance, contains a vehement rejection of dualism within the Deity, ascribing the roots of evil to Adam's "original sin." Based on the vehemence of his arguments, which have an almost polemical approach, we can postulate the existence of

---

[18]For an English version, see *Pirkey de-Rabbi Eliezer*, translated and annotated by Gerald Friedlander, New York Sepher-Hermon Press 1981.

dualistic concepts not found in extant texts. In my view, it is precisely Rabbi Ezra of Gerona's treatise that provides the earliest evidence of the eruption of forces inherent in kabbalah itself, leading to the formation of a pronounced dualistic mythology of the divine realm—even if we have no direct knowledge of the exact nature of these trends.

In Nachmanides' commentary, on the other hand, Samael appears for the first time as a cosmic force, identified with the "spirit of the sphere of Mars" and associated with destructive demonic forces.[19] Although Nachmanides' comments are obscure, if taken in conjunction with Rabbi Ezra's polemic, they point to the existence of a dualistic trend (albeit partly hidden) in the thought of the Gerona kabbalists. The anonymity of the material hinders the identification of its sources, leaving the scholar to establish through indirect proof that the appearance of dualistic tendencies in kabbalah did not result from historical contact with non-Jewish sources.

Unequivocal mythological dualism first appears openly in the works of Rabbi Isaac ben Jacob ha-Cohen of Soria (in the second half of the thirteenth century), especially in his Treatise on the Emanations on the Left and in *Taamei Taamim*. In other articles,[20] I have attempted to identify the sources utilized by Rabbi Isaac, which ranged from Pseudo-Ben Sira (gaonic period) to the works of Rabbi Judah the Pious and Rabbi Eleazar ben Judah of Worms, and to show how their concepts were adapted and transmuted. Examination of sources known to have been used by Rabbi Isaac ha-Cohen indicates that his creation of the myth of the "left emanation" and the hierarchy of the forces of evil is based on texts devoid of such concepts. The sources provided raw material for imagery, but the dualistic aspect was solely Rabbi Isaac's innovation. Moreover, the singularity of Rabbi Isaac's views is heightened by the fact that neither the writings of his brother, Rabbi Jacob ben Jacob ha-Cohen, nor

[19]For an English version, see Rabbi C. B. Chavel, trans., *Ramban Commentary on the Torah*, New York: Shilo 1974, Leviticus, p. 220.
[20]J. Dan, "Samael, Lilith, and the Concept of Evil in Early Kabbalah," *AJS Review* 5 (1980), pp. 17–40.

those of his father reflect these ideas. Rabbi Isaac's disciple and interpreter, Rabbi Moses ben Solomon of Burgos, minimized dualistic aspects, even in his presentation of the doctrine of the left emanation, The Left Pillar. The followers of the "Ha-Cohen brothers" like Todros Abulafia, author of the *Or Zarua*, similarly obscured the dualistic core of their mentors' thought. Rabbi Isaac's mythical doctrines come into their own only in the *Zohar* (but, surprisingly, not in the Hebrew treatises of Moses ben Shem Tov de Leon himself, nor of his colleague, Rabbi Joseph ben Abraham Gikatilla), where Rabbi Isaac's doctrine of the emanation on the left becomes the basis for the powerful myth of the *sitra ahra* (the "other side"—meaning evil).

THE EMANATIONS ON THE LEFT

Historically and phenomenologically, Rabbi Isaac's doctrine of the left emanation is at the core of any attempt to understand kabbalistic dualism and its relationship to gnostic dualism. Owing to the dominant role of the *Zohar*, this was the critical juncture at which the nature of the kabbalistic myth of evil was established, leaving its stamp on all later doctrines. Thus the questions posed earlier are crucial with respect to Rabbi Isaac ha-Cohen: (1) Was his dualism gnostic? (2) If so, did it result from historical contact with gnosticism? (3) In the absence of historical contact, can Rabbi Isaac's doctrine be phenomenologically defined as gnostic dualism? Unfortunately, limitations of space permit not a detailed discussion, but only presentation of essential points.

The similarity between the dualism of the left emanation and gnostic dualism is open to interpretation. On the one hand, the depiction of a world ruled by ten demonic forces identifiable by name and by individual characteristics, involved in a dynamic relationship centering on sexual rivalry (the competition between Samael and Asmoeus for Lilith's favors is one example), contains elements strongly resembling the concept of the Archons[21] in the most ex-

---

[21]See I. Gruenwald, "Jewish Mysticism and Gnosticism," *Studies in Jewish Mysticism*, p. 42.

treme gnostic doctrines, including the Manichaean. Other central
motifs paralleling gnostic themes are the never-ending battle of evil
against good leading to the exile of the forces of good, and anticipa-
tion of the decisive mythic battle between the Messiah and the forces
of evil. It is also notable that in Rabbi Isaac's doctrine, "original sin"
does not mark the emergence or the intensification of evil; evil has
a fully independent existence prior to creation. Emanations from
heavenly forces are the origin of evil, unrelated to man or his deeds.
The dissociation between evil and human actions (in sharp contrast
to the view of Rabbi Ezra ben Shlomo of Gerona) is intrinsically
gnostic in and of itself. It is also inimical to Jewish tradition in general, as well as to the Catholic tradition in Christianity.

On the other hand, it can be argued that significant differences
separate Rabbi Isaac's doctrine from typical gnostic dualism. For
example, evil powers play no demiurgic role in Rabbi Isaac's thought;
on the contrary, they defy creation, leading to the destruction of
the first worlds.[22] Although Rabbi Isaac's ideas lack clarity, the forces
of evil in his works can nonetheless be described as antithetical to
material existence, with only the final redemption freeing the world
from the bonds of evil and establishing the true creation. The conception of messianism as the redemption of the material world di-
verges from the gnostic view of redemption as the freeing of chosen
individuals from material existence and their unification with the
Good Deity, Who exists above and apart from the material world.
Thus, the absence of the demiurgic aspect from Rabbi Isaac's description of evil distinguishes it in principle from the usual gnostic systems.

Yet another innovative aspect of Rabbi Isaac's thought differentiates it from gnostic doctrines. In his Treatise on the Emanations
on the Left, Rabbi Isaac links, apparently for the first time in Jewish mystical literature, the adversities of human existence with the

---

[22]Based on midrashim relating the destruction of earlier worlds (see, for example
Midrash Rabbah 9:2). G. Scholem writes, "Isaac haKohen taught that the first worlds
that were destroyed were three dark emanations, which perished because of the
overly concentrated power of strict judgment that they contained," (Kabbalah,
Jerusalem: Keter 1974, pp. 123-124).

forces of evil—for example, attributing rabies and leprosy to the influence of Samael's servants. His dualistic approach divides material reality itself into good and evil without ascribing reality entirely to either the realm of good or evil. The world as created by God is essentially good; however, it contains harmful phenomena caused by the activities of evil powers. Apparently Rabbi Isaac here expands the view first expressed by Nachmanides, a view far removed from the gnostic doctrine of evil as the dominant force in created reality.

Another less strongly stated yet significant difference should also be stressed. Jewish mysticism, as an integral part of Jewish tradition, affirms man's role (including that of the mystic) as the servant of God, King of the universe, Scholem emphasized this element of divine sovereignty in his treatment of Hechalot and Merkavah mysticism; the "descenders to the chariot" (yordey ha-merkavah) achieved mystical ecstasy by joining the ranks of the servants of God in the upper realms and by serving God on Earth. Normative Judaism in general, and all branches of Jewish mysticism in particular, take divine sovereignty and human devotion for granted—a principle expressed by the centrality of prayer in Jewish mysticism, especially the kedushah.[23]

In contrast, in gnosticism the mystic aspires to spiritual-religious freedom from material reality which is enslaved by the forces of evil. Gnostic literature contains no positive descriptions of divine sovereignty, and the aspect of servitude always appears in its negative connotation of bondage to the forces of evil. Gnostic dualism embodies the longing for spiritual freedom; redemption is release, whereas Judaism, including its mystical aspect and even its starkest dualistic treatises, celebrates the value of human worship of God the creator. The exception to this is the well-known aspect of Sabbatianism.

In summation, while Rabbi Isaac ha-Cohen's dualism is clearly gnostic in nature, his theological doctrines are not identical with gnostic dualism. It is now incumbent on us to establish whether

---

[23]The blessing, based on the verse in Isaiah 6:3, which is central in the Jewish daily prayer.

historical contact with gnosticism shaped the similarities between Rabbi Isaac and gnostic dualism.

In his initial study of the doctrines of Rabbi Jacob and Rabbi Isaac ha-Cohen of Castile, Gershom Scholem tended to accept the possibility that gnostic sources influenced the theory of the left emanation. However, it should be noted that this view antedated the crystallization of Scholem's thesis regarding the date of composition of the *Zohar*. Therefore, he was inclined to interpret the gnostic symbols common to the *Zohar* and to Rabbi Isaac ha-Cohen as resulting from the mutual influence of earlier sources—Scholem then believing that the *Zohar* incorporated many earlier sources and was itself widely known prior to the medieval era—and not as the influence of the thirteenth-century kabbalist, Rabbi Isaac, on that work. Subsequent to his positive identification of Rabbi Moses ben Shem Tov de Leon as the author of the *Zohar*, Scholem did not return to a detailed analysis of the works of Rabbi Isaac ha-Cohen, nor did he examine the question of Rabbi Isaac's sources once the historical-philological structure of the *Zohar* had been established.

With regard to the question of the historical influence of gnosticism on Rabbi Isaac, the historian cannot argue *ex silentio*. It is impossible to prove beyond the shadow of a doubt that Rabbi Isaac ha-Cohen did not possess additional sources similar to the ones cited in his detailed description of the chain of tradition reaching him, and to his references to the esoteric writings, especially *Hechalot Zutarti*, [24] from which he ostensibly derived his ideas. Despite the absence of evidence, the contention that Rabbi Isaac may have utilized sources unknown to us retains its validity. Nonetheless, the weight of the argument turns up not a shred of evidence that Rabbi Isaac ha-Cohen derived his gnostic motifs from sources unknown to us and indicates that these motifs evidently represent his innovations. The strange names and innovative concepts used by Rabbi

---

[24]*Hechalot Zutarti*, "The Small Book of the Celestial Palaces," is a *Hechalot* tract whose main speaker is Rabbi Akiva. It contains a detailed description of the world of the "chariot," the ecstatic ascent to that world, and the techniques used to accomplish the ascent.

Isaac are comprehensible within the context of his commentary on traditional sources; for example, the names of the destroyed worlds, *Kamteil*, *Beliel*, and *Ittiel* are based on the phonemes of Job 22:16 (*kumtu belo eit*).[25] Where Rabbi Isaac utilized other sources known to us, the manner in which he injected dualism into texts totally lacking such principles is readily apparent.

Historically, Rabbi Isaac ha-Cohen is, in my opinion, the last figure among the formulators of the kabbalistic doctrine of evil for whom the question of the source of his doctrines is relevant. With regard to the subsequent development of the kabbalistic doctrine of evil, the obvious dependence of the *Zohar*, Lurianic kabbalah, and Sabbatianism on the doctrines of Rabbi Isaac and his followers makes this question extraneous. The problem can be presented *a minori ad majus*: If in the case of Rabbi Isaac no historical evidence exists for use of early gnostic sources, then *a fortiori* this is so with regard to the *Zohar*, Rabbi Isaac Luria, and Nathan of Gaza. Rabbi Isaac's doctrine in Treatise on the Emanations on the Left amounts to only a few dozen pages filled with obscurities. In contrast, the broad scope of the *Zohar* and Lurianic kabbalah, with their motifs reappearing in different contexts, facilitates analysis of their origin and development. Moreover, as the historical distance between the development of kabbalah and the flowering of gnosticism increases, the likelihood of the influence of gnostic sources unknown to us and of contact between kabbalists and adherents of gnosticism decreases.

Essentially, Rabbi Isaac is the pivotal figure in the formulation of the kabbalistic doctrine of evil. The features added in the *Zohar*, Lurianic kabbalah, and Sabbatianism are secondary to the revolutionary character of the theory of the left emanations in Jewish thought, and there is even less justification for their ascription to external influence. Thus, if Rabbi Isaac's doctrines are thought to be based on the sources known to us, it is far-fetched to assume the eruption of gnostic influences in later periods. Consequently, the

---

[25]According to Rabbi Isaac ha-Cohen, the previous worlds were evil, and he uses midrashic terms to denote a process of "inverse emanation." See J. Dan, "Samael, Lilith, and the Concept of Evil," p. 33.

question of possible contact between Rabbi Isaac ha-Cohen and gnostic sources is crucial for the history of Jewish thought. As seen from the above, I clearly lean toward the view that Rabbi Isaac ha-Cohen's doctrines are an immanent development of prekabbalistic thought.

BETWEEN HISTORY AND TYPOLOGY

The third question, namely, the phenomenological definition of Rabbi Isaac ha-Cohen's doctrine of evil, remains to be determined. Scholem certainly defined Rabbi Isaac's doctrine as typologically gnostic, regardless of whether he postulated the existence of historical influence as well. Whereas historical impact is accessible to historical and philological investigation, phenomenological assessment assigns greater weight to the preferences of the scholar. I intend to digress momentarily in order to present a concept pertinent to the understanding of this issue.

Nearly forty years ago, in his article, "Paths of Materialistic and Abstract Thought in Kabbalah," Isaiah Tishby demonstrated that kabbalah is subject to cyclical changes between "mythological" and "systematic" tendencies, with the latter displacing the mythological bases to a large extent.[26] Tishby correctly classified the dualistic understanding of evil as a mythological concept, since it represents the most acute mythological aspect of many of the doctrines under discussion. To illustrate the cyclical interchange of trends, Tishby contrasted *Sefer ha-Bahir*, a materialistic myth, with the outstanding abstraction found in the works of Rabbi Azriel of Gerona; the mythological aspect of the *Zohar* with the systematic approach of its interpreters, especially the doctrines of Rabbi Moses ben Jacob of Cordovero; and the extreme mythology of Lurianic kabbalah with the retreat from that approach by later commentators. Time has not detracted from the validity of Tishby's thesis; rather, it has been corroborated.

---

[26]See I. Tishby, "Mythological vs. Systematic Trends in Kabbalah," *Binah 2: Studies in Jewish Thought*, New York: Praeger 1989, pp. 121–130.

Building on Tishby's thesis, I wish to add that in the cyclical swing between mythology and abstraction, the dualistic myth in kabbalah does not return to the *status quo ante*; rather, at each stage of development of the kabbalah, the dualistic myth intensifies. The existence of scattered and undeveloped dualistic elements in *Sefer ha-Bahir* is incontrovertible. But, despite Rabbi Ezra of Gerona's subsequent rejection of this dualism, it reappears in more extreme form, first in the works of Nachmanides, followed by Rabbi Isaac ha-Cohen, and then in the *Zohar*, which now incorporates a mythological struggle between opposing divine forces of good and evil, based on sexual rivalry—beginning with a description of Lilith and culminating in the imprisonment of the *Shechinah* by the *sitra ahra*. This myth met with opposition on the part of fourteenth- to sixteenth-century kabbalists, first and foremost among them Rabbi Moses ben Jacob of Cordovero. Yet the reemergent myth in Lurianic kabbalah was even bolder. Moreover, if Lurianic kabbalah itself was tempered at the beginning of the seventeenth century, the eruption of Sabbatianism carried the myth to new summits. Rather than a cyclical model, I propose to view the process as cylindrical, with each ring on a higher plane than its predecessor.

The inescapable conclusion is that the gnostic element in the history of the kabbalistic doctrine of evil was not fixed, but rather was dynamic in nature, increasing in potency in proportion to its distance from historical gnosticism. The dualistic myth of Rabbi Isaac ha-Cohen was intensified by several degrees in the *Zohar*, and in Lurianic kabbalah acquired definite Manichaean elements. In Lurianic doctrine, on the one hand, the seeds of divine evil are contained in the precreation Deity, thus intensifying the theological basis for dualism. On the other hand, the myth of the fallen sparks awaiting redemption, which played a minor role in early kabbalah, becomes the focal point of that doctrine's mandates for daily life, morality, and observance of the *mitzvot*. Nathan of Gaza's dichotomy between the "light that contained thought" and the "light that did not contain thought" is also clearly gnostic, albeit inversely, since evil plays no demiurgic role. Older gnostic concepts are extended to their logical extreme in the Frankist doctrine of the total domination of the world by evil and in various manifestations of Sabbatianism.

It is precisely the inverse relationship between the phenomeno-logical intensification of the kabbalistic doctrine of evil and increased distance from historical gnosticism that illustrates the spiritual in-dependence and immanent development of kabbalah on the one hand, and the surprising phenomenological similarity, which in-creases with time, between later Jewish mystics and the Jewish and Gentile mystics of antiquity on the other. If Rabbi Isaac ha-Cohen's doctrine is original, it represents the closest phenomenological par-allel in kabbalah to the doctrine of evil espoused by some historical gnostic sects. By analogy, if the Lurianic doctrine of sparks could have evolved without direct gnostic influence, it is within the realm of possibility for Rabbi Isaac ha-Cohen's doctrine of the left emana-tion to be entirely the result of internal development.

In conclusion, I would like to suggest an entirely hypothetical construct to explain the close phenomenological parallels between kabbalah and gnostic doctrines, and to establish whether they rep-resent separate but parallel developments or the expansion of philo-sophical elements inherent within the very nature of Judaism itself. Recent studies have indicated that the origins of gnosticism—or at least of several of its central aspects—are to be found in the period of the destruction of the Second Temple. I suggested above that the source for the evil demiurge found in gnosticism may be derived from the God of Genesis (*yotzer bereshit*) who complements the Deity in Second Temple Judaism and the succeeding generations—the Jewish doctrine of "two divine powers" being transformed by the gnostics into a dualistic mythology of good versus evil.

Perhaps we can contend that the evolution of the doctrine of evil in kabbalah represents the activation of protognostic kernels within Judaism. While these elements developed rapidly within the gnostic sects outside Judaism, within Judaism itself they flowered slowly, in stages, coming to fruition one thousand years later in the doctrines of Rabbi Isaac ha-Cohen, and subsequently in the *Zohar*, Lurianic kabbalah, and in the thought of Nathan of Gaza and Jacob Frank.

Although this hypothesis cannot be summarily dismissed, it lies outside the purview of the historian, who must concern himself with the historical ties between texts and doctrines. The question of whether phenomenological parallels are evidence of hidden metahistorical ties, or emerge from the basic needs of the human soul, must concern the psychologist of religion, not the historian.

Index

About the Author

Professor Joseph Dan is the Gershom Scholem Professor of the Kabbalah at the Hebrew University of Jerusalem. Born in Bratislava, Slovakia in 1935, his parents immigrated to Jerusalem in 1938. He received his BA (1956), MA (1958), and Ph.D. (1963) from the Hebrew University. Professor Dan has served as the Head of the Institute of Jewish Studies in the Hebrew University, and as the Director of the Jewish University and National Library. He has also served as a visiting professor at UCLA, UC Berkeley, Brown University, Columbia University, Harvard University, Princeton Institute of Advanced Study, and University College, London. Other positions include editor of *Jerusalem Studies in Jewish Thought* and (with P. Schaefer) of *Jerusalem Studies Quarterly*. Professor Dan has published over 40 books in Hebrew and English, among them: *The Early Kabbalah* (Paulist Press, 1987), *Gershom Scholem and the Mystical Dimension in Jewish History* (NYU Press, 1986), *On Sanctity* (Hebrew, Magnes Press, 1997), and *Jewish Mysticism and Jewish Ethics* (2nd ed., Aronson, 1996), and over 600 articles. He was the recipient of the 1997 Israel Prize.